*British Politics
in the Nineteenth Century*

A volume
in
DOCUMENTARY HISTORY
of
WESTERN CIVILIZATION

DOCUMENTARY HISTORY OF WESTERN CIVILIZATION
Edited by Eugene C. Black and Leonard W. Levy

ANCIENT AND MEDIEVAL HISTORY OF THE WEST

Morton Smith: ANCIENT GREECE

A. H. M. Jones: A HISTORY OF ROME THROUGH THE FIFTH CENTURY
Vol. I: The Republic HR/1364
Vol. II: The Empire HR/1460

Deno Geanakoplos: BYZANTINE EMPIRE

Marshall W. Baldwin: CHRISTIANITY THROUGH THE THIRTEENTH CENTURY HR/1468

Bernard Lewis: ISLAM THROUGH SULEIMAN THE MAGNIFICENT

David Herlihy: HISTORY OF FEUDALISM

William M. Bowsky: RISE OF COMMERCE AND TOWNS

David Herlihy: MEDIEVAL CULTURE AND SOCIETY HR/1340

EARLY MODERN HISTORY

Hanna H. Gray: CULTURAL HISTORY OF THE RENAISSANCE

Florence Edler de Roover: MONEY, BANKING,
AND COMMERCE, THIRTEENTH THROUGH SIXTEENTH CENTURIES

V. J. Parry: THE OTTOMAN EMPIRE

Ralph E. Giesey: EVOLUTION OF THE DYNASTIC STATE

J. H. Parry: THE EUROPEAN RECONNAISSANCE: *Selected Documents* HR/1345

Hans J. Hillerbrand: THE PROTESTANT REFORMATION HR/1342

John C. Olin: THE CATHOLIC COUNTER REFORMATION

Orest Ranum: THE CENTURY OF LOUIS XIV

Thomas Hegarty: RUSSIAN HISTORY THROUGH PETER THE GREAT

Marie Boas Hall: NATURE AND NATURE'S LAWS HR/1420

Barry E. Supple: HISTORY OF MERCANTILISM

Arthur J. Slavin: IMPERIALISM, WAR, AND DIPLOMACY, 1550-1763

Herbert H. Rowen: THE LOW COUNTRIES

C. A. Macartney: THE HABSBURG AND HOHENZOLLERN DYNASTIES
IN THE SEVENTEENTH AND EIGHTEENTH CENTURIES HR/1400

Lester G. Crocker: THE AGE OF ENLIGHTENMENT HR/1423

Robert and Elborg Forster: EUROPEAN SOCIETY IN THE EIGHTEENTH CENTURY HR/1404

REVOLUTIONARY EUROPE, 1789-1848

Paul H. Beik: THE FRENCH REVOLUTION

David L. Dowd: NAPOLEONIC ERA, 1799-1815

René Albrecht-Carrié: THE CONCERT OF EUROPE   HR/1341

John B. Halsted: ROMANTICISM   HR/1387

R. Max Hartwell: THE INDUSTRIAL REVOLUTION

Mack Walker: METTERNICH'S EUROPE   HR/1361

Douglas Johnson: THE ASCENDANT BOURGEOISIE

John A. Hawgood: THE REVOLUTIONS OF 1848

NATIONALISM, LIBERALISM, AND SOCIALISM, 1850-1914

Eugene C. Black: VICTORIAN CULTURE AND SOCIETY   HR/1426

Eugene C. Black: BRITISH POLITICS IN THE NINETEENTH CENTURY   HR/1427

Denis Mack Smith: THE MAKING OF ITALY, 1796-1870   HR/1356

David Thomson: FRANCE: *Empire and Republic*, 1850-1940   HR/1378

Theodore S. Hamerow: BISMARCK'S MITTELEUROPA

Eugene O. Golob: THE AGE OF LAISSEZ FAIRE

Roland N. Stromberg: REALISM, NATURALISM, AND SYMBOLISM:
Modes of Thought and Expression in Europe, 1848-1914   HR/1355

Melvin Kranzberg: SCIENCE AND TECHNOLOGY

Jesse D. Clarkson: TSARIST RUSSIA: *Catherine the Great to Nicholas II*

Philip D. Curtin and John R. W. Smail: IMPERIALISM

Massimo Salvadori: MODERN SOCIALISM   HR/1374

THE TWENTIETH CENTURY

Jere C. King: THE FIRST WORLD WAR

S. Clough, T. and C. Moodie : ECONOMIC HISTORY OF EUROPE:
Twentieth Century   HR/1388

W. Warren Wagar: SCIENCE, FAITH, AND MAN:
European Thought Since 1914   HR/1362

Paul A. Gagnon: INTERNATIONALISM AND DIPLOMACY BETWEEN THE WARS, 1919-1939

Henry Cord Meyer: WEIMAR AND NAZI GERMANY

Michal Vyvyan: RUSSIA FROM LENIN TO KHRUSHCHEV

Charles F. Delzell: MEDITERRANEAN TOTALITARIANISM, 1919-1945

Donald C. Watt: THE SECOND WORLD WAR

British Politics
in the Nineteenth Century

Edited by
EUGENE C. BLACK

Harper & Row, Publishers
New York, Evanston, and London

BRITISH POLITICS IN THE NINETEENTH
CENTURY

Introduction, editorial notes, bibliographies, chronology,
and compilation copyright © 1969 by Eugene C. Black.

Printed in the United States of America.

First edition: HARPER PAPERBACKS, 1969, Harper & Row,
Publishers, Incorporated, 49 East 33rd Street, New York,
N. Y. 10016.

A clothbound edition of this book is published in the
United States and Canada by Walker and Company.

Library of Congress Catalog Card Number: 69-15562.

Contents

Introduction   1

I. Challenging the Constitution in Church and State   11
    1. A Divided, Unhappy Land: The Pentrich
        Rising of 1817   19
    2. The Establishment Reacts: The Grenvilles and
        Peterloo   26
    3. The Decline of Monarchy: The Queen's Case,
        1820   30
    4. Tory Reform: Canning's New World   37
    5. Tory Resistance: Eldon and the Test Act   41
    6. Political Knowledge and Participation:
        The Extraordinary Black Book   47
    7. An Eccentric King: William IV   54
    8. Remaking the Constitution: The Reform Act of
        1832   59

II. Reform and Social Stress   75
    9. Political Exploitation: Francis Place
        on Class Cooperation   82
    10. Direct Action: The Cold Bath Fields Manifesto   84
    11. Humanitarianism: The Abolition of Slavery   87
    12. Utilitarianism: The New Poor Law   94
    13. The White Man's Empire: The Durham Report   103
    14. Constitutional Delicacy: Melbourne, Victoria,
        and the Bedchamber Crisis   114
    15. Chartism: Jacobin Ideology and Armed Poverty   119
    16. Social Tension: The Attack upon
        Symbols of Privilege   136
    17. The Early Victorian Statesman: Bagehot on Peel   142

III. The Heyday of Victorianism   168
    18. World Power: Palmerston and Don Pacifico   175
    19. The Queen: Some Power and Much Influence   193
    20. The Middle-Class Franchise: A Mid-Victorian Election   198
    21. Liberalism: Gladstone and Democracy   202
    22. Conservatism: Disraeli's Platform   212
    23. The Limitations of Liberalism: John Bright   232
    24. The Rationalization of Institutions: The Fog of Chancery and Judicial Reform   243
    25. The Career Open to Talents: Civil Service   260
    26. Irish Nationalism: Problems in the Devolution of Power   277

IV. Toward Collectivism   288
    27. The New Radicalism: The Intrusion of Collectivism   297
    28. The Fabians: Toward Socialism—as Slowly as Possible   308
    29. The Logic of Socialism: The Unconscious Conversion   323
    30. The Revolution in Local Government: London   324
    31. Power and Fear: "Made in Germany"   335
    32. Jubilee: "The Captains and the Kings depart . . ."   340
    33. The Masses Emerge: Keir Hardie   346
    34. Jingoism: The Boer War   350
    35. The New Liberalism: Lloyd George, the Budget, and the Peers   363

General Bibliography   376
Chronology   *following page* 378
Index   379

Introduction

HISTORY cannot be segregated into neat, topical departments. The economic historian may nestle behind demographic data, terms of trade, and productivity indices, but he must acknowledge that government policies and social options are often crucial factors in economic decisions. G. M. Trevelyan once described social history as history with the politics left out. But any meaningful study of social history demands the consideration of political institutions and relationships if it is to have coherent form and substance. This volume is a selection of documents, in emphasis more narrowly political, that can most profitably be used with its companion volume *Victorian Culture and Society* [Harper Torchbooks, TB 1426]. Political issues, after all, derive from economic, social, ideological, even psychological elements, none of which should be assessed in a vacuum. Chartism was, at bottom, a futile challenge to a changing economic and social world, as was the Pentrich rising of 1817 before it. Gladstonian liberalism derived from ideological notions and religious-humanitarian values. Disraelian conservatism was similarly woven into the fabric of Victorian life.

The thrust of this volume is Victorian. The selections range from the last years of the reign of George III to the last years of Edward VII, but most of the material and the themes defined speak to the years of the good Queen's reign. Her death in 1901 is a clearer political dividing line than 1837, for Victoria ascended the throne in the midst of political tension and adjustment. The great Whig reforms—the Reform Act of 1832, the Municipal Corporations Act of 1835, the Abolition of Slavery (1833), the first meaningful Factory Act (1833), the social revolution of the new poor law (1834), and the first state grants for popular education, to mention but a few—are part of a continuing process of change,

1

to which the conservative Peel contributed with measures ranging from the Bank Charter Act (1844) to the repeal of the corn laws (1846) and the Ten Hours Act (1847).

These documents, with few exceptions, consider men, events, and institutions. Some touch more explicitly upon political ideas and constitutional theory than others, but political philosophy for its own sake receives short shrift, not because it is unimportant, but because space is limited and Victorian prose is not. The Victorians were ideologically fertile. They constructed systems grounded in felicitous calculus and the immutable laws of political economy; others premised upon economic or biological determinism and historical necessity; and some peered with unclouded if confused vision from the empyrean heights of positivism. I have therefore divided political philosophy between the applications and assertions found in this volume and the broader, more sweeping affirmations of ideas and values to be found in *Victorian Culture and Society*. I have tended to leave statements of imperial and foreign policy as well as socialist doctrine to the volumes in this series treating those themes.

The selection of individuals and themes must, in the end, be extremely subjective. The Victorians padded their furniture, their posteriors, and their prose. Neither this nor any volume could do justice to the full panoply of Victorian political theory and practice. Not only is the range so extensive and the figures so numerous, but also extensive pruning is necessary to bring Victorian prose under control, leaving the reader with snippets or paraphrases. Furthermore, I emphasize domestic politics, since other volumes in this series deal with some issues of foreign policy and empire. These problems can be fruitfully considered in comparative context in René Albrecht-Carrié, *The Concert of Europe* [Harper Torchbook, TB 1341], and the forthcoming *Imperialism* by Philip D. Curtin and John R. W. Smail in this series. Jere C. King will analyze Britain's involvement in 1914 in *The First World War* [forthcoming Harper Torchbook].

The Nineteenth-Century World

Britain was tired and confused at the end of the Napoleonic wars. Men governed who had with William Pitt. But it was no longer his world. It was larger, more productive, more dynamic, and more unstable. The new world of the nineteenth century demanded imagination and found uncertainty. This was not simply political ineptitude. Industrialists were not certain of their own values or even of the proper use of their own machinery. Those unknown souls, the farmers of England, were ambivalent about machine breaking and public order. Was social peace worth the price of drastic political change? Population growth and urban concentration outstripped the capacity of man to cope. An assertive, self-defining middle class was making itself heard and felt but lacked certainty about direction.

This was the world of Mr. Pickwick's flying coaches and the Turnpike Trusts and of Jane Austen's tight village society in which a journey of twenty miles was a formidable expedition. Both were to vanish in a puff of steam in the railroad revolution. Rapid mass transportation unified the nation in the years following 1830. The British road system never fully recovered, and gentry society was slowly submerged beneath the soot and cinders of the railroad, the industrial north, and the hearths of city masses. The cultural jolts were sporadic but cumulative. Changes in economic structure and social organization produced new values and political revolution.

A variety of causes and effects served to reinforce and intensify each other. Take three representative Victorian economic and social institutions—the railroad, the family or partnership industry, the respectable family. Each was itself shaken by aspects of the world it helped to make, and the vehicle for change in each instance was at least partially political. The railroad made possible economic regional specialization and thus dictated, at least in part, the flow of men and materials through the national bloodstream. The railroad made possible patterns of urban and suburban growth. The railroad smoothed the rough edges of localism by integrating the nation. Yet each of these achievements suggests that the railroad was a unitary institution, whereas it actually developed on a highly individualistic and inefficient basis. So strong was the myth of laissez faire that the railroads could successfully resist costly safety regulations after providing token social responsibility through guaranteed passenger service. In return, the government provided the railroads, those products of self-help, with guaranteed profits through excessive subsidies for carrying the post. The railroads even resisted efforts of the government to help them help themselves through such regulations as standardized gauge. Having preached laissez faire, the railroads found themselves trapped by their own logic. Parliament accepted the rhetoric and tended to reject amalgamations, although they were rational responses to the problem of inefficiency. Twentieth-century Britain inherited the problem of completing the rationalization and regulation of railroads. And by then it was too late. The internal combustion engine, a product of the industrial colossus the railroad had helped to build, changed the world in ways that were increasingly visible before the collapse of post-Victorian civilization in the First World War. The automobile, truck, and bus liberated Britons from Victorian patterns of growth. Emancipation from the steel ribbon of the railroad produced a new suburban, even an ex-urban life. The internal combustion engine also provided a new degree of individual freedom and initiative—the ability to wander wherever roads might lead at one's own convenience, provided it was not a Bank Holiday weekend.

Stringent provisions of British commercial law, modified in the 1820's but not rationalized until the 1850's, made economic development a product of individual, family, and partnership enterprise. The Bubble Act of 1720 limited a common partnership to seven members and provided that each owner was liable "to his last shilling and acre" for the debts of the concern. When the more stringent provisions had been dropped a century later, business enterprise was a safer, if still legally anomalous, form of investment. Prior to 1855 limited liability required a special act of Parliament, and the landed gentlemen who ran the state felt this to be a good thing. Relatively small-scale enterprise, therefore, created the industrial revolution. Once limited liability was available, most established firms were in little hurry to incorporate. As the second and third generation of entrepreneurial families went on to higher (or lower) things, British industry turned increasingly to larger, more professional, and more anonymous organization. Business practices and business management drew heavily upon American examples. Corporate attitudes, framed in individualistic rhetoric, gave a misleading impression of consistency while moving toward changes in economic, social, and political institutions.

Economic success and political legislation helped to shake that mainstay of Victorian values, the respectable family. Improvement in real wages and working conditions made it increasingly possible for working-class women to concentrate upon rearing a family rather than on supplementing family income—seemingly an expansion of the middle-class notion of the respectable family. But economic success also emancipated the Victorian woman and jeopardized the family as traditionally conceived. Married women secured the right to hold their own property, and with that right stripped away one of the principal social sanctions sustaining the patristic Victorian family. Divorce became available, although expensive, striking yet another small blow at the sanctity of the family. And there were increasing options to marriage. Single women found an expanding list of possible occupations under steadily improving conditions. There were even choices for respectable women. Slowly, very slowly, professional barriers fell, and women entered the sacred precincts of medical schools and law courts. Service industries expanded, and women were increasingly employed in retail trades and clerical positions. These extensions of independence generated new demands for political rights. Each element became self-multiplying.

The reforms of the Grey-Melbourne Whig administrations (1830–41) touched a wide range of institutions and had far-reaching social and political implications. They struck at privilege and inefficiency, although the administration was itself anything but a paragon of fiscal virtue. Some measures acerbated, others healed, social tensions. Invariably, perhaps inevitably, they were all beginnings. The Factory Act of 1833, with its system of factory inspectors, was the beginning, not the end, of government intervention in the industrial life of the nation. The abolition of slavery in 1833 acknowledged British responsibility for the oversight of human as well as economic relations in the Empire. It remained for Peel's government to find an escape from escalating social tensions in the repeal of the corn laws (1846)—far more important in satisfying middle-class aggressions than as a matter of commercial policy—and the Ten Hours Act of 1847. Both were ostensible class victories. Each pointed in opposite directions: to laissez faire with repeal, to collectivism with the Ten Hours Act. They symbolized the mid-Victorian balance. There was no revolution of 1848 in Britain, only stray shots in an Irish cabbage patch and a fiasco Chartist demonstration on Kennington Common.

Most nineteenth-century British development was geared, directly or indirectly, to the working of economic machinery. The

slow, erratic maturation of the economy during the pre-Victorian
and the early Victorian years was reflected in economic distress,
social tension, and political bitterness. The railroad rationalized the
nation between 1830 and 1850, providing employment, balancing
the elements of production, and establishing Britain's mid-century
economic hegemony. There were bad years and occasional hard
times between 1850 and 1873, but by the yardsticks economists
like to employ, it was a prosperous time. Productivity increased;
distribution costs dropped dramatically with the transportation
revolution; there was an extraordinary increase in savings and
investment; and net real income per head (ostensibly the best single
gauge of economic well-being) rose sharply.

The new middle classes began to assert themselves in the years
after the Great Exhibition of 1851, that monument to industry and
bad taste. These were not the radical industrialists of the 1830's and
1840's, exponents of the Manchester School out to dethrone what
Richard Cobden called the "booby aristocracy." They were not
revolutionaries but rather were elements who, once economically
established, sought social and political adjustments. Much of the
classic liberal legislation of Gladstone's great ministry (1868–74)
responded to these pressures. The new middle classes wanted
opportunity: state-supported education, responsibility and prudence in the conduct of national business, the elimination of
vestigial privileges, careers open to talents. Jacobinism looks so
tame three-quarters of a century later. Lower down the scale
among the artisan groups, the skilled trades, and the lower middle
classes, the practice of self help has led to their gradual engrossing
of the old mechanics institutes, the Polytechnic, and the opportunities for training and careers. We still understand, as G. M.
Young delighted to point out, exactly what the Victorians meant
when they referred to "the classes and the masses." Mid-Victorian
England was the England of the classes.

The radicalism of early Victorian England wore thin and was
replaced by a narrow, materialistic satisfaction. The British worked
off their aggressions on Russians, Chinese, and Indians rather than
on each other. Meanwhile, the economic machine ground out the
goods, and Britain played her most advantageous role in the world
market. But this age of contentment also was one of nagging
doubts. To be sure it was a prosperous world, but there was "the
submerged tenth," the Victorian underworld that never knew

subsistence—to which the workhouse was irrelevant, and for which private charity was helpless. The younger generation of the 1870's was already doing well. It wanted to do good, for the evolving *rentier* age was also an age of guilt. Beatrice Webb spoke of the "sense of social sin" among the propertied—an interesting secular resurrection of evangelical rhetoric.

Gladstone had completed the liberal revolution. The Second and Third Reform Acts in 1867 and 1884 had established household suffrage, which was protected by secret ballot after 1872. Both Liberals and Conservatives anticipated problems. The new democracy, invited into the political mansion at the onset of the Great Depression (1873–96), did not prove an attractive house guest. The newly enfranchised were much like other men, somewhat bellicose and self-seeking, concerned more with lording it (vicariously in most instances) over others than in coming to grips with their own complex problems. Radicals like Joseph Chamberlain, who demonstrated the potential range of municipal reform, and Sir Charles Dilke, who demonstrated that scandal was insupportable in a party sustained by the nonconformist conscience, attempted to shift the Liberal party to an advanced program of agrarian reform, graduated taxation, free education, Church disestablishment, and effective democracy in local government. But Gladstone's longevity and his ill-timed and incredibly bungled conversion to home rule for Ireland saved Britain for the Tory party.

The Conservatives did not even need their champion of Tory Democracy, Lord Randolph Churchill. Imperialism, with an occasional token measure of social welfare, proved enough to win elections. It also led to the Boer War. The Tory success was too great. The Conservatives gained the residual old Whigs who had chafed under Gladstonian liberalism and found Irish home rule a good excuse to defect to a conservative haven. From that point on, the House of Lords, always conservative, was overwhelmingly Tory. Gladstone also lost some moderates and many radicals, the Liberal Unionists. They brought to the Conservative party the intellectual weight and imagination it had lacked since the days of Peel, and did so at a time when the party was absorbing business and professional men. The Conservatives tended their mass flocks with a program of bread and circuses and a quasi-fraternal electioneering organization, the Primrose League. They neither solicited nor expected support from organized, politically active labor.

The evolving age of democracy and bureaucracy was neverthe-less characterized by an increasing concern with the quality of life. As the hand of the reformer reached from central to local govern-ment, the range of administrative concerns increased. Fabian social-ists delighted to point out that the process of institutional reform was pushing Britain "into an ever-deepening collectivist channel." Liberals, whose efforts to prevent the rise of a working-class party waned with the departure of Joseph Chamberlain, initially con-tracted rather than expanded their political concerns. The party became increasingly the whining voice of English nonconformity, anxious to press liquor licensing (a much-needed reform executed principally, in the end, by the brewers and the liquor interests themselves), secular education, and Church disestablishment. Lib-erals split on imperialism and found themselves essentially impotent for twenty years.

Conservative indifference and Liberal incompetence made the rise of a Labor party easier, but it was still a long, arduous process, and even the twenty-nine members who sat in the interests of the Labor Representation Committee after the election of 1906, had little sense of their future. Simultaneously a combination of eco-nomic pressures and the cumulative effect of political reform eroded the position of the landed aristocracy. Democracy, bureauc-racy, and the collapse of wheat prices all did their bit. The aristocracy was thrown more and more upon non-landed sources of income and came to share interests, values, and status with the plutocracy. Disraeli's "two nations"—the rich and the poor—had not ceased to be a problem; the prospective political alliances were redrawn. Conservatives worried less about aristocratic responsi-bility for the general welfare and became increasingly the party of British capitalism. Liberals slowly emancipated themselves from doctrinaire notions of laissez faire and drifted steadily toward collectivism.

The Boer War (1899–1902) looked good at first. Balfour at-tempted his famous "Khaki Election" in 1900—a modestly suc-cessful experiment tried with still greater success by Lloyd George in 1918 and with no success by Winston Churchill in 1945. The Liberals were hopelessly divided, easy game for the vicious "Every vote for the Liberals is a vote for the Boers." But soon the war looked less attractive. The concentration camps and systematic sweeping operations justified the critics. Nevertheless the war was won; the issue was resolved on magnanimous British terms. Joseph Chamberlain felt so confident of continued Conservative success that he launched the Tories down the road to tariff protection. A sixty-year-old issue—"dead and damned" as far as Disraeli was concerned—precipitated a wild election and the first modern land-slide—for the Liberals. The Liberal governments of Sir Henry Campbell-Bannerman and Herbert Asquith remade Britain in the eight years before the First World War.

So, with the Boer War, one form of tumult and shouting died. The little old lady wound her way through the narrow streets into the capacious hearts and fond memories of her subjects. The bunting fluttered farewell. The world she left was brassy, vulgar, crass, and cynical. A liberal century produced democracy, and the people sanctioned jingoism. Britain became a prisoner of escalating domestic and international conflict. "We want eight, and we won't wait!" chanted the voting masses in 1908 upon hearing that Germany was laying down four dreadnoughts. The outlines of the welfare state were being tortuously drawn as suffragettes bombarded the House of Commons with pepper, broke shop windows, and burned empty churches. Sir George Askwith refined government mediation for collective bargaining just as Britain confronted an ill-tempered rash of strikes. The peers finally paid for partisanship and folly with the Parliament Act of 1911. Irish home rule came belatedly, threatened to touch off civil war, and was set aside "for the duration."

"We want eight . . .
Winston Churchill established wage boards to bring fair rates to the sweated trades. The National Insurance Act of 1911 finally provided a measure of security for all against illness and disability.
    . . . and we won't wait!"
Six million Britons donned uniforms because the world would not wait: 750,000 died; another 1,700,000 were wounded. The troops that actually fought were almost exclusively volunteers. One out of every eleven of the most able, venturesome, and active men between the ages of twenty and forty-five could not come home. The nineteenth century was dead, and Britain never recovered.

I

Challenging the Constitution
in Church and State

Introduction

BRITAIN in 1815 was shell-shocked. Drained materially and emotionally by more than two decades of war, she faced the future with glazed eyes. The country gentlemen who had paid most of the bills demanded an immediate abolition of the income tax and a high, fixed protective tariff on grain, Vansittart's irresponsible Corn Law of 1815. Readjustment to a peacetime footing, a difficult process at best, was made worse by governmental incompetence and fear. The British championed responsibility in Europe and practiced irresponsibility at home. Yet the unimaginative Conservatives who dominated Parliament contributed unwittingly to the process of constitutional change. Their cumulative incapacity raised substantial questions about their capacity to govern, and their demands for economy in government—met by trimming administrative fat—reduced their capacity to rule. Ministries, lacking patronage, were thrown increasingly into the hands of organized public and enfranchised electoral opinion. Initially that posed no threat, since the government and the public agreed that the first task was to preserve property and public order.

There was less agreement on how best to do so. Programs of radical reform, nurtured long before the French Revolution but developed by increasingly artisan and lower-class elements, advocated substantial constitutional revision. Some of these proposals had gained considerable backing in Parliament. Most men of advanced views and many Conservatives believed that the Test and Corporation Acts, the seventeenth-century statutes that restricted government offices to communicants in the established church, should be repealed—initially for Protestant dissenters, but then for Roman Catholics. The Whigs, who tended to react to issues pragmatically rather than ideologically, accepted this proposal without conceding that the British constitution was a constitution in church and state. A change in one would surely mean remaking the other.

The small, noisy radical fringe of British political life is generally given too much importance in these early pre-Victorian years. Jeremy Bentham, that ostensible model of radicalism, wanted to work with the Tories and became a democrat (of a peculiar sort) only after those efforts failed. Robert Owen, the father of British socialism and the cooperative movement (of which he disapproved), was an authoritarian planner who had demonstrated that paternalism could pay substantial dividends. His record of unbroken successes after taking over the New Lanark mill in 1800 attracted domestic and foreign dignitaries. He had considerable influence, almost all of which he dissipated with a clumsy attack upon religion in 1819; and yet the Factory Act of that year, although it was unenforced, was a tribute to his work and a short step in the direction of government intervention in private economic affairs. The industrial middle classes in general were not hospitable to radical reform. They opposed Luddism, endemic outbursts of machine-breaking which peaked in 1811–12 and again in 1817, and were unlikely to favor remodeling the state before public order and security of property could be established. The conversion of these middle-class elements to constitutional reform, as William Cobbett observed in his *Political Register*, was both sudden and late, following rather than preceding the first great blows struck in 1828 and 1829 with the repeal of the Test Acts.

The incapacity of Tory administrations from 1815 to 1830 to adjust British institutions to the nineteenth century, not radical pressures, generated the sustained agitation and protest that culminated in a remodeled constitution. Every pre-Victorian Briton grew up with news of riot and revolution. The grim reality and darker legends of the French Revolution sharpened fears. Every unruly wage dispute, each political meeting, even the occasional outbursts of seditious words in public houses seemed to threaten upheaval. Britons were increasingly aware of demographic and economic change, but they had no guidelines and little comprehen-

sion of causes and effects to lead them through the early development of industrial civilization. Other nations could profit from
Britain's example. Britain could not. Instead there was growing
maladjustment, an increasing gap between political institutions and
the reality to which they were addressed.

These years of incapacity were also years of political development; some intentional, some fortuitous. Since the governing elements tended first to resist, then to consider, events, bitterness and
misunderstanding grew. Social divisions and maladjustment became
more acute. The Pentrich rising of 1817, a pathetic outburst, re-
vealed the depth of political incomprehension of social problems.[1]
Doubts grew within the charmed circle, and the clear ministerial
abuse of authority in the Peterloo massacre of 1819 precipitated
divisions within the establishment. Some leaders recognized this to
be the real danger. Artisan and working-class movements posed
little threat; but should part of the governing element defect and
set itself at the head of a popular force, political and social upheaval
must follow.[2]

This confrontation did not come in 1820. Instead, Whig and
Radical ire dispelled itself in the sordid comedy of royal scandal.
The lascivious details of the Queen's Case made *The Times* un-
readable for proper young ladies, entertained, then bored, people
of fashion, and demonstrated the triviality of the revolutionary
threat.[3] The London crowd indulged in its usual boisterous pas-
times, while glaziers did a roaring trade repairing broken windows
in ministerial houses. Queen Caroline had little staying power. As
one scribbler put it,

> Most gracious Queen, we thee implore,
> To go away, and sin no more.
> But if that effort be too great,
> To go away at any rate.

The institution of monarchy lost important ground, less in power
than in prestige. Neither George IV nor William IV after him
attempted to or could recover the lost ground. Their failures were
fundamentally failures of character.[4] By the time Victoria re-

[1] See Document 1.
[2] See Document 2.
[3] See Document 3.
[4] See Document 7.

covered the moral authority of the crown, its political role had been fundamentally circumscribed.[5]

Prior to the Reform Act of 1832, royal authority lay less in its capacity to make ministries than in its ability to influence elections. Windsor tradesmen would respond to royal influence under Victoria as readily as they did when George III darted from shop to shop stammering orders and electioneering, but the scope of vestigial royal electoral influence was significantly reduced by the Reform Act. The rotten boroughs and the family boroughs that remained lay principally in areas of aristocratic rather than governmental influence. The crown had ceased to be a free agent. In fact, it had not been so before. Royal preference was a factor of importance, but it was only one of many factors. Even George III could break, not make, ministries. No ruler could or would maintain his ministers against the electorate. But it remained for party finally to remove the crown from the center of politics, and the evolution of the modern party was a slow, uneven process.[6]

One prerequisite for party was the development of a meaningful program attractive to substantial portions of the electorate and to the political establishment. That was initially the contribution of Lord Liverpool's reshuffled administration after 1821, when Tory reform reached into most areas of British life. Trade unions were legalized (1824–25), although they continued to be harassed by the courts. Sir Robert Peel at the Home Office amended the worst aspects of the criminal code and provided London with a police system. His method of intensive investigation—marshaling all the facts and summarizing them in an objective report was as important as the results. Peel pioneered revolution by "blue books": in them problems were defined, and issues clarified, so that Parliament could proceed systematically with its consideration of the question at hand.

[5] See Documents 14, 19, and 32. See also *Victorian Culture and Society* [hereafter cited as *VC&S*], Document 1, "Queen Victoria as a Moral Force."

[6] R. Pares, *King George III and the Politicians* (Oxford, 1953); L. B. Namier, "Monarchy and the Party System," *Personalities and Powers* (London, 1964), and B. Kemp, *King and Commons 1660–1832* (London, 1957), discuss this problem at length. A. Aspinall (ed.), *The Formation of Canning's Ministry* (London, 1937), suggests the many considerations involved on that or any similar occasion during those transitional years. See also A. S. Foord, "The Waning of the 'Influence of the Crown,'" *English Historical Review*, Vol. LXII (1947), pp. 484–507.

The procedural change accompanied new men and new attitudes into Parliament. Little changed in the social structure of the House of Commons in pre-Victorian years, but much changed in the way these parliaments conducted their affairs. Some members continued to regard their seats as patrimony and attendance as a nuisance, but being a member of Parliament increasingly meant attending to business and understanding what it was about. Going to Parliament was becoming a time-consuming career. Members were more aware of the world in which they functioned. They tended to be informed though prejudiced, motivated, even if in wrong directions. The small house lacking issues and divisions became a thing of the past. Government jobs became tasks, not handouts.

Function and attitude of Parliament did not suddenly change. The alteration had begun in the eighteenth century, and the direction was evident after 1784 in the ministry of William Pitt and in the behavior of such private members as William Wilberforce, who campaigned tirelessly for the abolition of the slave trade (1807). It is easy, too easy, to ascribe this change to evangelical ethics, to a growing seriousness in affairs and increasing concern with duties. Whatever the explanation, there was a new world for parliamentary men, and the lines along which it developed became clear in the decade before the Reform Act.

Many pre-Victorian reforms ran counter to public prejudices or lacked widespread national support. Both right and left suspected Peel's police reform of 1829, and both pleaded invasion of traditional liberties. Religious liberalism was not the long suit of the English people, but the repeal of the Test and Corporation Acts (1828–29) was one of the most significant measures of Tory reform. Public ambiguity and ministerial uncertainty sometimes combined to make the worst of complex situations. William Huskisson, who, as president of the Board of Trade, did as much as any man to adjust British political and commercial institutions before 1830, fought rearguard and flanking actions against a host of vested interests, often without being quite certain where he was going. He sought to rationalize British tariffs and to develop a system of commerce adapted to current British needs. Country gentlemen resisted efforts to tamper with the corn laws, and Huskisson's sliding-scale compromise satisfied neither the manufacturing and commercial interests nor the agriculturalists. He sought to develop a system of reciprocal tariffs; but although he was encouraged by cotton men who were prepared for free trade, Huskisson was challenged by silk manufacturers and merchant shippers who were not. English fiscal institutions left much to be desired, while Scottish banking was sound. The panic of 1825 showed the frailty of country banking in England, but so deep-seated were English prejudices against general joint-stock organization and branch banking that Huskisson was forced into a series of odd, even inconsistent, reforms in 1826.

British policy had tended consistently, if relatively, toward liberalism in foreign affairs since 1815. Her role in the concert of Europe had been to balance the excessive reaction of Russia, Prussia, and Austria. The drift of France into the conservative camp, particularly over the liberal revolt in Spain, left Britain isolated and mistrustful of the Congress movement. A mixture of ideals and interests stimulated British support of Greek independence, but here British goals happened to coincide with those of France and Russia. Frustration over impotence to preserve the short-lived Spanish liberal regime ("liberal" being a relative term) led Britain to pursue a harder line in support of Latin American nationalism—clearly in the British interest—and of Portuguese liberalism—one of the few areas where British power could be effective.[7] George Canning's efforts in this sphere have secured him an entirely undeserved reputation for liberalism. He was, save on Catholic emancipation, indifferent or hostile to domestic measures of reform. Almost by default, Canning committed Britain to the support of European nationalism and liberal governments, although the policy was never consistently followed. This foreign policy was defended in the same terms as reforming domestic policy—adaptation to avoid upheaval and revolution.

Reformers and their foes played upon this point so much that an interesting myth developed: the notion that reforms were conceded under the implicit, occasionally explicit, threat of revolution. In some instances this was true. Catholic emancipation was wrested at gunpoint in 1829. It was a matter of English concession or civil war in Ireland, and England was too divided to press the point. This was not the case sixty years later, however, as the painful history of Irish home rule testifies.[8] England in 1829 had no lack of bitter-enders upholding the principles of inequality and bigotry

[7] See Document 4.
[8] See Document 26.

with a passion worthy of their twentieth-century successors. But there is a refreshing quality about the Lord Eldons of this world: they are outspoken and honest.[9]

The articulate world, however, increasingly saw a need for change. One group, the Benthamite utilitarians, had developed and was refining a program. These philosophical radicals were an inchoate group with internal ideological and generational differences. Historians, like contemporaries, have never developed a precise definition of either personnel or program. In the most general terms, Benthamite notions, augmented by selected principles of classical economy, provided general guidelines for a radical reconstruction of state and society. Some of these middle-class revolutionaries sought a root-and-branch excision of constitutional anomalies and the devolution of political control into the hands of those who made the new world work. Most, however, dealt pragmatically with situations as they arose, adapted institutions, respected traditional British conservatism, and concealed the full implications of proposed changes. Knowledge for them was the key to change, and the wide dissemination of truth must, they believed, carry all before it.[10] Man will work within economic laws once he understands them, instead of wasting his time on futile efforts to resist. Understand the workings of human psychology, and government can devote its energies to assisting man to help himself. All of this must work to produce the best of all possible worlds.

There was much radical pragmatism and little ideology behind the Reform Act of 1832. Whig opportunism, as much as anything else, produced what was simultaneously the first step toward and a rearguard action against democracy. Fortuitous timing enabled Lord Grey's government (1830–34) to benefit from Ultra-Tory fury with the Duke of Wellington for passing Catholic emancipation, from philosophical radical doctrine, middle-class aspirations and assertiveness, a genuinely revolutionary movement (although it was not effective) among the artisan and working classes, and the new King, William IV, who was not quite intelligent enough to understand what was happening.[11] The Reform Act was an expedient. It was one reform among many and was not the crucial

[9] See Document 5.
[10] See Document 6.
[11] See Document 8.

reform of the early nineteenth century. But it was necessary. It firmly established the principle of the supremacy of the Commons in place of the traditional doctrine of the balanced constitution, and it was the secular installment of undoing the constitution in church and state.

Recommended Reading

A. ASPINALL and E. A. SMITH, *English Historical Documents,* Vol. XI, *1783–1832* (London, 1959).

J. R. M. BUTLER, *Passing of the Great Reform Bill* (London, 1914).

D. CECIL, *Melbourne* (New York, 1954).

J. CLIVE, *Scotch Reviewers* (London, 1957).

G. D. H. COLE, *William Cobbett* (London, 1924).

F. O. DARVALL, *Popular Disturbances and Public Order in Regency England* (London, 1934).

H. W. C. DAVIS, *The Age of Grey and Peel* (Oxford, 1929).

N. GASH, *Mr. Secretary Peel* (London, 1961).

K. G. FEILING, *The Second Tory Party* (London, 1951).

J. HAMBURGER, *James Mill and the Art of Revolution* (London, 1963).

J. L. and B. HAMMOND, *The Town Labourer* (London, 1917).

———, *The Skilled Labourer* (London, 1919).

———, *The Village Labourer* (London, 1911).

E. HALÉVY, *The Growth of Philosophic Radicalism* (London, 1928).

H. JEPHSON, *The Platform,* 2 vols. (London, 1892).

B. KEMP, *King and Commons 1660–1832* (London, 1957).

W. L. MATHIESON, *England in Transition* (London, 1920).

C. W. NEW, *Life of Henry Brougham to 1830* (London, 1961).

D. READ, *Peterloo* (Manchester, 1958).

H. W. TEMPERLEY, *The Foreign Policy of Canning* (London, 1925).

E. P. THOMPSON, *The Making of the English Working Class* (London, 1963).

G. M. TREVELYAN, *Lord Grey and the Reform Bill* (London, 1920).

A. S. TURBERVILLE, *The House of Lords in the Age of Reform* (London, 1958).

G. S. VEITCH, *The Genesis of Parliamentary Reform* (London, 1913).

G. WALLAS, *Life of Francis Place* (London, 1898).

C. K. WEBSTER, *The Foreign Policy of Castlereagh*, 2 vols. (London, 1925).

R. J. WHITE, *Life in Regency England* (London, 1963).

————, *Waterloo to Peterloo* (London, 1957).

1. A Divided, Unhappy Land: The Pentrich Rising of 1817

LORD LIVERPOOL'S administration could boast that it had won the war and made Britain an arbiter of Europe, but each foreign triumph was offset by a domestic failure. Demographic and economic revolution were sweeping the land. A tired old order attempted to manage the boisterous, adolescent world of the nineteenth century with instruments, attitudes, and policies left over from another age. Lord Sidmouth, the Home Secretary, could find a Jacobin under every bed. He knew that revolution was imminent. He knew it in 1792 and unflaggingly prophesied it thereafter. All the food riots, wage disputes, Luddite machine-breaking, those endless radical plots would soon bring the confrontation between the forces of order and desperate anarchy. Some nervous country magistrates like the hysterical reactionary, Colonel Fletcher of Bolton, outdid Sidmouth in predicting disaster and, like Sidmouth, attempted to generate threats where they were wanting. Every word of alehouse sedition—and in bad times, like the postwar years, many were uttered—was another link in the devilish conspiracy.

Sidmouth got his revolution. It was not quite what he had predicted, but it would serve. Social and economic unrest unsettled the North and Midlands in the spring of 1817. The protest march of the Blanketeers in March 1817, the threats to Manchester, and the Ardwick Bridge conspiracy following on the heels of the Spa Fields riots in London in December 1816 could not be discrete events. Ironically, Sidmouth's *agent provocateur*, Oliver the Spy, unwittingly spent so much time rushing about postponing the date that most of the northern hotheads, despairing of ever seeing action, had cooled and returned home.

Jeremiah Brandreth, an unemployed stockinger on poor relief who had served an apprenticeship as Luddite, provided the action at Pentrich in the Peak district of Derbyshire on the night of June 9. He was a large, powerful man, frustrated and aggrieved, innocent of any political program, anxious to strike a blow, with little consideration of what it might be for and with only the vaguest notion of what it was against. There was much talk of rum, one hundred guineas for every man who reached Nottingham, band concerts, and riverboat parties, but there was never a whisper of suffrage or the constitution. Yet Brandreth avowed that he was to lead the Derbyshire branch of a "simultaneous operation" throughout the nation. No one else, particularly in the radical circles of Nottingham, seemed to be taking the revolution very seriously. Throughout June 8, Brandreth sat with his map at the White Horse Inn in Pentrich explaining his strategy and tactics to anyone who would listen. His auditors included two special constables who disregarded it as "all foolish talk."

Brandreth marched. His followers scoured the country rather inefficiently in search of recruits and arms. Brandreth did shoot a servant drawing on his boots—the only fatality of the revolution. Otherwise the results were disappointing. The manager of the Butterley Iron Works told the ragamuffin crowd to go home and save themselves a hanging. Some went, and Brandreth's authority never recovered. The last ten miles were a soggy march through pouring rain. A magistrate appeared with a party of hussars, and the revolution dissolved.

The trials were pitiful. The defense had a hopeless case; the government had its revolution. Twenty-three misguided countrymen were transported or imprisoned; twenty others were acquitted; Brandreth and three fellow leaders were sentenced to die. The defense defined the real basis of unrest, the economic grievances and social dislocation, but the argument was firmly rejected by the court and jury. Lord Chief Baron Richards of the Court of the Exchequer upheld the mission of the special commission. Jeremiah Brandreth, William Turner, and Issac Ludlam were hanged on November 7, 1817, to remind a divided, unhappy land about the realities of power and authority. The traditional political forces asserted their position. Social disorder was the threat used to sustain the constitution in church and state. Any reform, it was argued, invited revolution.

Recommended Reading

For Pentrich in context, there are a variety of possibilities, sentimental, ideological, and generally sound. Among others are: E. P. THOMPSON, *The Making of the English Working Class* (London, 1963); R. J. WHITE, *Waterloo to Peterloo* (London, 1957); and J. L. and B. HAMMOND, *The Town Labourer* (London, 1917). The soundest general study remains the first two volumes of ELIE HALÉVY, *A History of the English People in the Nineteenth Century: England in 1815* and *The Liberal Awakening, 1815–1830* (London, 1924–26). There are many subsequent editions.

SOURCE: "The Trial of Jeremiah Brandreth, *alias* John Coke, *alias* The Nottingham Captain [et al.], for High Treason . . . at Derby . . . the 16th . . . [through the] 25th October 1817,"

T. B. Howell, *A Complete Collection of State Trials*, Vol.
XXXII (London, 1824), cols. 874–877, 1391–1393.

Opening Statement for the Defense
by Counsel John Cross

But before I call your attention to the facts already proved, it
may be right that I should remind you of the state of the country
and the public mind at the time when these unhappy disturbances
occurred, and of the causes which led to them. You will remember,
we had just then attained to the close of a glorious and successful
war of nearly five and twenty years continuance, when the long
promised and expected fruits of peace were to come into immediate
enjoyment; it pleased Providence, however, that we should have a
most unfavourable season; the last year, you well know was a most
unfortunate one, a season of scarcity combined with a deficiency
of employment, so that our poor manufacturers had the misery to
find all their expectations of increased trade and prosperity at once
destroyed, and when they hoped to enjoy the fruits of peace,
"instead of fruit chewed bitter ashes."

The scarcity of food, and a general obstruction in the circulation
of property, occasioned by a variety of causes which have been the
subjects of much discussion and contention in other places, and to
which I would not willingly allude, had combined to drive a vast
number of honest and industrious manufacturers into a state
bordering upon absolute famine. There were people in this country
of far different dispositions from these miserable men, who did not
lose the opportunity of instilling into their minds, and those of all
the labouring classes, discontent against the government, and of
persuading them that the sole cause of all their misery was the
mismanagement of our public affairs, and the enormous weight of
public taxes, and that the only remedy was a change of the constitution of the House of Commons. Accordingly they fell, you
know, to petitioning the Prince Regent and the two Houses of
Parliament; and although from day to day the act against tumultuous petitioning was violated within the walls of the House of
Commons, the tender commiseration of that House for their real
sufferings prevented any person there from noticing such violation
of the law. I may possibly be mistaken when I state this, as I
perceive a learned member of that House, who appears not to

approve of what I say; I may have fallen into a mistake, but it has appeared to me, and I saw with some surprise that petitions, signed by hundreds and thousands, were presented to the House of Commons for an alteration of the laws, contrary to the statute against tumultuous petitioning. Far be it from me to presume to blame that forbearance: the House of Commons, as well as the prince, I have no doubt felt the utmost anxiety to relieve, to the best of their ability, those distresses which it had pleased Providence to inflict upon us. But it was not in the power of the prince or the parliament to create one single bushel of wheat more than the ordinary course of the seasons may have produced for the sustenance of man. They could only do their best to distribute the food, which it had pleased Providence to send us, in due proportion amongst all the people. The petitioners were, however, by artful and insidious publications, excited to a very unbecoming feeling towards those from whom they had sought relief in vain; and, by one in particular, to which I cannot help alluding, and earnestly directing your attention, as one of the most malignant and diabolical publications that ever issued from the English press. It was addressed to the labouring classes in the midst of their distresses! It is entitled—"An Address to the Journeymen and Labourers of England, &c." I will not shock the ears of this Court with stating what I here find as an excitement to this insurrection, and out of which I am persuaded it almost entirely grew. This publication was scattered into the hands of every unhappy (idle for want of employment) and every destitute artizan; it teaches such things as I hope and trust may, by the exertions of the attorney-general of England, be prevented at least from repetition. But all this went on in the face of day; this wicked author publicly avowed what he was doing, and his success in carrying on the wholesale trade of sedition. It was just on the commencement of the winter, in the month of November last, that that sanguinary publication first came forth; and, in the course of about a fortnight, it was followed up by another, which is styled—"An Address to the Luddites;" and it was there boasted—(I will read to you this writer's own words, and you will see, gentlemen, to what extent the minds of these unhappy and miserable people were acted upon; he has the impudence to put forth this advertisement)—"That he has reprinted" such and such matters, alluding to the one I have mentioned, "in a cheap form, price twopence retail, and 12s. 6d. per hundred wholesale: any number may be had by application through the post, or otherwise to the publisher, No. 192, Strand, London." The attorney-general shall know where to find him;—

> Parcels will be sent off by the coach to any part of the country upon a plain direction being sent to the publisher. If any person take one thousand copies or more, regularly, the price then will be only 11s. a hundred. But in all cases the money must be paid to the publisher weekly; that is to say, the sale is to be for ready money, which is perfectly reasonable, seeing how low the price is, and that the retail must necessarily be for ready money. Friends to truth,

friends to falsehood and misrepresentation he should have said, who live near country towns will doubtless point out the means of obtaining this publication to some persons in such towns, whether booksellers or others; booksellers and reading-room keepers may, perhaps, be afraid of parsons and taxing people; but shoemakers and other shopkeepers may not be afraid of them, and the profit on three or four hundred a week is sufficient to support a small family.—N. B. Forty-four thousand copies of No. 18 have been printed and sold, that is the detestable publication I have alluded to. Let the attorney-general of England look at these publications, and let me ask where was the attorney-general of that day? What were the magistracy of the country doing at that time?— Poor, miserable hawkers, wanting bread, were going up and down the country selling forty-four thousand of the most mischievous publications that were ever put into the hand of man, and the magistracy of the country looked on. I impute no blame to them on that account; this wicked and detestable wholesale and retail trade in sedition was so perfectly new, that the magistracy of the country did not know how to deal with it, and the mischief proceeded; the poor manufacturers were thus persuaded that all their miseries and distresses were owing to taxation, and that it was in the power of government and of his majesty's ministers to relieve those distresses at any hour if they ownly thought fit to do it: this they were taught; this they were suffered by the magistracy of the country to learn, and I am sorry to find they did learn it. At last, however, the attention of the secretary of state was called to these proceedings, and he thought it his duty (and such I conceive it was) to remind the magistracy of the country that there was no greater nuisance on earth than such detestable libels; and that a justice of the peace must not stand by till the assizes came round, but must abate the nuisance. Lord Sidmouth taught that duty to the magistracy, and I hope in future they will observe it. But, gentlemen, unfortunately it came too late. These unhappy men were without employment, and they had already been influenced by the powerful excitement of this seditious writer, who seems to have acquired an extraordinary facility in this way, and who writes in such a manner that it is not very easy for these poor illiterate persons either to refute or detect him. Such was the state of public feeling at the time when these outrages were committed, and such were the causes that led to them.

Sentence Pronounced by Lord Chief Baron Richards

Prisoners at the bar: To see so many persons, especially of your description, standing in the miserable condition in which you stand now before me, is indeed most melancholy; and you exhibit to the public, a spectacle, as afflicting as it is uncommon. I thank God it is extremely rare.

It must be most satisfactory to the world, and I hope administer some consolation to you, that you have had every assistance and advantage that any man labouring under any charge could have wished for. You have been defended by counsel of your own selection, who, without any the least interruption from any quarter, used every exertion in your favour, which their experience, their learning, and their great abilities could suggest to them;—I am speaking of such of you as persisted in the plea of not guilty. You who were tried, were tried by several juries, of as great respectability, as patient, and as attentive, as ever appeared in a British court of justice. During the whole of the investigation which has taken place upon this important and solemn occasion, every consideration has been paid by every side, to every thing that belonged to your defence. Those juries were compelled, by the clearest and most irresistible evidence, to find the four they tried, guilty of high treason. Those of you who were not tried by the juries, desired to be at liberty to withdraw your plea of not guilty;—you knew that your cases being the same, had been decided by the other cases; and that you were virtually condemned by the verdicts which were given, and the rectitude of which you were obliged to admit;—you were conscious of your guilt, and pleaded guilty: you are, therefore, all of you, guilty of high treason—the highest and greatest offense known to the law; it indeed in a manner includes every other. Your insurrection, I thank God, did not last long; but whilst it continued, it was marked with violent outrages, and by the murder of a young man, who did not offer even the least appearance of provocation to you; that conduct showed the ferocity of your purpose. Your object was, to wade through the blood of your countrymen, to extinguish the law and the constitution of your country, and to sacrifice the property, the liberties, and the lives of your fellow subjects, to confusion and anarchy, and the most complete tyranny. God be praised, your purpose failed.

It is not my intention to dwell upon this dreadful picture, which you exhibit; but I trust I may be allowed to express my sincere hope, and my earnest wishes, that the example which you furnish on this important day, may prevent others from yielding to the wild and frantic delusions of a rebellious spirit, and if there be such, deter them from becoming instruments in the hands of hellish agitators, if there are any behind, who, to gratify their own malignity, provoke and excite them, and plunge them into ruin in this world, and it is to be feared, in the next also! Let me beseech you to weigh well your conditions; your lives are become forfeit to the violated laws of your country; make the best use of the small remnant of those lives that you shall enjoy; endeavour to make some compensation to the society which you have injured, and pray God fervently for his forgiveness. I have nothing more to say upon this melancholy occasion, except that I must repeat my sincere wishes, that your example may serve as an useful lesson to others; and that the excellent advice which some of you received from Mr. Goodwin, may never be forgotten, "That the law is too strong for rebels, and that they always carry the halter round their necks." I hope others, by remembering what passes to-day, may avoid the dreadful situation in which you are placed.

I cannot trust myself with speaking more upon the subject, but I hasten to pronounce upon you the last and awful sentence of the law; That you, and each of you, be taken from hence to the gaol from whence you came, and from thence be drawn on a hurdle to the place of execution, and be there severally hanged by the neck until you be dead—and that afterwards, your heads shall be severed from your bodies, and your bodies divided into four quarters shall be disposed of as his majesty shall direct; and may the Lord God of all mercies have compassion upon you!

2.   *The Establishment Reacts:*
The Grenvilles and Peterloo

PETERLOO—the violence inflicted upon about fifty thousand onlookers at a mass meeting in St. Peter's Fields, Manchester, on August 16, 1819, by irresponsible magistrates, incompetent yeoman cavalry, and insensitive mounted troops—was the moral collapse of the cause of reaction. The irrepressible and quarrelsome Henry Hunt, the great radical orator, won no converts, but Sidmouth and other leaders of the extreme right within the British establishment began to lose ground. The defeat was far from apparent in the postscript to Peterloo. The Earl Fitzwilliam—no friend of radicalism but a great champion of a yeomanry properly employed and of order respectably maintained—led a significant group in protest to the government's silly congratulations to the Manchester magistrates. Divisions began to appear in a political elite bound by a common ideology, shared values, kinship, and friendship.

The Grenville clan—a small group uneasily attached to, and shortly to be detached from, the Whig connection—did not share Fitzwilliam's sentiments. Stern measures were the order of the day. The only danger could come from a significant defection within the establishment, and Thomas Grenville was industriously out on circuit attempting to maintain the connection of the establishment against radicalism of any sort at any time under any circumstances. The Grenvilles were properly concerned, for the reforms that trickled forth slowly in the years after 1820, turning into a constitutional and legislative torrent by the end of the decade, had to issue from the establishment and the instruments that it controlled.

The passage of the Six Acts that winter showed only that the traditionalists still commanded the votes. Two of the measures remain substantially in force, raising some question of their totally repressive nature. The preposterous Cato Street conspiracy and the Queen's Case in 1820 served to conceal a fault now running more consistently through the ranks of traditional power.

Recommended Reading

DONALD READ, *Peterloo* (Manchester, 1958), is the most complete study of the event. For the world of the great, consult ARTHUR BRYANT, *The Age of Elegance 1812–1822* (London, 1950). The Whigs connection is dissected and appraised in A. MITCHELL, *The Whigs in Opposition* (Oxford, 1967).

Source: Letters of Thomas Grenville to Lord Grenville, October
1–16, 1819, Historical Manuscripts Commission, *Report on the
Manuscripts of J. B. Fortescue, Esq. Preserved at Dropmore*,
Vol. X (London, 1927), pp. 447–451.

Thomas Grenville to Lord Grenville

Vale Royal
October 1, 1819

In this part of the country as in every other where I have been,
the Manchester Meeting engrosses the whole of the conversation of
all societies. The general opinion however seems to have in it less of
general alarm than I had expected; there is a great confidence in the
general mass of the people who, with the exception of the manufacturing districts, are said to be in no degree disaffected, and the
contemptible characters of the present leaders among the reformers
is another supposed security against any serious mischiefs from
them. I believe, with those who so talk, that the agricultural part of
the population has no ill intentions; indeed with this new code,
which has grown out of the Poor Laws, by which they think
themselves born to the inheritance of being supported, themselves
and their families, out of the Poor's Rates, as long as that lasts, I do
not see why they should wish for great radical changes; but this
does not quiet my apprehensions, because not only is the manufacturing part of the population extremely numerous, but, as far as
one can judge, their discontented leaders appear to be uncommonly
active in using all endeavours to give the most extensive circulation
to their mutinous language and to be extending their connections
into the most remote parts of the country; and it does not appear
that the prosecution of the three or four who are to be tried for
publishing and circulating seditious libels has in any perceptible
degree stopped the publication and circulation of them. Great
rumours prevail of endeavours among the disaffected to produce
before the winter what they call "a general rising" by which they
mean probably breaking out into tumult and riot in so many different districts at once, as to baffle any hopes of the civil authority
being effectually supported by the military. Whether they can or
cannot produce this combined and extended riot to the degree to
which it is talked of by them, may reasonably be doubted; but I see
no reason to doubt that such an intention may be carried into effect
to a degree quite sufficient to produce very frightful consequences,

if some early measures are not adopted for defence and security. Bills are talked of when Parliament meets, but Ministers do not talk, that I know, of assembling Parliament before February, which delay will leave the country for five months exposed to the dangers, whatever they are, that call for new measures of defence. The first obvious measure is that of inviting, through the Lord Lieutenants of counties, yeoman infantry and cavalry in such additions to the present force as could be made most practicable. The very thin ranks of the present yeomanry force not only makes them insufficient in point of number, but renders those who do appear less confident than they would feel if they were numerous enough to support each other with more effect; and further, I should think there would be less difficulty in augmenting them on the present occasion, since in many of the printed papers of the Radicals they attack "the middling orders" for their servility, and threaten them as well as the richer proprietors with equalisation of property. Mr. Banks, a very rich Cheshire gentleman, now in this house, says that he has just come from Manchester, and that the populace there daily insult all who have the appearance of gentlemen and ladies, but particularly the latter, so much, that several who lived in small villas near Manchester to which they had retired from successful business are selling their villas and quitting altogether that part of the country.

Hitherto, bad as the *Times*, *Chronicle*, and *Globe* have been, Opposition seems to have taken as a party no general or decided part for them, nor have I heard of any respectable names, with the exception of Lord Grosvenor's foolish letter and Lord Dundas's foolish speech at York; yet this last I read of with uneasiness, because it is difficult to believe that so decided a step could be taken at York without or against the concurrence of names much more respectable than the electioneering aldermen of the city.

Thomas Grenville to Lord Grenville

Wynnstay
October 14, 1819

It has given me very sincere pain to read the names which are affixed to the Yorkshire requisition, and I can still hardly believe my own eyes when I see them. The language that is circulated by the most moderate and sober-minded of them (if indeed that epithet can be truly applied to any who have joined in such a subscription) is to say that they are aware of the dangers of the times, and of the doctrines promulgated at these meetings, but that the safest way of parrying this danger is by the Whigs taking these meetings into their own hands instead of abandoning them to the Radical Reformers, etc. The childish folly and imbecility of this view of the subject is too provoking to allow of discussing it with any patience. If the history of all ages did not shew how constantly the moderates have in all revolutions been made first the tools, and then the victims of the most furious agitators, surely the recent example of the French Revolution, and the fate of the Brissotins [Girondins], is a lesson sufficiently instructive even to the weakest understandings. The rash step that has been taken by the Whigs in giving their countenance and support to such men and such measures as now fill the public eyes, is in my opinion likely to do the greatest mischief in the country, which their influence could have produced. That it has been done with so much tardy consideration and reflection aggravates in my mind the misconduct and folly of their proceedings. It is whispered to me that Lord G[rey] and his son-in-law went from the north to Doncaster races, and there produced the Yorkshire requisition.

Before that time I had passed a week at Worksop where I had much conversation with the master of the house, and I am glad to find that he has refused both his name and subscription to Lord F[itzwilliam], who visited him to ask it, and that, too, although his father had given both the one and the other. I left him augmenting his yeomanry, which is a measure that I still think has not been sufficiently promoted and encouraged by the Ministers. I had much conversation with Charles yesterday who sees the whole of this subject just as we do; he is gone to Welsh Pool to meet his yeomanry, and writes to-night to offer through the Lord Lieutenant to augment his numbers and to extend their services; and Watkin writes a similar letter to Lord Sidmouth with a similar offer to-night. I very much wish this course was more generally adopted. It would give an opportunity of displaying a constitutional desire to support the laws and the Government of the country, and would furnish at the same time the most efficient means of substantial defence.

Thomas Grenville to Lord Grenville

Llanvorda
October 16, 1819

I find Lord Carrington here, expressing great satisfaction at Lord Buckingham's letter, and still more at hearing what he had presumed to be your opinions confirmed by my account of them. He approves as much as I do of the meeting of Parliament, intends to be there on the first day, and trusts that he shall meet you there, a confidence in which I hope he will not be disappointed. Surely there never was a time in which it was more necessary for every man, according to his means and abilities, to set his shoulder to the wheel. D[uke] of Devonshire, L[or]d Carlisle, L[or]d Morpeth, L[or]d Surr[e]y are names well saved from the disgrace of the Yorkshire requisition, but I am afraid by what I hear from Henry that his brother-in-law does not agree with Lord Carrington on this subject, and I am not without great apprehension of our two lordly nephews, though I have as yet heard nothing positive of them.

I met at Wynnstay a Lancashire gentleman who is a magistrate, who told me that last year he had evidence upon oath that schools in his neighbourhood, recently instituted, and where not less than 2,000 children are educated, are in the hands and under the direction of these Radical Reformers, and that at more than one of them their master had publicly burnt the Bible before them; and that some of the speechifying Radical ladies of these latter meetings he knew to have placed children in these schools in order to have these opinions taught to them. My authority is Mr. Brook, a gentleman of very large estate living at twelve miles from Manchester.

3. *The Decline of Monarchy: The Queen's Case, 1820*

THE PRESSURES beneath the surface of British political life that exploded in such diverse rows as Peterloo and the Cato Street conspiracy were dramatically eased by an important event in the decline of British monarchy, the divorce case of Queen Caroline in 1820. It was a tawdry

matter but of immediate political and long-range constitutional significance. The Hanoverian dynasty contributed stolid, rather uninspiring
and uninspired sovereigns. Queen Victoria stands apart, but only after
her apotheosis and reappearance in her Disraelian role of imperial
mother. She was a small woman. But her great uncle was not a small
man. He was Falstaffian—weak, impetuous, egotistic—but he was the
only Hanoverian of real aesthetic sensitivity. He patronized the great
architects of his age, like Nash; the great painters, like Turner. He had
a feeling for music and literature, which we forget when we see the
painted, corseted voluptuary.

George IV, as Regent and King, presided over an era of fundamental
constitutional change, much of which he never perceived and almost
all he did perceive he disliked. The "influence of the crown," that
century-old Country party bugaboo, was waning. The sovereign—as
George III may slowly have realized as he descended into the merciful
oblivion of insanity—was ceasing to be a political free agent. Parliament and the country were increasingly dictating the course of
national policy and selecting the royal servants to conduct it. George
IV had not totally lost the political initiative, but his use of it was
almost invariably bad. He clung to his father's consistent, hysterical
opposition to Roman Catholic emancipation and, had he not been a
coward retreating under the pressure of Wellington and Peel, would
have plunged England into civil war in Ireland.

The disintegrating estate of British monarchy was not merely a
matter of constitutional changes deriving from a new political situation. It was also a matter of character. George III had gone mad.
George IV showed that intelligent inattention might be as bad as
stupid concentration. Moreover, as W. E. H. Lecky observed of
Queen Victoria, the monarch functioned as a moral force. He no
longer merely set the style for a court; he set an example for the
nation. George IV added color but no conscience to an age of
increasing seriousness which avowed dedication and discipline in human affairs.

George unfortunately had an aggressive Brunswick for a wife. She
shared her husband's melodramatic and amorous proclivities. Caroline
offered an even less suitable example for moral guidance, for her taste
in lovers was more democratic. The King and the Queen had separated; and she had lived on the Continent for some years. Spurred on
by some political adventurers, she came flying back to England when
George took it into his head to have her name stricken from the
Anglican liturgy, to divorce her, and to marry the plump but pleasing
Lady Conyngham. The tawdry divorce case became a party issue. The
disaffected of England used Caroline to purge their grievances and
release their aggressions. Brougham and Denman, two of the ablest trial
counsels of the day, acted on her behalf. The London crowds cheered
her on her way.

Scandal, even royal scandal, loses its piquancy. It has limited theatrical value, and the dull scenes played out in the upper house through the summer of 1820 found the Queen—as Lord Holland put it—who formerly slept with her footman, now sleeping with the Lords. The ministry got a bare majority in the House of Lords and knew it could never face the Commons. The divorce bill was dropped, Caroline's name vanished from the liturgy, and she was bought with a pension of fifty thousand pounds. Her popularity collapsed; the King's rose. But the damage was irrevocable. The sovereign was increasingly a symbolic contradiction in his own age. Through madness, stupidity, and immorality Victoria's three predecessors lowered the stock of monarchy. Only thirty years of the narrow domestic virtues of Queen Victoria finally retrieved the symbolic luster of the sovereign. Meanwhile the political function and the constitutional role had been changed.

The world changed in the Regency and reign of George IV; but save as a patron of the arts (itself no small matter), he contributed little of merit. As a contemporary critic observed,

> If, in examining closer, we find that where open and absolute violation of established morality was not practised, there existed low debauchery, debasing indulgencies, vain and haughty insolence of demeanour, and an overweening self-estimation, we have little to induce us to believe that the small portion of the royal life not yet laid bare to public inspection, would do credit to the late King, or add much support to the too-willing eulogium of his admirers.[1]

He was the end of an era even as his reign was the end of a system.

Recommended Reading

In addition to the usual HALÉVY citations, there are the usual popular *qua* sensationalist biographies which emphasize the wrong things. A. ASPINALL, who has edited the King's correspondence, has the best range of material in his *English Historical Documents*, Vol. XI, *1783–1832* (London, 1959). The problem is also discussed in L. B. NAMIER, "Monarchy and the Party System," which can be found in several collections, including *Crossroads of Power* (London, 1962). The most perceptive analysis of the subtle elements of constitutional change is A. S. FOORD, "The Waning of 'the Influence of the Crown,' " *English Historical Review*, Vol. LXII (1947), pp. 484–507.

SOURCE: Charles Cavendish Fulke Greville, *The Greville Memoirs: a Journal of the Reigns of King George IV and King Wil-*

[1] Robert Huish, *Memoirs of George the Fourth*, Vol. II (London, 1831), p. 420.

liam IV, edited by Henry Reeve (New York, 1875), pp. 24–28, 30–33.

June 7th.—The Queen arrived in London yesterday at seven o'clock. I rode as far as Greenwich to meet her. The road was thronged with an immense multitude the whole way from Westminster Bridge to Greenwich. Carriages, carts, and horsemen followed, preceded, and surrounded her coach the whole way. She was everywhere received with the greatest enthusiasm. Women waved pocket-handkerchiefs, and men shouted wherever she passed. She traveled in an open landau, Alderman Wood sitting by her side, and Lady Ann Hamilton and another woman opposite. Everybody was disgusted at the vulgarity of Wood in sitting in the place of honor, while the Duke of Hamilton's sister was sitting backward in the carriage. The queen looked exactly as she did before she left England, and seemed neither dispirited nor dismayed. As she passed by White's she bowed and smiled to the men who were in the window. The crowd was not great in the streets through which she passed. Probably people had ceased to expect her, as it was so much later than the hour designated for her arrival. It is impossible to conceive the sensation created by this event. Nobody either blames or approves of her sudden return, but all ask, "What will be done next? How is it to end?" In the House of Commons there was little said; but the few words which fell from Creevy, Bennett, or Denman, seem to threaten most stormy debates whenever the subject is discussed. The King in the mean time is in excellent spirits, and the Ministers affect the greatest unconcern and talk of the time it will take to pass the Bills to "settle her business." "Her business," as they call it, will in all probability raise such a tempest as they will find it beyond their powers to appease; and for all His Majesty's unconcern the day of her arrival in England may be such an anniversary to him as he will have no cause to celebrate with much rejoicing.

June 9th. . . . The mob have been breaking windows in all parts of the town and pelting those who would not take off their hats as they passed Wood's door. Last night Lord Exmouth's house was assaulted and his windows broken, when he rushed out, armed with sword and pistol, and drove away the mob. Frederick Ponsonby saw him. Great sums of money have been won and lost on

34CHALLENGING THE CONSTITUTION

the Queen's return, for there was much betting at the clubs. The alderman showed a specimen of his taste as he came into London; when the Queen's coach passed Carlton House he stood up and gave three cheers.

June 16th.—There was some indiscipline manifested in a battalion of the 3d Guards the day before yesterday; they were dissatisfied at the severity of their duty and at some allowances that had been taken from them, and on coming off guard they refused to give up their ball-cartridges. They were ordered off to Plymouth, and marched at four yesterday morning. Many people went from the ball at Devonshire House to see them march away. Plymouth was afterward changed for Portsmouth in consequence of their good behavior on the route. [The Marquis of] Worcester met many of them drunk at Brentford, crying out, "God save Queen Caroline!" There was some disturbance last night in consequence of the mob assembling round the King's mews, where the rest of the battalion that had marched to Portsmouth still remained.

June 25th.—The Queen's refusal to comply with the desire of the House of Commons keeps conjecture afloat and divides opinions as to the opening of the bag [of evidence about her conduct]. The Opposition call her answer a very good one; those of the other party I have seen think it too long, and not neatly and clearly worded. Brougham declined advising her as to her answer; he told her she must be guided by her own feelings, and was herself the only person capable of judging what she had best do. The discussion of the Queen's business is now become an intolerable nuisance in society; no other subject is ever talked of. It is an incessant matter of argument and dispute what will be done and what ought to be done. All people express themselves tired of the subject, yet none talk or think of any other. It is a great evil when a single subject of interest takes possession of society; conversation loses all its lightness and variety, and every drawing-room is converted into an arena of political disputation. People even go to talk about it from habit long after the interest it excited has ceased.

July 6th.—Since the report of the Secret Committee public opinion is entirely changed as to the result of the proceedings against the Queen. Everybody thinks the charges will be proved and that the King will be divorced. It is impossible to discover what effect the report may have in the country; it is certain hitherto that all ranks of men have been decidedly favorable to the

Queen, and disbelieve the charges against her. The military in London have shown alarming symptoms of dissatisfaction, so much so that it seems doubtful how far the Guards can be counted upon in case of any disturbance arising out of this subject. Luttrell says that "the extinguisher is taking fire."

July 14th.—I have been at Newmarket, where I had the first fortunate turn this year. The conversation about the Queen begins to subside; everybody seems to agree that it is a great injustice not to allow her lists of the witnesses; the excuse that it is not usual is bad, for the proceedings are anomalous altogether, and it is absurd to attempt to adhere to precedent; here there are no precedents and no analogies to guide to a decision. London is drawing to a close, but in August it will be very full, as all the Peers must be here. They say the trial will last six months. . . .

The town is still in an uproar about the trial, and nobody has any doubt that it will finish by the Bill being thrown out and the Ministers turned out. Brougham's speech was the most magnificent display of argument and oratory that has been heard for years, and they say that the impression it made upon the House was immense; even his most violent opponents (including Lord Lonsdale) were struck with admiration and astonishment.

October 15th. . . . Since I have been in the world I never remember any question which so exclusively occupied everybody's attention, and so completely absorbed men's thoughts and engrossed conversation. In the same degree is the violence displayed. It is taken up as a party question entirely, and the consequence is that everybody is gone mad about it. Very few people admit of any medium between pronouncing the Queen quite innocent and judging her guilty and passing the Bill. Until the evidence of Lieutenant Hownam it was generally thought that proofs of her guilt were wanting, but since his admission that Bergami slept under the tent with her all unprejudiced men seemed to think the adultery sufficiently proved. The strenuous opposers of the Bill, however, by no means allow this, and make a mighty difference between sleeping dressed under a tent and being shut up at night in a room together, which the supporters of the Bill contend would have been quite or nearly the same thing. The Duke of Portland, who is perfectly impartial, and who has always been violently against the Bill, was so satisfied by Hownam's evidence that he told me that after that admission by him he thought all further proceedings useless, and that it was ridiculous to listen to any more evidence, as the fact was proved; that he should attend no longer to any evidence upon the subject. This view of the case will not, however, induce him to vote for the Bill, because he thinks that upon grounds of expediency it ought not to pass. The Ministers were elated in an extraordinary manner by this evidence of Hownam's. The Duke of Wellington told Madame de Lieven that he was very tired; "mais les grands succès fatiguent autant que les grands revers [but great successes are as tiring as great defeats]." They look upon the progress of this trial in the light of a campaign, and upon each day's proceedings as a sort of battle, and by the impression made by the evidence they consider that they have gained a victory or sustained a defeat. Their anxiety that this Bill should pass is quite inconceivable, for it cannot be their interest that it should be carried; and as for the King, they have no feeling whatever for him. The Duke of Portland told me that he conversed with the Duke of Wellington upon the subject, and urged as one of the reasons why this Bill should not pass the House of Lords the disgrace that it would entail upon the King by the recrimination that would ensue in the House of Commons. His answer was "that the King was degraded as low as he could be already." The vehemence with which they pursue this object produces a corresponding violence in their language and sentiments. Lady Harrowby, who is usually very indifferent upon political subjects, has taken this up with unusual eagerness. In an argument which I had with her the day before yesterday, she said that if the House of Lords was to suffer itself to be influenced by the opinions and wishes of the people, it would be the most mean and pusillanimous conduct, and that after all what did it signify what the people thought or what they expressed if the army was to be depended upon? I answered that I never had expected that the day would come when I should be told that we were to disregard the feelings and wishes of the people of this country, and to look to our army for support.

4. Tory Reform:
Canning's New World

TORYISM was not synonymous with reaction and repression. The old age of acute tensions left over from the French and Napoleonic wars abroad and the persecution of radicalism at home seemed to pass after the purgation of the Queen's Case. Sidmouth finally left the Home Office in 1821. Castlereagh committed suicide in 1822. The way was open for the reconstruction of Lord Liverpool's government along new lines—and strikingly new they were. William Huskisson, as the new president of the Board of Trade, worked on the problem of adjusting British policy and institutions to the industrial age. Sir Robert Peel at the Home Office executed spectacular reforms in the criminal code and provided London, at last, with a civilized police force.

British foreign policy, like domestic policy, underwent basic changes in the years following the defeat of Napoleon. Here there was less of a break between old and new. Castlereagh and Canning despised each other, but Canning made his foreign policy sound more like a break with his predecessor's than it was. The failure of the Congress movement, from the British point of view, was as clear to Castlereagh as it was to Canning; and Castlereagh had already begun the process of British disengagement from the system. The Duke of Wellington walked out of the Congress of Verona (1822) as the French prepared to walk into Spain to restore the contemptible Ferdinand to his throne.

Canning's response to French intervention in Spain was English intervention in Portugal. English troops appeared to be marching to support a liberal constitution against a reactionary conspiracy. So, in fact, they were, but Canning's principal interest was to restore the balance of power. Support of liberal nationalism was a convenience, not a principle—in Portugal, Greece, and Latin America. But it did come to be a policy (how and in what ways Document 18 suggests) over the next twenty years, although not one consistently pursued. The "New World" that Canning summoned to redress the balance of the old was the new world of British interests quite as much as of British ideals.

Recommended Reading

On the general problem, R. W. SETON-WATSON, *Britain in Europe, 1789–1914* (London, 1937); and H. W. V. TEMPERLEY, *The Foreign*

Policy of Canning, 1822–1827 (London, 1925). For the British context, in addition to E. HALÉVY, *The Liberal Awakening,* consult W. R. BROCK, *Lord Liverpool and Liberal Toryism* (London, 1941).

SOURCE: George Canning, "Speech on the King's Message Relative to the Affairs of Portugal, December 12th, 1826," *The Speeches of George Canning,* edited by R. Therry, Vol. VI (London, 1828), pp. 106–112.

    I do not see how the withdrawing of the French troops from Spain, could effect our present purpose. I believe, Sir, that the French army in Spain is now a protection to that very party which it was originally called in to put down. Were the French army suddenly removed at this precise moment, I verily believe that the immediate effect of that removal would be, to give full scope to the unbridled rage of a fanatical faction, before which, in the whirl-wind of intestine strife, the party least in numbers would be swept away.

    So much for the *immediate* effect of the demand which it is proposed to us to make, if that demand were instantly successful. But when, with reference to the larger question of a military occupation of Spain by France, it is averred, that by that occupation the relative situation of Great Britain and France is altered; that France is thereby exalted and Great Britain lowered, in the eyes of Europe;—I must beg leave to say, that I dissent from that averment. The House knows—the country knows—that when the French army was on the point of entering Spain, His Majesty's Government did all in their power to prevent it; that we resisted it by all means, short of war. I have just now stated some of the reasons why we did not think the entry of that army into Spain, a sufficient ground for war; but there was, in addition to those which I have stated, this peculiar reason,—that whatever effect a war, commenced upon the mere ground of the entry of a French army into Spain, might have, it probably would not have had the effect of getting that army out of Spain. In a war against France at that time, as at any other; you might, perhaps, have acquired military glory; you might, perhaps, have extended your colonial posses-sions; you might even have achieved, at great cost of blood and treasure, an honourable peace; but as to getting the French out of Spain, *that* would have been the one object which you, almost certainly, would not have accomplished. How seldom, in the whole history of the wars of Europe, has any war between two great powers ended, in the obtaining of the exact, the identical object, for which the war was begun!

Besides, Sir, I confess I think, that the effects of the French occupation of Spain have been infinitely exaggerated.

I do not blame those exaggerations; because I am aware that they are to be attributed to the recollections of some of the best times of our history; that they are the echoes of sentiments, which in the days of William and of Anne, animated the debates and dictated the votes of the British Parliament. No peace was in those days thought safe for this country while the crown of Spain continued on the head of a Bourbon. But were not the apprehensions of those days greatly overstated?—Has the power of Spain swallowed up the power of maritime England?—Or does England still remain, after the lapse of more than a century, during which the crown of Spain has been worn by a Bourbon,—niched in a nook of that same Spain—Gibraltar; an occupation which was contemporaneous with the apprehensions that I have described, and which has happily survived them?

Again, Sir,—is the Spain of the present day the Spain of which the statesmen of the times of William and Anne were so much afraid? Is it indeed the nation whose puissance was expected to shake England from her sphere? No, Sir, it was quite another Spain—it was the Spain, within the limits of whose empire the sun never set—it was Spain *"with the Indies"* that excited the jealousies and alarmed the imaginations of our ancestors.

But then, Sir, the balance of power!—The entry of the French army into Spain disturbed that balance, and we ought to have gone to war to restore it! I have already said, that when the French army entered Spain, we might, if we chose, have resisted or re-sented that measure by war. But were there no other means than war for restoring the balance of power?—Is the balance of power a fixed and unalterable standard? Or is it not a standard perpetually varying, as civilization advances, and as new nations spring up, and take their place among established political communities? The balance of power a century and a half ago was to be adjusted between France and Spain, the Netherlands, Austria, and England. Some years afterwards, Russia assumed her high station in Euro-pean politics. Some years after that again, Prussia became not only a substantive, but a preponderating monarchy.—Thus, while the balance of power continued in principle the same, the means of adjusting it became more varied and enlarged. They became enlarged, in proportion to the increased number of considerable states—in proportion, I may say, to the number of weights which might be shifted into the one or the other scale. To look to the policy of Europe, in the times of William and Anne, for the purpose of regulating the balance of power in Europe at the present day, is to disregard the progress of events, and to confuse dates and facts which throw a reciprocal light upon each other.

It would be disingenuous, indeed, not to admit that the entry of the French army into Spain was, in a certain sense, a disparagement—an affront to the pride—a blow to the feelings of England: —and it can hardly be supposed that the Government did not sympathize, on that occasion, with the feelings of the people. But I deny that, questionable or censurable as the act might be, it was one which necessarily called for our direct and hostile opposition. Was nothing then to be done?—Was there no other mode of resistance, than by a direct attack upon France—or by a war to be undertaken on the soil of Spain? What, if the possession of Spain might be rendered harmless in rival hands—harmless as regarded us—and valueless to the possessors? Might not compensation for disparagement be obtained, and the policy of our ancestors vindicated, by means better adapted to the present time? If France occupied Spain, was it necessary, in order to avoid the consequences of that occupation—that we should blockade Cadiz? No. I looked another way—I sought materials of compensation in another hemisphere. Contemplating Spain, such as our ancestors had known her, I resolved that if France had Spain, it should not be Spain "*with the Indies*." I called the New World into existence, to redress the balance of the Old.

It is thus, Sir, that I answer the accusation brought against His Majesty's Government, of having allowed the French army to usurp and to retain the occupation of Spain. That occupation, I am quite confident, is an unpaid and unredeemed burden to France. It is a burden of which, I verily believe, France would be glad to rid herself. But they know little of the feelings of the French Government, and of the spirit of the French nation, who do not know, that, worthless or burdensome as that occupation may be, the way to rivet her in it would be, by angry or intemperate representations, to make the continuance of that occupation a point of honour. . . .

In conclusion, Sir, I shall only once more declare, that the object of the Address, which I propose to you, is not war:—its object is to take the last chance of peace. If you do not go forth, on this occasion to the aid of Portugal, Portugal will be trampled down, to your irretrievable disgrace:—and then will come war in the train of national degradation. If, under circumstances like these, you wait till Spain has matured her secret machinations into open hostility, you will in a little while have the sort of war required by the pacifitors:—and who shall say where that war will end?

5. Tory Resistance:
Eldon and the Test Act

JOHN SCOTT, first Earl of Eldon (1751–1838), was a reactionary in the most meaningful sense of the term. He did not merely resist the future. He actively sought a retreat to the past. He was the son of a Newcastle coal merchant, and Eldon always fancied himself a self-made man. His attitude toward his many honors was that of the frightened parvenu, but honors he accumulated. He opposed the American Revolution, the French Revolution, and the industrial revolution and attempted to repeal the nineteenth century. Yet he was one of the great Lord Chancellors (1801–06, 1807–27), responsible for much of the equity doctrine and judicial obfuscation that characterized the Court of Chancery. He had focused his penetrating, but narrow, mind on the law and resisted all other forms of cultivation or interest. He was an unpleasant man who in Harold Twiss had the singular good fortune to find a biographer even more politically and culturally Neanderthal than himself.

Eldon characteristically confused obstinacy with firmness, prejudice with value, and narrowness with character.

The leading principle of his political life was attachment to the establishments of the country, especially in the Church. He opposed the Dissenters and the Roman Catholics, not because he looked at them through any jaundice of theological dislike, but simply because he believed that the Church Establishment would be undetermined by their admission to the functions of the State. He endeavoured to restrain the eagerness with which the advocates of the Negroes, in 1804 and in 1806, were pressing the abolition of the Slave Trade, not because he was friendly to tyranny or oppression, but because he doubted the efficacy of the measure even for its own objects, and held it unjust precipitately to unsettle the great masses of property which had been invested on the faith of the then existing law.[1]

His inveterate resistance to Catholic emancipation made him briefly a sort of folk hero. His biographer claims that he presented over 900 petitions against Catholic relief in the 1829 debates. For once his prejudices and those of the great mass of Englishmen coincided. "No Popery!" remained sound middle-class doctrine. Lord John Russell could still win a general election with it in the middle of the century.

Roman Catholics secured their rights in England through the threat of Irish rebellion and Civil War. The Catholic Association and Daniel O'Connell mobilized a nation and won British civil rights. Ironically the Duke of Wellington and Sir Robert Peel, who had organized their government with right-wing support, found themselves the unwitting victims of their previous rhetoric. Their "betrayal" on the issue led to substantial Ultra-Tory defections in the election of 1830 and provided some right-wing support for constitutional reform.[2]

In a sense, the Ultras at least possessed the virtue of consistency. They understood that the traditional constitution was a constitution in Church and state. It could suffer no change without jeopardizing the whole, and the political structure was the final expression of the social world and cultural values of the aristocracy.

Recommended Reading

Beyond previous suggestions, one should consult: G. Best, "Popular Protestantism," in R. Robson, *Ideas and Institutions of Victorian Britain* (London, 1967), pp. 115–142; O. J. Brose, *Church and Parliament* (Stanford, 1959); N. Gash, *Mr. Secretary Peel* (London, 1959); U. Henriques, *Religious Toleration in England 1787–1833* (Toronto, 1961); A. McIntyre, *The Liberator* (London, 1965); P. Reynolds, *The Catholic Emancipation Crisis in Ireland* (New Haven, 1954).

Source: John Scott, Lord Eldon, "Speech on the Roman Catholic Relief Bill, 10 April 1829," *Hansard's Parliamentary Debates*, New Series, Vol. XXI, cols. 633–640.

The noble and learned lord, after some further observations, which were inaudible, said, that the question was partly political,

---

[1] H. Twiss, *The Public and Private Life of Lord Chancellor Eldon* (London, 1844), Vol. III, p. 490.

[2] On this intriguing point, see the elaborate argument of D. C. Moore, "The Other Face of Reform," *Victorian Studies*, Vol. V (1961), 7–34.

and partly religious, and of mighty import in both points of view. He firmly believed, that the high moral and religious character of the great bulk of the people who formed the community in England was owing to the abolition of indulgencies, absolution, penance, commutation of trial on payment of money, and all the other abominable doctrines which belonged to the church of Rome. The advocates of the measure contended, that little danger was to be apprehended from it, because it was not likely that a Protestant king would place a Roman Catholic in any important office of trust. What would be the consequence? Why, that instead of the feeling of dissatisfaction on the part of the Catholics being directed against the law of the country as heretofore, the king would be placed in such a situation, that it must be directed against him. He had heard lord Hardwicke, lord Loughborough, lord Kenyon, and lord Ellenborough declare their opinion of the necessity of every government providing an established church, and incorporating it with the state; and when he looked at the history of the country, and saw that the contest between the reformed and the Roman Catholic religion had debilitated every nerve, and destroyed every sinew, until it was terminated by the Revolution of 1688, he was the more confirmed in the correctness of that opinion. His opinion had always been, that there should be in this country an established church, carrying with it political power, and giving to all other religions a toleration hardly knowing a limit. God forbid that he should harbour any ill-feeling towards Roman Catholics and Dissenters on account of their religious opinions; but he would rather that their lordships would establish another religion, and give toleration to those of the Protestant persuasion, than pass a measure which, in his soul and conscience, he believed would first destroy the established church in Ireland—(which was part of the united established church of England and Ireland)—and finally leave us with a system of political power regulated in no manner by religious opinions.

This question had always been considered as one which affected the constitution as established in 1688. He really did not know what formed the constitution of a country, unless those established laws which were stated to be fundamental laws formed the constitution. He begged their lordships to look at what he might call the compact entered into between king William and the people of this country; he begged of them to attend to what that monarch had said, with respect to admitting persons to offices of political trust, other than those who belonged to the established church;—he begged of their lordships to look at the Bill of Rights, the very first clause of which declared, that this was to be a Protestant kingdom, and then to tell him how this was to continue a Protestant kingdom, if they acted on a principle which would destroy its character as a Protestant kingdom? He begged of their lordships to tell him, what was the meaning of imposing on the sovereign the solemn oath which he had taken, that he would, to the very utmost of his power, support the Protestant reformed religion. Would their lordships tell him how it happened that, after king William had said all he had said, with respect to removing the tests—among which were the tests removed last year, and that which it was proposed now to remove, that his object was not carried into effect? Now, he could not find an act passed in the course of king William's reign—even that with respect to indulgences to what were called tender consciences—which did not require some disclaimer against the power of foreign princes and potentates. From the whole of the acts of parliament then passed, it was quite clear, that a bargain was then made between the prince and the people, to the intent, that their liberties might not be endangered.

He now came to the act of Union with Scotland. . . . It was his decided opinion, that it was a part of that act, that no papist should elect or be elected. . . . It was the law of the land that no papist should have any thing to do with the throne, or fill any office whatsoever. . . . The articles of the treaty declared, that the clauses respecting the churches of England and Scotland should be inviolable. He had said, over and over again, and he would now repeat, that the mere declaration of any thing to be inviolable, unless means were at the same time enacted to preserve it inviolable, was worth nothing. . . . Now, whether their lordships called these laws the laws which formed the constitution—whether they called them established and fundamental laws, or gave them any other name they pleased—he besought their lordships to allow him to ask if, to use a modern phrase, they were to be delighted with the idea of "settling the question," whether those laws, at the time they were passed, were not considered a settlement of the question—laws which were enacted, as it was therein declared, that our religion and liberties might not be again endangered. Their lordships had now, for twenty years, refused to endanger that liberty and that religion. . . .

He had before stated his opinion of the Catholic Association, and should not fatigue the House by repeating it. With respect to the Disfranchisement bill, there was one point which he wished to explain. It was very true that he was not present at the debate upon that bill, and his reason was this;—he looked upon it as a measure of vast importance, and as possessing an influence over the condition of society in Ireland which, perhaps, even yet, had not been estimated. . . . With respect to the disputed power of parliament to interfere with the right of franchise, his opinion was this—that it was fully competent to parliament to make any alteration which it thought fit in the elective franchise of the people; and, further, that when it appeared to them fitting to make such alterations, the public good and common interest were not to be overridden by the terms of the act of Union. This was his opinion, right or wrong. If right, he claimed no merit from it; if wrong, he hoped the House would have the courtesy to believe that, though he might be wrong, he was not obstinate.

And now, my lords (continued the noble and learned lord), "I think I have given my humble answer to most of the arguments on this subject, and stated my humble opinion upon most of the topics which have been introduced into the discussion of this bill. I was not present at any debate upon it while it was in the committee, and in this, perhaps, I may have been wrong; but it appeared to me that I should gain no good end by attending, because I knew that no alteration would be permitted to be made in the bill, and that it would be only waste of time to propose any thing. But I cannot help saying now, that this measure will and must have the effect of utterly beating down those principles of justice upon which the great compact was first made between a Protestant prince and a Protestant people, and that it will lead to the ruin of the purest church, and the purest system of Christianity which the world ever saw, if I were to vote for it, my lords, it would be against my decided opinion of its injustice, and against my well-considered and well-founded apprehensions of its danger to the church of England and Ireland. I do not believe that, if the church of Ireland were to be made distinct from that of England, it would be possible for it to survive this measure. My own opinion is, that it cannot survive it. . . . Those of your lordships who suppose that the Catholic bishops are willing to admit the Protestant church, have not read the oath taken by these bishops. That oath is a sufficient answer to the question of, whether they acknowledge the church or no? and

I believe I may take the extract which I have just read as expressing the sentiments of all Catholics towards our church. You may flatter yourselves that these consequences will not follow—and God forbid that I should say you are wrong, if, in voting for the third reading of this bill, you do not conscientiously believe that you are placing in danger those Protestant establishments which ought to have, but which will not have, if this bill pass, a Protestant king and a Protestant parliament. Those with whom we have to deal with are much too wary to apprize us, by any immediate conduct, of our danger; but that they will triumph—not to-day, nor to-morrow, but when I shall have been consigned to the urns and sepulchres of mortality—I have no more doubt than that I now stand here. I, therefore, my lords, pray to God that those evils may be averted which I foresee. I say to you—and I pray you to hearken to the words of a man who must soon go to his last great account—that before I can bring myself to give my vote for this bill, I must first pray to God to forgive me for having outraged every notion which I have ever conceived should regulate my conduct, and every notion of the sacred nature of the oaths and declarations which I had ever taken. I think I know something of the Catholic clergy, and of their feelings towards our Protestant church. I have long entertained certain opinions of them, and though this is late in life to alter one's opinion, yet I should be willing to think better of these clergy if I could. But I do declare, my lords, that I would rather hear at this moment, that to-morrow morning I was to cease to exist—an illustration, however, which I do not put as one of great force, for I should look upon it as any thing but an affliction—I say, that, after all the consideration which I have been able to give to this question, rather than consent to an alteration of laws which I hold to be fundamental, and which I think to be essential to the support of the throne, the safety of the church, the good of the aristocracy, and the preservation of the constitution of the country, in kings, lords, and commons, I would rather hear that I was not to exist to-morrow morning, than awake to the reflection, that I had consented to an act, which had stamped me as a violator of my solemn oath, a traitor to my church, and a traitor to the constitution.

6. Political Knowledge and Participation: The Extraordinary Black Book

THE POWER of information is measureless. If a man knows, he will be able to do. So runs at least part of the liberal argument derived from radical sources of the eighteenth century. The aristocracy maintained its control, institutions ran badly if at all, attitudes were confused, morals were debased through an insufficiency of knowledge. Utilitarian political philosophy emphasized the need for knowledge to make rational choices. The practical problem of surviving in a changing world demanded information and awareness. The theme constantly recurs: let people know, and they will do what must be done.

English radicalism grew from domestic roots but foreign branches were grafted on its trunk. English Jacobin ideology antedated the French Revolution, but *sans culottes* rhetoric augmented the vocabulary and glorified the threat from the left. Again in 1830–32, radical elements in the reform crisis drew upon French and American doctrine as well as finding some degree of inspiration in the French revolution of 1830. English radicals were essentially anti-establishment. They consistently argued in terms of history and precedent—the restoration of the unblemished Anglo-Saxon constitution, repeated appeals to "our ancient liberties and rights"—but they struck principally at establishments in church and State, specifically at any privileged element, or what they conceived to be the corrupt sources of Establishment support.

Radical pamphleteering and journalism became effective and general in the era of intense reaction. When in 1816 William Cobbett shifted from his one-shilling newspaper, *The Political Register*, to a small pamphlet costing twopence, he found a mass market awaiting him. For the next half-century others emulated his example, bringing an unprecedented range of views and information to an expanding reading public. Even widespread illiteracy, running over 40 per cent in some counties, did not prevent the rapid dissemination of sensible and eccentric notions. The political pamphlet or newspaper became and remained a favorite medium for propaganda and proselytizing. A persistent campaign ran for the total elimination of tax stamps on newspapers and the lesser duties on pamphlets: proponents and foes divided roughly along the lines of adaptability to social and political change. Moderates, in other words, thought a low but moderate duty a good thing.

Radicals had no interest in compromise on this point. *The Extraordi-*

nary Black Book of 1831, a marvel of political muckraking, gave freedom of publication first priority. In this section of the chapter on the "State of the Representation," the author(s) probably overstate the case for the efficacy of pamphleteering and the radical press, but not by much. They were enshrining "the right to know" as a fundamental liberal freedom.

Recommended Reading

In addition to the general and specific titles mentioned before, see W. H. WICKWAR, *The Struggle for the Freedom of the Press, 1819– 1832* (New York, 1928); R. K. WEBB, *The British Working-Class Reader* (New York, 1955); J. DERRY, *The Radical Tradition* (London, 1967); M. HAMBURGER, *James Mill and the Art of Revolution* (London, 1963); and biographies of the principal radical writers.

SOURCE: *The Extraordinary Black Book* (London, 1831), pp. 345– 349.

Irresponsible, and occasionally oppressive power, exercised by the Times, and the defects in its management as a public journal, fully, in our opinion, exemplify the abuses which may grow up under the present system of the Press. For the correction of these evils we know nothing so appropriate as *opening the trade*, by means of minor publications. The suppression of the cheap political pamphlets by lord Castlereagh always appeared to us both unjust and impolitic. Sedition and licentiousness might have been effectually restrained without destroying an instrument which, ultimately, might have been made subservient to the attainment of the most salutary ameliorations. It is the imposition of the *stamp duty*, not the demand of security of which we complain; the former completely interdicting, to a vast majority of the community, a source of amusement and intellectual improvement.

Some of the most dangerous popular errors, we are convinced, were eradicated solely by the agency of the cheap political tracts. Among these we reckon the prevailing opinions on *Catholic Emancipation*. Before the establishment of the weekly pamphlets the mass of the population was decidedly anti-catholic, and hardly less obstinate in their prejudices than Lord Eldon or Sir C. Wetherall. A prodigious change was effected in the character of the people in another respect. During a scarcity, or high prices, the rage of the labouring classes was mostly vented on the butcher, baker, and farmer; such senseless outrages are now never heard of.

Besides the diffusion of political knowledge and the principles of religious toleration, other advantages, tending to the security of property and the commercial prosperity of the country, resulted from the circulation of cheap pamphlets. We allude to the introduction of *machinery*. This, for obvious reasons, was opposed by the mass of the people. It was impossible they should at first be reconciled to inventions which, though tending to the general advantage, by the multiplication of commodities at a cheaper rate, yet, if they did not deprive some classes of the means of subsistence, degraded them for ever into lower stations. It was natural, therefore, they should resist this innovation; and, in so doing, we believe, they did no more than the legal, ecclesiastical, or any other class would have done, had their interests been sacrificed, though that sacrifice were made for the general good. It was necessary, however, the principle should triumph. The people resisted; severer laws were made against frame-breakers, and a terrible sacrifice was made at York: but all this would have been ineffectual, had not another cause interfered. This cause, we verily believe, was the introduction of the *two-penny trash;* which demonstrated that, however injurious the employment of machinery might be to particular branches of industry, yet, inasmuch as it augmented the supply of food and clothing, consequently rendered them cheaper to all classes, it must be ultimately beneficial. Here, then, was another advantage resulting from pamphlet-writing.

One more remark may be made on this subject. It was unceasingly represented, at the time, that the weekly writers were solely occupied on those subjects most likely to *inflame* and *delude* their readers: had this been their only object, it is strange they did not more frequently allude to the subject of *machinery*. Here, indeed, was a fine field both for inflaming and deluding the people. Thousands of unhappy men might have been found in the manufacturing districts, whose passions it were easy to inflame, and whose vengeance it were easy to direct to the destruction of machinery, as the cause of their sufferings. But among the cloud of publications issuing from the press, not one contained the least allusion to this popular topic of discontent: among all the *incendiary*, *inflammatory*, and *designing* writers, as they were called, there was not one base enough, whose love of mischief, whose desire to avail himself of distress, to inflame the discontents of the people were such as to induce him to resort to the expedient of representing machinery as the cause of, or its destruction the means whereby their sufferings might be alleviated. We are convinced, if pamphlet-writing had been in as full activity this winter as it was ten years ago, the county of Kent would not have been the scene of outrages directed against the machinery and property of individuals who suffer as much as the unfortunate peasantry from the burthens and oppressions of the Borough System.

Much has been said about the pernicious, dangerous, and absurd doctrines which were propagated. Possibly, this might be the case; possibly, with many important truths, error also might be inculcated; possibly, ideas beneficial to society might be accompanied with others of a contrary tendency. This, however, was matter of opinion; and a more proper subject for discussion than coercion. Admitting that cheap publications were injurious as well as beneficial, it afforded no argument whatever for their suppression. The same objection might be made to plays, novels, romances, and almost every other publication; the same objection might be urged against the amusements of the theatre: all these, no doubt, are productive of evil as well as good to the community; but who ever, on that account, thought that they should be suppressed? Who ever expects to see any thing which is not accompanied with some portion of evil? The only principle in this, as in every other case, is to balance the good against the evil; and it was on this principle the fate of the cheap publications ought to have been determined.

It is unnecessary, we think, to say any thing more in defence of political pamphlets. We were desirous of submitting a few observations at present, because it appears likely an attempt will be made to revive them; and, contemporary with that, probably an attempt to stop their circulation. We were also anxious to undeceive many well-meaning persons, whose fears were artfully excited on a former occasion, and who were taught to look upon this portion of the press as an unmixed source of disorder and immorality. Important advantages, however, it is clear, resulted from its labours; not merely were many valuable truths in political economy disseminated, and the prejudices of bigotry and intolerance rooted out, but property secured, and a prodigious change wrought in the moral and intellectual character of the people. On the revilers and slanderers of the Reformers, we are aware, these arguments will make little impression; we shall have rather excited their fears than conciliated their esteem: their security is in the slavery and ignorance of the population; and they look to the diffusion of the principles of liberty and knowledge through the great mass of society with the same horror the wicked await the day of judgment and retribution.

These calumniators represent the present struggle as one betwixt *property* and *no-property;* whereas, it is a struggle betwixt that importance the people are acquiring, and which they ought to acquire, and the unprincipled usurpations of their rulers. The people have become much too enlightened for the present system. They have discovered its abuses, defects, and injustice. Their resistance to the Oligarchy is not a feverish excitement; it is not a transitory burst of enthusiasm, resulting from some brutal outrage of arbitrary power, but a permanent feeling, originating in a deliberate investigation of the causes of their privations. Such being the nature of the present discontents, they are not likely to subside. Time will rather increase than abate their force. To attempt to stifle them is chimerical. Coercion, while it irritates and prejudices men against its authors, invariably strengthens and confirms them in their opinions. Ministers may narrow the channel of information; but they cannot recall that stream of light which has been shed into every village, hamlet, and workshop of the kingdom. The people have little more to learn in respect of the present government. There is now scarcely an individual any way connected with its abuses whose name is not familiarly known in every part of the country. No factious juggle; no pretended zeal for religion, social order, and the security of property can now deceive. All the different classes—legal or ecclesiastical, their motives, interests, and hypocritical professions, have been fully exposed. But this is not all: the people are not only acquainted with the vices of the system, but also the most safe and effectual remedies. Formerly, they were the victims of spies and informers; they were deluded into abortive attempts against a system too strong in its corruptions, in the fears of some and the venality of others, to be pulled down by open disorganized violence; but caution, perseverance, and indestructible hatred to boroughmongering, an unceasing hostility to every thing tending to its support, are now the maxims of reformers.

Reform may be delayed for a time by the apathy of the middling classes. Something may be said in extenuation of the backwardness of this part of the community. Many of them, in a great measure, have acquired their wealth and importance under what is denominated the Pitt System;[1] and they look to that system, with a sort of filial gratitude, as the author of their being. But it is an egregious error to suppose that they are indebted for their wealth and advantages to the policy of Mr. Pitt. To that minister England owes nothing but her wars, her debt, her taxes, and poor-rates. These were the distinguishing features of his system; and they cannot be considered conducive to commercial prosperity. In fact, it is to the people, not to the government,—it is to the discoveries of Watt, Arkwright, and Wedgewood, that the merchants and manufacturers are indebted for their wealth; and that they have been enabled, in spite of stamp-duties, excises, taxes, and imposts, to maintain an ascendancy in every market of the world.

To Church and State the people owe little but their calamities. Even for their religious and moral character they are indebted solely to themselves. Certainly it is not to the formularies, the ostentation, and the principles of the ecclesiastical establishment, that they would look for either the forms or precepts of Christianity; and as little would they expect to find examples of morality in the licentious lives of non-resident incumbents, or in the bribery, drunkenness, and perjury of our representative system.

We shall now conclude our observations on the newspaper stamp-duties and the efforts of the Aristocracy to stop reform by the Vandal expedient of taxing knowledge. All their endeavours will prove abortive. They might as well try to shut out the light of the sun as to prevent the diffusion of intelligence. Will they not learn even from experience? . . . Efforts to prevent the exposition of abuses would do more to confirm men in a belief of their existence, and the unprincipled nature of the system, than could be done by cheap publications in a century; and they admit their criminality in shrinking from investigation.

Knowledge is the great instrument by which the rights of the people are to be acquired; and, of course, it is against this powerful engine all the efforts of tyranny are directed. The chief objects sought to be attained in legislating against the Press are, to enfeeble the spirit of public discussion, and narrow the circle of political information, by the joint operation of fear and vexatious restric-

[1] The system of government and administration developed by Pitt under the unreformed constitution between 1784 and 1806.

tions. According to the laws now in force, every printer is compelled to print his name and place of abode at the bottom of every thing he prints; he is compelled to keep a copy, in order to its being produced, if called for, to the secretary of state; the printers and proprietors of a newspaper, or political periodical, are compelled to go to the stamp-office, and swear that they are so; they are obliged also to make oath to their several places of abode; and the publisher is obliged to deposit one copy of every number of the paper in the stamp-office, where it is ready to be produced against all the parties, in case of any prosecution for a libel.

To these impediments, in the way of political publications, may be added, the arbitrary and tyrannical powers of the attorney-general. This officer can, at any time, file an information; he can bring a man to trial, or put the trial off, and may thus keep a prosecution hanging over a man for an indefinite period. When a man is brought into court, he can stop the proceedings, or go on with them. If two men are prosecuted and convicted for the same thing, he may bring one up for punishment, and suffer the other to escape without any punishment at all. In 1809, Sir Vicary Gibbs introduced the dangerous practice of holding to bail, or sending to prison in default of bail, immediately an ex-officio information is filed; and this may be done without bringing, or having any intention to bring, the party to trial.

Supposing our legislators ever so successful in an attempt to fetter the Press, what advantages would they derive from it? Would it ensure prosperity to commerce and manufactures? Would it reduce the debt or the poor-rates? Would it relieve the distress of the rural population, or fill the coffers of the Chancellor of the Exchequer? Unless it would accomplish some of these, it would do nothing. *It would not stop the progress of reform.* That cause must and will triumph. The truths disseminated cannot be rooted out by the hand of power. It is not now a problematical, but a demonstrated truth that the calamities of the country flow from overwhelming taxation, originating in non-representation; that they are the effect of a shameless waste of the public money, participated in and supported by a corrupt House of Commons. This is the conviction of at least nine-tenths of the community; and it cannot be destroyed by gagging-bills.

7. *An Eccentric King: William IV*

GEORGE IV died in 1830, almost universally unmourned. Lady Conyngham regretted the material advantages he provided, but few missed him. The Duke of Wellington found it much easier to work with the new king. Lord Eldon could never forgive George his cowardice on Catholic emancipation. But the new King was confusing. The former Duke of Clarence had been shunted aside and not very well provided for. He was crude, amoral, and more than a little silly. Social and political tensions had been so acute under George that William received a totally undeserved popular reputation for liberality. Its only basis in fact was William's contempt for his brother, the vicious, reactionary Duke of Cumberland who became ruler of Hanover upon Victoria's accession. William's brief career as Lord High Admiral earned him the soubriquet "Sailor Billy," which may have fortified the democratic myth but had shown him to no advantage.

William's behavior suggested that he might imitate George III and go mad. His political instincts drew him to Wellington's Tories, but he was not doctrinaire and had no hatred or guilt about the Whigs. His accession required a new general election, and the timing of that election made possible the reform Parliament. In the long struggle for the Reform Act, the King's role proved significant. Before the House of Lords would acquiesce, he had to threaten to invoke the royal prerogative and to create sufficient peers to guarantee passage in that House. But he did this most grudgingly, and his one actual employment of prerogative in parliamentary politics was to bring in Peel in 1834. While Peel had minority support in the Commons, he argued that as the King's choice he had the right to a chance. The house concurred, but Peel was unable to carry a general election that year.

SOURCE: Charles Cavendish Fulke Greville, *The Greville Memoirs: a Journal of the Reigns of King George IV and King William IV*, edited by Henry Reeve, Vol. I (New York, 1875), pp. 357–361, 363–366.

London, July 16th—I returned here on the 6th of this month, and have waited these ten days to look about me and see and hear what is passing. The present King and his proceedings occupy all attention, and nobody thinks any more of the late King than if he had been dead fifty years, unless it be to abuse him and to rake up all his vices and misdeeds. Never was elevation like that of King William IV. His life has been hitherto passed in obscurity and neglect, in miserable poverty, surrounded by a numerous progeny of bastards, without consideration or friends, and he was ridiculous from his grotesque ways and little, meddling curiosity. Nobody ever invited him into their house, or thought it necessary to honor him with any mark of attention or respect; and so he went on for above forty years, till Canning brought him into notice by making him Lord High Admiral at the time of his grand Ministerial schism. In that post he distinguished himself by making absurd speeches, by a morbid official activity, and by a general wildness which was thought to indicate incipient insanity, till shortly after Canning's death and the Duke's accession, as is well known, the latter dismissed him. He then dropped back into obscurity, but had become by this time somewhat more of a personage than he was before. His brief administration of the navy, the death of the Duke of York, which made him heir to the throne, his increased wealth and regular habits, had procured him more consideration, though not a great deal. Such was his position when George IV broke all at once, and after three months of expectation William finds himself King.

July 18th.—King George had not been dead three days before everybody discovered that he was no loss, and King William a great gain. Certainly nobody ever was less regretted than the late King, and the breath was hardly out of his body before the press burst forth in full cry against him, and raked up all his vices, follies, and misdeeds, which were numerous and glaring enough.

The new King began very well. Everybody expected he would keep the Ministers in office, but he threw himself into the arms of the Duke of Wellington with the strongest expressions of confidence and esteem. He proposed to all the Household, as well as to the members of Government, to keep their places, which they all did except Lord Conyngham and the Duke of Montrose. He soon after, however, dismissed most of the equerries, that he might fill their places with the members of his own family. Of course such a King wanted not due praise, and plenty of anecdotes were raked up of his former generosities and kindnesses. His first speech to the Council was well enough given, but his burlesque character began even then to show itself. Nobody expected from him much real grief, and he does not seem to know how to act it consistently; he spoke of his brother with all the semblance of feeling, and in a tone of voice properly softened and subdued, but just afterward, when they gave him the pen to sign the declaration, he said, in his usual tone, "This is a damned bad pen you have given me." My worthy colleague, Mr. James Buller, began to swear Privy Councillors in the name of "King George IV—William, I mean," to the great diversion of the Council.

A few days after my return I was sworn in, all the Ministers and some others being present. His Majesty presided very decently, and looked like a respectable old admiral. The Duke [of Wellington] told me he was delighted with him—"If I had been able to deal with my late master as I do with my present, I should have got on much better"—that he was so reasonable and tractable, and that he had done more business with him in ten minutes than with the other in as many days. . . .

He began immediately to do good-natured things, to provide for old friends and professional adherents, and he bestowed a pension upon Tierney's widow. The great offices of Chamberlain and Steward he abandoned to the Duke of Wellington. There never was any thing like the enthusiasm with which he was greeted by all ranks; though he has trotted about both town and country for sixty-four years, and nobody ever turned round to look at him, he cannot stir now without a mob, patrician as well as plebeian, at his heels. All the Park congregated round the gate to see him drive into town the day before yesterday. But in the midst of all this success and good conduct certain indications of strangeness and oddness peep out which are not a little alarming, and he promises to realize the fears of his Ministers that he will do and say too much, though they flatter themselves that they have muzzled him in his approaching progress by reminding him that his words will be taken as his Ministers', and he must, therefore, be chary of them.

At the late King's funeral he behaved with great indecency. That ceremony was very well managed, and a fine sight, the military part particularly, and the Guards were magnificent. The attendance was not very numerous, and when they had all got together in St. George's Hall a gayer company I never beheld; with the exception of Mount Charles, who was deeply affected, they were all as merry as grigs. The King was chief mourner, and, to my astonishment, as he entered the chapel directly behind the body, in a situation in which he should have been apparently, if not really, absorbed in the melancholy duty he was performing, he darted up to Strathaven, who was ranged on one side below the Dean's stall, shook him heartily by the hand, and then went on nodding to the right and left. . . .

The King's good-nature, simplicity, and affability to all about him, are certainly very striking, and in his elevation he does not forget any of his old friends and companions. He was in no hurry to take upon himself the dignity of King, nor to throw off the habits and manners of a country gentleman. . . . The Queen, they say, is by no means delighted at her elevation. She likes quiet and retirement and Bushy (of which the King has made her Ranger), and does not want to be a Queen. However, "l'appétit viendra en mangeant [an appetite will come with eating]." He says he does not want luxury and magnificence, has slept in a cot, and he has dismissed the King's cooks, "renversé la marmite." He keeps the stud (which is to be diminished) because he thinks he ought to support the turf. He has made Mount Charles a Lord of the Bedchamber, and given the robes to Sir C. Pole, an admiral. Altogether he seems a kind-hearted, well-meaning, not stupid, burlesque, bustling old fellow, and if he doesn't go mad may make a very decent King, but he exhibits oddities. . . .

July 20, 1830– . . . All this was very well; no great harm in it; more affable, less dignified, than the late King; but when this [first council] was over, and he might very well have sat himself quietly down and rested, he must needs put on his plainer clothes and start on a ramble about the streets, alone too. In Pall Mall he met Watson Taylor, and took his arm and went up St. James's Street. There he was soon followed by a mob making an uproar, and when he got near White's a woman came up and kissed him. Belfast (who had been sworn in Privy Councilor in the morning), who saw this from White's, and Clinton, thought it time to interfere, and came out to attend upon him. The mob increased, and, always holding W. Taylor's arm, and flanked by Clinton and Belfast, who got shoved and kicked about to their inexpressible wrath, he got back to the Palace amid shouting and bawling and applause. When he got home he asked them to go in and take a quiet walk in the garden, and said, "Oh, never mind all this; when I have walked about a few times they will get used to it, and will take no notice."

July 24, 1830— . . . Yesterday he went to the House of Lords, and was admirably received. I can fancy nothing like his delight at finding himself in the state coach surrounded by all his pomp. He delivered the speech very well, they say, for I did not go to hear him. He did not wear the crown, which was carried by Lord Hastings. Etiquette is a thing he cannot comprehend. He wanted to take the King of Würtemberg with him in his coach, till he was told it was out of the question. In his private carriage he continues to sit backward, and when he goes with men makes one sit by him, and not opposite to him. Yesterday, after the House of Lords, he drove all over the town in an open calèche with the Queen, Princess Augusta, and the King of Würtemberg, and coming home he set down the King (*dropped him*, as he calls it) at Grillon's Hotel. The King of England dropping another king at a tavern! It is impossible not to be struck with his extreme good-nature and simplicity, which he cannot or will not exchange for the dignity of his new situation and the trammels of etiquette; but he ought to be made to understand that his simplicity degenerates into vulgarity, and that without departing from his natural urbanity he may conduct himself so as not to lower the character with which he is invested, and which belongs not to him, but to the country.

At his dinner at St. James's the other day more people were invited than there was room for, and some half-dozen were forced to sit at a side-table. He said to Lord Brownlow, "Well, when you are flooded (he thinks Lincolnshire is all fen) you will come to us at Windsor." To the Freemasons he was rather good. The Duke of Sussex wanted him to receive their address in a solemn audience, which he refused and when they did come he said, "Gentlemen, if my love for you equaled my ignorance of every thing concerning you, it would be unbounded," and then he added something good-humored. The consequence of his trotting about, and saying the odd things that he does, is that there are all sorts of stories about him which are not true, and he is always expected everywhere. In the mean time I believe that politically he relies implicitly on the Duke [of Wellington], who can make him do any thing.

8.   Remaking the Constitution:
The Reform Act of 1832

THE REFORM ACT of 1832 was once defined as the crucial step in the modernization of Britain. More recent scholarship has tended to minimize the importance of what it was and what it did. Historians have been at some pains to demonstrate that the traditional constitution was a constitution in church and state, and thus that the repeal of the Test and Corporation Acts in 1828 and 1829 must stand in equal importance to the Reform Act of 1832. Whatever else it might have done, the Reform Act did not abolish rotten boroughs or the corrupt political practices of the unreformed constitution. At least fifty rotten boroughs (many of them Whig-controlled) remained, not to mention the many constituencies that returned at least one member from the same family throughout the period. The new device of registration became a source of new corrupt or dubious practices. Taper and Tadpole, Disraeli's fictitious Tory party agents, know they have lost when they have voted all of their dead and are but a dozen votes ahead. Certainly the gentry-aristocracy continued to dominate both principal political parties. Changes in the electorate did not mean alterations in management.

Yet the Reform Act was important. It did shift the constitution from its fixed, historically sanctioned base to a new one of social utility. Both Radicals and Tories knew that this was but a first step down the path to democracy. The Whigs did not agree. Lord John Russell outlined their philosophy of reform in his speech introducing the first reform bill, which was essentially the same as the second and third bills, the last of which passed into law. Committed to some measure of parliamentary reform, the Whigs opted, under the prodding of their younger, more advanced wing, for a big bill far less striking for its limitations than for its strength. It was a more extensive measure than most contemporaries expected, as well as a successful gamble which captured radical support without losing too many aristocratic or disaffected Tory partisans.

The Reform Act initially attacked the most vulnerable features of the unreformed constitution: nomination boroughs, wildly disparate urban franchises, unrepresented cities, neglected national interests (like the new manufacturers), and regional under or overrepresentation. It struck at rotten boroughs, overly small and overly corrupt. Some were salvaged through the simple expedient of franchise extension or territorial expansion, often both. Others, like Old Sarum—the grass knoll that sent two members to Parliament—were to vanish; their seats were appropriated for unenfranchised industrial towns and under-represented countries. Such redistribution, incidentally, served the interests of the established landed classes as much as it satisfied the demands of new urban elements. Enfranchising Manchester and Birmingham pulled those cities out of the counties and helped to restore to the gentry-aristocracy unchallenged control in those seats.

As the initial reaction of hysterical fury subsided, the principles and criteria of reform became clear but not consistent. The sociology of reform was another matter. The Whig compromise was the £10 household franchise for all boroughs: the householder whose premises were assessed for a rental value of at least £10 per year, which meant the substantial middle classes in 1832. When Lord John Russell spoke of adding half a million voters, he stressed the fact that they were all men of property. This was the Whig version of John Adams' case for "the rich, the well born, and the able." Only a few noisy radicals rejected the notion of the representation of interests and clamored for personal representation. Neither theory nor practice admitted the idea.

Lord John could not leave well enough alone. He argued—perhaps he had to in order to carry the Whigs—that this bill was a final constitutional settlement. Twenty years later "Finality Jack" was again searching for another perfect formula—perhaps £8? Neither the £10 household franchise nor the other vaunted claims for social utility could conceal obvious limitations and patent contradictions, as Lord Carnarvon pointed out to the Duke of Wellington.

If I have a freehold garden at Dorchester of the value of 50s. a year it gives me a vote for Dorset.

If I build a cottage upon it, and inhabit it, the value becoming *about* 10l. [£] a year, it is doubtful whether I am to vote for the county or borough. The registering barrister for Dorchester thinks it worth more, and gives me a vote for the borough.

The barrister for Dorset thinks it worth less, and gives me a vote for the county.

And so I have two votes, which is plainly contrary to the Act.

The next year the same question arises, and both barristers being changed, each decides contrary to his predecessor, and so I have no vote, which is equally contrary to the Act.

If I let my house and garden for 9l. 19s., I have a vote for the county, and my tenant none; if for 10l. 1s., I have no vote at all, and my tenant gets one for Dorchester.

If I let my house to A. and my garden to B., A. loses his vote for Dorchester, and I recover mine for Dorset.

If I make the house alone worth 10l. a year, I retain my vote for the county, and A. acquires one for the borough.

How admirably must this system work![1]

[1] Carnarvon to Wellington, ? January 1832, Wellington, *Despatches,* Vol. VIII, pp. 193–194.

Neither contemporary quibbling nor revisionist historiography can in the end reduce the importance of the Reform Bill of 1832, although both can help to place it in proper perspective. It represented a substantial alteration in the franchise and in the rationale of representation. Nothing more could have gone through a Parliament which, after all, was voting to extinguish its privileged if obsolete self. For while the pressure of the country was new both in extent and in degree, parliamentary reform was voluntary, not coerced. It satisfied few but mollified many and proved, not a final settlement, but a way station on the road to democracy and the modernization of the British state.

Recommending Reading

The general and monographic literature on the Reform Bill is vast enough to resist quick selection, but try: E. HALÉVY, *The Triumph of Reform* (London, 1926, and many subsequent editions); J. R. BUTLER, *The Passing of the Great Reform Bill* (London, 1914); and the useful set of selections edited by W. H. MAEHL, JR., *The Reform Bill of 1832* (New York, 1967), which defines the general areas of controversy.

SOURCE: Lord John Russell, "Speech on the Introduction of the First Reform Bill, March 1, 1831," *Hansard's Parliamentary Debates*, Third Series, Vol. II, cols. 1061–1089.

Mr. Speaker:—I rise, Sir, with feelings of deep anxiety and interest, to bring forward a question, which, unparalleled as it is in importance, is likewise unparalleled in difficulty, without my apprehension in the least degree being removed by the reflection that I have, on former occasions, brought this question before the consideration of the House; for if, on the other occasions, I have called the attention of the House of Commons to this subject, it has been upon my own responsibility—unaided by any one—involving no one in the failure of the attempt—though often completely gratified by partial success. But, Sir, the measure I have now to bring forward, is a measure, not of mine, but of the Government, in whose name I appear—the deliberate measure of a whole Cabinet, unanimous upon this subject, and resolved to place their measure before this House, in redemption of their pledge to their Sovereign, the Parliament, and to their country. It is, therefore, with great anxiety that I venture to explain their intentions to the House upon a subject, the interest of which is shewn by the crowded audience assembled here, but still more by the deep interest that is felt by millions out of this House, who look with anxiety—who look with hope—who look with expectation, to the result of this day's deliberations. . . .

[Lord John goes to great pains to indicate that this is a government measure approved by the cabinet.]

Sir, much cavil has been raised upon expressions of the noble Lord whom I have mentioned, that he would endeavour to frame such a measure as might satisfy the public mind, without at the same time endangering the settled institutions of the country. "Do you mean," it has been asked on one hand, "by the settled institutions of the country the close and rotten boroughs?" I think we shall shew in the course of the explanation we are about to make, that is is not the close and rotten boroughs that were intended by the settled institutions of the country. On the other hand, it is said by another party, "Can you pretend to satisfy the public mind without endangering the settled institutions of the country? If you attempt to satisfy the public mind, you must shake the public institutions." Sir, we are of opinion, that the very reverse of this will take place; to attempt to satisfy the public mind will not endanger the settled institutions of the country; but not to satisfy that, will endanger them. We are of opinion, that these institutions, resting as they ever have done on the confidence and love of Englishmen, must continue to rest on the same foundation: and while we discard the notion of complying with violent and extravagant remarks, we at the same time wish to place such a measure before the House, that every reasonable man, both in this House and in the country, may be satisfied with it. We wish to place ourselves between the two hostile parties. Neither agreeing with the bigotry of the one, that no Reform is necessary, nor agreeing with the fanaticism of the other, that only some particular kind of Reform can by any means be satisfactory to the people; we place ourselves between the two, and fix ourselves on what is, I hope, firm and steadfast ground, between the abuses we wish to amend, and the convulsions we hope to avert. It will not be necessary, on this occasion, that I should go over the arguments which have been so often urged in favour of Parliamentary Reform: but it is due to the question, that I should state shortly the chief points of the general argument on which the reformers rest their claim. . . .

[Russell makes a brief dash through the original functions and conceptions of the House of Commons.]

There can be no doubt, however, that at the beginning of the period I have alluded to, the House of Commons did represent the people of England. No man of common sense pretends that this Assembly now represents the commonalty or people of England. If it be a question of right, therefore, right is in favour of Reform.

Let us now look at the question as one of reason. Allow me to imagine, for a moment, a stranger from some distant country, who should arrive in England to examine our institutions. All the information he had collected would have told him that this country was singular for the degree which it had attained in wealth, in science, and in civilization. He would have learned, that in no country have the arts of life been carried further, no where the inventions of mechanical skill been rendered more conducive to the comfort and prosperity of mankind. He would have made himself acquainted with its fame in history, and above all, he would have been told, that the proudest boast of this celebrated country was its political freedom. If, in addition to this, he had heard that once in six years this country, so wise, so renowned, so free, chose its Representatives to sit in the great Council, where all the ministerial affairs were discussed and determined; he would not be a little curious to see the process by which so important and solemn an operation was effected.

What then would be his surprise, if he were taken by his guide, whom he had asked to conduct him to one of the places of election, to a green mound and told, that this green mound sent two Members to Parliament—or, to be taken to a stone wall, with three niches in it, and told that these three niches sent two Members to Parliament—or, if he were shown a green park, with many signs of flourishing vegetable life, but none of human habitation, and told that this green park sent two Members to Parliament? But his surprise would increase to astonishment if he were carried into the North of England, where he would see large flourishing towns, full of trade and activity, containing vast magazines of wealth and manufactures, and were told that these places had no Representatives in the Assembly which was said to represent the people. Suppose him, after all, for I will not disguise any part of the case, suppose him to ask for a specimen of popular election, and to be carried, for that purpose, to Liverpool; his surprise would be turned into disgust at the gross venality and corruption which he would find to pervade the electors. After seeing all this, would he not wonder that a nation which had made such progress in every kind of knowledge, and which valued itself for its freedom, should permit so absurd and defective a system of representation any longer to prevail? But whenever arguments of this kind have been urged, it has been replied, and Mr. Canning placed his opposition to Reform on this ground, "We agree, that the House of Commons is not, in fact, sent here by the people—we agree that, in point of reason, the system by which it is sent is full of anomaly and absurdity—but Government is a matter of experience, and so long as the people are satisfied with the actual working of the House of Commons, it would be unwise to embark in theoretical change." Of this argument, I confess, I always felt the weight, and so long as the people did not answer the appeals of the friends of Reform, it was indeed an argument not to be resisted. But what is the case at this moment? The whole people call loudly for Reform. That confidence, whatever it was, which formerly existed in the constitution of this House, exists no longer—it is completely at an end. Whatever may be thought of the particular acts of the House of Commons, I repeat that the confidence of the country in the construction and constitution of the House of Commons is gone—and gone for ever. I would say more—I affirm that it would be easier to transfer the flourishing manufactories of Leeds and Manchester to Gatton and Old Sarum, than to re-establish the confidence and sympathy between this House and those whom it calls its constituents. I end this argument, therefore, by saying, that if the question be one of right, right is in favour of Reform—if it be a question of reason, reason is in favour of Reform—if it be a question of policy and expediency, policy and expediency speak loudly for Reform.

I come now to the most difficult part of this subject—the explanation of the measure, which, representing the King's Ministers, I am about to propose to the House. Those Ministers have thought, and, in my opinion, justly, that it would not be sufficient to bring forward a measure which should merely lop off some disgusting excrescences, or cure some notorious defects; but would still leave the battle to be fought again with renewed and strengthened discontent. They have thought that no half measures would be sufficient—that no trifling, no paltering, with so great a question could give stability to the Throne—authority to the Parliament— or satisfaction to the Country. Let us look, then, at what have been the chief grievances in the representation, of which the people have complained. And here let me observe, that there is great difference between the complaint of a grievance, and the suggestion of a remedy. On matter of grievance we ought to regard with deference the expressed opinions of the people; but in suggesting remedies, those who are called to the business of legislation should follow the deliberate result of their own judgment.

But not to digress any further. The chief grievances of which the people complain are these;—First, the nomination of Members by individuals. Second, the Elections by close Corporations; third, the Expense of Elections. With regard to the first—the nomination by individuals—it may be exercised in one of two ways; either over a place containing scarcely any inhabitants, and with a very extensive right of election, or over a place of wide extent and numerous population, but where the franchise is confined to very few residents. Gatton is an example of the first, and Bath of the second. At Gatton, the right is popular, but there is nobody to exercise it: at Bath, the inhabitants are numerous, but very few of them have any concern in the result of an election. We have addressed ourselves to both these evils, because we have thought it essential to apply a remedy to both; but they must, of course, be dealt with in different ways. With regard to Boroughs where there are scarcely any inhabitants, and where the elective franchise is such as to enable many individuals to give their voices in the choice of Members for this House, it would be evidently a mere farce to take away the right from the person exercising it, and to give it to the borough; and the only Reform that can be justly recommended is, to deprive the borough of its franchise altogether. I am perfectly aware, that in making this proposition we are proposing a bold and decisive measure. I am perfectly aware, and I should myself vote upon that persuasion, that on all ordinary occasions, rights of this kind ought to be respected, and it would be no small interest, no trifling consideration, which would justify the invasion of them. . . . [Lord John discusses his rationale for reform. Sixty boroughs of less than 2,000 inhabitants will lose their right to elect members. Forty-seven or less than 4,000 will lose one, making 168 vacancies. In addition the government proposes to remove the right of election from those closed corporations currently exercising it.] I contend, that it is important to get rid of these complicated rights—of these vexatious questions, and to give to the real property and to the real respectability of the different cities and towns the right of voting for Members of Parliament. . . . We therefore propose that the right of voting shall be given to householders paying rates for, or occupying a house of, the yearly value of 10*l* and upwards. Whether he be the proprietor, or whether he only rent the house, the person rated will have the franchise upon certain conditions hereafter to be named. At the same time, it is not intended to deprive the present electors of their privilege to vote, provided they be resident. With regard to non-residence, we are of opinion that it produces much expense, that it is the cause of a great deal of bribery, and that it occasions such manifold and manifest evils, that electors who do not live in a place ought not to be permitted to retain their votes. At the same time, I do not believe that we are inflicting even upon this class any injury, for nearly all, either in one place or in another, will possess a franchise as belonging to the great mass of householders. With regard to resident voters, we propose that they shall retain their right during life, but that no vote shall be allowed hereafter, excepting on the condition I have before stated, that the person claiming the right must occupy a house of the value of 10*l* a year.

I shall now proceed to the manner in which we propose to extend the franchise in counties. The Bill I wish to introduce will give all copyholders to the value of 10*l* a year, qualified under [Peel's] bill to serve on Juries, and all leaseholders for not less than twenty-one years, whose leases have not been renewed within two years, a right to vote for the return of Knights of the Shire. [*Sir R. Peel asked, across the Table, the amount of rent which was necessary.*] The right will depend upon a lease for twenty-one years, where the annual rent is not less than fifty pounds. [Lord John observes that 168 vacancies will be created, but since the House of Commons is uncomfortably large, some seats will just be cut.]

But it is obvious, that whenever a Member has a certain number of constituents watching his actions, and looking to his votes, in order that the people's money be not given for purposes inconsistent with the people's interests, his attendance will be much more regular. Therefore, when we propose a great change, by cutting off a number of Members, the effect will be, to facilitate public business, to the manifest advantage of the country. We propose, however, to fill up a certain number of the vacancies, but not the whole of them. We intend that seven large towns shall send two Members each, and that twenty other towns shall send one Member each. [Lord John then lists the twenty-seven towns.]

It is well known, that a great portion of the Metropolis and its neighbourhood, amounting in population to 800,000 or 900,000, is not represented, and we propose to give eight Members to the unrepresented, by dividing them into the following districts each of which is to have two: [Russell lists them].

Next we propose an addition to the Members for the larger counties—a species of Reform always recommended, and which, I believe, Lord Chatham was almost the first to advocate. Those counties contain a variety of interests, and form an admirable constituency; in some, as in Staffordshire, there is a large manufacturing population, better represented in this way than perhaps in any other; and as County Members have unquestionably the most excellent class of constituents, they form of themselves a most valuable class of Representatives. The Bill I shall beg leave to introduce will give two additional Members to each of twenty-seven counties, where the inhabitants exceed 150,000. [This, too, is detailed, with the addition of one Member for the Isle of Wight.]

I will now proceed to another part of the subject. I spoke at first of the evils connected in the minds of the people with the power of nomination by individuals, and with the power of election by a few persons in very small and close Corporations. The remedies I have already detailed are pointed against these defects.

I now beg leave to direct the attention of the House to that part of the plan which relates to the expense of long protracted polls, and which, while it removes that evil, also greatly facilitates the collection of the sense of the elective body. The names of electors are to be enrolled, by which means we hope that the disputes regarding qualification will be in a great measure avoided. We propose that all electors in counties, cities, towns, or boroughs, shall be registered, and for this purpose, machinery will be put in motion very similar to that of the Jury Act. [Lord John outlines an annual registration procedure which will simplify polling and enable elections to be completed in two days.]

In some of the boroughs, to which the right of representation is to be continued, the number of electors is exceedingly small. We shall, therefore, insert in the Bill which we propose to submit to Parliament, a clause, giving to Commissioners, nominated under that bill, authority to enable the inhabitants of the adjoining parishes, and chapelries, to take part in the elections, when the number of electors in such Boroughs shall be less than 300. . . .

[Lord John proposes a Committee of the Privy Council as the proper agency but states his readiness to hear alternatives.]

I have now only one thing more to say with regard to the Representation of England. In all those new towns to which we propose to give the right of sending Members to Parliament, all persons who are in them entitled by their property to vote, are to be excluded from the right to vote for the Representatives of the county, by virtue of the same property. At the same time that the towns will have themselves a proper share in the representation, we do not intend that they shall interfere with the representation of the counties. It is not intended to interfere with the franchise of those freeholders who are at present entitled to vote. I believe I have now concluded the statement of all the alterations which are intended to be made in the representation of England.

With respect to the right of the forty-shilling freeholders in the counties, I do not think that there should be any alteration; for I consider that they are a class of persons eminently qualified to have the trust of electing committed to them. By the smallness of the property which constitutes their qualification, they are especially calculated to give the Representation that extended basis which it is most desirable that it should have.—[*An hon. Member, here called on Lord John Russell to name the disfranchised boroughs*]—It is proposed to take away the right of electing Members to serve in Parliament from all towns and boroughs which do not contain 2,000 inhabitants. . . .

[Lord John lists sixty boroughs to be completely disfranchised and forty-seven to lose one seat.]

With regard to Wales, the only alteration I propose to make besides introducing the same right of franchise into all the boroughs there which we propose for England, consists in adding to the towns in Wales, which already send Members, the neighbouring unrepresented towns, so as to give them a share in the representation. [He specifies the cases.]

I now come to the representation of Scotland; and if the representation of England wants Reform, certainly the same thing may be said, with additional reason, as regards the representation of Scotland. If we have close boroughs in England, we have also popular elections, and popular representation in many of those boroughs; but in Scotland there is not a vestige of popular representation. Indeed there is no such thing known in that country as a popular election; consequently, the wealth, the respectability, and the intelligence, for which the inhabitants of that country are so distinguished, are virtually unrepresented. In the counties of Scotland, there are 3,253 persons, who appear on the lists as qualified to vote, but, from various causes, a number of those electors cannot vote; so that the whole number of electors, by which the county Members of Scotland are returned, does not exceed 2,340 persons. . . .

What I propose in the counties of Scotland is, that every one possessing what is there called the *dominum utile*, or what we should call a beneficial interest, in lands or houses, to the amount of 10*l.*, in the nature of a freehold or copyhold, shall be entitled to a vote. We propose, likewise, that leaseholders in possession, and having a written lease for a term of nineteen years, or any longer period, to the value of 50*l.*, shall be entitled to vote; provided, as the Bill provides for England, that the lease has not been renewed for two years before the election. We have fixed on nineteen years, because leases are generally granted for that term in Scotland. All the details of the measure for England, as already described, will be applicable, with some trifling alteration, to the elections for Scotland. [Lord John proceeds to explain the arrangements.]

As to the right of voting in the boroughs and towns of Scotland, it will be founded on the principle of property, arising from the occupation of houses rented or rated to taxes at not less than 10*l.* per year. . . .

I now proceed to Ireland, where a reform in the Representation, though necessary, will be more simple than that proposed with respect to the representation of England and Scotland. . . . I propose that the inhabitants of those boroughs generally shall have the right of electing their Representatives in the same manner as in England, although that right is to be ascertained differently. I propose that property or occupancy, to the value of 10*l.* per annum, should give every man a vote who resides in one of these boroughs. I am convinced that this arrangement will be attended with the greatest benefit to Ireland. I know that the people of that country have suffered the greatest inconvenience and injury from the political rights being in the hands of a few. . . . The qualification of voters in counties in Ireland is not to be altered, except, that beneficed Clergymen are to be entitled to vote as freeholders. The arrangement as to elections is to be the same as in England. The county elections must be concluded within six days from the time of their commencement, as in England, and all persons at present entitled to vote will continue to have that right. I think there is no other alteration of any importance as regards Ireland.

Having gone through the several alterations proposed in England and Wales, in Scotland and Ireland, I now come to the result. The number of Members now belonging to this House is

The number of Members now belonging to this House is	658
The number to be disfranchised	168
Number remaining	490
Additional Members for Scotland	5
Additional Members for Ireland	3
Additional Member for Wales	1
Additional Members for the metropolis	8
New Members for large towns in England	34
Additional Members for counties in England	55
Total additional Members	106
Members of the House not to be disfranchised	490
Total	596

Making a decrease of sixty-two Members in the total number of Representatives.

I will now state the number of additional persons who, I suppose, will be entitled to votes for counties, towns, and boroughs under this Bill:—

	Persons
The number in towns and boroughs in England already sending Members, will be increased by	110,000
The electors of towns (in England) sending Members for the first time I estimate at	50,000
Electors in London, who will obtain the right of voting	95,000
Increase of electors in Scotland	60,000
In Ireland, perhaps	40,000
Increase in the counties of England probably	100,000

It is my opinion, therefore, that the whole measure will add to the constituency of the Commons House of Parliament, about half a million of persons, and these all connected with the property of the country, having a valuable stake amongst us, and deeply interested in our institutions. They are the persons on whom we can depend in any future struggle in which this nation may be engaged, and who will maintain and support Parliament and the Throne in carrying that struggle to a successful termination. I think that those measures will produce a farther benefit to the people, by the great incitement which it will occasion to industry and good conduct. For when a man finds, that by industrious exertion, and by punctuality, he will entitle himself to a place in the list of voters, he will have an additional motive to improve his circumstances, and to preserve his character amongst his neighbours. I think, therefore, that in adding to the constituency, we are providing for the moral as well as for the political improvement of the country. . . .

I arrive at last at the objections which may be made to the plan we propose. I shall be told, in the first place, that we overturn the institutions of our ancestors. I maintain, that in departing from the letter, we preserve the spirit of those institutions. Our opponents say, our ancestors gave Old Sarum Representatives, therefore we should give Old Sarum Representatives.—We say, our ancestors gave Old Sarum Representatives, because it *was* a large town; therefore we give Representatives to Manchester, which *is* a large town. I think we are acting more as our ancestors would have acted, by letting in Representatives for our great commercial and manufacturing towns, than by excluding such Representatives. . . .

It has been asserted also, if a Reform were to be effected, that many men of great talents, who now get into this House for close boroughs, would not be able to procure seats. I have never entertained any apprehensions of the sort, for I believe that no Reform that can be introduced will have the effect of preventing wealth, probity, learning, and wit, from having their proper influence upon elections. My learned and hon. friend near me, his Majesty's Attorney General, is an illustrious instance that, in large and populous boroughs, lawyers of eminence, and gentlemen of great talents and public spirit, will be spontaneously chosen.

It may be said too, that one great and injurious effect of the measures I propose will be, to destroy the power and privileges of the aristocracy. This I deny. I utterly deny that this plan can have any such effect. Wherever the aristocracy reside, receiving large incomes, performing important duties, relieving the poor by charity, and evincing private worth and public virtue, it is not in human nature that they should not possess a great influence upon public opinion, and have an equal weight in electing persons to serve their country in Parliament. Though such persons may not have the direct nomination of members under this Bill, I contend that they

will have as much influence as they ought to have. But if by aristocracy those persons are meant who do not live among the people,
who know nothing of the people, and who care nothing for
them—who seek honours without merit, places without duty, and
pensions without service—for such an aristocracy I have no sympathy; and I think, the sooner its influence is carried away with the
corruption on which it has thriven, the better for the country, in
which it has repressed so long every wholesome and invigorating
influence. Language has been held on this subject, which I hope
will not be heard in future. A call has been made upon the aristocracy—all who are connected with it have been summoned to make
a stand against the people. Some persons have even ventured to say,
that they, by their numerical strength, could put down what they
call sedition. But the question at issue does not respect the putting
down of sedition.

The real question is, whether, without some large measure of
Reform, the business of the country can be carried on with the
confidence and the support of the people? I shall not ask whether
you can resist Reform, but I say, that it has become a question
whether or not the Constitution would now perish if Reform be
deferred. This House, in its unreformed state, has nothing to look
to but the sympathy, confidence, and support of the nation. If it
now refuses Reform, that sympathy will be withheld—that support will be denied. I ask you, then, whether, when his Majesty's
Ministers are convinced that Reform is necessary, and when they
have the approbation of their gracious Sovereign for bringing this
proposition before the House; when they declare that Reform is
indispensable; when multitudes of petitions pour upon your Table,
and myriads of voices out of doors put forth a just request for
Reform—will this House say, "We are the judges of our own
honesty, we despise the advice of the Crown, and disregard at once
the warning of Ministers, and the demands of the people, whom we
presume to represent?" Will this House say, "We will keep our
power, keep it how we may; we regard not the petitions of the
people, and are ready to abide by all the consequences of our refusal." I appeal, Sir, in my turn, to the aristocracy. The gentlemen
of England have never been found wanting in any great crisis.
When the country was engaged in war against the national enemy
—when the honour and security of the country were assailed—
they were ever foremost. When burthens were to be borne, they

were ever as ready to bear their share as any other class of the
community. I ask them now, when a great sacrifice is to be made,
to show their generosity—to convince the people of their public
spirit—and to identify themselves for the future with the people.
Upon the gentlemen of England, then, I call. I ask them to come
forward, and, by their conduct on this occasion, to give security to
the Throne, stability to Parliament and the Constitution, and
strength and peace to the country. The question is to be decided
by this House. Whatever may be the result of this proposition, the
King's Ministers will feel that they have done their duty. They
have hitherto pursued an even and straightforward line, consulting
no particular class or party, but acting according to the dictates of
what they considered their duty. Wherever the line of duty has led
them, they have not hesitated to encounter any difficulties by
which they were met. I need only refer to their firm and vigorous
exertions of the laws, by which those disturbances, which unhappily prevailed throughout the country when they took office, have,
I may say, been entirely put an end to. By the vigorous exertion of
law, passed before they came into office by another Ministry, they
have been enabled to put down that system of agitation which had
commenced in the sister kingdom, and which threatened such fatal
results. In neither of those instances, I may venture to say, has there
been anything like a bending to popular clamour on the part of his
Majesty's Ministers, or a desire to ingratiate themselves with the
people, for the mere sake of obtaining popular and transient
favour. I therefore think I am justified in saying, that we are to be
believed when we come forward and state, that we consider some
effectual measure of Reform to be necessary. I say, that we have a
right to be believed when we assert that it is not for any sinister
end of our own we bring forward the present measure, but because
we are interested in the future welfare of this country, which
welfare we conceive to be best consulted by the adoption of a
timely and an effective Reform—because we think, that, by such a
course alone we shall be enabled to give permanency to that
Constitution which has been so long the admiration of nations, on
account of its popular, spirit, but which cannot exist much longer,
unless strengthened by an additional infusion of popular spirit,
commensurate with the progress of knowledge and the increased
intelligence of the age [To establish the Constitution on a firm
basis, you must show that you are determined not to be the repre-

sentatives of a small class, or of a particular interest; but to form a body, who, representing the people, springing from the people, and sympathising with the people, can fairly call on the people to support the future burthens of the country, and to struggle with the future difficulties which it may have to encounter;] confident that those who call upon them are ready to join them heart and hand: and are only looking, like themselves, to the glory and welfare of England. I conclude, Sir, by moving for leave to bring in a Bill for amending the state of the Representation in England and Wales.

II

Reform and Social Stress

Introduction

MANY Britons came to recognize that they were not the benefi-
ciaries of constitutional reform. Some had known it all the time—
the radical artisans of London, the stockingers of Nottingham, the
handloom weavers of the West Riding; they had fought for one
generation and were prepared to fight for another.[1] Others came
to understand what had and had not happened only with the
passing of time. The nineteenth century was a religious age. A
man's faith often swayed his politics, and the repercussions amending the constitution in both church and state were many and
various. Dissenters found that repeal of the Test and Corporation
Acts merely began a long battle, never completely won, for equality in the state. Their campaign had undeserved casualties like
public education, for dissenters with a taste for social martyrdom
resisted any state-supported school system that would mean some
degree of Anglican control. Meanwhile arid conflicts between
Tractarians and their foes deflected considerable Church of England energy and social purpose. Evangelical enthusiasm, while
morally repressive and often repugnant, had stimulated campaigns
for social welfare—for chimney sweeps, factory children, the
insane, slaves, aborigines in imperial domains. The Broad Church
movement, associated with such men as Dr. Thomas Arnold, the
reforming headmaster of Rugby, sought to define an ethical community with a maximum of content and a minimum of dogma—a
worthy point which Thomas Hughes and the Christian Socialists
demonstrated in different ways. The Oxford movement, on the
other hand, detracted much from social purpose and added little

[1] See Documents 1 and 2.

beyond the introduction of modest qualifications for Anglican ordination.[2]

Lacking sustained spiritual leadership and a consistent sense of purpose, evangelical values sank to the lowest common denominator. They were secularized as a code of respectability to which lip service and often little more was paid. Cant, always near, became respectable. Reforming impulses tended increasingly to be secular. Workingmen and radicals, particularly those involved in the agitation of 1830–1832, pressed for more reform. The shape and scale of radical activity encouraged the upper classes to resist further constitutional reform and to suspect any proposal for change. The course of reform after 1832 sharpened class divisions and consciousness. By 1837 this hostility exploded in Chartism and the middle-class agitation of the Anti-Corn Law League.

The country gentlemen who dominated Parliament swallowed substantial doses of reform. The abolition of slavery meant that the British humanitarian was prepared to draw upon his purse as well as his conscience to right a moral wrong.[3] The Factory Act of 1833 had a rocky beginning, but manufacturers came to realize that it was an asset, not a threat. Factory inspectors, who were among the first busy bees of reform bureaucracy, began to amass the data needed to understand industrialism and to adjust national policy to social and economic needs. Other starts were symbolic, rather than substantial. The ill-enforced provision for factory schools and the modest grant of £20,000 to assist the Anglican and principal dissenting educational association schools were a half-hearted step in the direction of state-supported education. There was little demand for more. Working-class parents needed family income to make do. Middle-class parents, once education came to be a concern, preferred private schools. As the established social orders already had their privileged system of education, they were content with no public education.

Sir Robert Peel could have set the Conservative party against social adjustment and political change. He elected otherwise, accepted the principles of 1832 in his famous Tamworth Manifesto of 1834 and articulated a program for modest, pragmatic extensions. Most of the senior members of the Liberal party served their political apprenticeship under Peel rather than under Grey and

[2] See Document 24, "Religious Belief and Reform." *VC&S*
[3] See Document 11.

Melbourne.[4] Parties were new institutions superimposed upon a persistent political order. All the old tricks were still used in the game of politics, and new ones were refined for the occasion. It was the age of club government, the Tory Carlton and the Whig-Liberal Reform, where the food was better and the quarrels noisier. So long as local power elites controlled their constituencies, party control retained a flavor of Regency group bargaining. But in spite of continued aristocratic control, the established classes chose to define themselves increasingly in terms of party, although the party had no modern array of sanctions to keep malcontents in line.[5]

Party structure remained sufficiently loose to give Radicals a disproportionate weight in Parliament between the first Reform Act in 1832 and the second in 1867. The Conservative schism in 1846 and the subsequent three-party political tangle gave the Radicals a still larger role. From 1852 to 1867 franchise reform measures emanated from Whigs and Tories in an effort to secure Radical support. The last bill—Disraeli's offering as it happened—passed almost by accident. The Radicals also tended to be in touch with the most dynamic and articulate elements in the country. They became, for every administration, a line of communication between the nation and its Parliament. They tended to be—as they lost no occasion to remind the House of Commons—the chosen channels for public pressure, and they reveled in their role.

Early Victorian political history is fundamentally the story of assaults on privilege. The strongest drives were liberal in the broadest sense of the term. The effort to secure careers open to talents usually meant just that. Education and skill competed on equal terms with birth and privilege. Yet opening careers to competitive examination and clever lads from school or university can choke off social mobility. Initially it expanded the diameter of the charmed circle from which Britain's governors were chosen, and thus created a new elite, those who could secure the advantages of public school and university education. Small changes are often indicative. The property qualification for members of Parliament was amended in 1838 to count movables as well as income from land in the required £300. Twenty years later this modified privilege was struck entirely with the abolition of property qualifica-

[4] See Document 17.
[5] See Document 20.

tions. Anyone could sit in Parliament, but members were unpaid: the door was symbolically open and effectively shut.

The old sacred cows were marked for selective slaughter. Nothing was done to the monarchy, since it seemed to be discrediting itself. The crown had lost power through "economical" reform and had accepted the primacy of the Commons with the Reform Act of 1832. William IV, whose character added no luster to the crown, promptly squandered prerogative powers by abusing them. He tossed out Melbourne in 1834 and summoned Peel to form a government. Peel insisted upon his chance to prove himself as the King's minister: the electorate rejected him. Victoria, too, had her bad moments at the start, and none was constitutionally worse than to repeat William IV's mistake. The Bedchamber crisis was viewed as a matter of royal confidence. Peel declined to form a government. Melbourne defended royal prerogative in contradiction to all Whig principles and was crushed in the subsequent general election of 1841.[6] The fault was Melbourne's, not Victoria's, but the lesson was not lost. As Victoria and Albert retrieved royal prestige in the next two decades, they used great care about political intervention. Meddle they did, but principally because the fractionated party system offered, even invited, them to do so.[7]

The powers of the House of Lords, like those of the crown, were circumscribed by the reform bill crisis. In case of a dispute between the two houses, the peers must give way. Wellington led their retreat in 1846 on the issue of repeal of the corn laws, although some wished to stand and fight. Most sensible magnates recognized that the corn laws were not essential to their position, and that they could surrender the symbol and retain the substance of power.[8] Not until the 1880's—as the cumulative pressure of democracy and bureaucracy weakened their authority, and the partial collapse of English agriculture undercut their position and resources—did the aristocracy react irrationally. The peers had by then become hopelessly unrepresentative: they spoke for the most exclusive part of one class and for the most conservative wing of one party. Their capacity to hamstring legislation tempted them into ever more dangerous waters, until Lloyd George wrecked them on the shoals of his 1909 budget.[9]

[6] See Document 14.
[7] See Document 19.
[8] See Document 16.
[9] See Document 35. For the position and problems of the landed classes, see VC&S, Documents 7, 15, and 16.

Aristocratic and oligarchic political vested interests were strongest in parish, town, and county administrations. The initial radical assault struck at the general principle of amateur control of local administration through the revolutionary Poor Law Amendment Act of 1834. Benthamite-utilitarian in conception and execution, the measure swept away two centuries of independent parochial administration by amalgamating parishes into unions managed by elected boards of guardians. Habits of deference and authority could be and were maintained in spite of elections over the short run, but traditional power was still circumscribed. Authority and final decisions lay in the hands of the Poor Law Commission in London, and commission orders spelled out in meticulous detail the conditions and circumstances of poor relief.[10] Inspectors, assistant commissioners, even clerical help were recruited on the basis of merit and competitive examination. The new bureaucracy, into whose hands greater administrative power was voted by Parliament, was of necessity becoming professional long before regular civil service reform.

The more direct confrontation with local vested interests came with the Municipal Corporations Act of 1835, the companion piece to the Reform Act of 1832. The old, co-optive oligarchies were broken, provisions were made for rotation of office, and the municipal franchise was given to all resident ratepayers. Results here were less dramatic than many radicals hoped and conservatives feared. A broader "shopocracy" (as a Manchester Tory put it) replaced the older oligarchy. The great age of municipal reform waited for the 1870's, but the structure of municipal politics was substantially changed. This shift and expansion of the center of power was undoubtedly a principal attraction of party to Britain's traditional governors as a medium of political organization.

Two non-doctrinaire parties moved pragmatically and inconsistently. They tried repression with the trade unionists at home and the Irish across the water. They attempted to bargain with established and evolving national interests. Over and over again, however, Radicals secured more than their share of results. They had a program, promotional skill, and a capacity to adapt themselves to the politically possible and expedient. Some of the most striking examples of Radical success were imperial rather than domestic. Sir James Stephen brought evangelical values and utilitarian doctrine to the Colonial Office, where his dynamic, pushing, occasionally

[10] See Document 12.

officious activities earned him the soubriquets of "Mr. Over-Secretary" and "Mr. Mother Country."[11]

Melbourne, who was Whig Prime Minister in 1834 and from 1835 to 1841, disliked Radical reforming pressure ("Why can't they leave it alone?"); he attempted to find expedient answers to two problems and found himself redefining the imperial relationship. Lord Durham—"Radical Jack" of reform bill days—was threatening to organize the disparate radical monomaniacs into a party or a substantial group within the Whig party. Canada in 1837 was in a state of virtual insurrection. Durham was dispatched with his friend and colleague Charles Buller to find answers. They did, and the Durham report of 1839 became the Magna Carta of the Commonwealth.

All of the achievements—and they were substantial—were too little and too late, sometimes even steps in the wrong direction, for many Britons. Northern industrial workers sought limitation of hours of factory work through parliamentary legislation. Their "short-time committees" organized the industrial heartland, but the Factory Act of 1833 was not the result they wanted. Trade union failures coupled with the doctrinaire application of the new Poor Law at the onset of an industrial slump brought the men out in thousands. Handloom weavers, the displaced persons of the industrial revolution, sought to repeal machinery. Urban slum dwellers revolted against the industrial city. The ideological program was simple and specific: the six points of the People's Charter; it promised political action to secure economic and social betterment and security.[12]

Middle-class malcontents sought the victory they had not won in 1832 in the repeal of the corn laws. In a brilliantly organized and well-financed campaign, they succeeded in concealing the patent group and class interests involved and in rousing support along a broad front. To some degree they cut across potential chartist support; and repeal, when it came, drew off much of the politically explosive social tension in the nation. Chartists found themselves divided and diverted. The repeal of the corn laws in 1846 followed

[11] P. Knaplund, *Sir James Stephen and British Colonial Policy* (Madison, 1953); E. Stokes, *The English Utilitarians and India* (Oxford, 1959); P. Mason [Woodruff], *The Men Who Ruled India*, Vol. I, *The Founders* (London, 1953).
[12] See Document 16.

by the Ten Hours Act of 1847 were effective political responses to social grievances. A return to relative prosperity coupled with the damping down of social tension made possible the uneasy but real opening of "an age of equipoise."

Recommended Reading

I. ANSTRUTHER, *The Knight and the Umbrella* (London, 1963).

G. F. A. BEST, *Shaftsbury* (London, 1964).

————, *Temporal Pillars* (London, 1964).

A. BRIGGS, *Chartist Studies* (London, 1959).

O. BROSE, *Church and Parliament* (London, 1959).

D. CECIL, *Melbourne* (New York, 1954).

G. KITSON CLARK, *Making of Victorian England* (Cambridge, Mass., 1962).

G. D. H. COLE, *Robert Owen* (London, 1930).

E. DOLLÉANS, *Le Chartisme* (Paris, 1949).

C. DRIVER, *Tory Radical* (London, 1952).

R. D. EDWARDS and T. D. WILLIAMS, *The Great Famine* (New York, 1957).

F. ENGELS, *Condition of the Working Class in England in 1844*, ed. by W. O. HENDERSON and W. H. CHALONER (London, 1958).

S. E. FINER, *The Life and Times of Sir Edwin Chadwick* (London, 1952).

N. GASH, *Politics in the Age of Peel* (London, 1953).

————, *Reaction and Reconstruction in English Politics* (Oxford, 1965).

J. HAMBURGER, *Intellectuals in Politics* (New Haven, 1965).

J. L. and B. HAMMOND, *The Age of the Chartists* (London, 1930).

M. HOVELL, *The Chartist Movement* (Manchester, 1918).

N. LONGMATE, *King Cholera* (London, 1966).

N. McCORD, *The Anti-Corn Law League* (London, 1958).

O. MacDONAGH, "The Nineteenth-Century Revolution in Government: a Reappraisal," *Historical Journal*, Vol. I (1958), pp. 52–67.

————, *A Pattern of Government Growth* (London, 1961).

F. C. MATHER, *Public Order in the Age of the Chartists* (Manchester, 1959).

C. NEW, *Lord Durham* (London, 1929).

H. PARRIS, *Government and Railroads in Nineteenth-Century Britain* (Toronto, 1965).

————, "The Nineteenth-Century Revolution in Government: a Reappraisal Reappraised," *Historical Journal*, Vol. III (1960), pp. 19–39.

D. ROBERTS, *Victorian Origins of the British Welfare State* (New Haven, 1960).

A. R. SCHOYEN, *The Chartist Challenge* (London, 1958).

A. J. TAYLOR, "Progress and Poverty in Britain 1780–1850: a Reappraisal," *History*, Vol. XLV (1960), pp. 16–31.

J. T. WARD, *The Factory Movement* (London, 1962).

R. F. WEARMOUTH, *Methodism and the Working-Class Movements of England* (London, 1937).

R. K. WEBB, *The British Working Class Reader* (London, 1955).

————, *Harriet Martineau* (New York, 1960).

D. WILLIAMS, *Life of John Frost* (Cardiff, 1939).

C. WOODHAM-SMITH, *The Great Hunger* (New York, 1962).

9.   Political Exploitation:
Francis Place on Class Cooperation

FRANCIS PLACE, perhaps the first great "labor" politician, made a career of politcial agitation, organization, and analysis. He was schooled in London artisan Jacobin radicalism in the days of the French Revolution and became an unqualified Benthamite utilitarian. He was a kingpin in one of the first modern political machines, the Westminster Committee, and he played a significant role in most London-based reform agitation. While he has certainly overstated his importance in the matter, he played a leading role in the investigation that led to the repeal of the Combination Acts prohibiting trade unions in 1824. His shop at Charing Cross was a gathering place for respectable radicals; his phenomenal library of press cuttings and papers, now in the British Museum, was a mine worked by researchers in the cause of progress. Place knew, or he could find out.

To augment the continuing agitation of the political unions for the reform bill, Place enticed some liberally inclined and ambitious young gentlemen into the new Parliamentary Candidates Society, which had been formed to provide reformist candidates for seats in Parliament and seats for reformist candidates. The simplest way to confront the problem was to have the temerity to publish voting records of current members of Parliament. This proved too much.

> The mean pitiful miserable notions of these half and half gentry, [wrote an angry Place] their timidity, their fears of giving offence, to those whom if they had the power of correct appreciation they would never for a moment consider of any importance, and whom, when deference is paid to them, always either succeed in producing failures, or in dwindling down every proposal to a very small matter, but who never the less almost always stand as bug-a-boo before these absurdly genteel people and palsy them completely. It is not so with the tories in public political matters[;] they persuade themselves that every thing they do is genteel and the most atrocious acts if committed only against the people are sure to be encouraged and applauded.[1]

Place is often accused of knuckling under to the governing classes: in fact he only appreciated political reality, having long schooled himself in the facts of life. Place had no use for those who were "afraid to compromise their gentility by doing what would be condemned as going much too far, by their friends,—the half dandy, half idiot fashionable people, who sometimes condescended to notice them; or with whom they usually associated, as well as by the fools who would call them vulg-a-r-r fellows."[2] The leisure and social station of these liberal dilettantes made them indispensable, but it also accentuated the inner hostility and contempt that Place and his class-conscious peers felt toward them. English radicalism rested upon insecure foundations.

Recommended Reading

Consult the works listed for the Reform Act of 1832 and G. WALLAS, *Life of Francis Place* (London, 1898; often reprinted); and W. E. S. THOMAS, "Francis Place and Working Class History," *Historical Journal*, Vol. V (1962), pp. 61.79.

SOURCE: Francis Place on Middle-class Radicals and the Parliamentary Candidates Society, March–April 1831, British Museum, Additional Manuscript 27,789, folios 338–339.

The working classes, who are of little importance in any useful political proceeding unless countenanced by those called their betters, might have been made useful to the public cause, and themselves been somewhat instructed in many particulars. The

[1] Additional Ms. 27, 789, folios 335–336.
[2] *Ibid.*, folio 337.

shopkeeping men, and such as they, who are among the most despicable people in the nation, in a public point of view, might be of as much importance and in some particulars of more importance than an equal number of persons in almost any class;—ought on this occasion to have been and might have been turned to good account, had the men who have leisure and considerable requirements been in other respects qualified to have proceeded in the right direction; but they were not, the curse of gentility is upon them all, and this induces them to attend to minor objects, to neglect major objects, to trifle with matters the most serious, and when any considerable difficulty occurred to shuffle away from it, and then when reproached with such pitiful conduct to make an off hand lying excuse which an honest boy or girl would be ashamed to make. These people, whenever they interfere in liberal political affairs endeavour to accomplish two incompatible things, 1st—to go on with the public matter. 2   not to lose caste with their fashionable friends and acquaintance[s], this being impossible the first is sacrificed invariably, they shrink back as it were into their shells and get rid of their uneasy sensation by the comfort they find in their snug retreat. Not one of them has the courage to cut his drawing room friends and become as he ought to be a highly useful and important man.

10.   Direct Action: The Cold Bath Fields Manifesto

SAVE as a demonstration that reforming Whigs could preserve order with the same rigor as intransigent Tories, the Cold Bath Fields disorders should have vanished into an obscure, if amusing footnote in monographic studies. The Alice in Wonderland qualities of Messrs. Mee and Dee (who were even appropriately named), the triviality of the event, and the relative inconsequence of that fringe of radical agitators known as the Rotundanists minimize the actual importance of the event. But the Cold Bath Fields meeting was symptomatic of a tradition that reached back into the 1790's and forward to Chartism. The program was revolutionary. There was no notion of amendment, no past to which these agitators appealed. This was English republicanism—not the effete tradition of Sir Philip Sidney—derived from an ill-sorted English populism.

These revolutionaries—Owenites, agrarian radicals, Spenceans, followers of Thomas Hodgskin—were a ragtag lot. They were the only genuine subversives in the nation. They seized upon a reformist device, the national convention, and dressed it in revolutionary clothing. There was in Britain, from the past and in the future, a minute group that owed no allegiance to standing institutions. Never important in itself, it did color the views and thought of men and movements that were to matter.

Recommended Reading

In addition to the more conventional authorities on British socialism, E. P. THOMPSON makes an extensive argument for the integration of this line into the evolution of working-class consciousness in *The Making of the English Working Class* (London, 1963). W. H. G. ARMYTAGE discusses some aspects in *Heavens Below* (Toronto, 1961). Among some interesting individual studies are: E. HALÉVY, *Thomas Hodgskin* (London, 1956) and M. BEER, *History of British Socialism* (London, 1940).

SOURCE: Minutes of Evidence Taken before the Select Committee on the Cold Bath Fields Meeting, 18 July 1833, *Parliamentary Papers*, 1833, Vol. XIII, Q. 191.

A National Convention, the Only Proper Remedy

FELLOW CITIZENS, The majority of the hereditary legislators obstinately and impudently oppose our just claims to representation. Treat their opposition with contempt; set the privileged villains and usurpers at defiance. This political club of hereditary self-elected law-makers has no proper authority either to concede or to withhold our just and irrefragable right to representation. Their privilege of nullifying the expressed will of the majority of the nation is an unjustifiable usurpation, repugnant to reason and justice, which ought not to be tolerated for an instant longer.

By the recent audacious prank of the hereditary hospital of incurable national nuisances, this gang opposes itself to the public good. Every thing opposed to the public good ought to be annihilated; therefore the political existence of the hereditary House of Lords ought to be instantly destroyed. From this time no honest reformer will recognize this self-constituted gang as a legislative assembly. At all events, it has no just authority to interfere with the reform of what ought to be the House of Representatives. The only persons who have a right to interfere are the unrepresented.

With regard to the King, he is not authorized to reject or to assent to a reform of the representation of the people. By the humbug Constitution it appears he is permitted to oppose or yield to the decree of the nation, according as he may be "graciously pleased!!!" The deluded old gentleman who at present holds the hereditary (monstrous) office of Chief Magistrate, might peaceably have exercised this privilege for the benefit of his fellow citizens or "subjects," as we are insolently and drolly called; this Royal Person, however, has employed this privilege against the unrepresented in favour of the boroughmongering, tyrannical, bloodthirsty, plundering, execrable anti-reform aristocrats. This the "glorious" damnable Constitution privileged him to do; but this Constitution was not made by the unrepresented, consequently it is not their affair.

It may be remarked *en passant*, that the hereditary kingship is deservedly brought into contempt, and is almost universally denounced by reformers in consequence of the recent conduct of the quondam patriot. Alas, poor William Guelph! [William IV] he is merely the puppet of a base scoundrelocracy. Suffice it for the present to maintain, that neither the hereditary puppet of the aristocrats nor the hereditary self-constituted law-makers can actually prevent the unrepresented from acquiring their elective rights.

Every man has a right to vote in electing those who make the laws which he is required to observe; if that incontrovertible right be denied him, he is a despicable slave. Let all honest and sincere reformers, who desire to be superior to such a wretched and degraded position, now stand forward. Never was a more favourable opportunity for a simultaneous movement in the good cause.

In the first place, it must be constantly remembered that taxation without representation is tyranny, and ought to be resisted; therefore of course every consistent reformer will refuse to pay what are called King's Taxes, until he is represented in the assembly in which the taxes are imposed.

Then follows the question of how are the unrepresented to obtain an immediate representation?

Represent yourselves!

This is the shortest, easiest and most simple method. Let every city, town and considerable borough elect delegates for each place and its vicinity, to be deputed to sit and legislate for their constituents in the place now occupied by the mock representatives boroughmongers' creatures, and nominees of the national nuisances or Lords. These usurpers have almost unanimously condemned themselves of mock representation in addition to being found guilty by the unrepresented; therefore, nothing could be more feasible than for the real representatives to turn out the mock representatives; in fact, they are only waiting for notice to quit.

The gang of plundering parliamentary usurpers being superseded by the representatives, the National Convention would be complete.

This is practicable, and the most simple and rational mode of settling the reform of the representation. It cannot be prevented if the reformers are unanimous on the subject. Who can prevent it? Not the military dictator, citizen Arthur Wellesley, for this antireformer, or very moderate reformer, has not even the majority of the man-butchers on his side, were he so ridiculously mad as to attempt to resort to violence.

The unrepresented have the remedy in their own hands. Let them employ it without delay. That remedy, the sole, proper and decisive remedy, is the election of delegates, to be formed into a—

NATIONAL CONVENTION.

JAMES HENRY BADEN LORYMER,
(Editor of the Republican)

Member of the National Political Union, and of the National Union of the Working Classes and others.

Hetherington, Printer, Kingsgate-street, Holborn, London; from whom this Circular can be had in any quantity in every town in Great Britain and Ireland, at 4*d*. per dozen for general distribution.

11.   Humanitarianism:
The Abolition of Slavery

PARLIAMENTARY reform may not have been a necessary prerequisite for the emancipation of slaves in the British West Indies, but it helped. Undoubtedly the most important element deferring emancipation so long after the abolition of the slave trade in 1807 was the long-continued deflection of reformist energy into the crucial constitutional reforms—Catholic emancipation and parliamentary reform. Temporizing and local option legislation passed in the 1820's had failed to move West Indian whites a step nearer to emancipation. If anything, their success in emasculating, perverting, or defeating reform proposals raised their confidence and stiffened their resistance. But the mobilized forces of conscience and humanitarianism pressed with vigor and unanimity to undo a wrong. The fact that the situation was thousands of miles away encouraged sanctimoniousness. The cure for moral wrong is most clearly perceived from afar; it is easier to redress someone else's error than our own.

The sweep of humanitarian reform, however, touched domestic life with but little less unanimity. Chimney sweeps, debtors, the sick, the insane—the underprivileged and abused of society, helpless to aid themselves, were repeated objects of moral beneficence. But the first blow was struck at slavery. Edward Stanley, later fourteenth Earl of Derby (1799–1869), made his mark at Oxford, on the turf, and in politics. The "Rupert of Debate," as he was called, was never too happy a member of the Whig reforming government and was shortly, after an epic quarrel with Daniel O'Connell, to gravitate to the Tories. Stanley sought to modify the reform bill in cabinet, although he finally gave it grudging support. On slavery, too, he had no doctrinaire position. He opposed it. Even men of Stanley's incredible social arrogance generally concurred in the belief that slavery was a bad thing. But planters were aristocrats, and slaves a form of property. He feared—and West Indian partisans played upon his fears—that the next attack on those institutions might come closer to home.

Sir James Stephen, an ardent evangelical and then legal counselor for the Colonial Office, helped to draw (he may entirely have drawn it) the government abolition bill. Stanley presented the general proposal in a stirring speech, dwelling at length on the failure of West Indian proprietors and legislatures to come to grips with the problem. The measure, displaying the great characteristic of English reform legislation, satisfied no extreme. It abolished slavery as an institution, although, rather than a loan of £15,000,000, it awarded £20,000,000 as a gift to the planters as compensation for their loss. The term of apprenticeship, which looked very much like slavery in practice if not at law, was reduced to seven years (later to four).

Britain moved to emancipation before any other major state. Moreover, the British taxpayer was willing to pay for his principles in hard cash. The abolition of slavery was the most dramatic, probably the most important, humanitarian reform in the Empire. It was not unique. In Africa, in India, in Australia, the British conscience mobilized by evangelical groups meeting in Exeter Hall fundamentally altered the character and the content of life, touching native and white alike. God, as seen by his British Protestant children of light, had given them the Empire as a moral responsibility.

Recommended Reading

The literature on evangelicalism, Empire, and abolition is so extensive that selection is at best random. G. F. A. Best, *Lord Shaftesbury*
(London, 1964), suggests the range of concerns of one great evangelical reformer. W. L. Mathieson, *British Slavery and Its Abolition*
(London, 1926), is a sound, conventional account. E. Williams, *Capitalism and Slavery* (London, 1964), presents quite a different analysis.
P. Knaplund, *James Stephen and the British Colonial System* (Madison, 1953), deals with the interrelations of evangelical and other
imperial concerns. On Derby, see W. D. Jones, *Lord Derby and Victorian Conservatism* (Oxford, 1956).

Source: Edward Stanley, "Speech Introducing the Ministerial Proposal for the Emancipation of Slaves," May 14, 1833, *Hansard's
Parliamentary Debates*, Third Series, Vol. XVII, cols. 1216–
1217, 1222–1228.

I know that people will tell me we do not wish to perpetuate
slavery—we merely wish to postpone it till the negroes are fit for
freedom—till they manifest a disposition for laborious industry
sufficient to qualify them for the privileges of free men. That
argument, if it proves anything, proves too much. Do men ever
show a disposition to labour until population presses upon food;
and will that ever take place, so long as the depopulating influence
of slavery prevails? We are told that the negroes own no domestic
ties; nor will they, so long as you keep them in that state of slavery
which debases their principles, and which deprives them of fore-
sight, and which takes away from them the motives to industry.
The slaves have no education, and you deny them any; for, as
slaves, they can have none. They have hitherto been treated as
chattels attached to the soil—do you think they can be made fit for
freedom, till freedom has exercised its influence upon their minds
and upon their moral character? The treatment of the West-India
negroes is a stain upon a Christian age, and upon a country professing itself Christian. If the slaves be made acquainted with religion,
they must learn that slavery is inconsistent with the Christian
religion; and will you shut out religion, in order that you may
maintain slavery? Other countries have read us a severe lesson
upon this subject. In colonies belonging to Catholic countries, no

man was allowed to possess a slave, who did not provide the means of instructing him in the Catholic faith. Be that, however, as it may, this I will say, that this House will ill discharge its duty, if it does not forthwith put forth a declaration of religious freedom, as respects the colonies, and does not compel the local authorities to leave to every negro within their limits, the free, independent, and inviolable right of adopting whatever form of Christianity he may think proper.

I trust the House will now feel, that it is necessary to act in a different way, and that they will not think it sufficient to promise freedom for future generations, but to provide freedom for the present. I am prepared to offer freedom to the existing generation; I would not condemn them to that state of despair in which Mr. Canning supposed the hon. Gentleman wished to leave them; but I agree with the prudent language which was used in the discussions of 1823 and 1824, that the slaves should not be made free by one hasty step—that the shackles should not be burst at once—that they should not be flung forth suddenly from slavery to freedom, for which they may be unfit. But am I prepared to say, that we ought to wait for any given period, for one or two years, and that then the slaves should be immediately emancipated? I say there would be still greater danger if such a course were pursued, because the slaves would be unsettled, by having the prospect of liberty so long set before them. The intermediate period would undoubtedly be a period of great excitement, a period of tyranny on the one hand, and of defiance on the other, and the slaves would be abandoned to irrepressible disobedience and want of control. I propose a safer and a middle course, which will give to the slave all the essentials of freedom, will gradually sweep away slavery, and remove the slaves from the restrictions imposed upon them by Colonial Legislatures, but leave them still subject to such regulations as will operate as an incentive to the acquisition of industrious habits. I propose, that every slave, on the passing of this Act, shall immediately, not in one year, nor two years, have the power of claiming to be put in a situation in which they may enjoy all the privileges of freemen—in which they may wear no servile badge, and be subject to no corporal punishment—in which they may be entitled to the full enjoyment of all the comforts of their domestic ties—in which those who are nearest and dearest to them may not be liable to cruel punishments—in which their evidence in courts may not be disputable—in which their rights of property may be as full and as complete as those of their masters—a state, in short, in which they would be entitled to every right and every privilege of freemen, subject to this condition, and to this condition alone—that, for a certain period, they shall contract to labour under their present owners but their then employers. If I am asked how I propose to meet all those acts of the Colonial Legislatures which control the actions of slaves? Why, I say, if you pass a measure of this kind, you sweep all these acts away at once. These regulations are enacted for slaves; but the negroes will be no longer slaves. They will be entitled to every right of person, of property, of religion, to which a freeman is entitled—subject to this one only condition, and that but for a limited period. I cannot believe, even if the matter stood thus, and thus only, that this condition would be considered such an infraction of the freedom of the labourer as would give the smallest reason for the opponents of slavery to withhold their assent from the measure. Those who are anxious that this House should proceed to the immediate abolition of slavery, and who wish that every trace of slavery should vanish in a few years, would do well to reflect in what condition the agricultural labourer in England is placed, when he works upon contract—bound, as he is, to provide for himself lodging, clothes, and food, for which his wages are so inadequate. In what state is it proposed to place the negroes? The master will be bound to supply him with food and clothing, or to give him money to provide them, if it should be thought more advisable that it should be done by the negro himself. For this, three-fourths of the negro's time are to be given to his former owner—the day being considered as consisting of ten hours; and seven hours and a-half cannot be considered any very exorbitant demand for these advantages. For the remaining fourth part of his time, whether it be taken as portions of the day, or of the week, the negro shall be at liberty to transfer his services where he pleases; but with this advantage, that the master is bound to employ him at a rate of wages proportionate to the value which he originally sets upon him. . . .

I do not credit what some people say about the negro character; but I do credit what is said about the slave character. I know the effect of a tropical climate. The effect of the state of slavery in these countries is to inculcate upon the slave, that labour is the greatest of all curses, and that the removal of labour is the greatest

of all blessings. To throw the slave suddenly into freedom would
be to destroy all his inclinations to industry; it would be exposing
him to the temptation of recurring to his primitive habits of savage
life, from which he has but lately been reclaimed. Therefore some
restriction is necessary for a time, both for the masters, and for the
good of the slaves themselves. I know no better security which can
be devised, than that which I propose, by obliging the masters to
fix a value upon their slaves, and afterwards regulating the rate of
wages by that value. In what other way is it possible that the rate
of wages can be fixed? Should it be referred to a committee of
planters to determine the rate of wages according to the cost of
maintenance, and the price of the necessaries of life? . . . There
is . . . no mode of doing equal justice, except by imposing upon
the planter the necessity of fixing the price of the wages in this
way; because the relation between the wages and the price fixed
would operate as a check upon the planter's valuation. If he fixes a
high price, he pays a high rate of wages; if he fixes a low price, the
easier it is for the negro to obtain his freedom. I propose, therefore,
that the labourer shall have a right to claim employment of his
master for one-fourth of his time, according to a fixed scale of
wages; that during such one-fourth of his time the labourer shall be
at liberty to employ himself elsewhere; that the master shall fix a
price upon the labourer at the time of his apprenticeship; that the
wages to be paid by the master shall bear such a proportion to the
price fixed by him; that for the whole of his spare time, if given to
the master, the negro shall receive one-twelfth of his price annually, and in proportion for each lesser term. . . . Is it right or just,
that on [the West-India proprietor] alone should be thrown the
whole burthen of repairing the injustice which has been done to
the negro, with the concurrence of the national Legislature for
ages? The question must not be looked upon as confined entirely
to property, however fully the species of property in question may
be sanctioned by law; however frequently it may be made the
subject of legal decision. I will not enter into the abstract question,
whether one man ever can, consistently with the principles of
natural justice, acquire a property in another man; but I proceed
upon the principle, that if one man employs the labour of another,
he is bound to give him support, and to take upon himself a portion
of the risk attending the employment of the other. . . .

We propose to advance a loan to the planters, amounting to ten years purchase of those profits. We propose a loan to the West-India Planters of 15,000,000*l*. It will be a question for Parliament to decide in what manner and on what conditions that loan shall be granted, and how it shall be repaid—and further, if they shall be prepared to go so far as to say that they will not require repayment, it will be for Parliament, if it shall think fit to do so, to convert the loan into a gift. In the first instance, however, our proposition is to advance to the planter a loan of 15,000,000*l*. in consideration of the sacrifice on his part of the fourth of the labour of his slaves. With that fourth of his labour the negro will be able in twelve years (if we have not fixed the rate of wages too high, which I do not think is the case) to purchase the other three-fourths of his time. From the labour of the negro, in the first instance, the planter will have the means of paying Government the sum advanced; and at the end of twelve years the purchase money of the whole labour of the negro will be at his disposal. I do not state this proposition as wishing to bind the House with respect to it—on the contrary, I wish that both the amount of relief which the planter is to obtain, and the means of repayment, may be fully open to consideration. I also wish to leave to the consideration of the House whether we shall or shall not call upon the negro labourer to contribute his share to the repayment of the sum advanced to the planter. It is quite clear, that the repayment must be borne either by the produce of negro labour, or by the revenue of this country; it cannot in justice be borne by the planter. One or other of those alternatives must be adopted. There is certainly a middle course, but into that consideration I will not at present enter. For my own part, I think a great object would be gained by calling on the negro to contribute his share to the repayment of the advance. I think it likely that the negro will be encouraged to continue his industry and exertions, if out of his wages for the fourth of his labour, some deduction should be made for the purpose I have adverted to. To tell him that out of the produce of the fourth of his labour something should be paid up for that purpose, would certainly be more conducive to create in him habits of industry and of self denial, than if, having all his wants provided for by the planter in consideration of three-fourths of his labour, he should feel that the only object of employing the remaining fourth would be, at his own option, to provide himself with superfluities. In the latter case there would not be such a stimulus to active exertion as in the former. I, therefore, do not think that to exempt the negro from contributing his share of the repayment is by any means desirable. . . .

There is also another object on which I am sure his Majesty's Government will not appeal in vain to the House or to the country. I feel perfect confidence in calling upon this House to pledge itself, whether in aid of the Local Legislatures of the colonies, or without any aid from those Legislatures, to establish a religious and moral system of education for the negroes. We are about to emancipate the slaves; the old, after a trial of their industrious and other good qualities—the young immediately. With the young, therefore, our responsibility will immediately commence. If we place them in a state of freedom, we are bound to see that they are fitted for the enjoyment of that state; we are bound to give them the means of proving to themselves that the world is not for merely animal existence—that it is not the lot of man merely to labour incessantly from the cradle to the grave—and that to die is not merely to get to the end of a wearisome pilgrimage. We must endeavour to give them habits, and to imbue them with feelings calculated to qualify them for the adequate discharge of their duties here: and we must endeavour to instil into them the conviction, that when those duties shall be discharged, they are not "as the brutes that perish."

12. Utilitarianism: The New Poor Law

THE POOR Law Amendment Act of 1834 was a far-reaching revolution in local government and statutory assertion of social values. It is not merely an example, but the best example, of Benthamite legislation in the early Victorian era. Experts investigated, defined the problems, and proposed reforms. Parliament responded. Administrative experts applied a law conceived on sound principles. The Benthamism was more than the presence of Edwin Chadwick, Bentham's secretary during his last years, or of the distinguished political economist, Nassau Senior, on the royal commission of investigation. The new poor law rested upon Benthamite assumptions ("Man strives to find pleasure and avoid pain") and employed Benthamite devices (the workhouse test and the principle of "less eligibility").

The Whig administration deserves credit for its daring. The massive project was initiated in 1832 while the reform bill crisis was still hot. The problem of the Poor Law was the thorniest administrative issue of the day; the poor rate was the most substantial tax levy in peacetime. The crisis in poor relief, it appeared to proponents of reform, had reached such proportions that only dramatic action could work. The underlying problem was the use of poor relief as a supplement for inadequate wages in a variety of ways, usually according to formulas derived from the Speenhamland plan. This expedient, developed by Berkshire justices of the peace in 1795 (a crisis year in food prices), made up inadequate wages out of the poor rate on an allowance system adjusted to the cost of provisions and the size of the recipient's family. The free movement of labor was retarded by the seventeenth-century Act of Settlement and Removal, which authorized magistrates to remove any person liable to become a burden on their poor rates to the parish of his last legal settlement. Thus make-up systems tended slowly to drive wages down and the poor rate up, in effect to develop and intensify pockets of poverty.

All this, argued the reformers, would be changed by consolidating the more than fifteen thousand parishes into manageable Poor Law unions, ending outdoor relief for the able-bodied (the workhouse test) and, to make choice easy, making the regimen and conditions of life in the workhouse less desirable ("less eligibility") than life outside. Only the truly desperate, those for whom there were no options, would enter the workhouse and be a burden upon the rates. Those who can be gainfully employed should be. The system should hold out inducements to work, not to be idle. The new poor law was intended to provide economy, rationality, and morality. It was the ideal Victorian law.

The revolutionary implications of the measure, however, were by no means limited to the poor. The act began the formal process of breaking the power of the traditional classes in their local communities, and this local strength was the most important base of aristocratic and gentry strength. The squires and lords could assert their local sway to be returned as members of the boards of guardians of their Poor Law unions, but the local board no longer had control of policy. Not only general principles but specific administrative standards were defined by three Poor Law commissioners (after 1847 the Poor Law Board whose president sat in Parliament). Assistant commissioners made regular, routine inspections of each union. The hand of professional bureaucracy began to brush away the free and easy amateur administration of the nation.

The initial reaction to the new poor law was favorable, for it was first applied in the troubled southern agricultural counties. There where the worst abuses had been unearthed, improvements followed much as predicted. Wages rose and poor rates fell. Demoralization appeared to be checked. But the problem was quite different with the doctrinaire effort to apply the act in the industrial North. Neither the history nor the substance of the question of poor relief justified rigid Benthamite answers. Yet in 1837 the assistant commissioners took to the road. Riot and violence greeted them in the West Riding of Yorkshire and in South Lancashire. One industrial enlightened despot, John Fielden of Todmorden, master cotton spinner and radical M.P., blocked the formation of a local union for years. An assistant commissioner in Bradford was pursued to the roof of the town hall by an angry mob and was saved only by repeated charges of dragoons. Forces mobilized to fight for a ten-hour act became anti-poor-law organizations. Failing here, the same groups drifted to Chartism. The new poor law was a principal element in the alienation of classes in early Victorian England.

Theoretically the Poor Law commissioners would have preferred to end outdoor relief altogether, but that was impossible. Instead, they regulated it as closely as possible in an effort to allow for the fewest possible exceptions. The Workhouse Rules as defined in 1841 are more than bureaucratic fiats; they are statements of Victorian morality and values.

Recommended Reading

Works speaking fairly precisely to this problem are DAVID ROBERTS, *The Victorian Origins of the British Welfare State* (New Haven, 1960), and his article "How Cruel Was the Victorian Poor Law?" *Historical Journal*, Vol. VI (1963), pp. 97–107. URSULA HENRIQUES takes quite a different view in an article with the same title in *Historical Journal*, Vol. XI (1968), pp. 365–371. S. E. FINER, *The Life and Times of Edwin Chadwick* (London, 1952), is an excellent study of the man and the measure. MARK BLAUG, "The Myth of the Old Poor Law and the Making of the New," *Journal of Economic History*, Vol. XXIII (1963), pp. 151–184, challenges the assumptions and evidence of the commission and concludes that Speenhamland did not produce the conditions for which it stands indicted.

SOURCE: Eighth Annual Report of the Poor Law Commissioners, *Parliamentary Papers*, 1842, Vol. XIX, Appendix, pp. 47–51.

No. 3. General Order—Workhouse Rules

WE, THE POOR LAW COMMISSIONERS, do hereby, . . . rescind so much of every order heretofore issued by the Poor Law Commissioners . . . as relates to the government of the workhouse, or the powers and duties of the officers for such workhouse, except in so far as the said orders, or any of them, may have authorized the appointment of the existing officers, or may have prescribed a

dietary for the use of the inmates of the workhouse, or the times of
labour and the intervals for meals.

And We do hereby order, direct, and declare, . . . with respect
to the government of the workhouse in the said Unions and
parishes respectively, as follows . . .

CLASSIFICATION OF THE PAUPERS

Art. 9.   The paupers, so far as the workhouse admits thereof,
shall be classed as follows, subject nevertheless to such arrangements as the Board of Guardians may deem necessary with regard
to persons labouring under any disease of body or mind, or for the
further subdivision of any of such classes:

Class 1.   Men infirm through age or any other cause.
Class 2.   Able-bodied men, and youths above the age of 15
            years.
Class 3.   Boys above the age of 7 years, and under that of 15.
Class 4.   Women infirm through age or any other cause.
Class 5.   Able-bodied women, and girls above the age of 15
            years.
Class 6.   Girls above the age of 7 years, and under that of 15.
Class 7.   Children under 7 years of age.

To each class shall be assigned that ward or separate building and
yard which may be best fitted for the reception of such class, and
each class of paupers shall remain therein, without communication
with those of any other class.

DISCIPLINE AND DIET OF THE PAUPERS

Art. 13.   All the paupers in the workhouse, except the sick and
insane, and the paupers of the first, fourth, and seventh classes shall
rise, be set to work, leave off work, and go to bed at the times
mentioned in the Form marked A, hereunto annexed, and shall be
allowed such intervals for their meals as are therein stated; and
these several times shall be notified by the ringing of a bell; provided always that the Guardians may, with the consent of the Poor
Law Commissioners, make such alterations in any of the said times
or intervals as the Guardians may deem fit.

Art. 14.   Half an hour after the bell shall have been rung for
rising, the names of the paupers shall be called over by the master

and matron respectively in the several wards provided for the second, third, fifth, and sixth classes, when every pauper, belonging to the respective wards, must be present and must answer to his name, and be inspected by the master and matron respectively.

Art. 15.   The meals shall be taken by all the paupers except the sick, the children, persons of unsound mind, wayfarers, and vagrants, and the paupers of the first and fourth classes, in the dining-hall, or day-room, and in no other place whatever, and during the time of meals, order and decorum shall be maintained, and no pauper of the second, third, fifth, or sixth classes shall go to or remain in his sleeping-room, either in the time hereby appointed for work, or in the intervals allowed for meals, except by permission of the master or matron.

Art. 16.   The master and matron of the workhouse shall (subject to the directions of the Board of Guardians) fix the hours of rising and going to bed for the paupers of the first, fourth, and seventh classes, and determine the occupation and employment of which they may be capable; and the meals for such paupers shall be provided at such times and in such manner as the Board of Guardians may direct.

Art. 17.   The paupers of the respective sexes shall be dieted with the food and in the manner described in the dietary table which may be prescribed for the use of the workhouse, and in no other manner.

Provided, however, that the medical officer for the workhouse may direct in writing such diet for any individual pauper as he shall deem necessary, and the master shall obey such direction until the next ordinary meeting of the Board of Guardians, when he shall report the same in writing to the Guardians. And if the medical officer for the workhouse shall at any time certify that he deems a temporary change in the diet essential to the health of the paupers in the workhouse, or of any class or classes thereof, the Guardians shall cause a copy of such certificate to be entered on the minutes of their proceedings, and shall be empowered forthwith to order, by a resolution, the said diet to be temporarily changed according to the recommendation of the medical officer, and shall forthwith transmit a copy of such certificate and resolution to the Poor Law Commissioners.

Art. 18.   If any pauper shall require the master or matron to weigh the allowance of provisions served out at any meal, the master or matron shall forthwith weigh such allowance in the presence of the pauper complaining, and of two other persons.

Art. 19. No pauper shall have or consume any liquor, or any food or provision other than is allowed in the said dietary table, unless by the direction in writing of the medical officer; such direction to be obeyed and reported by the master, as in Article 17.

Art. 20. The clothing to be worn by the paupers in the workhouse shall be made of such materials as the Board of Guardians may determine.

Art. 21. The paupers of the several classes shall be kept employed according to their capacity and ability; and no pauper shall receive any compensation for his labour. Provided always that the Guardians may, without any direction of the medical officer, make such allowance of food as may be necessary to paupers employed as nurses, or in the household work; but they shall not allow to such paupers any fermented or spirituous liquors.

Art. 22. The boys and girls who are inmates of the workhouse shall, for three of the working hours at least every day, be respectively instructed in reading, writing, arithmetic, and the principles of the Christian religion, and such other instruction shall be imparted to them as shall fit them for service, and train them to habits of usefulness, industry, and virtue.

Art. 23. Any pauper may quit the workhouse upon giving to the master, or (during his absence or inability to act) to the matron, a reasonable notice of his wish to do so: and in the event of any able-bodied pauper, having a family so quitting the house, the whole of such family shall be sent with him unless the Board of Guardians shall for any special reason otherwise direct, and such directions shall be in conformity with the regulations of the said Commissioners with respect to out-door relief in force for the time being.

Art. 24. Provided nevertheless that the Board of Guardians shall make such regulations as they may deem fit, subject to the approval of the Poor Law Commissioners, to enable the master of the workhouse to allow any pauper to quit the workhouse, for some urgent or special reason, without giving any such notice as is required in Article 23, and to return after a temporary absence only; every such allowance shall be reported by the master to the Board of Guardians at their next ordinary meeting.

Provided also that nothing herein contained shall prevent the master of the workhouse from allowing the paupers of each sex

under the age of 15, subject to such restrictions as the Board of
Guardians may impose, to quit the workhouse under the care and
guidance of himself, or the matron, schoolmaster, schoolmistress,
porter, or some one of the assistants and servants of the workhouse,
for the purpose of exercise.

Art. 25.   Any person may visit any pauper in the workhouse by
permission of the master, or (in his absence) of the matron, subject
to such conditions and restrictions as the Board of Guardians may
prescribe; such interview to take place, except where a sick pauper
is visited, in a room separate from the other inmates of the workhouse, in the presence of the master, matron, or porter.

Art. 26.   No written or printed paper of an improper tendency,
or which may be likely to produce insubordination, shall be allowed to circulate, or be read aloud among the inmates of the
workhouse.

Art. 27.   No pauper shall play at cards, or at any game of chance
in the workhouse; and it shall be lawful for the master to take from
any pauper, and keep until his departure from the workhouse, any
cards, dice, or other articles relating to games of chance, which
may be in his possession.

Art. 28.   No pauper shall smoke in any room of the workhouse,
except by the special direction of the medical officer, or shall have
any matches or other articles of a highly combustible nature in his
possession.

Art. 29.   Any licensed minister of the religious persuasion of any
inmate of the workhouse who shall at any time in the day, on the
request of any inmate, enter the workhouse for the purpose of
affording religious assistance to him, or for the purpose of instructing his child or children in the principles of his religion, shall give
such assistance or instruction so as not to interfere with the good
order and discipline of the other inmates of the workhouse; and
such religious assistance or instruction shall be strictly confined to
inmates who are of the religious persuasion of such minister, and to
the children of such inmates, except in the cases in which the Board
of Guardians may lawfully permit religious assistance and instruction to be given to any paupers who are Protestant dissenters by
licensed ministers who are Protestant dissenters.

Art. 30.   No work, except the necessary household work and
cooking, shall be performed by the paupers on Sunday, Good
Friday, and Christmas-day.

Art. 31.   Prayers shall be read before breakfast and after supper every day, and Divine Service shall be performed every Sunday in the workhouse (unless the Guardians, with the consent of the Poor Law Commissioners shall otherwise direct), at which all the paupers shall attend, except the sick, persons of unsound mind, the young children, and such as are too infirm to do so; provided that those paupers who may object so to attend, on account of their professing religious principles differing from those of the Church of England, shall also be exempt from such attendance.

Art. 32.   The Guardians may make such regulations as they deem expedient to authorise any inmate of the workhouse, being a member of the established church, and not being an able-bodied female pauper having an illegitimate child, to attend public worship at a parish church or chapel, on every Sunday, Christmas-day, and Good Friday, under the controul and inspection of the master or porter of the workhouse, or other officer.

Art. 33.   The Guardians may also make such regulations as they deem expedient to authorise any inmate of the workhouse, being a dissenter from the established church, and not being an able-bodied female pauper having an illegitimate child, to attend public worship at any dissenting chapel in the neighbourhood of the workhouse, on every Sunday, Christmas-day, and Good Friday.

PUNISHMENTS FOR MISBEHAVIOUR OF THE PAUPERS

Art. 34.   Any pauper who shall neglect to observe such of the regulations herein contained as are applicable to and binding on him;—

> Or who shall make any noise when silence is ordered to be kept;
> Or shall use obscene or profane language;
> Or shall by word or deed insult or revile any person;
> Or shall threaten to strike or to assault any person;
> Or shall not duly cleanse his person;
> Or shall refuse or neglect to work, after having been required to do so;
> Or shall pretend sickness;
> Or shall play at cards or other game of chance;
> Or shall enter or attempt to enter, without permission, the

ward or yard appropriated to any class of paupers other
than that to which he belongs;

Or shall misbehave in going to, at, or returning from public
worship out of the workhouse, or at prayers in the workhouse;

Or shall return after the appointed time of absence, when allowed to quit the workhouse temporarily;

Or shall wilfully disobey any lawful order of any officer of
the workhouse;

Shall be deemed DISORDERLY.

Art. 35.   Any pauper who shall, within seven days, repeat any
one or commit more than one of the offences specified in Article
34;

Or who shall by word or deed insult or revile the master or
matron, or any other officer of the workhouse, or any of
the Guardians;

Or shall wilfully disobey any lawful order of the master or
matron after such order shall have been repeated;

Or shall unlawfully strike or otherwise unlawfully assault any
person;

Or shall wilfully or mischievously damage or soil any property whatsoever belonging to the Guardians;

Or shall wilfully waste or spoil any provisions, stock, tools, or
materials for work, belonging to the Guardians;

Or shall be drunk;

Or shall commit any act of indecency;

Or shall wilfully disturb the other inmates during prayers or
divine worship;

Shall be deemed REFRACTORY.

Art. 36.   It shall be lawful for the master of the workhouse, with
or without the direction of the Board of Guardians, to punish any
disorderly pauper by substituting, during a time not greater than
forty-eight hours, for his or her dinner, as prescribed by the
dietary, a meal consisting of eight ounces of bread, or one pound of
cooked potatoes, and also by withholding from him during the same
period, all butter, cheese, tea, sugar, or broth, which such pauper
would otherwise receive, at any meal during the time aforesaid.

Art. 37.   It shall be lawful for the Board of Guardians, by a special direction to be entered on their minutes, to order any *re-fractory* pauper to be punished by confinement in a separate room, with or without an alteration of diet, similar in kind and duration to that prescribed in Art. 36 for *disorderly* paupers; but no pauper shall be so confined for a longer period than twenty-four hours, or, if it be deemed right that such pauper should be carried before a justice of the peace, and if such period of twenty-four hours should be insufficient for that purpose, then for such further time as may be necessary for such purpose.

13. The White Man's Empire: The Durham Report

RADICAL doctrine found its most unqualified expression defining constitutional relation overseas rather than at home. Most Britons did not realize or would not admit the extent to which the balanced constitution of crown, Lords, and the Commons had been upset. When Lord Durham (1792–1840) drew his proposal for resolving the Canadian crisis of 1837–39, he stated clearly and concisely the principles of responsible government. His contemporaries did not understand that he was doing little more than adapt British practice to his reading of Canadian conditions; and the implementation of the report proved a most sensitive task, requiring infinite patience and good will on the part of governors general, colonial secretaries, and British governments.

Durham, Charles Buller, and their associates spent just long enough in Canada to gain some impression of the complex situation, but not long enough to allow them to perceive qualifications and problems within problems. The ascendancy of a few families in upper Canada (Ontario) could be broken by improving the land system and local government institutions. The British economic ascendancy in lower Canada (Quebec) should be reinforced. Like many radicals, Durham in power behaved like an authoritarian. He exiled the leaders of the rebellion, placated the more powerful disaffected groups, and improved relations with the United States.

His basic proposals were two: anglicization and self-determination; the one, in his mind, was a necessary condition for the other. Durham had no sympathy with French-Canadian nationalism. He thought the French-Canadians hopelessly retrograde, economically useless, culturally barren. They could only be saved by becoming "Englishmen" overseas. A union of the provinces and a crash program of emigration would secure British ascendancy. Durham, like other English radicals, was shockingly innocent of the nature or the force of nationalism. Self-government was—he argued in the most strikingly perceptive parts of his report—entirely consistent with the status of mother country and colony. The governor must select his council from groups that can command a majority of the elected houses.

Although Anglo-Saxon superiority was not established and the path to Canadian comity proved to be federation, not union, Durham's proposal became the Magna Carta of the Empire. It was, of course, for white colonies of settlement only. Imperial policy in India, for example, ran to increasing authoritarianism and control. The results of self-government within the dominions were not necessarily well received at home. Canada and Australia began to tinker with tariffs, while Britain preached free trade to the world. New Zealand found that self-government meant paying the bills for internal defense, and did not like it.

Durham had shown the British a way out of the American dilemma of 1775; and thanks to twenty years of sound implementation, his proposal worked. Intangible bonds of loyalty grew as each dominion evolved its own institutions and national life. Perhaps the greatest irony was the unwillingness of the British to concede to the Irish what they gave to Canadians, Australians, New Zealanders, and the Cape Colony.

Recommended Reading

Beyond the conventional literature on the Empire and imperial policy, see A. P. THORTON, *Doctrines of Imperialism* (New York, 1965); C. NEW, *Lord Durham* (London, 1929); and R. L. SCHUYLER, *The Durham Report* (New York, 1939).

SOURCE: Lord Durham, Report on the Affairs of British North America, *Parliamentary Papers*, 1839, Vol. XVII, pp. 100–106.

It is not by weakening, but strengthening the influence of the people on its Government; by confining within much narrower bounds than those hitherto allotted to it, and not by extending the interference of the imperial authorities in the details of colonial affairs, that I believe that harmony is to be restored, where dissension has so long prevailed; and a regularity and vigour hitherto unknown, introduced into the administration of these Provinces. It needs no change in the principles of government, no invention of a new constitutional theory, to supply the remedy which would, in my opinion, completely remove the existing political disorders. It needs but to follow out consistently the principles of the British constitution, and introduce into the Government of these great Colonies those wise provisions, by which alone the working of the representative system can in any country be rendered harmonious and efficient. We are not now to consider the policy of establishing representative government in the North American Colonies. That has been irrevocably done; and the experiment of depriving the people of their present constitutional power, is not to be thought of. To conduct their Government harmoniously, in accordance with its established principles, is now the business of its rulers; and I know not how it is possible to secure that harmony in any other way, than by administering the Government on those principles which have been found perfectly efficacious in Great Britain. I would not impair a single prerogative of the Crown; on the contrary, I believe that the interests of the people of these Colonies require the protection of prerogatives, which have not hitherto been exercised. But the Crown must, on the other hand, submit to the necessary consequences of representative institutions; and if it has to carry on the Government in unison with a representative body, it must consent to carry it on by means of those in whom that representative body has confidence.

In England, this principle has been so long considered an indisputable and essential part of our constitution, that it has really hardly ever been found necessary to inquire into the means by which its observance is enforced. When a ministry ceases to command a majority in Parliament on great questions of policy, its doom is immediately sealed; and it would appear to us as strange to attempt, for any time, to carry on a Government by means of ministers perpetually in a minority, as it would be to pass laws with a majority of votes against them. The ancient constitutional remedies, by impeachment and a stoppage of the supplies, have never, since the reign of William III, been brought into operation for the purpose of removing a ministry. They have never been called for, because, in fact, it has been the habit of ministers rather to anticipate the occurrence of an absolutely hostile vote, and to retire, when supported only by a bare and uncertain majority. If Colonial Legislatures have frequently stopped the supplies, if they have harassed public servants by unjust or harsh impeachments, it was because the removal of an unpopular administration could not be effected in the Colonies by those milder indications of a want of confidence, which have always sufficed to attain the end in the mother country.

The means which have occasionally been proposed in the colonies themselves appear to me by no means calculated to attain the desired end in the best way. These proposals indicate such a want of reliance on the willingness of the Imperial Government to acquiesce in the adoption of a better system, as, if warranted, would render an harmonious adjustment of the different powers of the State utterly hopeless. An elective executive council would not only be utterly inconsistent with monarchical government, but would really, under the nominal authority of the Crown, deprive the community of one of the great advantages of an hereditary monarchy. Every purpose of popular control might be combined with every advantage of vesting the immediate choice of advisers in the Crown, were the Colonial Governor to be instructed to secure the co-operation of the Assembly in his policy, by entrusting its administration to such men as could command a majority; and if he were given to understand that he need count on no aid from home in any difference with the Assembly, that should not directly involve the relations between the mother country and the Colony. This change might be effected by a single despatch containing such instructions; or if any legal enactment were requisite, it would only be one that would render it necessary that the official acts of the Governor should be countersigned by some public functionary. This would induce responsibility for every act of the Government, and, as a natural consequence, it would necessitate the substitution of a system of administration, by means of competent heads of departments, for the present rude machinery of an executive council. The Governor, if he wished to retain advisers not possessing the confidence of the existing Assembly, might rely on the effect of an appeal to the people, and, if unsuccessful, he might be coerced by a refusal of supplies, or his advisers might be terrified by the prospect of impeachment. But there can be no reason for apprehending that either party would enter on a contest when each would find its interest in the maintenance of harmony; and the abuse of the powers which each would constitutionally possess, would cease when the struggle for larger powers became unnecessary. . . .

I know that it has been urged, that the principles which are productive of harmony and good government in the mother country, are by no means applicable to a colonial dependency. It is said that it is necessary that the administration of a colony should be carried on by persons nominated without any reference to the wishes of its people; that they have to carry into effect the policy, not of that people, but of the authorities at home; and that a colony which should name all its own administrative functionaries, would, in fact, cease to be dependent. I admit that the system which I propose would, in fact, place the internal government of the colony in the hands of the colonists themselves; and that we should thus leave to them the execution of the laws, of which we have long entrusted the making solely to them. Perfectly aware of the value of our colonial possessions, and strongly impressed with the necessity of maintaining our connexion with them, I know not in what respect it can be desirable that we should interfere with their internal legislation in matters which do not affect their relations with the mother country. The matters, which so concern us, are very few. The constitution of the form of government,—the regulation of foreign relations, and of trade with the mother country, the other British Colonies, and foreign nations—and the disposal of the public lands, are the only points on which the mother country requires a control. This control is now sufficiently secured by the authority of the Imperial Legislature; by the protection which the Colony derives from us against foreign enemies; by the beneficial terms which our laws secure to its trade; and by its share of the reciprocal benefits which would be conferred by a wise system of colonization. A perfect subordination, on the part of the Colony, on there points, is secured by the advantages which it finds in the continuance of its connexion with the Empire. It certainly is not strengthened, but greatly weakened, by a vexatious interference on the part of the Home Government, with the enactment of laws for regulating the internal concerns of the Colony, or in the selection of the persons entrusted with their execution. The colonists may not always know what laws are best for them, or which of their countrymen are the fittest for conducting their affairs; but, at least, they have a greater interest in coming to a right judgment on these points, and will take greater pains to do so than those whose welfare is very remotely and slightly affected by the good or bad legislation of these portions of the Empire. If the colonists make bad laws, and select improper persons to conduct their affairs, they will generally be the only,

always the greatest, sufferers; and, like the people of other countries, they must bear the ills which they bring on themselves, until
they choose to apply the remedy. But it surely cannot be the duty
or the interest of Great Britain to keep a most expensive military
possession of these Colonies, in order that a Governor or Secretary
of State may be able to confer colonial appointments on one rather
than another set of persons in the Colonies. For this is really the
only question at issue. . . . Whatever inconvenience a consequent
frequency of changes among the holders of office may produce, is a
necessary disadvantage of free government, which will be amply
compensated by the perpetual harmony which the system must
produce between the people and its rulers. Nor do I fear that the
character of the public servants will, in any respect, suffer from a
more popular tenure of office. For I can conceive no system so
calculated to fill important posts with inefficient persons as the
present, in which public opinion is too little consulted in the
original appointment, and in which it is almost impossible to
remove those who disappoint the expectations of their usefulness,
without inflicting a kind of brand on their capacity or integrity.

My own observation convinces me, that the predominant feeling
of all the English population of the North American Colonies is
that of devoted attachment to the mother country. I believe that
neither the interests nor the feelings of the people are incompatible
with a Colonial Government, wisely and popularly administered.
The proofs, which many who are much dissatisfied with the existing administration of the Government, have given of their loyalty,
are not to be denied or overlooked. The attachment constantly
exhibited by the people of these Provinces towards the British
Crown and Empire, has all the characteristics of a strong national
feeling. They value the institutions of their country, not merely
from a sense of the practical advantages which they confer, but
from sentiments of national pride; and they uphold them the more,
because they are accustomed to view them as marks of nationality,
which distinguish them from their Republican neighbours. I do not
mean to affirm that this is a feeling which no impolicy on the part
of the mother country will be unable to impair; but I do most
confidently regard it as one which may, if rightly appreciated, be
made the link of an enduring and advantageous connexion. The
British people of the North American Colonies are a people on

whom we may safely rely, and to whom we must not grudge power. For it is not to the individuals who have been loudest in demanding the change, that I propose to concede the responsibility of the Colonial administration, but to the people themselves. . . .

The important alteration in the policy of the Colonial Government which I recommend, might be wholly or in great part effected for the present by the unaided authority of the Crown; and I believe that the great mass of discontent in Upper Canada, which is not directly connected with personal irritation, arising out of the incidents of the late troubles, might be dispelled by an assurance that the government of the Colony should henceforth be carried on in conformity with the views of the majority in the Assembly.

[Durham stresses the need for greater security through a union of the Canadian provinces.]

It is necessary that I should also recommend what appears to me an essential limitation on the present powers of the representative bodies in these Colonies. I consider good government not to be attainable while the present unrestricted powers of voting public money, and of managing the local expenditure of the community, are lodged in the hands of an Assembly. As long as a revenue is raised, which leaves a large surplus after the payment of the necessary expenses of the civil Government, and as long as any member of the Assembly may, without restriction, propose a vote of public money, so long will the Assembly retain in its hands the powers which it every where abuses, of misapplying that money. The prerogative of the Crown which is constantly exercised in Great Britain for the real protection of the people, ought never to have been waived in the Colonies; and if the rule of the Imperial Parliament, that no money vote should be proposed without the previous consent of the Crown, were introduced into these Colonies, it might be wisely employed in protecting the public interests, now frequently sacrificed in that scramble for local appropriations, which chiefly serves to give an undue influence to particular individuals or parties.

The establishment of a good system of municipal institutions throughout these Provinces is a matter of vital importance. A general legislature, which manages the private business of every parish, in addition to the common business of the country, wields a power which no single body, however popular in its constitution, ought to have; a power which must be destructive of any constitutional balance. The true principle of limiting popular power is that apportionment of it in many different depositaries which has been adopted in all the most free and stable States of the Union. Instead of confiding the whole collection and distribution of all the revenues raised in any country for all general and local purposes to a single representative body, the power of local assessment, and the application of the funds arising from it, should be entrusted to local management. It is in vain to expect that this sacrifice of power will be voluntarily made by any representative body. The establishment of municipal institutions for the whole country should be made a part of every colonial constitution; and the prerogative of the Crown should be constantly interposed to check any encroachment on the functions of the local bodies, until the people should become alive, as most assuredly they almost immediately would be, to the necessity of protecting their local privileges.

The establishment of a sound and general system for the management of the lands and the settlement of the Colonies, is a necessary part of any good and durable system of government. . . .

A plan by which it is proposed to ensure the tranquil government of Lower Canada, must include in itself the means of putting an end to the agitation of national disputes in the legislature, by settling, at once and for ever, the national character of the Province. I entertain no doubts as to the national character which must be given to Lower Canada; it must be that of the British Empire; that of the majority of the population of British America; that of the great race which must, in the lapse of no long period of time, be predominant over the whole North American Continent. Without effecting the change so rapidly or so roughly as to shock the feelings and trample on the welfare of the existing generation, it must henceforth be the first and steady purpose of the British Government to establish an English population, with English laws and language, in this Province, and to trust its government to none but a decidedly English Legislature. . . .

I must not, however, assume it to be possible that the English Government shall adopt the course of placing or allowing any check to the influx of English immigration into Lower Canada, or any impediment to the profitable employment of that English capital which is already vested therein. The English have already in their hands the majority of the larger masses of property in the country; they have the decided superiority of intelligence on their side; they have the certainty that colonization must swell their numbers to a majority; and they belong to the race which wields the Imperial Government, and predominates on the American Continent. If we now leave them in a minority, they will never abandon the assurance of being a majority hereafter, and never cease to continue the present contest with all the fierceness with which it now rages. In such a contest they will rely on the sympathy of their countrymen at home; and if that is denied them, they feel very confident of being able to awaken the sympathy of their neighbours of kindred origin. . . .

I am far from wishing to encourage indiscriminately those pretensions to superiority on the part of any particular race; but while the greater part of every portion of the American Continent is still uncleared and unoccupied, and while the English exhibit such constant and marked activity in colonization, so long will it be idle to imagine that there is any portion of that Continent into which that race will not penetrate, or in which, when it has penetrated, it will not predominate. It is but a question of time and mode; it is but to determine whether the small number of French who now inhabit Lower Canada shall be made English, under a Government which can protect them, or whether the process shall be delayed until a much larger number shall have to undergo, at the rude hands of its uncontrolled rivals, the extinction of a nationality strengthened and embittered by continuance.

And is this French Canadian nationality one which, for the good merely of that people, we ought to strive to perpetuate, even if it were possible? I know of no national distinctions marking and continuing a more hopeless inferiority. The language, the laws, the character of the North American Continent are English; and every race but the English (I apply this to all who speak the English language) appears there in a condition of inferiority. It is to elevate them from that inferiority that I desire to give to the Canadians our English character. I desire it for the sake of the educated classes, whom the distinction of language and manners keeps apart from the great Empire to which they belong. At the best, the fate of the educated and aspiring colonist is, at present, one of little hope, and little activity; but the French Canadian is cast still further into the shade, by a language and habits foreign to those of the Imperial Government. A spirit of exclusion has closed the higher professions on the educated classes of the French Canadians, more, perhaps, than was absolutely necessary; but it is impossible for the utmost liberality on the part of the British Government to give an equal position in the general competition of its vast population to those who speak a foreign language. I desire the amalgamation still more for the sake of the humbler classes. Their present state of rude and equal plenty is fast deteriorating under the pressure of population in the narrow limits to which they are confined. If they attempt to better their condition, by extending themselves over the neighbour-ing country, they will necessarily get more and more mingled with an English population: if they prefer remaining stationary, the greater part of them must be labourers in the employ of English capitalists. In either case it would appear, that the great mass of the French Canadians are doomed, in some measure, to occupy an inferior position, and to be dependent on the English for employ-ment. The evils of poverty and dependence would merely be aggravated in a ten-fold degree, by a spirit of jealous and resentful nationality, which should separate the working class of the com-munity from the possessors of wealth and employers of labour.

But their present proprietary and inactive condition is one which no political arrangements can perpetuate. Were the French Cana-dians to be guarded from the influx of any other population, their condition in a few years would be similar to that of the poorest of the Irish peasantry.

There can hardly be conceived a nationality more destitute of all that can invigorate and elevate a people, than that which is exhib-ited by the descendants of the French in Lower Canada, owing to their retaining their peculiar language and manners. They are a people with no history, and no literature. The literature of Eng-land is written in a language which is not theirs; and the only literature which their language renders familiar to them, is that of a nation from which they have been separated by eighty years of a foreign rule, and still more by those changes which the Revolution and its consequences have wrought in the whole political, moral and social state of France. Yet it is on a people whom recent his-tory, manners and modes of thought, so entirely separate from them, that the French Canadians are wholly dependent for almost all the instruction and amusement derived from books: it is on this essentially foreign literature, which is conversant about events, opinions and habits of life, perfectly strange and unintelligible to them, that they are compelled to be dependent. Their newspapers are mostly written by natives of France, who have either come to try their fortunes in the Province, or been brought into it by the party leaders, in order to supply the dearth of literary talent available for the political press. In the same way their nationality operates to deprive them of the enjoyments and civilizing influence of the arts. Though descended from the people in the world that most generally love, and have most successfully cultivated the drama—though living on a continent, in which almost every town, great or small, has an English theatre, the French population of Lower Canada, cut off from every people that speaks its own language, can support no national stage.

In these circumstances, I should be indeed surprised if the more reflecting part of the French Canadians entertained at present any hope of continuing to preserve their nationality. Much as they struggle against it, it is obvious that the process of assimilation to English habits is already commencing. The English language is gaining ground, as the language of the rich and of the employers of labour naturally will. It appeared . . . that there are about ten times the number of French children in Quebec learning English, as compared with the English children who learn French. A considerable time must, of course, elapse before the change of a language can spread over a whole people; and justice and policy alike require, that while the people continue to use the French language, their Government should take no such means to force the English language upon them as would, in fact, deprive the great mass of the community of the protection of the laws. But, I repeat that the alteration of the character of the Province ought to be immediately entered on, and firmly, though cautiously, followed up; that in any plan, which may be adopted for the future management of Lower Canada, the first object ought to be that of making it an English Province; and that, with this end in view, the ascendancy should never again be placed in any hands but those of an English population. . . .

14.   Constitutional Delicacy:
Melbourne, Victoria, and the Bedchamber Crisis

WILLIAM IV's ill-advised attempt to invoke his prerogative to select his ministers against the will of the country as represented in Parliament had circumscribed the constitutional powers of the crown. After Peel's failure in 1834, the crown never again attempted to run counter to public opinion. Sovereigns recommended, warned, cautioned, but did not attempt to impose. The negative side of the issue remained to be resolved. Granted the ruler could not impose his choice. What concessions had he to make to show contentment with a ministry he disliked?

This problem was brought to a head in an amusing but serious way early in the reign of the young Queen Victoria. She ascended the throne in 1837, ill-prepared and frightened. The stature of monarchy had slipped, sometimes imperceptibly, occasionally precipitately through the past half-century. Criticism ranged from waspish comments about expense to outright republicanism, a challenge to the utility and right of the institution. George IV and William IV offered no moral inspiration or sound leadership. They had not even produced legitimate children, surely one of the principal functions of royalty. This, at least, was an oversight that Victoria would decisively redress. Initially, however, the new Queen found herself dependent upon Lord Melbourne, not merely as prime minister but as a father figure and intimate friend.

Melbourne's second administration (1835-41) was less manageable than his first. The fact that he was dependent upon Radical and Irish support to maintain his majority goes far to explain why the Municipal Corporations Act of 1835 was a more radical measure than its companion piece, the Reform Act of 1832. This awkward coalition was perpetually crumbling, now here, now there. By 1839 it was past repointing. Peel was summoned to form a new government. Since his support would be marginal, he sought to obviate criticism of royal disfavor by having the Queen reconstruct her household offices along nonpartisan, if not Conservative, lines. All went well until it came to the matter of ladies of the bedchamber. Victoria insisted on retaining all of them; Sir Robert viewed this as a want of confidence in him and declined to form a government. Melbourne and the Whigs, in an ironical twist of positions, found themselves compelled to stand for royal prerogative. Crude bargaining with the Radicals provided enough parliamentary support to enable the government to limp through to the election of 1841, when it was decisively defeated.

Peel was properly concerned that Melbourne might use his personal position with the Queen to undercut any Conservative government, and he sought to minimize the degree to which Whig partisan interests monopolized royal attention. Fortunately Albert was just appearing on the scene. He was to educate Victoria and himself to sounder constitutional practice.

Recommended Reading

There is a range of material both general and specific, but the broad background of the constitutional problem is best studied in BETTY KEMP, *King and Commons* (London, 1957). For a variety of reasons every student should read Lord DAVID CECIL, *Melbourne* (New York, 1954), and ELIZABETH LONGFORD, *Queen Victoria: Born to Succeed* (New York, 1965), although the latter has not completely superseded LYTTON STRACHEY, *Queen Victoria* (New York, 1921).

SOURCE: Charles Cavendish Fulke Greville, *The Greville Memoirs (Second Part). A Journal of the Reign of Queen Victoria from 1837 to 1852*, edited by Henry Reeve, Vol. I (London, 1885), pp. 130–131, 207–211.

September 12th [1838].—George Villiers, who came from Windsor on Monday, told me he had been exceedingly struck with Lord Melbourne's manner to the Queen, and hers to him: his, so parental and anxious, but always so respectful and deferential; hers, indicative of such entire confidence, such pleasure in his society. She is continually talking to him; let who will be there, he always sits next her at dinner, and evidently by arrangement, because he always takes in the lady-in-waiting, which necessarily places him next her, the etiquette being that the lady-in-waiting sits next but one to the Queen. It is not unnatural, and to him it is peculiarly interesting. I have no doubt he is passionately fond of her as he might be of his daughter if he had one, and the more because he is a man with a capacity for loving without having anything in the world to love. It is become his province to educate, instruct, and form the most interesting mind and character in the world. No occupation was ever more engrossing or involved greater responsibility. I have no doubt that Melbourne is both equal to and worthy of the task, and that it is fortunate she has fallen into his hands, and that he discharges this great duty wisely, honourably, and conscientiously. There are, however, or rather may be here-after, inconveniences in the establishment of such an intimacy, and in a connexion of so close and affectionate a nature between the young Queen and her Minister; for whenever the Government, which hangs by a thread, shall be broken up, the parting will be painful, and their subsequent relations will not be without embar-rassment to themselves, nor fail to be the cause of jealousy in others. It is a great proof of the discretion and purity of his conduct and behaviour, that he is admired, respected, and liked by all the Court.

May 12th 1839.—The Cabinet met yesterday, and resolved to take the Government again; they hope to interest the people in the Queen's quarrel, and having made it up with the Radicals they think they can stand. It is a high trial to our institutions when the wishes of a Princess of nineteen can overturn a great Ministerial combination, and when the most momentous matters of Govern-ment and legislation are influenced by her pleasure about her Ladies of the Bedchamber. The Whigs resigned because they had no longer that Parliamentary support for their measures which they deemed necessary, and they consent to hold the Government without the removal of any of the difficulties which compelled them to resign, for the purpose of enabling the Queen to exercise her pleasure without any control or interference in the choice of the Ladies of her household. This is making the private gratifica-tion of the Queen paramount to the highest public considerations: somewhat strange Whig doctrine and practice! With respect to the question of unfettered choice, a good deal may be said on both sides; but although it would be wrong and inexpedient for any Minister to exercise the right, unless in a case of great necessity, I think every Minister must have the power of advising the Queen to remove a Lady of her Court, in the same way as he is admitted to have that of removing a man. Notwithstanding the transaction of 1812, and Lord Moira's protection of George IV. in the retention of his household, it is now perfectly established in practice that the Royal Household is at the discretion of the Minister, and it must be so because he is responsible for the appointments; in like manner he is responsible for every appointment which the Sovereign may make; and should any of the Ladies conduct herself in such a manner as to lead the public to expect or require her dismissal, and the Queen were to refuse to dismiss her, the Minister must be responsible for her remaining about the Royal person.

The pretension of the Queen was not merely personal, *pro hâc vice* [for this occasion], and one of arrangement, but it went to the establishment of a principle unlimited in its application, for she declared that she had felt bound to make her stand where she did, in order once for all to resist the encroachments which she anticipated, and which would lead, she supposed, at last to their insisting on taking the Baroness Lehzen herself from her. In a constitutional point of view, the case appears to me to be much stronger than in that of a Queen Consort, for the Minister has nothing to do with a Queen Consort; he is not responsible for her appointments, nor for the conduct of her officers, and she is a *feme sole* possessed of independent rights which she may exercise according to her own pleasure, provided only that she does not transgress the law. It was a great stretch of authority when Lord Grey insisted on the dismissal of Lord Howe, Queen Adelaide's Chamberlain; but he did so upon an extraordinary occasion, and when circumstances rendered it, as he thought, absolutely necessary that he should make a public demonstration of his influence in a Court notoriously disaffected to the Reform Bill.

The origin of the present mischief may be found in the objectionable composition of the Royal Household at the Accession. The Queen knew nobody, and was ready to take any Ladies that Melbourne recommended to her. He ought to have taken care that the female part of her household should not have a political complexion, instead of making it exclusively Whig as, unfortunately for her, he did; nor is it little matter of wonder that Melbourne should have consented to support her in such a case, and that he and his colleagues should have consented to act the strange, anomalous, unconstitutional part they have done. While they really believed that she had been ill-used, it was natural they should be disposed to vindicate and protect her; but after the reception of Peel's letter they must have doubted whether there had not been some misapprehension on both sides, and they ought in prudence, and in justice to her, even against her own feelings, to have sifted the matter to the bottom, and have cleared up every existing doubt before they decided on their course. But to have met as a Cabinet,

and to have advised her what answer to send to the man who still
held her commission for forming a Government, upon points relating to its formation, is utterly anomalous and unprecedented, and a
course as dangerous as unconstitutional.[1] The danger has been
sufficiently exemplified in the present case; for, having necessarily
had no personal cognisance of the facts, they incurred the risk of
giving advice upon mistaken grounds, as in this instance has been
the case. *She* might be excused for her ignorance of the exact limits
of constitutional propriety, and for her too precipitate recurrence
to the counsels to which she had been accustomed; but *they* ought
to have explained to her, that until Sir Robert Peel had formally
and finally resigned his commission into her hands, they could
tender no advice, and that her replies to him, and her resolutions
with regard to his proposals, must emanate solely and spontaneously from herself. As it was, the Queen was in communication
with Sir Robert Peel on one side, and Lord Melbourne on the
other, at the same time; and through them with both their Cabi-
nets; the unanimous resolutions of the former being by her conveyed to, and her answer being composed by, the latter. The
Cabinet of Lord Melbourne discussed the proposals of that of Sir
Robert Peel, and they dictated to the Queen the reply in which she
refused to consent to the advice tendered to her by the man who
was *at that moment* her Minister, and it was this reply which
compelled him to resign the office with which she had entrusted
him.

May 13th.—Lord Tavistock went on Saturday to Buckingham
Palace; found Melbourne was not there, and followed him to his
house, where the Cabinet was sitting. He wrote him a letter, in
which he said that he had seen the Duke, and that his impression
was that there had been a misunderstanding between Peel and the
Queen; and suggested to Melbourne that he should see the Duke,
who was very willing, if he pleased, to talk the matter over with
him. This letter was taken in to the Cabinet, and they discussed its

[1] Melbourne explains away this objection by alleging that the negotiation
with Peel was over at six on Thursday; that the Queen sent for him to tell
him so; that he was again become her Minister; and that he and his colleagues properly advised the terms in which she should convey her final
decision. This explanation seems to have gone down, but I can't imagine
how: the decision to persist in refusing Peel's demands became *their* decision, when they advised the letter in which it was conveyed. I know not
why more was not made of this part of the case.

contents.[2] Melbourne was not indisposed to see the Duke; but, after a careful consideration of Peel's letter, they came to the conclusion that there was no difference between the Queen's statement to them and Peel's to her, and, therefore, no misconception to correct. The Chancellor accordingly gave his opinion, that there was no ground for an interview between Melbourne and the Duke; so then ended the last hope of a readjustment.

The question (they say) was all along one of *principle*, and never of the *application* of the principle; but the extraordinary part of it is that they admit that the principle is not maintainable, yet declare that they were bound *as gentlemen*, when the Queen had recourse to them, to support her. This is strange doctrine in Whig mouths. They have, in my opinion, abandoned their duty to the country and to the Queen, and they ought to have been impressed with the paramount obligation of instructing her in the nature and scope of her constitutional obligations and duties, and the limits of her constitutional rights, and to have advised her what she ought to do, instead of upholding her in doing that which was agreeable to her taste and inclination.

15. Chartism:
Jacobin Ideology and Armed Poverty

CHARTISM was armed poverty, claimed John Walter, the owner of *The Times*. So it was. But such an explanation, simultaneously simple and complex, was insufficient. This attempt to mount a mass democratic movement in the opening years of Victoria's reign was different things to different men. To London artisan radicals Chartism was another installment in a long struggle for the means of political self-help. The six points of the People's Charter drawn by William Lovett and Francis Place—universal manhood suffrage (women were dropped to preserve unanimity), vote by ballot, elimination of property qualifications for members of Parliament, payment of members, standard-sized single-member constituencies, and annual elections—were more than sixty years old. They were outgrowths of a "commonwealth" tradi-

---

[2] LORD Grey was at Melbourne's house; Melbourne sent for him, and consulted him, and he remained in another room while the Cabinet was in deliberation. Lord Grey took it up very warmly, and was strongly for supporting the Queen, saying they could not do otherwise.

tion, a peculiarly English form of jacobinism, that reached back to the civil war of the seventeenth century. Chartist rhetoric, organization, and methods derived from late eighteenth-century reform agitation. Engels read the situation correctly in Manchester, where Chartism was an expression of industrial class conflict between cotton masters and men. But no generalization follows from that example. Across the Pennines in Leeds, Chartism grew from a political alliance of owners and workers and was, as a result, a different, more moderate movement. In other towns and villages of the Midlands, Yorkshire, and Lancashire, starving and desperate handloom weavers, victims of a revolution in technology and of a change in clothing style, found Chartism a vehicle for their violent frustration.

Chartism was almost exclusively an urban and industrial phenomenon. Traditional loyalties, intimidation, and more widespread political insensitivity each contributed to the relatively feeble Chartist impact upon agricultural labor in the more traditional environment of the countryside. The very term Chartism suggests a greater degree of sociological, political, and geographical unity than the movement ever had. Only the six points, the political sublimation of very different grievances were held in common.

Other causes, usually short-term failures, provided most Chartist support. Industrial workers, like those in Manchester, had taken a serious beating on trade unionism and failed in their initial attempts to win a statutory ten-hour day. Outdoor relief, the traditional form of unemployment insurance and social security in the industrial North, was officially (and officiously) banned under the Poor Law Amendment Act of 1834—the bitterly hated new poor law first implemented in the North during the recession of 1836–38. The protest movement of South Lancashire and Yorkshire flowed swiftly into Chartism. Champions of paper money, advocates of an unstamped (untaxed) press, agrarian socialists, and a wide spectrum of reforming monomaniacs were drawn to franchise reform as a panacea. If only the people were enfranchised, the masses would support their several causes.

Essential middle-class support was lacking. The compromise of the Reform Act of 1832 had siphoned off much class discontent. The more aggressive bourgeois elements were fighting their own psychological class war in the campaign of the Anti-Corn-Law League. While they recruited lower class partisans, the leaguers were hostile to Chartism, better organized, and strikingly successful in translating a fiscal issue into a moral cause. The remaining potential leadership for Chartism was quarrelsome and confused. The dignified democrats had no alternative when peaceful petitions were rejected by the House of Commons. Chartist holidays, proposed general strikes, were unlikely to succeed in the economic doldrums of the hungry forties. Advocates of physical force and direct action revolution fought better campaigns in the columns of Feargus O'Connor's *Northern Star* or in hysterical

harangues from the hustings than they did in the field. The one serious
outburst, that associated with John Frost in Wales in 1839, collapsed
within hours.

The threat of revolution remained real. The fact that England
avoided violence, that no barricades went up in the streets of London
or Manchester, that the red flag animated George Harney's imagination rather than tens of thousands of handloom weavers must never
conceal the essential fact. Englishmen believed they were poised on the
brink of a revolutionary abyss. Trouble in the North was avoided to
no small extent by having in General Napier a military district
commander who understood the basis of discontent and sympathized
with the Chartists. Still, during the Chartist trials of 1848 artillerymen
were standing to their guns at the doors of the court with glowing
linstocks in their hands.

But 1848 was also the catharsis of Chartism. Only fear or fantasy
made the Chartist rally on Kennington Common seem a real threat to
public order. In 1848 specters were too often real, and even the exiled
Louis Napoleon took his place as a volunteer London special constable.
The rally, the petition, its rejection were all an anticlimax. The slow
return of business prosperity, the elimination of some and the irrele-
vance of other sources of Chartism, and the emotional exhaustion after
a decade of sustained agitation, all contributed to the dispersion, rather
than to the destruction, of Chartism. Retrospectively it is easy to see
that Chartism posed little serious threat after 1842, but contemporaries
did not view the problem that way. The Victorian age began on the
rumbling note of revolution. The echoes were to be heard for decades.

Recommended Reading

There is so much Chartist literature that it is hard to know where to
begin. Good places to start are: A. BRIGGS, ed., *Chartist Studies*
(London, 1959); G. D. H. COLE, *Chartist Portraits* (London, 1941);
J. L. and B. HAMMOND, *The Age of the Chartists* (London, 1930), or its
abridged Penguin edition entitled *The Bleak Age;* M. HOVELL, *The
Chartist Movement* (London, 1918); and A. R. SCHOYEN, *The Chartist
Challenge* (London, 1958).

SOURCE: Documents A and B: William Lovett, *The Life and
    Struggles of William Lovett* (London, 1876), pp. 174–180, 469–
    473. Document C: Report of the Commissioners for Inquiry into
    the Conditions of Unemployed Hand-Loom Weavers in the
    United Kingdom, *Parliamentary Papers*, 1841, Vol. X, pp. 187–
    189. Document D: Report from the Committee on Public Pe-
    titions on the Chartist Petition, April 13, 1848, *Hansard's Parlia-
    mentary Debates*, Third Series, Vol. XCVIII, col. 285.

A. London Working Men's Association, Address to the Public
(1838)

Fellow-Countrymen,—Having great faith in the inherent excellence of humanity, and believing that more of the mental and moral incongruities of men are to be attributed to erroneous convictions than to interested perversions of truth and justice, we should belie our opinions were we to make any foolish attack on the press or its conductors.

We rather lament that such a powerful instrument towards man's political and social redemption should be constrained by interest or party, to shut out truth from its pages and make error a marketable speculation; or that men, so competent to direct aright the public mind, should be employed to mystify and mislead it.

But we think that the many notorious changes and conversions recently witnessed, the skilful balancing of opinions, the fear-to-offend and desire-to-please disposition which have characterized so great a portion of those papers who call themselves *"liberal,"* should open the eyes of all those who desire to see the Press as consistent in practice, as it ought to be honest in principle.

Such eccentric courses, and such conduct, in men professing liberality of sentiment and honesty of intention, can only be countenanced by the public's disregard of all principle, or the private encouragement of those who maintain their fraudulent position by unworthy means.

We would be the last to restrict the freedom of thought, or the most unbounded expressions that could be given in opposition to our own opinions, as we consider that truth can only be elicited through the severest test of mental conflict; but when, in the same paper, we see the most ultra-political principles set forth in the strongest language to-day, pertinaciously defended by the most cogent arguments to-morrow, and the most sweeping condemnation and invective bestowed on them the day following, we confess we do not think it free discussion, but direct apostasy.

We are induced to put forth these observations from the conduct of a great portion of the press, ever since the recent agitation that has commenced in favour of the "People's Charter and the National Petition," embracing, as they do, the principles of Universal Suffrage, as well as the other essentials which we believe necessary to a just representative system. Without, however, *individualizing* any paper, or noticing their scurrility or abuse, we will proceed to answer some of the objections they have urged against us, or our principles.

They say that we are "adopting and imitating the mischievous conduct of our oppressors, in seeking to make men free and happy by means of legislation!" What, we would ask, but legislation has made the difference between democratic America, despotic Russia, and pauperised and oppressed England? If the will of the American people, expressed through their legislature, has raised them from such a poor and heterogeneous origin, to become a nation "better educated than any other under the sun—where two-thirds of the adults are proprietors, and while most of the others have the prospect of becoming so"—what, we would ask the gentlemen who make those admissions, is there in the character of Englishmen to prevent them from realizing similar advantages, were the same political rights conferred on them as on their American brethren?

They say that our *"ignorance and poverty* should preclude us from the franchise." We beg to refer them back to the "beautiful democracy" and all its results, which they admit to exist in America, and ask them whether the intelligence and prosperity of that country *preceded* their political rights, or whether they are not the consequence of their having obtained them?

Granting that a number of our countrymen are in poverty, can these gentlemen show, by any valid reasoning, the absolute necessity of their being so, especially in a country blessed by nature with such abundant resources? Nay, can they trace the existence of that poverty to any other source than corrupt and exclusive legislation? Granting too, that ignorance to a great extent prevails, to what other cause can it be attributed than to those who have legislated to keep knowledge from the people? And, therefore, is it not as immoral as it is unjust to make the *effects* of corruption a pretence for upholding the *cause* of it? We would call upon any reflecting individual to take up the history of his country, and to investigate the true cause of all the wars, the superstitions, the oppressions, and the persecutions, which leave so many stains upon our national character, and he will find it to be an exclusive and corrupt government; and he will find that in proportion as the spirit of democracy has forced its influence on the legislature, so have the venomous influences of later times abated.

Warned, therefore, by the experience of the past, and cheered by the example of modern democracy, whether in Switzerland, Norway, or America, we think that every lover of his species ought to exert his influence to remove that prolific source of evil—*corrupt legislation*. It is not so much by *forms* of government that evils are generated or removed, as by the principles of exclusive or responsible representation; the former acts for itself, the latter for the people. Therefore, according to our humble abilities, in seeking to remedy the evils we complain of, we believe the most effective means will be those we have embodied in the People's Charter.

We are told that "Universal Suffrage would produce universal confusion"; that "the people would only substitute noisy demagogues for an idle aristocracy," and that therefore "we had better suffer the ills we know, than fly to others that we know not of." Those who talk of present ills, we presume, are not among the suffering classes, and they only expose their own selfishness and heartlessness in showing such a disregard to the misery of others. As to the kind of men we should choose, if Universal Suffrage prevailed, that will need experience to test it; but where it has been tested by the descendants of Englishmen, such "demagogues" as Washington, Jefferson, Franklin, and others equally efficient, seem to cast a doubt upon the prophecy. The "confusion," too, likely to flow from removing corruption would, by the same test, be proved more imaginative than real. America had an adventurous and speculative race to begin with, intermingled with fanatics and convicts from Britain, and for the last half century the poor and oppressed of all the countries of Europe have sought and found an asylum on her hospitable shores. The greedy speculator, the ruined bankrupt, the broken down insolvent, and the felon pursued by justice, have also transferred their vices to her soil, but her salutary laws and institutions, *springing from Universal Suffrage*, have enabled her to reform, instruct, and purify the mass, and in despite of that black *remnant of kingly dominion*—"SLAVERY," she is the most prosperous and free of all the nations of the earth.

We have been gravely assured that "the best test of intelligence is property"—that "the outward mark of ascertaining the existence of property is house-rent"—that "a still surer indication of property is direct taxation," and "that therefore the present electoral body is a guarantee for fair legislation." While we, in part, admit the truth of some of these propositions, to the extent that wealth will *give the means* of knowledge, we deny that property is any fair criterion for intelligence. We know of hundreds of rich fools, and thousands of housekeepers whose knowledge does not extend beyond their counters, and who are no more qualified to judge of any man's political capabilities than the most ignorant ploughman, whose common sense would not at least be subject to such influence as the fear of losing a wealthy customer. If *wealth alone* formed "a sufficient guarantee for just government," the benevolent portion of mankind would not for so many years have been striving to rescue the enslaved negro from the mercenary grasp of the wealthy planter of India, and the Southern slaveowner of America; nay, further, if *intelligence alone* were sufficient, we should not have such a catalogue of bad laws to complain of.

The great boast of England is "Trial by Jury"—but why do we prefer the less intelligent jury to the more intelligent judge, who fully knows the law, and is a more competent judge of evidence? Simply, *because honesty is not always united with intelligence.* We have found out that wealthy and intelligent judges cannot even be trusted in a court of law, and we are therefore pleased to submit to the occasional blunders of an unbiassed jury, rather than trust our lives to a designing judge. If men without responsibility were strictly virtuous, a few intelligent individuals would be found sufficient to make and execute the laws; but as they are not so, we must endeavour to make them honest by making them accountable and responsible for their actions.

But we are told that "we are virtually represented"—that "our interests are identified with those who represent us." This is very false philosophy. Man does not always pursue *his own* real interests; if he did, he would never commit so many crimes and blunders as he does; on the contrary, he pursues an imaginary interest, as passion or circumstances determine; and hence the necessity for laws to regulate his conduct. So with men collectively, so with classes—they uphold the interest of their class according to their power or inclinations; and it is only by a mutual reliance on, and *responsibility to each other*, that oppression can be guarded against.

Land, labour, and capital are the great sources of wealth; without land and labour capital would be unproductive; without capital and land labour could not be employed; and, without labour, both land and capital would be useless. Here, then, is a mutual necessity for mutual interests; and, being so dependent, each upon the other, justice demands that in all the arrangements necessary for production and distribution, equality in legislation should prevail. But, no; we are told that "the capitalists dread the labourers, and therefore will oppose giving them their rights." We would here stop to ask these very consistent gentlemen, who talk of "virtual representation," what just cause have English capitalists to dread, or to oppose the English labourer, more than American capitalists have to fear the power of Universal Suffrage in that country. The people there find it to their interest to protect and encourage capital as *the best seed for future production,*—they find it equally beneficial to remove monopolies and develop their own resources, taking care that, as the public cause is promoted, individual interests shall not suffer. They know that *knowledge* is the surest promoter of peace and order, and therefore seek to extend it,— they find that poverty is the most fruitful source of crime, and therefore seek to remove it. Do the opponents of Universal Suffrage imagine that Englishmen would be less wise in pursuing their own interests than Americans are?

But there are a class of reasoners who, when foiled by truth and compelled to admit the justice of principles, will fall back upon that old subterfuge of error, *expediency*. We are told that, admitting Universal Suffrage to be just, "we must demonstrate its expediency." In answer to which we would say, if the evils of which most classes complain, can be traced to any one cause, it is as *expedient* as it is just to remove that cause. And if we can show that the removal of a similar cause has produced beneficial results in another country, it is "expedient" to make the trial in our own. We are next informed that "Household Suffrage would be a more respectable suffrage" than that which we propose; in reply to which, we think honesty preferable to respectability, and believe that all the ignorance which they say they fear would be embodied in Household Suffrage, *to the exclusion of the intelligence of the towns*, would be embodied in Universal Suffrage.

But, as a last resource, the opponents to our rights think it necessary to mislead and misdirect us from our object. They tell us that "the repeal of the Corn Laws is of much more importance than the Suffrage," as it would even "give cheap bread, more trade, promote morality, upset the priesthood, and destroy cant." That the Corn Laws are highly mischievous we admit, but they are only *one of the effects* of the great cause we are seeking to remove; and in justice we think the question of their repeal ought to be argued *by the representatives of all the people*, and not by a faction. If they had existed so long that people had forgotten the state of things previous to their enactment, we might be induced to have faith in all the blessed promises now made us; but the year 1815 is not of very great antiquity. And when we find the following bit of advice given by these "kindly disposed persons," we think it exhibits their hollowness and hypocrisy. "All those who want *to stave off* as long as possible the trial of strength between the proprietary and the working classes, ought to direct the meeting, that is to be held in Palace Yard, to pass resolutions for the repeal of the Corn Laws and to move an amendment to the People's Charter." This is evidently an attempt to sow divisions and dissensions, in no ways warranted by the disposition of a patient, long-suffering, industrious people; nor by any supposed interest in opposition to persons or to property. But we would caution such advisers against making such "trials of strength," and warn them also against exciting prejudices it should be their duty to dispel. In arousing the passions they silence reason, and the weapon they would enlist in their service might be fatal to themselves.

B. The People's Charter

NATIONAL PETITION

Unto the Honourable the Commons of the United Kingdom of Great Britain and Ireland in Parliament assembled, the Petition of the undersigned, their suffering countrymen,

HUMBLY SHEWETH,

That we, your petitioners, dwell in a land whose merchants are noted for enterprise, whose manufacturers are very skilful, and whose workmen are proverbial for their industry.

The land itself is goodly, the soil rich, and the temperature wholesome; it is abundantly furnished with the materials of commerce and trade; it has numerous and convenient harbours; in facility of internal communication it exceeds all others.

For three-and-twenty years we have enjoyed a profound peace. Yet, with all these elements of national prosperity, and with every disposition and capacity to take advantage of them, we find ourselves overwhelmed with public and private suffering.

We are bowed down under a load of taxes; which, notwithstanding, fall greatly short of the wants of our rulers; our traders are trembling on the verge of bankruptcy; our workmen are starving; capital brings no profit, and labour no remuneration; the home of the artificer is desolate, and the warehouse of the pawnbroker is full; the workhouse is crowded, and the manufactory is deserted.

We have looked on every side, we have searched diligently in order to find out the causes of a distress so sore and so long continued.

We can discover none in nature, or in Providence.

Heaven has dealt graciously by the people; but the foolishness of our rulers has made the goodness of God of none effect.

The energies of a mighty kingdom have been wasted in building up the power of selfish and ignorant men, and its resources squandered for their aggrandisement.

The good of a party has been advanced to the sacrifice of the good of the nation; the few have governed for the interest of the few, while the interest of the many has been neglected, or insolently and tyrannously trampled upon.

It was the fond expectation of the people that a remedy for the greater part, if not for the whole, of their grievances, would be found in the Reform Act of 1832.

They were taught to regard that Act as a wise means to a worthy end; as the machinery of an improved legislation, when the will of the masses would be at length potential.

They have been bitterly and basely deceived.

The fruit which looked so fair to the eye has turned to dust and ashes when gathered.

The Reform Act has effected a transfer of power from one domineering faction to another, and left the people as helpless as before.

Our slavery has been exchanged for an apprenticeship to liberty, which has aggravated the painful feeling of our social degradation, by adding to it the sickening of still deferred hope.

We come before your Honourable House to tell you, with all humility, that this state of things must not be permitted to continue; that it cannot long continue without very seriously endangering the stability of the throne and the peace of the kingdom;

and that if by God's help and all lawful and constitutional appliances, an end can be put to it, we are fully resolved that it shall speedily come to an end.

We tell your Honourable House that the capital of the master must no longer be deprived of its due reward; that the laws which make food dear, and those which by making money scarce, make labour cheap, must be abolished; that taxation must be made to fall on property, not on industry; that the good of the many, as it is the only legitimate end, so must it be the sole study of the Government.

As a preliminary essential to these and other requisite changes; as means by which alone the interests of the people can be effectually vindicated and secured, we demand that those interests be confided to the keeping of the people.

When the state calls for defenders, when it calls for money, no consideration of poverty or ignorance can be pleaded in refusal or delay of the call.

Required as we are, universally, to support and obey the laws, nature and reason entitle us to demand, that in the making of the laws, the universal voice shall be implicitly listened to.

We perform the duties of freemen; we must have the privileges of freemen.

WE DEMAND UNIVERSAL SUFFRAGE.

The suffrage to be exempt from the corruption of the wealthy, and the violence of the powerful, must be secret.

The assertion of our right necessarily involves the power of its uncontrolled exercise.

WE DEMAND THE BALLOT.

The connection between the representatives and the people, to be beneficial must be intimate.

The legislative and constituent powers, for correction and for instruction, ought to be brought into frequent contact.

Errors, which are comparatively light when susceptible of a speedy popular remedy, may produce the most disastrous effects when permitted to grow inveterate through years of compulsory endurance.

To public safety as well as public confidence, frequent elections are essential.

WE DEMAND ANNUAL PARLIAMENTS.

With power to choose, and freedom in choosing, the range of our choice must be unrestricted.

We are compelled, by the existing laws, to take for our representatives, men who are incapable of appreciating our difficulties, or who have little sympathy with them; merchants who have retired from trade, and no longer feel its harassings; proprietors of land who are alike ignorant of its evils and their cure; lawyers, by whom the honours of the senate are sought after only as means of obtaining notice in the courts.

The labours of a representative, who is sedulous in the discharge of his duty, are numerous and burdensome.

It is neither just, nor reasonable, nor safe, that they should continue to be gratuitously rendered.

We demand that in the future election of members of your Honourable House, the approbation of the constituency shall be the sole qualification; and that to every representative so chosen, shall be assigned, out of the public taxes, a fair and adequate remuneration for the time which he is called upon to devote to the public service.

Finally, we would most earnestly impress on your Honourable House, that this petition has not been dictated by any idle love of change; that it springs out of no inconsiderate attachment to fanciful theories; but that it is the result of much and long deliberation, and of convictions, which the events of each succeeding year tend more and more to strengthen.

The management of this mighty kingdom has hitherto been a subject for contending factions to try their selfish experiments upon.

We have felt the consequences in our sorrowful experience—short glimmerings of uncertain enjoyment swallowed up by long and dark seasons of suffering.

If the self-government of the people should not remove their distresses, it will at least remove their repinings.

Universal suffrage will, and it alone can, bring true and lasting peace to the nation; we firmly believe that it will also bring prosperity.

May it therefore please your Honourable House to take this our petition into your most serious consideration; and to use your utmost endeavours, by all constitutional means, to have a law passed, granting to every male of lawful age, sane mind, and unconvicted of crime, the right of voting for members of Parliament; and directing all future elections of members of Parliament to be in the way of secret ballot; and ordaining that the duration of Parliaments so chosen shall in no case exceed one year; and abolishing all property qualifications in the members; and providing for their due remuneration while in attendance on their Parliamentary duties.

And your petitioners, &c.

C. J. Fletcher on the Weavers of Coventry

The weavers of Coventry and its neighbourhood are not only aware that political institutions must have some effect on their welfare, but, like the labouring classes of England generally, regard the defects which may exist in those of their own, as of every other country, as the direct cause of evils, in the production of which they have scarcely any, if the remotest, influence. Though possessing a far larger share of political privileges than most labourers of their class, they complain that their class generally is insufficiently represented in the legislature; that they are depressed in mass by taxation; that justice is not equal; and that wealth is not equitably distributed; the latter evil being a consequence of the preceding political defects, to remedy which they propose the adoption of *universal suffrage*, with supplementary measures which shall keep the Commons' house of parliament constantly subject to the votes of the people.

Richard Holmes, an undertaker, speaking for the Foleshill weavers, says:—

If the labourers had the elective franchise, there would be a legislature which would be more likely to promote their interests than the present. The franchise should therefore be extended to the limit of *universal suffrage*.

The corn-laws themselves are evidence of this.

The general feeling throughout the working men of this, as of other manufacturing districts, is a total want of confidence in the legislature; and many have come to the full determination never again to address the legislature with petitions.

Were the legislature such as would do equal justice, it should make laws that *would give to the working men the position in society that they ought to hold.*

Measures should be passed *which will secure a more equitable division of the wealth created by them.* Knows of no law extant directed to such a purpose; but society has advanced to a new state, which demands new laws.

Cannot suggest any measures for the more equitable distribution of wealth, because the opinions entertained by himself on that subject are only private opinions, not entertained by the weavers generally, and he is only expressing their opinion. Needless to express his own, *for society is not prepared for the adoption of them.*

These were obviously of a socialist character, which unfortunately pervades the notions of those among the weavers of either town or country who think at all on political subjects. But, however unclear their ideas of administration may be, the desire for universal suffrage, with the supplementary contrivances for giving it full effect, has strong hold of the popular feelings in this district. Disregarding for the moment the visionary schemes to which men like the witness above quoted vainly suppose that the franchise might be applicable (schemes, the propagation of which is as hurtful to the immediate purpose of their entertainers, as they would ultimately be destructive to civil society), I cannot but express my warm concurrence in the views of Malthus on this subject, who justly regards the value of political privileges to the labouring classes as consisting in their indirect moral influence, far more than in their direct legislative efficacy. Their possession is assuredly the only *political* guarantee which a population can have for equal justice; but an enlightened public opinion is a *moral* security far more effective; one which governments of every form must respect; and one of which the labouring classes of England ought to appreciate the value in their own country; for without it the mere political forms of liberty can neither be acquired, usefully exercised, nor even maintained. . . .

Political institutions, which issue the mandates of legislation, hold the scales of justice, use the arm of police, give external security, and perform a few public services which private associations cannot well discharge, are based where the moral strength of society lies; and, in so closely compacted and civilized a community as that of England, where mutual forces are instinctively known and calculated upon, the resort to violence to attain a political object is certain proof of the feebleness of the cause. It may be attempted, but must miserably fail; for, wherever solid power exists, its violent exercise is needless. Men who are grossly ignorant, improvident, drunken, and almost without domestic virtues, like many of the unfortunate people engaged in the single-hand ribbon trade, can no more assert a claim to political privileges than they could rationally exercise them if granted. But their want of moral strength, which makes such populations feeble for any purpose of good to themselves, can never deprive them of the power of mischief to others; and the ultimate ruin of society would be as surely accomplished by the quiet abasement of the whole body of our unskilled labourers, as it would by the shocks of revolution. Whether it receive the legal recognition of a right to vote or not, every body of labourers has a political existence in this power of mischief, which intelligence alone can convert into a power of good; and it is vain in those who have strengthened this political power of mischief by enlarged industrial combinations, and in all the classes who have benefited by it, to suppose that they can securely enjoy the augmented power and profit which these have brought to them, without advancing the moral, and, consequently, the physical condition of the labouring masses. Happily, this is a law of nature which will assert its supremacy wherever a country is inhabited but by one free race. Only by a system of instruction which shall awaken the labourer to his true position and duties as a citizen, since no longer a domestic, can the peace of society be sufficiently preserved for agriculture, manufactures, or commerce to prosper.

Disaffection and the wildest theories prevail among the labouring classes not here only, but throughout large portions of England; and the modern industrial changes have unfortunately produced an alienation of classes, which various witnesses endeavoured to describe; but they were themselves too much involved in the local passions to take a fair view of their position. Their evidence pointed to the altered social relations in the agriculture as well as the manufactures of the district, consequent on the change from the small farm and undertaking systems, under resident landlords and manufacturers, to large farming and agency, growing and manufacturing for distant proprietors and capitalists. And that important moral and political phenomena result from these industrial changes cannot be doubted, however little they may generally be perceived and understood, even by the parties most immediately interested. To tamper with the industrial organization of society, or restrain its recourse to more economical arrangements, never belonged to political power in a free country; but it may avert consequent dangers of the gravest character by giving to its moral elements a development commensurate with its material progress.

Neighbourhood to propertied classes, especially if these be their employers, is an important element in the well-being of a low-skilled population. This neighbourhood alone is a political element; and when, as in the case of the Coventry city weavers, it has the full voice of the political franchise, it places the men in a position for being as liberally treated by their masters as the competition of other places, or the fear of it, can possibly permit; and, were the same influences elsewhere in operation, I cannot doubt that the men would everywhere be gradually raised in character and in comforts; for the demoralization of bribery at elections results chiefly from the possession of the parliamentary franchise by the labouring classes being *peculiar* to a few cities. The extension of the franchise must, however, be attendant on an extension of instruction, which might possibly be made the passport to its enjoyment.

So strongly am I impressed with the importance of the influences upon the condition of unskilled labourers, arising from the union of masters and men in the same local communities, that, were it possible to organize society politically according to their industrial occupations, I should most earnestly wish it. The representation of towns and counties respectively had in its origin much of the character which would be sought in such an expedient: in the boroughs themselves, which comprised all the manufacturing populations, the municipal organization was very commonly based upon trades; and the assessment of the community of employers to the burthens of poor's-rates arising from the families of their men, in lieu of the accidental locality of their residence, would be an object worthy of employing the best administrative talents in its attainment. So great, indeed, are the evils resulting from the municipal dissociation of large bodies of our manufacturing population from their employers, that laws, calling upon the latter to bear whatever burthens of poor's-rates might arise from their work-people, or any other laws that could be devised with a tendency to congregate them around their premises, would be of enormous benefit to the whole community, whatever might be the slight check which the discharge of moral duties might impose upon a few branches of trade. Any such injury would be far more than compensated by the saving to the whole community, from the check given to a thriftless and demoralized population. The misery, abandonment, and demoralization which prevail in the single-hand ribbon-trade, I believe to be the natural and necessary result of this dissociation, and the dispersion of the workpeople. Their sole connexion with the great community around them is their weekly resort to the master's warehouse, which is assuredly no powerful means of civilization; and beyond this they are almost alienated from all society. The influences which reach them are those only of a religious character; and the feebleness of these has been already shown. The great body of the weaving and framework-knitting populations are similarly dispersed, and similarly depressed; and the *absenteeism* of so many of the employers, except agents, who are not the real capitalists, will, I doubt not, be found everywhere to have a great, though not always an obvious, effect on the condition of the labouring people; working their depression, not actively, but through the want of the moral bonds which should attach them to society at large. Neighbourhood and a poor's-rate would afford to employers admonitions which would ultimately have the effect of limiting the number of their people to that which could subsist by the trade in order and decency. The contrary system makes discontent national instead of local; and, as in Ireland, turns upon the government tumults which ought to have assailed only the municipality or the masters.

D. Report from the Committee on Public Petitions on the Chartist Petition, April 13, 1848

The House, on the 26th of November last, directed your Committee, in all cases, to set forth the number of signatures to each petition; and also, having regard to the powers delegated to them, to report their opinion and observations thereupon to the House, and they have agreed to the following special report: That on the 10th of April last, a petition for universal suffrage, &c., from the inhabitants of the British Isles, and subjects of the British Crown, was presented to the House. Your Committee strongly feel the value of the right of petition, and they consider that the exercise of it is one of the most important privileges of the subjects of this realm. They feel the necessity of preserving the exercise of such a privilege from abuse; and having also due regard to the importance

of the very numerously signed petition forming the subject of the
present report, they feel bound to represent to the House, that in
the matter of signatures there has been, in their opinion, a gross
abuse of the privilege. The hon. Member for Nottingham [Feargus
O'Connor] stated, on presenting the petition, that 5,706,000 names
were attached to it; but, upon the most careful examination of the
number of signatures in the Committee-room, and at which examination thirteen law-stationers' clerks were engaged upwards of
seventeen hours, with the person ordinarily employed in counting
the numbers appended to petitions, under the superintendence of
the clerk of your Committee, the number of signatures has been
ascertained to be 1,975,496. It is further evident to your Committee, that on numerous consecutive sheets the signatures are in one
and the same handwriting. Your Committee also observed the
names of distinguished individuals attached to the petition, who
can scarcely be supposed to concur in its prayer: among which
occurs the name of Her Majesty, as Victoria Rex, April 1st, F. M.
Duke of Wellington, Sir Robert Peel, &c., &c. Your Committee
have also observed, in derogation of the value of such petition, the
insertion of numbers of names which are obviously fictitious, such
as "No Cheese," "Pug Nose," "Flat Nose." There are others included, which your Committee do not hazard offending the House
and the dignity and decency of their own proceedings by report-
ing. It may be added that there are other signatures appended
obviously belonging to the name of no human being.

16.   Social Tension:
The Attack upon Symbols of Privilege

THE NEWLY enfranchised substantial middle class of the Reform Act of
1832 proved obstreperous and assertive. They discovered that their
constitutional victory had given them the forms, not the substance, of
power. The classes who had dominated British politics before the
Reform Act continued to do so. The dynamic industrial entrepreneurs
believed that they could win a simultaneous victory for their interests
and their class. The corn laws, which protected British agriculture
from imported grain, had long been a subject for debate. David

Ricardo had stigmatized the landlord as a parasite collecting his un-earned increment, economic rent, from the productive classes of the nation. British manufacturing and commercial interests saw an end-lessly expanding market if they could just cut through the restrictions of tariffs. Thus the case for repeal had a well-defined and generally accepted place in economic thought. Prudent business interest pointed in the same direction. But the most important need served by the Anti-Corn Law League was psychological. The corn laws were the symbol of the privileged position of the landed classes of Britain. End protec-tion, thought many repealers, and the old order is through. We who are forging the new Britain shall then assume our rightful place.

Richard Cobden, George Wilson (the league's president), and John Bright believed much of what they said as the Anti-Corn Law League campaign took hold in 1838 and after. But they were also conscious of the fact that they were forging a new radical program on the fortui-tous issue of cheap food. Idealists they may have been, but they were also opportunists of the first order. The Anti-Corn-Law League con-ducted a brilliant, overwhelming campaign to rouse the country. They contended that tariff policy was a moral issue, and they hired some of the leading nonconformist preachers to prove it. The league even dabbled irresponsibly with the more violent northern agitation usually associated with Chartism. It shares some of the responsibility for the plug riot of 1842, and its "pay no taxes" resolutions looked much like a call for massive civil disobedience.

The campaign of the Anti-Corn-Law League did not bring repeal. That was a direct result of the Irish famine and a policy choice by Sir Robert Peel. The league wielded little influence inside Parliament and much less than it wished in the constituencies. Moveover, repeal, when it came, proved an empty victory. As the Duke of Wellington implied to the House of Lords, they could sacrifice the symbols of privilege without relinquishing power. But the repeal of the corn laws (1846), like the passage of the Ten Hours Act (1847), drew off much of the poison of social tension that had reached such a pitch during the first decade of Victoria's reign.

Other results followed the campaign and repeal. Benjamin Disraeli rose to dominate the Conservative party by leading the Tory back-benchers against almost all of their leaders. He hated Peel and reveled in the opportunity of the moment to confront the issue in league terms and to insult his former chief.

Recommended Reading

Consult the standard studies and: G. KITSON CLARK, "The Repeal of the Corn Laws and the Politics of the Forties," *Economic History Review*, Second Series, Vol. IV (1951); C. R. FAY, *The Corn Laws and Social England* (Cambridge, 1932); N. GASH, *Reaction and Recon-struction in English Politics* (Oxford, 1965); W. D. GRAMPP, *The*

Manchester School of Economics (Stanford, 1960); and N. McCord, *The Anti-Corn Law League* (London, 1958).

Source: Benjamin Disraeli, Speech on the Corn Importation Bill, May 4, 1846, *Hansard's Parliamentary Debates,* Third Series, Vol. LXXXVI, cols. 83–87.

I am ready to meet the real question without any evasion. If the measures of the Government have not a tendency to occasion a great displacement of labour, a displacement of that kind of labour which is of the most permanent character—if they have not by that displacement a tendency to occasion great social suffering, and, ultimately, great political disaster, then I say they are good measures, and I for one am not prepared to oppose them. But that is the whole question, and that question at the right moment, at the fitting opportunity, with the permission and indulgence of the House, I am prepared to discuss. If I do not meet it now, I hope that no one will for a moment suppose that I admit the justice of the series of assumptions with which we have been favoured by the right hon. Gentleman. The right hon. Gentleman alluded to the state of Ireland, that 534,000 farmers are without capital, and then he turns round, in the manner of his great master, and says, "See what protection has produced." I shall be prepared, upon the proper occasion, to prove that protection has not produced the present condition of Ireland. That is an enormous assumption. I might as well turn round to the right hon. Gentleman and say, "Had it not been for protection, those 534,000 farmers would not have existed." Nothing is so easy as to take instances of wretchedness and say protection has produced them. There is the eternal instance of the Wiltshire labourer with his 6s. or 7s. a week; and it is said, "See what protection has produced." I go into Lincolnshire, and I find the labouring man with ample means and flourishing— may I not turn round and say, "See what protection has produced?" These are questions which cannot be entered into without more time than, in an incidental debate like the present, can be appropriated to them; but when the right hon. Gentleman takes this occasion, with his great authority, to scatter arguments which, of course, influence public opinions, or rather to make statements —for he has not condescended to reason to-night, he has rather taken refuge in rhetoric—it is absolutely necessary they should be noticed, however partially.

The right hon. Gentleman says, "How can you justify your system of protection, even if it did benefit to the agriculturist, to the manufacturer?" I can justify it; I resist altogether the inference that is sought to be drawn from the question put by the right hon. Gentleman. I say, unless by the system of protection, as described in this debate, the benefit to manufactures is as great as the benefit to agriculture, I agree with him, the objection to it is fatal, and he would not be a wise statesman that would not earnestly consider the consequences of it. I take this to be the case of the manufacturer. The late war and some preceding wars destroyed existing manufactures in many countries. Those in Europe and the United States are of modern origin. In no instance have those manufactures sprung from any other source than the capital that the system of protection allowed the landed proprietors to accumulate. It is that capital which has formed our own manufactures. That noble industry of the north of England, which is so often the subject of discussion in this House, the cotton manufacture, is as much owing to the agricultural capital of England, as it is to the genius of its great mechanical inventions, and even to its unprecedented local advantages which unite mines of coal and iron. In the early state of the cotton manufacture, it was the capital of Lombard Street that promoted the immense development of that fabric. And what was the capital of Lombard Street? It was the capital of the farmers of Norfolk and Lincolnshire, which had found its way into Lombard Street, and was thence distributed by the great bankers and billbrokers. I am speaking of transactions when a house like Gurney's, for example, would discount bills to the amount of half a million, all drawn upon and accepted by one firm, for the purchase of Manchester goods. It was that farmers' capital which gave the principal development to the industry of Lancashire. I am very glad that the industry of Lancashire has outlived the necessity of such support; but it must not be forgotten that it received that support, any more than it must be forgotten that it received, when necessary, the protection of the Legislature.

This brings me to the point of the right hon. Gentleman, who said—and the noble Lord too, inferentially—"If manufactures require no protection, how can the agricultural interest demand it?" As an abstract principle I protest against this reasoning. It is not sound as a mere argument. The business of a statesman is, not to inquire why one interest is protected, and another is not, but whether the protection enjoyed by any particular interest is required. Are the circumstances in which agriculture and manufactures are respectively placed the same? I have heard a great deal said about the peculiar burdens on land. I confess I have never held that a sufficient ground for what is called protection to agriculture; but no one will deny that the manufactures of England have peculiar advantages—at least, no hon. Gentleman opposite will deny it, because they are always getting up and telling us of them. They perpetually assure us that they have no fear of competition, because the unrivalled advantages of their soil from the interstratification of coal and iron, independently of their machinery, alone exempts them from all rivalry. The farmers have no such peculiar advantages; they do not, therefore, meet upon equal ground. To say, therefore, that one interest should not be protected, because another does not require protection, is, in fact, quite illogical. It is not an argument; it is a mere appeal—a sentimental appeal: it does for the hustings and for popular assemblies, but it will not bear the examination of the closet, and is unworthy of this assembly. I am not now asserting that the farmers of England do require protection, for that is too great a subject to enter upon now; but I will venture hereafter to approach it if opportunity is given to me. I shall then be prepared to meet the arguments that are put forward by Her Majesty's Ministers, and which in reality is the case of their great master. I would address my arguments to the creative minds and manly energies that are really responsible for them.

We have heard to-night a great deal about territorial aristocracy. There may be some doubts whether we have a territorial aristocracy in this country; but there is none whatever that we have an aristocracy of wealth. We all feel it, and I believe that the measures of Her Majesty's Ministers have a tendency to increase that power in a degree I believe not beneficial to the people; but suppose there were in England what is called a territorial aristocracy, I utterly protest against the rhetorical position taken up by the right hon. Gentleman, and also touched upon by the noble Lord. The right hon. Gentleman has argued upon the case as if the aristocracy of England were a privileged aristocracy. What privileges have they? I have on more than one occasion risen in this House to uphold the cause of what I call our territorial constitution, not imagining by such a word I was maintaining the mere interests of peers and esquires. I certainly should not have risen had I thought I was pleading only their cause. But this territorial constitution which I have defended, has given to this country public liberty and the blessings of local and self-government. It appeals to all; it has immense ramifications; it touches every class of the community.

I have talked myself of the necessity of maintaining the preponderance of the agricultural interest, and I remember somebody or other saying, "Can any thing be more improper than thus holding up the necessity of the predominance of a class in the country?" I do not imagine for a moment that the agricultural interest is constituted merely of the proprietors of land. The agricultural interest is that great body of people who are the cultivators of the earth; and if you materially change the balance between the populations that depend upon the two great interests of this country, you shake to its centre that territorial constitution, you destroy the security for local government—you subvert the guarantee for public liberty—you change, in fact, the character of England; you bring about that social revolution which the right hon. Gentleman always reminded us would be the consequence of following the policy of the school of Manchester.

Sir, there is nothing exclusive or restrictive in this territorial constitution, or I am sure it would not be tolerated for a moment in England. From the days of Sir Robert Walpole to the present moment, with one solitary exception, all those who have realized large fortunes in our great seats of industry, have deposited the results of their successful enterprise in the soil of their country. The power of acquiring territorial possessions is open to every man. The fact that every family which has acquired great wealth has invested that wealth in the purchase of land, affords the best possible proof that in our territorial constitution there is nothing alien or adverse to the interests of commerce or manufactures. Respecting the county in which I myself live, I can state from my own experience, within the last twenty years, that not less than one-third of the land of that county has changed hands; and I may add that even some portion of that land has been purchased by Gentlemen who subscribed to the funds of the Anti-Corn Law League.

Away, then, with this declamation about a territorial aristocracy, as if it were a body distinguished from all other classes. The

Constitution of this country has invested the proprietors of land
with certain duties and certain rights, which all may acquire, and
aspire to fulfil. It has secured to us at all times, and under all
circumstances, leaders who have saved us from that despotism
which has too often been the fate of other countries. It affords to
every man this position to which his property and intelligence
entitle him: no man need despair of obtaining the highest place in
our free aristocracy—even the sons of the humblest may find a
place in this or the other House of Parliament. I have no wish to
enter further into this question at present.

17.   The Early Victorian Statesman:
Bagehot on Peel

WALTER BAGEHOT (1826–1877) was England's most incisive political
observer; Sir Robert Peel (1788–1850) one of the most capable Victorian statesmen. Peel dominated early Victorian England in many
ways more completely than Palmerston, Gladstone, or Disraeli would
dominate the later years. Bagehot was simultaneously drawn to and
repelled by Sir Robert. He acknowledged him to be a fitting man for
his times in both his strengths and his weaknesses. Peel's father had
begun in textiles and turned to improving landlordship. The son was
educated at Harrow and Christ Church, Oxford in the tradition of the
imperial purple. Sir Robert entered Parliament in 1809 and became
undersecretary for War and the Colonies the subsequent year. While
he began with advantages, he mounted to the top on ability. Initially
even his prejudices were politically fortuitous. A staunch foe of
Roman Catholic political emancipation, he earned the soubriquet
"Orange Peel" as Chief Secretary in Ireland. But he proved to be one
of the more progressive ministers in Lord Liverpool's Tory administration. From 1822 he began to overhaul the criminal code and introduced
the modern police system. He pioneered revolution by blue book—
reforms developed from the recommendations derived from an exhaustive investigation by experts. Although he remained unenthusiastic
about Catholic emancipation, he helped the Duke of Wellington push
it through in 1829.

The Conservative party, Peel's reconstructed Tory party after the
Reform Act of 1832, learned to adopt moderate reform within the
spirit of the constitution in church and state. Both the Conservative

party and Peel's Tamworth Manifesto of 1834 could mean much or little, but Sir Robert demonstrated his leadership in the modernization of Britain during his great 1841–46 administration. He was the only Conservative leader to win a national election with the votes of the propertied classes enfranchised by the first Reform Act. This most successful party leader showed his mettle by placing the needs of his country above partisan considerations. The Irish famine precipitated the repeal of the corn laws, the protective tariff on wheat and ostensibly the symbol of the privileged position of the landed classes. The dispute shattered the Conservative party, catapulted Disraeli forward as leader of the Tories, and left the Peelites generals without an army.

But Sir Robert performed yet one more service. He mediated subsequent political developments and aided in the construction of those elements that would contribute much substance and talent to the future Liberal party. The greatest Liberal statesman, Gladstone, began as Peel's lieutenant.

The political critic, Walter Bagehot, was one of the first great alumni of University College, London. He made a lasting mark as an economist, a journalist, and a political commentator. A self-styled liberal-conservative, he has much in common with his great French contemporary, Alexis de Tocqueville. Bagehot was concerned about the content and the quality of contemporary British life. He viewed the advent of democracy with no enthusiasm, although he readily admitted the problems of the world as it was. He was a realist, a practiced man of the world who appeared to have few illusions: in fact he had many, but he concealed them well—even from himself. The great G. M. Young called him "the most Victorian of Victorians," and his current editor, Norman St. John-Stevas, styles him "Victorian England's most versatile genius." Both pitch his claims rather high, but Bagehot was an acute observer. And he is fun.

Recommended Reading

There is an extensive literature on Peel and early Victorian politics. See, among other titles: G. KITSON CLARK, *Peel and the Conservative Party* (London, 1929); N. GASH. *Mr. Secretary Peel* (London, 1961), *Politics in the Age of Peel* (London, 1953), and *Reaction and Reconstruction in English Politics* (Oxford, 1965).

There is no satisfactory study of Walter Bagehot. The best substitute is the substantial introduction by NORMAN ST. JOHN-STEVAS to *Walter Bagehot: a Study of His Life and Thought Together with a Selection from His Political Writings* (London, 1959). I also strongly recommend G. M. YOUNG, "The Greatest Victorian," *Victorian Essays*, ed. by W. D. HANDCOCK (London, 1962), pp. 123–128; and the penetrating critique in A. BRIGGS, *Victorian People* (Chicago, 1955), ch. iv.

SOURCE: Walter Bagehot, "The Character of Sir Robert Peel," *National Review* (July, 1856), pp. 146–174.

A constitutional statesman is in general a man of common opinions and uncommon abilities. The reason is obvious. When we speak of a free government, we mean a government in which the sovereign power is divided, in which a single decision is not absolute, where argument has an office. The essence of the *gouvernement des avocats*, as the Emperor Nicholas called it, is that you must persuade so many persons. The appeal is not to the solitary decision of a single statesman; not to Richelieu or Nesselrode alone in his closet; but to the jangled mass of men, with a thousand pursuits, a thousand interests, a thousand various habits. Public opinion, as it is said, rules; and public opinion is the opinion of the average man. Fox used to say of Burke: "Burke is a wise man; but he is wise too soon." The average man will not bear this. He is a cool, common person, with a considerate air, with figures in his mind, with his own business to attend to, with a set of ordinary opinions arising from and suited to ordinary life. He can't bear novelty or originalities. He says: "Sir, I never heard such a thing *before* in my life"; and he thinks this is a *reductio ad absurdum*. You may see his taste by the reading of which he approves. Is there a more splendid monument of talent and industry than *The Times*? No wonder that the average man—that any one—believes in it. As Carlyle observes: "Let the highest intellect able to write epics try to write such a leader for the morning newspapers, it cannot do it; the highest intellect will fail." But did you ever see anything there you had never seen before? Out of the million articles that everybody has read, can any one person trace a single marked idea to a single article? Where are the deep theories, and the wise axioms, and the everlasting sentiments which the writers of the most influential publication in the world have been the first to communicate to an ignorant species? Such writers are far too shrewd. The two million, or whatever number of copies it may be, they publish, are not purchased because the buyers wish to know new truth. The purchaser desires an article which he can appreciate at sight; which he can lay down and say, "An excellent article, very excellent; exactly my own sentiments." Original theories give trouble; besides, a grave man on the Coal Exchange does not desire to be an

apostle of novelties among the contemporaneous dealers in fuel;—
he wants to be provided with remarks he can make on the topics of
the day which will not be known *not* to be his; that are not too
profound; which he can fancy the paper only reminded him of.
And just in the same way, precisely as the most popular political
paper is not that which is abstractedly the best or most instructive,
but that which most exactly takes up the minds of men where it
finds them, catches the floating sentiment of society, puts it in such
a form as society can fancy would convince another society which
did not believe—so the most influential of constitutional statesmen
is the one who most felicitously expresses the creed of the moment, who administers it, who embodies it in laws and institutions,
who gives it the highest life it is capable of, who induces the
average man to think, "I could not have done it any better if I had
had time myself."

It might be said, that this is only one of the results of that
tyranny of commonplace which seems to accompany civilisation.
You may talk of the tyranny of Nero and Tiberius; but the real
tyranny is the tyranny of your next-door neighbour. What law is
so cruel as the law of doing what he does? What yoke is so galling
as the necessity of being like him? What *espionage* of despotism
comes to your door so effectually as the eye of the man who lives
at your door? Public opinion is a permeating influence, and it
exacts obedience to itself; it requires us to think other men's
thoughts, to speak other men's words, to follow other men's habits.
Of course, if we do not, no formal ban issues, no corporeal pain, no
coarse penalty of a barbarous society is inflicted on the offender;
but we are called "eccentric"; there is a gentle murmur of "most
unfortunate ideas," "singular young man," "well-intentioned, I
dare say; but unsafe, sir, quite unsafe." The prudent, of course,
conform. The place of nearly everybody depends on the opinion
of every one else. There is nothing like Swift's precept to attain the
repute of a sensible man, "Be of the opinion of the person with
whom, at the time, you are conversing." This world is given to
those whom this world can trust. Our very conversation is in-
fected. Where are now the bold humour, the explicit statement,
the grasping dogmatism of former days? They have departed, and
you read in the orthodox works dreary regrets that the *art* of
conversation has passed away. It would be as reasonable to expect
the art of walking to pass away. People talk well enough when

they know to whom they are speaking. We might even say that the art of conversation was improved by an application to new circumstances. "Secrete your intellect, use common words, say what you are expected to say," and you shall be at peace. The secret of prosperity in common life is to be commonplace on principle.

Whatever truth there may be in these splenetic observations might be expected to show itself more particularly in the world of politics. People dread to be thought unsafe in proportion as they get their living by being thought to be safe. "Literary men," it has been said, "are outcasts"; and they are eminent in a certain way notwithstanding. "They can say strong things of their age; for no one expects they will go out and act on them." They are a kind of ticket-of-leave lunatics, from whom no harm is for the moment expected; who seem quiet, but on whose vagaries a practical public must have its eye. For statesmen it is different—they must be thought men of judgment. The most morbidly agricultural counties were aggrieved when Mr Disraeli was made Chancellor of the Exchequer. They could not believe he was a man of solidity; and they could not comprehend taxes by the author of *Coningsby*, or sums by an adherent of the Caucasus. "There is," said Sir Walter Scott, "a certain hypocrisy of action, which, however it is despised by persons intrinsically excellent, will nevertheless be cultivated by those who desire the good repute of men." Politicians, as has been said, live in the repute of the commonalty. They may appeal to posterity; but of what use is posterity? Years before that tribunal comes into life, your life will be extinct. It is like a moth going into Chancery. Those who desire a public career must look to the views of the living public; an immediate exterior influence is essential to the exertion of their faculties. The confidence of others is your *fulcrum*. You cannot, many people wish you could, go into parliament to represent yourself. You must conform to the opinions of the electors; and they, depend on it, will not be original. In a word, as has been most wisely observed, "under free institutions it is necessary occasionally to defer to the opinions of other people; and as other people are obviously in the wrong, this is a great hindrance to the improvement of our political system and the progress of our species."

Seriously, it is a calamity that this is so. Occasions arise in which a different sort of statesman is required. A year or two ago we had one of these. If any politician had come forward in this country, on the topic of the war, with prepared intelligence, distinct views, strong will, commanding mastery, it would have brought support to anxious intellects, and comfort to a thousand homes. None such came. Our people would have statesmen who thought as they thought, believed as they believed, acted as they would have acted. They had desired to see their own will executed. There came a time when they had no clear will, no definite opinion. They reaped as they had sown. As they had selected an administrative tool, of course it did not turn out a heroic leader.

If we wanted to choose an illustration of these remarks out of all the world, it would be Sir Robert Peel. No man has come so near our definition of a constitutional statesman—the powers of a first-rate man and the creed of a second-rate man. From a certain peculiarity of intellect and fortune, he was never in advance of his time. Of almost all the great measures with which his name is associated, he attained great eminence as an opponent before he attained even greater eminence as their advocate. On the corn-laws, on the currency, on the amelioration of the criminal code, on Catholic emancipation . . . he was not one of the earliest labourers or quickest converts. He did not bear the burden and heat of the day; other men laboured, and he entered into their labours. As long as these questions remained the property of first-class intellects, as long as they were confined to philanthropists or speculators, as long as they were only advocated by austere, intangible Whigs, Sir Robert Peel was against them. So soon as these same measures, by the progress of time, the striving of understanding, the conversion of receptive minds, became the property of second-class intellects, Sir Robert Peel became possessed of them also. He was converted at the conversion of the average man. His creed was, as it had ever been, ordinary; but his extraordinary abilities never showed themselves so much. He forthwith wrote his name on each of those questions, so that it will be remembered as long as they are remembered.

Nor is it merely on these few measures that Sir Robert Peel's mind must undoubtedly have undergone a change. The lifetime of few Englishmen has been more exactly commensurate with a change of public opinion—a total revolution of political thought. Hardly any fact in history is so incredible as that forty and a few years ago England was ruled by Mr Perceval [1809–1812]. It seems almost the same as being ruled by the *Record* newspaper. He had the same poorness of thought, the same petty Conservatism, the same dark and narrow superstition. His quibbling mode of oratory seems to have been scarcely agreeable to his friends; his impotence in political speculation moves the wrath—destroys the patience—of the quietest reader now. Other ministers have had great connections, or great estates, to compensate for the contractedness of their minds. Mr Perceval was only a poorish *nisi prius* lawyer; and there is no kind of human being so disagreeable, so teasing, to the gross Tory nature. He is not entitled to any glory for our warlike successes: on the contrary, he did his best to obtain failure by starving the Duke of Wellington, and plaguing him with petty vexations. His views in religion inclined to that Sabbatarian superstition which is of all creeds the most alien to the firm and genial English nature. The mere fact of such a premier being endured shows how deeply the whole national spirit and interest was absorbed in the contest with Napoleon, how little we understood the sort of man who should regulate its conduct—"in the crisis of Europe," as Sydney Smith said, "he safely brought the Curates' Salaries Improvement Bill to a hearing"—and it still more shows the horror of all innovation which the recent events of French history had impressed on our wealthy and comfortable classes. They were afraid of catching revolution, as old women of catching cold. Sir Archibald Alison to this day holds that revolution is an infectious disease, beginning no one knows how, and going no one knows where. There is but one rule of escape, explains the great historian, "Stay still, don't move; do what you have been accustomed to do, and consult your grandmother on everything." In 1812 the English people were all persuaded of this theory. Mr Perceval was the most narrow-minded and unaltering man they could find: he therefore represented their spirit, and they put him at the head of the state.

We cannot, however, believe that, even if Mr Perceval had lived, his power would have very long endured. It passed to milder and quieter men. It passed to such men as Lord Liverpool and Mr Peel. The ruling power at that time in England, as for many years before, as even in some measure, though far less, now, was the class of aristocratic gentry; by which we do not mean to denote the House of Lords exclusively, but to indicate the great class of hereditary landed proprietors, who are in sympathy with the upper house on cardinal points, yet breathe a somewhat freer air, are more readily acted on by the opinion of the community, more contradictable by the lower herd, less removed from its prejudices by a refined and regulated education. From the time of the revolution, more or less, this has been the ruling class in the community; the close-borough system and the county system giving them mainly the control of the House of Commons, and their feelings being in general, as it were, a mean term between those of the higher nobility and the trading public of what were then the few large towns. The rule of the House of Lords was rather mediate than direct. By the various means of influence and social patronage and oppression which are familiar to a wealthy and high-bred aristocracy, the highest members of it, of course, exercised over all below them a sure and continual influence: it worked silently and commonly on ordinary questions and in quiet times; yet it was liable to be overborne by a harsher and ruder power when stormy passions arose, in the days of wars and tumults. The largest amount of administrative power has indeed been rarely in the hands of the highest aristocracy, and in a great measure for a peculiar reason: that aristocracy will rarely do the work, and can rarely do the work. The enormous pressure of daily-growing business which besets the governors of a busy and complicated community is too much for the refined habits, delicate discrimination, anxious judgment, which the course of their life develops in the highest classes, and with which it nourishes the indolence natural to those who have this world to enjoy. The real strain of the necessary labour has generally been borne by men of a somewhat lower grade, trained by an early ambition, a native aptitude, a hardy competition, to perform its copious tasks. Such men are partakers of two benefits. They are rough and ready enough to accomplish the coarse enormous daily work; they have lived with higher gentlemen enough to know and feel what such persons think and want. . . .

Sir Robert's father and grandfather were two of the men who created Lancashire. No sooner did the requisite machinery issue from the brain of the inventor than its capabilities were seized on by strong, ready, bold men of business, who erected it, used it, devised a factory system, combined a factory population—created, in a word, that black industrial region, of whose augmenting wealth and horrid labour tales are daily borne to the genial and lazy south. Of course it cannot be said that mill-makers invented the middle classes. The history of England perhaps shows that it has not for centuries been without an unusual number of persons with comfortable and moderate means. But though this class has ever been found among us, and has ever been more active than in any other similar country, yet to a great extent it was scattered, headless, motionless. Small rural out-of-the-way towns, country factories few and far between, concealed and divided this great and mixed mass of petty means and steady intelligence. The huge heaps of manufacturing wealth were not to be concealed. They at once placed on a level with the highest in the land—in matters of expenditure, and in those countless social relations which depend upon expenditure—men sprung from the body of the people, unmistakably speaking its language, inevitably thinking its thoughts. It is true that the first manufacturers were not democratic. Sir Robert Peel, the statesman's father—a type of the class—was a firm, honest, domineering Conservative; but, however on such topics they may so think, however on other topics they may try to catch the language of the class to which they rise, the grain of the middle class will surely show itself in those who have risen from the middle class. If Mr Cobden were to go over to the enemy, if he were to offer to serve Lord Derby *vice* Disraeli disconcerted, it would not be possible for him to speak as the hereditary landowner speaks. It is not that the hereditary landowner knows more;—indeed, either in book-learning or in matters of observation, in acquaintance with what has been, or is going to be, or what now is, the owners of rent are not superior to the receivers of profits; yet their dialect is different—the one speaks the language of years of toil, and the other of years of indolence. A harsh laboriousness characterises the one, a pleasant geniality the other. The habit of industry is ingrained in those who have risen by it; it modifies every word and qualifies every notion. They are the βάναυσοι [vulgarity] of work. Vainly, therefore, did the first manufacturers struggle to be Conservatives, to be baronets, to be peers. The titles they might obtain, their outward existence they might change, themselves in a manner they might alter; but a surer force was dragging them and those who resembled them into another region, filling them with other thoughts, making them express what people of the middle classes had always obscurely felt, pushing forward this new industrial order by the side, or even in front, of the old aristocratic order. The new class have not, indeed, shown themselves republican. They have not especially cared to influence the machinery of government. Their peculiarity has been, that they wish to see the government administered according to the notions familiar to them in their business life. They have no belief in mystery or magic; probably they have never appreciated the political influence of the imagination; they wish to see plain sense applied to the most prominent part of practical life. In his later career, the second Sir Robert Peel was the statesman who most completely and thoroughly expressed the sentiments of this new dynasty;—instead of being the nominee of a nobility, he became the representative of a transacting and trading multitude.

Both of these two classes were, however, equally possessed by the vice or tendency we commented on at the outset. They each of them desired to see the government carried on exactly according to their own views. The idea on which seems to rest our only chance of again seeing great statesmen, of placing deep deferential trust in those who have given real proofs of comprehensive sagacity, had scarcely dawned on either. The average man had, so to say, varied; he was no longer of the one order, but of an inferior; but he was not at all less exacting or tyrannical. Perhaps he was even more so; for the indolent gentleman is less absolute and domineering than the active man of business. However that may be, it was the fate of Sir Robert Peel, in the two phases of his career, to take a leading share in carrying out the views, in administering the creed, first of one and then of the other.

Perhaps in our habitual estimate of Peel we hardly enough bear this in mind. We remember him as the guiding chief of the most intelligent Conservative government that this country has ever seen. We remember the great legislative acts which we owe to his trained capacity, every detail of which bears the impress of his practised hand; we know that his name is pronounced with applause in the great marts of trade and seats of industry; that even yet it is muttered with reproach in the obscure abodes of squires and rectors. We forget that his name was once the power of the Protestant interest, the shibboleth by which squires and rectors distinguished those whom they loved from those whom they hated; we forget that he defended the Manchester Massacre, the Six Acts, the Imposition of Tests, the rule of Orangemen. We remember

Peel as the proper head of a moderate, intelligent, half-commercial community; we forget that he once was the chosen representative of a gentry untrained to great affairs, absorbed in a great war, only just recovering from the horror of a great revolution.

In truth, the character of Sir Robert Peel happily fitted him both to be the chosen head of a popular community, imperiously bent on its own ideas, and to be the head of that community in shifting and changing times. Sir Robert was at Harrow with Lord Byron, who has left the characteristic reminiscence: "I was always in scrapes, Peel never." And opposed as they were in their fortunes as boys and men, they were at least equally contrasted in the habit and kind of action of their minds. Lord Byron's mind gained everything it was to gain by one intense, striking effort. By a blow of the imagination he elicited a single bright spark of light on every subject; and that was all. And this he never lost. The intensity of the thinking seemed to burn it on the memory, there to remain alone. But he made no second effort; he gained no more. He always avowed his incapability of continuous application: he could not, he said, learn the grammar of any language. In later life he showed considerable talent for action; but those who had to act with him observed that, versatile as were his talents, and mutable as his convictions had always seemed to be, in reality he was the most stubborn of men. He heard what you had to say; assented to all you had to say; and the next morning returned to his original opinion. No amount of ordinary argumentative resistance was so hopeless as that facile acquiescence and instantaneous recurrence. The truth was, that he was—and some others are similarly consti- tuted—unable to retain anything which he did not at any rate *seem* to gain by the unaided single rush of his own mind. The ideas of such minds are often not new, very often they are hardly in the strictest sense original; they really were very much suggested from without, and preserved in some obscure corner of memory, out of the way and unknown; but it remains their characteristic, that they seem to the mind of the thinker to be born from its own depths, to be the product of its latent forces. There is a kind of eruption of ideas from a subter-conscious world. The whole mental action is volcanic; the lava flood glows in *Childe Harold;* all the thoughts are intense, flung forth vivid. The day after the eruption the mind is calm; it seems as if it could not again do the like; the product only remains, distinct, peculiar, indestructible. The mind of Peel was the exact opposite of this. His opinions far more resembled the daily accumulating insensible deposits of a rich alluvial soil. The great stream of time flows on with all things on its surface; and slowly, grain by grain, a mould of wise experience is unconsciously left on the still, extended intellect. You scarcely think of such a mind as acting; it seems always acted upon. There is no trace of gushing, overpowering, spontaneous impulse; everything seems acquired. The thoughts are calm. In Lord Byron, the very style—dashing, free, incisive—shows the bold impulse from which it came. The stealthy accumulating words of Peel seem like the quiet leavings of an outward tendency, which brought these, but might as well have brought others. There is no peculiar stamp either in the ideas. They might have been any one's ideas. They belong to the general diffused stock of observations which are to be found in the civilised world. They are not native to the particular mind, nor "to the manner born." Like a science, they are credible or incredible by all men equally. This *secondary* order, as we may call it, of intellect, is evidently most useful to a statesman of the constitutional class, such as we have described him. He insensibly and inevitably takes in and imbibes, by means of it, the ideas of those around him. If he were left in a vacuum, he would have no ideas. The primary class of mind that strikes out its own belief would here be utterly at fault. It would want something which other men had; it would discover something which other men would not understand. Sir Robert Peel was a statesman for forty years; under our constitution, Lord Byron, eminent as was his insight into men, and remarkable as was his power, at least for short periods, of dealing with them, would not have been a statesman for forty days.

It is very likely that many people may not think Sir Robert Peel's mind so interesting as Lord Byron's. They may prefer the self-originating intellect, which invents and retains its own ideas, to the calm receptive intellect which acquires its belief from without. The answer lies in what has been said—a constitutional statesman must sympathise in the ideas of the many. As the many change, it will be his good fortune if he can contrive to change with them. It is to be remembered that statesmen do not live under hermetical seals. Like other men, they are influenced by the opinions of other men. How potent is this influence, those best know who have tried to hold ideas different from the ideas of those around.

In another point of view also Sir Robert Peel's character was exactly fitted to the position we have delineated. He was a great administrator. Civilisation requires this. In a simple age work may be difficult, but it is scarce. There are fewer people, and everybody wants fewer things. The mere tools of civilisation seem in some sort to augment work. In early times, when a despot wishes to govern a distant province, he sends down a satrap on a grand horse, with other people on little horses; and very little is heard of the satrap again unless he send back some of the little people to tell what he has been doing. No great labour of superintendence is possible. Common rumour and casual complaints are the sources of intelligence. If it seems certain that the province is in a bad state, satrap No. 1 is recalled, and satrap No. 2 is sent out in his stead. In civilised countries the whole thing is different. You erect a *bureau* in the province you want to govern; you make it write letters and copy letters; it sends home eight reports per diem to the head *bureau* in St Petersburg. Nobody does a sum in the province without somebody doing the same sum in the capital, to "check him," and see that he does it correctly. The consequence of this is, to throw on the heads of departments an amount of reading and labour which can only be accomplished by the greatest natural aptitude, the most efficient training, the most firm and regular industry. Under a free government it is by no means better, perhaps in some respects it is worse. It is true that many questions which, under the French despotism, are referred to Paris, are settled in England on the very spot where they are to be done, without reference to London at all. But as a set-off, a constitutional administrator has to be always consulting others, finding out what this man or that man chooses to think; learning which form of error is believed by Lord B, which by Lord C; adding up the errors of the alphabet, and seeing what portion of what he thinks he ought to do, they will all of them together allow him to do. Likewise, though the personal freedom and individual discretion which free governments allow to their subjects seem at first likely to diminish the work which those governments have to do, it may be doubted whether it does so really and in the end. Individual discretion strikes out so many more pursuits, and some supervision must be maintained over each of those pursuits. No despotic government would consider the police force of London enough to keep down, watch, and superintend such a population; but then no despotic government would have such a city as London to keep down. The freedom of growth allows the possibility of growth; and though liberal governments take so much less in proportion upon them, yet the scale of operations is so much enlarged by the continual exercise of civil liberty, that the real work is ultimately perhaps as immense. While a despotic government is regulating ten per cent of ten men's actions, a free government has to regulate one per cent of a hundred men's actions. The difficulty, too, increases. Anybody can understand a rough despotic community;—a small buying class of nobles, a small selling class of traders, a large producing class of serfs, are much the same in all quarters of the globe; but a free, intellectual community is a complicated network of ramified relations, interlacing and passing hither and thither, old and new— some of fine city weaving, others of gross agricultural construction. You are never sure what effect any force or any change may produce on a framework so exquisite and so involved. Govern it as you may, it will be a work of great difficulty, labour, and responsibility; and no man who is thus occupied ought ever to go to bed without reflecting that from the difficulty of his employment he may, probably enough, have that day done more evil than good. What view Sir Robert Peel took of these duties he has himself informed us.

Take the case of the Prime Minister. You must presume that he reads every important despatch from every foreign court. He cannot consult with the Secretary of State for Foreign Affairs, and exercise the influence which he ought to have with respect to the conduct of foreign affairs, unless he be master of everything of real importance passing in that department. It is the same with respect to other departments; India for instance: How can the Prime Minister be able to judge of the course of policy with regard to India, unless he be cognisant of all the current important correspondence? In the case of Ireland and the Home Department it is the same. Then the Prime Minister has the patronage of the Crown to exercise, which you say, and justly say, is of so much importance and of so much value; he has to make inquiries into the qualifications of the persons who are candidates; he has to conduct the whole of the communications with the Sovereign, he has to write, probably with his own hand, the letters in reply to all persons of station who address themselves to him; he has to receive deputations on public business; during the sitting of parliament he is expected to attend six or seven hours a day, and for four or five days in the week; at least, he is blamed if he is absent.

The necessary effect of all this labour is, that those subject to it have no opinions. It requires a great deal of time to have opinions. Belief is a slow process. That leisure which the poets say is necessary to be good, or to be wise, is needful for the humbler task of allowing respectable maxims to take root respectably. The "wise passiveness" of Mr Wordsworth is necessary in very ordinary matters. If you chain a man's head to a ledger, and keep him constantly adding up, and take a pound off his salary whenever he stops, you can't expect him to have a sound conviction on Catholic emancipation, tithes, and original ideas on the Transcaucasian provinces. Our system, indeed, seems expressly provided to make it unlikely. The most benumbing thing to the intellect is routine; the most bewildering is distraction: our system is a distracting routine. You see this in the description just given, which is not exhaustive. Sir Robert Peel once asked to have a number of questions carefully written down which they asked him one day in succession in the House of Commons. They seemed a list of every thing that could occur in the British empire, or to the brain of a member of parliament. A premier's whole life is a series of such transitions. It is rather wonderful that our public men have any minds left, than that a certain unfixity of opinion seems growing upon them.

We may go further on this subject. A great administrator is not a man likely to desire to have fixed opinions. His natural bent and tendency is to immediate action. The existing and pressing circumstances of the case fill up his mind. The letters to be answered, the documents to be filed, the memoranda to be made, engross his attention. He is angry if you distract him. A bold person who suggests a matter of principle, or a difficulty of thought, or an abstract result that seems improbable in the case "before the board," will be set down as a speculator, a theorist, a troubler of practical life. To expect to hear from such men profound views of future policy, digested plans of distant action, is to mistake their genius entirely. It is like asking the broker of the Stock Exchange what will be the price of the funds this day six months! His whole soul is absorbed in thinking what that price will be in ten minutes. A momentary change of an eighth is more important to him than a distant change of a hundred eighths. So the brain of a great administrator is naturally occupied with the details of the day, the passing dust, the granules of that day's life; and his unforeseeing temperament turns away uninterested from reaching speculations, from vague thought, and from extensive and far-off plans. Of course, it is not meant that a great administrator has absolutely no general views; some indeed he must have. A man cannot conduct the detail of affairs without having some plan which regulates that detail. He cannot help having some idea, vague or accurate, indistinct or distinct, of the direction in which he is going, and the purpose for which he is travelling. But the difference is, that this plan is seldom his own, the offspring of his own brain, the result of his own mental contention; it is the plan of some one else. Providence generally bestows on the working adaptive man a quiet adoptive nature. He receives insensibly the suggestions of others; he hears them with willing ears; he accepts them with placid belief. An acquiescent credulity is a quality of such men's nature; they cannot help being sure that what every one says must be true; the *vox populi* is a part of their natural religion. It has been made a matter of wonder that Peel should have belonged to the creed of Mr Perceval and Lord Sidmouth. Perhaps, indeed, our existing psychology will hardly explain the process by which a decorous young man acquires the creed of his era. He assumes its belief as he assumes its costume. He imitates the respectable classes. He avoids an original opinion, like an *outré* coat; a new idea, like an unknown tie. Especially he does so on matters of real concern to him, on those on which he knows he must act. He acquiesces in the creed of the orthodox agents. He scarcely considers for himself; he acknowledges the apparent authority of dignified experience. He is, he remembers, but the junior partner in the firm; it does not occur to him to doubt that those were right who were occupied in its management years before him. In this way he acquires an experience which more independent and original minds are apt to want. There was a great cry when the Whigs came into office, at the time of the Reform Bill, that they were not men of business. Of course, after a very long absence from office, they could not possess a technical acquaintance with official forms, a trained facility in official action. This Sir Robert Peel acquired from his apprenticeship to Mr Perceval. His early connection with the narrow Conservative party has been considered a disadvantage to him; but it may well be doubted whether his peculiar mind was not more improved by the administrative training than impaired by the contact with prejudiced thoughts. He never could have been a great thinker; he became what nature designed, a great agent.

In a third respect also Sir Robert Peel conformed to the type of a constitutional statesman; and that third respect also seems naturally to lead to a want of defined principle, and to apparent fluctuation of opinion. He was a great debater; and of all pursuits ever invented by man for separating the faculty of argument from the capacity of belief, the art of debating is probably the most effectual. Macaulay tells us that, in his opinion, this is

> the most serious of the evils which are to be set off against the many blessings of popular government. The keenest and most vigorous minds of every generation, minds often admirably fitted for the investigation of truth, are habitually employed in producing arguments such as no man of sense would ever put into a treatise intended for publication—arguments which are just good enough to be used once, when aided by fluent delivery and pointed language. The habit of discussing questions in this way necessarily reacts on the intellects of our ablest men, particularly of those who are introduced into Parliament at a very early age, before their minds have expanded to full maturity. The talent for debate is developed in such men to a degree which, to the multitude, seems as marvellous as the performances of an Italian *improvisatore*. But they are fortunate indeed if they retain unimpaired the faculties which are required for close reasoning, or for enlarged speculation. Indeed, we should sooner expect a great original work on political science—such a work, for example, as *The Wealth of Nations*—from an apothecary in a country town, or from a minister in the Hebrides, than from a statesman who, ever since he was one and twenty, had been a distinguished debater in the House of Commons.

But it may well be doubted whether there is not in the same pursuit a deeper evil, hard to eradicate, and tending to corrupt and destroy the minds of those who are beneath its influence. Constitutional statesmen are obliged, not only to employ arguments which they do not think conclusive, but likewise to defend opinions which they do not believe to be true. Whether we approve it or lament it, there is no question that our existing political life is deeply marked by the habit of advocacy. Perhaps fifteen measures may annually, on an average, be brought in by a cabinet government of fifteen persons. It is impossible to believe that all members of that cabinet agree in all those measures. No two people agree in fifteen things; fifteen clever men never yet agreed in anything; yet they all defend them, argue for them, are responsible for them. It is always quite possible that the minister who is strenuously defending a bill in the

House of Commons may have used in the cabinet the very arguments which the Opposition are using in the House; he may have
been overruled without being convinced; he may still think the
conclusions he opposes better than those which he inculcates. It is
idle to say that he ought to go out; at least, it amounts to saying
that government by means of a cabinet is impossible. The object of
a committee of that kind is to agree on certain conclusions; if every
member after the meeting were to start off according to the individual bent and bias of his mind, according to his own individual
discretion or indiscretion, the previous concurrence would have
become childish. Of course, the actual measure proposed by the
collective voice of several persons is very different from what any
one of these persons would of himself wish; it is the result of a
compromise between them. Each, perhaps, has obtained some concession; each has given up something. Every one sees in the actual
proposal something of which he strongly disapproves; every one
regrets the absence of something which he much desires. Yet, on
the whole, perhaps, he thinks the measure better than no measure;
or at least he thinks that if he went out, it would break up the
government; and imagines it to be of more consequence that the
government should be maintained than that the particular measure
should be rejected. He concedes his individual judgment. . . .

It is evident, too, that this necessarily leads to great apparent
changes of opinion—to the professed belief of a statesman at one
moment being utterly different from what it seems to be at another
moment. When a government is founded, questions A, B, C, D, E,
F, are the great questions of the day—the matters which are
obvious, pressing—which the public mind comprehends. X, Y, Z,
are in the background, little thought of, obscure. According to the
received morality, no statesman would hesitate to sacrifice the last
to the first. He might have a very strong personal opinion on X,
but he would surrender it to a colleague as the price of his co-
operation on A or B. A few years afterwards times change. Question A is carried, B settles itself, E and F are forgotten, X becomes
the most important topic of the day. The statesman who conceded
X before, now feels that he no longer can concede it; there is no
equivalent. He has never in reality changed his opinion, yet he has
to argue in favour of the very measures which he endeavoured
before to argue against. Everybody thinks he has changed, and
without going into details, the secrecy of which is esteemed essen-

tial to confidential co-operation, it is impossible that he can evince
his consistency. It is impossible to doubt that this is a very serious
evil, and it is plainly one consequent on, or much exaggerated by, a
popular and argumentative government. It is very possible for a
conscientious man, under a bureaucratic government, to co-operate
with the rest of a council in the elaboration and execution of
measures, many of which he thinks inexpedient. Nobody asks him
his opinion; he has not to argue, or defend, or persuade. But a free
government boasts that it is carried on in the face of day. Its principle is discussion; its habit is debate. The consequence is, that those
who conduct it have to defend measures they disapprove, to object
to measures they approve, to appear to have an accurate opinion on
points on which they really have no opinion. The calling of a
constitutional statesman is very much that of a political advocate;
he receives a new brief with the changing circumstances of each
successive day. It is easy to conceive a cold sardonic intellect,
moved with contempt at such a life, casting aside the half-and-half
pretences with which others partly deceive themselves, stating
anything, preserving an intellectual preference for truth, but regarding any effort at its special advocacy as the weak aim of foolish
men, striving for what they cannot attain. . . . One can conceive,
too, a cold and somewhat narrow intellect, capable of forming, in
any untroubled scene, an accurate plain conviction, but without
much power of entering into the varying views of others; little
skilled in diversified argument; understanding its own opinion, and
not understanding the opinions of others;—one can imagine such a
mind pained, and cracked, and shattered, by endeavouring to lead a
life of ostentatious argument in favour of others' opinions, of half-
concealment of its chill, unaltering essence. . . .

Sir Robert Peel was exactly fit for this life. The word which
exactly fits his oratory is—specious. He hardly ever said anything
which struck you in a moment to be true; he never uttered a
sentence which for a moment anybody could deny to be plausible.
Once, when they were opposed on a railway bill, the keen irascibil-
ity of Lord Derby stimulated him to observe "that *no one* knew
like the right honourable baronet how to *dress up* a case for that
House." The art of statement, the power of detail, the watching
for the weak points of an opponent, an average style adapting itself
equally to what the speaker believed and what he disbelieved, a
business air, a didactic precision for what it was convenient to

make clear, an unctuous disguise of flowing periods, and "a deep sense of responsibility" for what it was convenient to conceal, an enormous facility, made Sir Robert Peel a nearly unequalled master of the art of political advocacy. For his times he was perhaps quite unequalled. He might have failed in times of deep, outpouring patriotic excitement; he had not nature enough to express it. He might have failed in an age when there was nothing to do, and when elegant personality and the *finesse* of artistic expression were of all things most required. But for an age of important business, when there was an unusual number of great topics to be discussed, but none great enough to hurry men away from their business habits, or awaken the most ardent passion or the highest imagination, there is nothing like the oratory of Peel—able but not aspiring, firm but not exalted, never great but ever adequate to great affairs. It is curious to know that he was trained to the trade.

Soon after Peel was born, his father, the first baronet, finding himself rising daily in wealth and consequence, and believing that money in those peculiar days could always command a seat in Parliament, determined to bring up his son expressly for the House of Commons. When that son was quite a child, Sir Robert would frequently set him on the table and say, "Now, Robin, make a speech, and I will give you this cherry." What few words the little fellow produced were applauded; and applause stimulating exertion produced such effects that, before Robin was ten years old, he could really address the company with some degree of eloquence. As he grew up, his father constantly took him every Sunday into his private room and made him repeat, as well as he could, the sermon which had been preached. Little progress in effecting this was made, and little was expected *at first*, but by steady perseverance the habit of attention grew powerful, and the sermon was repeated almost *verbatim*. When at a very distant day the senator, remembering accurately the speech of an opponent, answered his arguments in correct succession, it was little known that the power of so doing was originally acquired in Drayton Church.

A mischievous observer might say, that something else had remained to Sir Robert Peel from these sermons. His tone is a trifle sermonic. He failed where perhaps alone Lord John Russell has succeeded—in the oratory of conviction.

If we bear in mind the whole of these circumstances; if we picture in our minds a nature at once active and facile, easily acquiring its opinions from without, not easily devising them from within, a large placid adaptive intellect, devoid of irritable intense originality, prone to forget the ideas of yesterday, inclined to accept the ideas of to-day—if we imagine a man so formed cast early into absorbing, exhausting industry of detail, with work enough to fill up a life, with action of itself enough to render speculation almost impossible—placed too in a position unsuited to abstract thought, of which the conventions and rules require that a man should feign other men's thoughts, should impugn his own opinions—we shall begin to imagine a conscientious man destitute of convictions on the occupations of his life—to comprehend the character of Sir Robert Peel.

That Sir Robert was a very conscientious man is quite certain. It is even probable that he had a morbid sense of administrative responsibility. . . . Sir Robert had an anxious sense of duty in detail. Lord Wellesley . . . on an occasion when it would have been at least equally natural to speak of administrative capacity and efficient co-operation, mentions only "the real impressions which your kindness and high character have fixed in my mind." The circumstances of his end naturally produced a crowd of tributes to his memory, and hardly any of them omit his deep sense of the obligations of action. . . . As a conspicuous merit, the Duke of Wellington, oddly enough according to some people's notions at the time, selected Peel's veracity. . . . Simple people in the country were a little astonished to hear so strong a eulogy on a man for not telling lies. They were under the impression that people in general did not. But those who have considered the tempting nature of a statesman's pursuits, the secrets of office, the inevitable complication of his personal relations, will not be surprised that many statesmen should be without veracity, or that one should be eulogised for possessing it. It is to be remarked, however, in mitigation of so awful an excellence, that Sir Robert was seldom in "scrapes," and that it is on those occasions that the virtue of veracity is apt to be most severely tested. The same remark is applicable to the well-praised truthfulness of the duke himself.

In conjunction with the great soldier, Sir Robert Peel is entitled to the fame of a great act of administrative conscience. He purified the Tory party. There is little doubt that, during the long and secure reign which the Tories enjoyed about the beginning of the century, there was much of the corruption naturally incident to a strong party with many adherents to provide for, uncontrolled by an effective Opposition, unwatched by a great nation. Of course, too, any government remaining over from the last century would inevitably have adhering to it various *remanet* corruptions of that curious epoch. There flourished those mighty sinecures and reversions, a few of which still remain to be the wonder and envy of an unenjoying generation. The House of Commons was not difficult then to manage. There is a legend that a distinguished Treasury official of the last century, a very capable man, used to say of any case which was hopelessly and inevitably bad: "Ah, we must apply our majority to this question"; and no argument is so effectual as the mechanical, calculable suffrage of a strong, unreasoning party. There were doubtless many excellent men in the Tory party, even in its least excellent days; but the two men to whom the party, as such, owes most of purification were the Duke of Wellington and Sir Robert Peel. From the time when they became responsible for the management of a Conservative government, there was no doubt, in office or in the nation, that the public money and patronage were administered by men whom no consideration would induce to use either for their personal benefit; and who would, as far as their whole power lay, discourage and prevent the corrupt use of either by others. . . .

The changes of opinion which Sir Robert Peel underwent are often cited as indications of a want of conscientiousness. They really are, subject of course to the preceding remarks, proofs of his conscientiousness. We do not mean in the obvious sense of them being opposed to his visible interest, and having on two great occasions destroyed the most serviceable party organisation ever ruled by a statesman in a political age: but in a more refined sense, the timeliness of his transitions may, without overstraining, be thought a mark of their *bona fides*. He could not have changed with such felicitous exactness, if he had been guided by selfish calculation. The problems were too great and too wide. There have, of course, been a few men—Talleyrand and Theramenes are instances—who have seemed to hit, as if by a political sense, the fitting moment to leave the side which was about to fall, and to join the side which was about to rise. But these will commonly be found to be men of a very different character from that of Peel. Minds are divided into open and close. Some men are so sensitive to extrinsic impressions, pass so easily from one man to another, catch so well the tone of each man's thought, use so well the opportunities of society for the purposes of affairs, that they are, as it were, by habit and practice, metrical instruments of public opinion. Sir Robert was by character, both natural and acquired, the very reverse. He was a reserved, occupied man of business. In the arts of society, in the easy transition from person to person, from tone to tone, he was but little skilled. If he had been left to pick up his rules of conduct by mere social perception and observation, his life would have been a life of miscalculations; instead of admiring the timeliness of his conversions, we should wonder at the perversity of his transitions. . . . His changes, as it has been explained, are to be otherwise accounted for. He was always anxious to do right. An occupied man of business, he was converted when other men of business in the nation were converted.

It is not, however, to be denied that a calm and bland nature like that of Peel is peculiarly prone to self-illusion. Many fancy that it is passionate, imaginative men who most deceive themselves; and of course they are more tempted—a more vivid fancy and a more powerful impulse hurry them away. But they know their own weakness. "Do you believe in ghosts, Mr Coleridge?" asked some lady. "No, ma'am, I have seen too many," was the answer. A quiet, calm nature, when it is tempted by its own wishes, is hardly conscious that it is tempted. These wishes are so gentle, quiet, as it would say, so "reasonable," that it does not conceive it possible to be hurried away into error by them. Nor *is* there any hurry. They operate quietly, gently, and constantly. Such a man will very much believe what he wishes. Many an imaginative outcast, whom no man would trust with sixpence, really forms his opinions on points which interest him by a much more intellectual process—at least, has more purely intellectual opinions beaten and tortured into him—than the eminent and respected man of business, in whom every one confides, who is considered a model of dry judgment, of clear and passionless equanimity. Doubtless Sir Robert Peel went on believing in the corn laws, when no one in the distrusted classes even fancied that they were credible.

It has been bitterly observed of Sir Robert Peel, that he was "a Radical at heart"; and, perhaps, with a similar thought in his mind, Mr Cobden said once, at a League meeting, "I do not altogether like to give up Peel. You see he is a Lancashire man." And it cannot be questioned that, strongly opposed as Sir Robert Peel was to the Reform Bill, he was really much more suited to the reformed than to the unreformed House of Commons. The style of debating in the latter was described by one who had much opportunity for observation, Sir James Mackintosh, as "continuous, animated, after-dinner discussion." The House was composed mainly of men trained in two great schools, on a peculiar mode of education, with no great real knowledge of the classics, but with many lines of Virgil and Horace lingering in fading memories, contrasting oddly with the sums and business with which they were necessarily brought side by side. These gentlemen wanted not to be instructed, but to be amused; and hence arose what, from the circumstance of their calling, may be called the class of conversationalist states-men. . . .

The old delicate parliament is gone, and the gladiatorship which it loved. The progress of things, and the Reform Bill which was the result of that progress, have taken, and are taking, the national representation away from the university classes, and conferring it on the practical classes. Exposition, arithmetic, detail, reforms—these are the staple of our modern eloquence. The old boroughs which introduced the young scholars are passed away; and even if the young scholars were in parliament, the subjects do not need the classic tact of expression. Very plain speaking suits the "passing tolls," "registration of joint-stock companies," finance, the Post-office. The petty regulation of the details of civilisation, which happily is the daily task of our Government, does not need, does not suit, a *recherché* taste or an ornate eloquence. As is the speech, so are the men. Sir Robert Peel was inferior to Canning in the old parliament; he would have been infinitely superior to him in the new. The aristocratic refinement, the nice embellishment, of the old time, were as alien to him as the detail and dryness of the new era were suitable. He was admirably fitted to be where the Reform Bill placed him. He was fitted to work and explain; he was not able to charm or to amuse.

In its exact form this kind of eloquence and statesmanship is peculiar to modern times, and even to this age. In ancient times the existence of slavery forbade the existence of a middle-class elo-quence. The Cleon who possessed the tone and the confidence of the people in trade was a man vulgar, coarse, speaking the senti-ments of a class whose views were narrow and whose words were mean. So many occupations were confined to slaves, that there was scarcely an opening for the sensible, moderate, rational body whom we now see. It was, of course, always possible to express the sentiments and prejudices of people in trade. It is new to this era, it seems created for Sir Robert Peel to express those sentiments, in a style refined, but not too refined; which will not jar people of high cultivation, which will seem suitable to men of common cares and important transactions.

In another respect Sir Robert Peel was a fortunate man. The principal measures required in his age were "repeals." From changing circumstances, the old legislation would no longer suit a changed community; and there was a clamour, first for the repeal of one important Act, and then of another. This was suitable to the genius of Peel. He could hardly have created anything. His intellect, admirable in administrative routine, endlessly fertile in suggestions of detail, was not of the class which creates, or which readily even believes an absolutely new idea. As has been so often said, he typified the practical intelligence of his time. He was prone, as has been explained, to receive the daily deposits of insensibly-changing opinion; but he could bear nothing startling; nothing bold, original, single, is to be found in his acts or his words. Nothing could be so suitable to such a mind as a conviction that an existing law was wrong. The successive gradations of opinion pointed to a clear and absolute result. When it was a question, as in the case of the Reform Bill, not of simple abolition, but of extensive and difficult reconstruction, he "could not see his way." He could be convinced that the anti-Catholic laws were wrong, that the currency laws were wrong, that the commercial laws were wrong; especially he could be convinced that the *laissez-faire* system was right, and the real thing was to do nothing; but he was incapable of the larger and higher political construction. A more imaginative genius is necessary to deal with the consequences of new creations, and the structure of an unseen future.

This remark requires one limitation. A great deal of what is called legislation is really administrative regulation. It does not settle what is to be done, but *how* it is to be done; it does not prescribe what our institutions shall be, but directs in what manner existing institutions shall work and operate. Of this portion of legislation Sir Robert Peel was an admirable master. Few men have fitted administrative regulations with so nice an adjustment to a prescribed end. The Currency Act of 1844 was an instance of this. If you consult the speeches by which that bill was introduced and explained to parliament, you certainly will not find any very rigid demonstrations of political economy, or dry compactness of abstract principle. Whether the abstract theory of the supporters of that Act be sound or unsound, no exposition of it ever came from the lips of Peel. He assumed the results of that theory; but no man saw more quickly the nature of the administrative machinery which was required. The separation of the departments of the Bank of England, the limitation of the country issues, though neither of them original ideas of Sir Robert's own mind, yet were not, like most of his other important political acts, forced on him from without. There was a general agreement among the received authorities in favour of a certain currency theory; the administrative statesman saw a good deal before other men what was the most judicious and effectual way of setting it at work and regulating its action.

We have only spoken of Sir Robert Peel as a public man; and if you wish to write what is characteristic about him, that is the way to do so. He was a man whom it requires an effort to think of as engaged in anything but political business. Disraeli tells us that some one said that Peel was never happy except in the House of Commons, or doing something which had some relation to something to be done there. In common life, we continually see men scarcely separable as it were from their pursuits; they are as good as others, but their visible nature seems almost all absorbed in a certain visible calling. When we speak of them we are led to speak of it, when we would speak of it we are led insensibly to speak of them. It is so with Sir Robert Peel. So long as constitutional statesmanship is what it is now, so long as its function consists in recording the views of a confused nation, so long as success in it is confined to minds plastic, changeful, administrative—we must hope for no better man. You have excluded the profound thinker; you must be content with what you can obtain—the business gentleman.

III

The Heyday of Victorianism

Introduction

BRITAIN was the strongest power in the world by the middle of the nineteenth century. Her economic superiority and strategic location secured her position. Potential competitors, moreover, had counted themselves out or had not yet become principals in the international reckoning. France, torn by dissension, did not fully recover under Louis Napoleon. The Crimean War (1854–56), a product of diplomatic miscalculations, created crises of confidence for Britons at home but eliminated Russia from Europe for a generation. The United States plunged into the bloodbath of its civil war. Between 1864 and 1871 the Germans were unified—or conquered, depending upon one's point of view—by Prussian power. Palmerston defended the assertion of British power through Europe.[1] Proconsuls showed the flag abroad—successfully in Burma, poorly in Afghanistan. Cumulative resentment against British social and political policies boiled over in the Indian mutiny of 1857. A mixture of force and reason re-established British control as "Clemency" Canning laid the foundations for successful imperial development. In Hong Kong, Sir John Bowring, Jeremy Bentham's literary executor, showed that radicals also had teeth. He used the *Arrow* incident, an even less savory cause than the Pacifico affair, as an excuse to bombard Canton in another installment of the Opium Wars (1856–58).

Britain's dominant position gave her no control of European politics. A British fleet made life easier for Garibaldi, but a French army did the serious fighting for a unified Italy. Britain did not

[1] See Document 18.

intervene on behalf of either Denmark for Schleswig-Holstein or the Confederate States of America for cotton. Both were salutary decisions based upon a realistic assessment of British power as well as on considerations of British interests. Britain was a spectator at the Austro-Prussian War in 1866. The Franco-Prussian War (1870–71) settled the European issue on Bismarck's terms, while the British sat by in stunned silence. The new German Reich dominated the Continent. The British had been so obsessed with the notion that Europe would fall under Russian domination if France were broken, and so concerned to keep the French from attempting to reassert European hegemony, that they failed to consider the possible emergence of a new force able to hold its own against both France and Russia. The elimination of Russia from Europe, as A. J. P. Taylor observes, was crucial in making possible the unification of Italy and of Germany.[2] But the British were slow to realize what they had made possible, and even then they were not certain what it meant.

Britons were generally individualistic, and to that extent the mid-Victorian age was a middle-class age. While most Victorians would have specific reservations about John Stuart Mill's argument in *On Liberty* (1859), they could not have agreed more with the general line of argument. From Anthony Trollope to Samuel Smiles, worth was measured in terms of the man, not of the group. Herbert Spencer presented an ideological caricature of mid-Victorian individualism, but his works were not so far removed from reality as to be ridiculous.[3]

The radical edge of the 1830's and 1840's had worn relatively smooth. The increasing range and substance of middle-class opportunities offered new and old groups potential status without social upheaval. There were greater skills, higher standards, and more status for professionals. The Medical Act of 1858 established standards for physicians and surgeons. Barristers had always cared for themselves through the Inns of Court, but solicitors attained substantial respectability with the growing need for legal advice and the increasing complexity of industrial civilization. The new

[2] A. J. P. Taylor, "Crimea: the War That Would Not Boil," reprinted in E. C. Black, *European Political History 1815–1870: Aspects of Liberalism* (New York, 1967).
[3] See *VS&C*, Documents 21, "A Definition of Liberalism"; 28, "Morley Assesses Carlyle"; 29, "Smiles on Self-Help"; 30, "Tennyson on Neglect."

world of industry and commerce developed its own professionals with accountants, engineers, and managers. Increasing government services while paying due regard to a budget-conscious Parliament led to more opportunities for talent and education in the civil service even before the Order in Council of 1870.[4] The growing demand for education and the establishment of institutions for teacher training improved the status and numbers of teachers, although masters (in public schools) clearly ranked above teachers (national or state-supported schools). Intellectuals, as Noel Annan demonstrated, developed their own elaborate social hierarchy.[5] Their aristocracy mingled on easy terms with the best society, sharing the virtues of gentlemanly birth and upbringing with business wealth. It had intelligence and skill, recognized and rewarded it in others, and came increasingly to engross the senior civil service both at home and in the Empire, academic positions at the best schools and universities, some areas of journalism, and even made inroads into politics.

The political rationalization of the mid-century developed parallel to and was, to a considerable degree, a response to these social changes. The lower middle classes expanded as adjuncts and mimics of their betters. The frock-coated law clerk, the industrial draftsman, the shop superintendent, the junior clerk at the metropolitan board of works, the grammar school genius with dreams of a university fellowship shared middle- and upper middle-class aspirations and values. Nor was there any sharp line of demarcation as one bestrode the border zone of middle and lower classes. The most characteristic institutional expression of these elements, particularly in the North and in Scotland, was the Co-Operative Movement. The humble beginnings by a handful of artisans in a shop in Toad Lane, Rochdale, in 1844 grew to such proportions that by the 1870's every important town, and many towns of no consequence, had its own co-operative. The co-operators were the owners and purchased their shares for one pound, often putting a shilling down and paying off the balance at threepence per week. There was interest on the shares and—the secret of co-operative success—the "divi," the patronage refund which grew the more one purchased. The petty bourgeois and skilled artisan types who

[4] See Document 25.
[5] N. Annan, "The Intellectual Aristocracy," *Studies in Social History Presented to G. M. Trevelyan,* ed. by J. H. Plumb (London, 1955).

managed the co-operatives practiced mutual self-help. By the 1860's they had expanded into wholesale lines of products they merchandised; by the 1880's they were in manufacturing. Profits were also invested in housing for co-operators or mortgage money for co-operator home purchase. By the 1870's co-operatives were beginning to invest more generally in the British economy.

Trade unions also adopted "middle-class ways." They were selective, restrictive, and conservative. Unions specialized—engineers (machinists), carpenters and joiners, shipwrights—organized their crafts, and developed strong national organizations. They acted as both trade union and friendly society, a dual role which simultaneously increased their role in the life of the workingman, strengthened their financial position, and reinforced conservative attitudes and values. Trade unions refined collective bargaining into a fine art. It was Robert Applegarth's proudest boast that he had never had an angry word with management either as an employee or as a trade union leader. Applegarth was one of the most important figures in mid-Victorian trade union leadership and an active participant in the First International.[6] Marx never understood him.

The unionized workingmen did much to soften the attitudes of Liberals by their patent respectability and extraordinary restraint during the cotton famine created by the American Civil War. The workingman, as Radicals and Liberals observed, had a better sense of what that war was about than did many of England's governors. But labor was a class apart. Fear of the masses still haunted men who remembered days of violence and revolution. Grudgingly and by accident, Britain stumbled into democracy, first in the towns (1867) and then in the country (1884). As before, parliamentary reform made little immediate difference in the constituencies or in parliament.

Yet the Britain of Palmerston was politically different from the Britain of Gladstone and Disraeli. For one thing, the legacy of 1846 to 1867 was a "three-party" system: Whig-Liberals, Peelites, and Conservatives. Palmerston, as he demonstrated in the election of 1857, was almost above party.[7] Ministerial instability provided

[6] For a retrospective review of trade unions, see *VS&C*, Document 14, "Trade Unions." Asa Briggs has an excellent chapter on Applegarth in *Victorian People* (London, 1954).
[7] See Document 20.

Victoria and Albert the chance to enter extensive opinions on men and measures. Albert would have liked the crown to play the role of arbiter between parties, but events never offered a real opportunity to experiment. The monarchy, moreover, viewed Palmerston as a menace to European peace, and Palmerston behaved with Whig disregard for royal sensitivity. Since Palmerston was the most popular man in Parliament and the country, Victoria and Albert could only fret and complain.[8]

The Reform Act of 1867 opened the great era of party government and completed the process of removing the crown from the center of politics. There was no ground left for mediation and royal influence. Elections were clearly won and lost by Liberals and Conservatives. Gladstone and Disraeli shared the parliamentary spotlight in a way two politicians never have before or since. Gladstonian liberalism represented the fruition of ideals and aspirations that had sprouted during the pre-Victorian liberal awakening.[9] Early and mid-Victorian radicalism was played out,[10] leaving the question of where liberalism consolidates its own victory. Institutional anomalies, even as cumbersome as the majesty of the law, demanded reform and were finally resolved.[11] The role of privilege in English political life was circumscribed by the establishment of professional requirements and the elimination of the more blatant forms of privilege and favoritism. The government abolished the purchase of commissions (a much belated reform set in motion by the Crimean War), established requirements for the ordination of Anglican clergymen, and established civil service practices in every government department but the Foreign Office.[12] There a pedigree was still considered to be a necessary qualification until 1919.

Disraeli's new conservatism, on the other hand, was less concerned with programmatic consistency. Having no doctrinaire commitment to laissez faire, Disraeli could indulge the newly enfranchised masses with public housing, public health, and a pure food and drug act. These were fulfillments of election pledges.[13]

[8] See Document 19.
[9] See Document 21.
[10] See Document 23.
[11] See Document 24.
[12] See Document 25.
[13] See Document 22.

More important to Disraeli was the matter of defending the institutions of the country—by which he meant preserving as many privileges as possible for the Queen, the peers, and the Church—and promoting the Empire. He purchased the Suez shares, wandered into another installment of that foreign policy nightmare, the Eastern question, and proclaimed Victoria Empress of India. Whether in doing so he had enhanced Britain's world position is another question. "Peace with honor" accompanied an increasingly bellicose foreign and imperial policy.

In one area the problem of empire was crucial. Irish difficulties, endemic since the Act of Union (1801), reached crisis proportions. Disraeli showed no interest in grappling with that thorny issue. Gladstone, on the other hand, came increasingly to define it as the principal issue in British politics and the one that he must resolve before he could leave politics. The results were almost fatal for the Liberal party, and the Irish question in its new and stormy phase closed the epic era of Victorian politics.[14]

Recommended Reading

O. ANDERSON, *A Liberal State at War* (London, 1967).

N. ANNAN, *Leslie Stephen* (Cambridge, Mass., 1952).

P. APPLEMAN, W. A. MADDEN, and M. WOLFE, *1859: Entering an Age of Crisis* (Bloomington, Ind., 1959).

H. AUSUBEL, *John Bright* (New York, 1966).

T. W. BAMFORD, *The Rise of the Public Schools* (London, 1967).

D. BEALES, *England and Italy* (London, 1961).

H. C. F. BELL, *Lord Palmerston*, 2 vols. (London, 1936).

R. BLAKE, *Disraeli* (London, 1966).

A. BRIGGS, *Victorian People* (London, 1954).

BRITISH BROADCASTING CORPORATION, *Ideas and Beliefs of the Victorians* (London, 1959).

W. L. BURN, *The Age of Equipoise* (London, 1964).

T. CHRISTENSEN, *Origins and History of Christian Socialism* (Copenhagen, 1962).

G. D. H. COLE, *A Century of Co-operation* (London, 1945).

W. C. COSTIN, *Great Britain and China* (London, 1937).

M. COWLING, *1867: Disraeli, Gladstone and Revolution* (London, 1967).

[14] See Document 26.

R. Fulford, *The Prince Consort* (London, 1949).

J. Gallagher, R. Robinson, and A. Denny, *Africa and the Victorians* (London, 1961).

———, "The Imperialism of Free Trade," *Economic History Review*, 2d Series, Vol. VI (1953), pp. 1–15.

F. E. Gillispie, *Labor and Politics* (Cambridge, Mass., 1927).

J. L. Hammond, *Gladstone and the Irish Nation* (London, 1938).

H. J. Hanham, *Elections and Party Management* (London, 1959).

R. Harrison, *Before the Socialists* (London, 1965).

C. Hobhouse, *1851 and the Crystal Palace*, new ed. (London, 1950).

A. H. Imlah, *Economic Elements in the Pax Britannica* (Cambridge, Mass., 1958).

R. J. Lambert, *Sir John Simon and English Social Administration* (London, 1963).

E. Longford, *Queen Victoria* (New York, 1965).

F. S. L. Lyons, *The Fall of Parnell* (London, 1960).

———, *The Irish Parliamentary Party* (London, 1951).

P. Magnus, *Gladstone* (London, 1954).

R. B. Martin, *The Dust of Combat* (London, 1959).

D. Newsome, *Godliness and Good Learning* (London, 1961).

C. C. O'Brien, *Parnell and His Party* (London, 1957).

M. St. J. Packe, *John Stuart Mill* (London, 1954).

N. St. John-Stevas, *Walter Bagehot* (London, 1959).

R. W. Seton-Watson, *Disraeli, Gladstone and the Eastern Question* (London, 1935).

R. T. Shannon, *Gladstone and the Bulgarian Agitation, 1876* (London, 1963).

F. B. Smith, *The Making of the Second Reform Bill* (London, 1966).

D. Southgate, *The Most English Minister* (London, 1966).

M. Sturt, *The Education of the People* (London, 1967).

J. Vincent, *The Formation of the Liberal Party* (London, 1966).

C. K. Webster, *The Foreign Policy of Palmerston* (London, 1951).

C. Woodham-Smith, *Florence Nightingale* (London, 1951).

———, *The Reason Why* (London, 1953).

18. World Power:
Palmerston and Don Pacifico

LORD PALMERSTON (1784–1865) dominated British foreign policy during the middle third of the nineteenth century. After the premature death of Sir Robert Peel in 1850, he also, as much as any man, stood ascendant in British politics. Yet Palmerston was curiously detached from party in the modern sense. He was a Whig, but he was not part of its aristocratic cult of "great-grandmotherhood." He was a Liberal, but cared little for domestic innovation and nothing for radical programs. He had no coterie of personal followers in the tradition of the eighteenth century or the Regency, although he was clearly a Regency survival in the Victorian age. He became the idol of the serious middle-class electorate enfranchised by the Reform Act of 1832, although his personal morals left much to be desired, and he could behave quite flippantly about many grave matters of state.

He was a man of many principles who never hesitated to proclaim them. He also embodied the confidence and bounce of mid-century Britain. Much of this is apparent throughout his speech. The debate revolved around the affair of a Portuguese Jew born in Gibraltar, David Pacifico (1784–1854), who transacted somewhat shady business in Greece; in 1847 he was attacked by an Athenian mob which was abetted, if not provoked, by the Greek authorities. Pacifico claimed British protection and aid in securing compensation as a British subject by right of birth. Palmerston acted forcefully by taking Greek reprisals and skirting close to a rupture with France. The nights of debate, of which this was the second, involved a wide-ranging discussion of British policy and the principles under which it was and should be conducted. Almost every one of the great debaters of the day opposed Palmerston—many, a historian might argue, with right on their side. But Palmerston beat them back.

Palmerston owed his victory in some measure to the simple fact that his policy was the one the mass of the British electorate wanted. Albert and the Queen might have preferred things done in other ways; certainly they would have preferred a different diplomatic and political style. Gladstone, Disraeli, Graham, and Cobden would have done things differently even if they had not, in the end, done different things. All of which demonstrated the broad agreement on the general lines and goals of British politics at mid-century. Dissenters, like Cobden on the Opium Wars and Bright over Crimea, were a minority with clearly limited national support.

Not until the disputes between Gladstone and Disraeli over the Eastern question in the later 1870's would significant differences be raised to the level of national debate. Even then the moral issues of the Midlothian campaign faded all too quickly into the more cynical, self-seeking diplomacy of imperialism.

Since Palmerston spoke most of the night and reviewed many aspects of policy in extraordinary detail, I have made substantial, indicated cuts in the text.

Recommended Reading

The Palmerston literature is extensive, and the best place to begin, save for the biographies by SOUTHGATE (1966) and BELL (1936), is A. J. P. TAYLOR's refreshing essay "Palmerston," *Englishmen and Others* (London, 1956), pp. 36–44. C. K. WEBSTER has a ponderous, complete study of *The Foreign Policy of Palmerston* (London, 1951).

SOURCE: Henry John Temple, Third Viscount Palmerston, The Pacifico Affair, June 25, 1850, *Hansard's Parliamentary Debates*, Third Series, Vol. CXII, cols. 380–383, 394, 396–398, 410–418, 421–424, 431–434, 438–440, 443–444.

When I say that this is an important question, I say it in the fullest expression of the term. It is a matter which concerns not merely the tenure of office by one individual, or even by a Government; it is a question that involves principles of national policy, and the deepest interests as well as the honour and dignity of England. I cannot think that the course which has been pursued, and by which this question has assumed its present shape, is becoming those, by whose act it has been brought under discussion of Parliament, or such as fitting the gravity and the importance of the matters which they have thus led this House and the other House of Parliament to discuss. For if that party in this country imagine that they are strong enough to carry the Government by storm, and to take possession of the citadel of office; or, if without intending to measure their strength with that of their opponents, they conceive that there are matters of such gravity connected with the conduct of the Government, that it becomes their duty to call upon Parliament solemnly to record its disapprobation of what has passed, I think that either in the one case or in the other, that party ought not to have been contented with obtaining the expression of the opinion of the House of Lords, but they ought to have sent down their resolution for the consent and concurrence of this House; or, at least, those who act with them in political co-operation here, should themselves have proposed to this House to come to a similar resolution. But, be the road what it may, we have come to the same end; and the House is substantially considering whether they will adopt the resolution of the House of Lords, or the resolution which has been submitted to them by my hon. and learned Friend, the Member for Sheffield.

Now, the resolution of the House of Lords involves the future as well as the past. It lays down for the future a principle of national policy, which I consider totally incompatible with the interests, with the rights, with the honour, and with the dignity of the country; and at variance with the practice, not only of this, but of all other civilised countries in the world. Even the person who moved it was obliged essentially to modify it in his speech. But none of the modifications contained in the speech were introduced into the resolution adopted by the other House. The country is told that British subjects in foreign lands are entitled—for that is the meaning of the resolution—to nothing but the protection of the laws and the tribunals of the land in which they happen to reside. The country is told that British subjects abroad must not look to their own country for protection, but must trust to that indifferent justice which they may happen to receive at the hands of the Government and tribunals of the country in which they may be.

The House of Lords has not said that this proposition is limited to constitutional countries. The House of Lords has not said that the proposition is inapplicable, not only to arbitrary and despotic countries, but even to constitutional countries where the courts of justice are not free; although these limitations were stated in the speech. The country is simply informed by the resolution, as it was adopted, that, so far as foreign nations are concerned, the future rule of the Government of England is to be, that, in all cases, and under all circumstances, British subjects are to have that protection only, which the law and the tribunals of the land in which they happen to be, may give them.

Now, I deny that proposition; and I say it is a doctrine on which no British Minister ever yet has acted, and on which the people of England never will suffer any British Minister to act. Do I mean to say that British subjects abroad are to be above the law, or are to be taken out of the scope of the laws of the land in which they live? I mean no such thing; I contend for no such principle. Undoubtedly, in the first instance, British subjects are bound to have recourse for redress to the means which the law of the land affords them, when that law is available for such purpose. That is the opinion which the legal advisers of the Crown have given in numerous cases; and it is the opinion on which we have founded our replies to many applications for our interposition in favour of British subjects abroad. And allow me, at the first moment when I have occasion to mention the legal advisers of the Crown, to say, that I heard with pain aspersions cast from a quarter from which they ought not to have come, upon the person who is the legal adviser of the office which I have the honour to hold. I should have thought that a person who by his own experience must have known, not only the learning, but the independence of mind, and the sense of justice that characterise the distinguished individual who holds the office of Queen's Advocate, would have abstained from those aspersions which have been cast upon that meritorious officer.

Perhaps I may have deviated from the strict orders of the House in what I have said; but I felt it due to an honourable-minded man to give my testimony on the earliest occasion that presented itself, to the independence and integrity of his character.

I say then, that if our subjects abroad have complaints against individuals, or against the Government of a foreign country, if the courts of law of that country can afford them redress, then, no doubt, to those courts of justice the British subject ought in the first instance to apply; and it is only on a denial of justice, or upon decisions manifestly unjust, that the British Government should be called upon to interfere. But there may be cases in which no confidence can be placed in the tribunals, those tribunals being, from their composition and nature, not of a character to inspire any hope of obtaining justice from them. It has been said, "We do not apply this rule to countries whose Governments are arbitrary or despotic, because there the tribunals are under the control of the Government, and justice cannot be had; and, moreover, it is not meant to be applied to nominally constitutional Governments, where the tribunals are corrupt." But who is to be the judge in such a case, whether the tribunals are corrupt or not? The British Government or the Government of the State from which you demand justice? . . .

I say, then, that our doctrine is, that, in the first instance, redress should be sought from the law courts of the country; but that in cases where redress cannot be so had—and those cases are many—to confine a British subject to that remedy only, would be to deprive him of the protection which he is entitled to receive.

Then we come to the claim of M. Pacifico—a claim which has been the subject of much unworthy comment. Stories have been told, involving imputations on the character of M. Pacifico; I know nothing of the truth or falsehood of these stories. All I know is, that M. Pacifico, after the time to which those stories relate, was appointed Portuguese consul, first to Morocco and afterwards at Athens. It is not likely that the Portuguese Government would select for appointments of that kind, a person whose character they did not believe to be above reproach. But I say, with those who have before had occasion to advert to the subject, that I don't care what M. Pacifico's character is. I do not, and cannot admit, that because a man may have acted amiss on some other occasion, and in some other matter, he is to be wronged with impunity by others.

The rights of a man depend on the merits of the particular case; and it is an abuse of argument to say, that you are not to give redress to a man, because in some former transaction he may have done something which is questionable. Punish him if you will—punish him if he is guilty, but don't pursue him as a Pariah through life.

[Palmerston spells out the details of the mob attack (which included the sons of the Greek Minister of War), Don Pacifico's inability to secure protection, the futility of seeking legal redress, and the unwillingness of the Greek government to arbitrate.]

Whether M. Pacifico's statement of his claim was exaggerated or not, the demand was not for any particular amount of money. The demand was, that the claim should be settled. An investigation might have been instituted, which those who acted for us were prepared to enter into, fairly, dispassionately, and justly.

M. Pacifico having, from year to year, been treated either with answers wholly unsatisfactory, or with a positive refusal, or with pertinacious silence, it came at last to this, either that his demand was to be abandoned altogether, or that, in pursuance of the notice we had given the Greek Government a year or two before, we were to proceed to use our own means of enforcing the claim. "Oh! but," it is said, "what an ungenerous proceeding to employ so large a force against so small a Power!" Does the smallness of a country justify the magnitude of its evil acts? Is it to be held that if your subjects suffer violence, outrage, plunder in a country which is small and weak, you are to tell them when they apply for redress, that the country is so weak and so small that we cannot ask it for compensation? Their answer would be, that the weakness and smallness of the country make it so much the more easy to obtain redress. "No," it is said, "generosity is to be the rule." We are to be generous to those who have been ungenerous to you; and we cannot give you redress because we have such ample and easy means of procuring it.

Well, then, was there anything so uncourteous in sending, to back our demands, a force which should make it manifest to all the world that resistance was out of the question? Why, it seems to me, on the contrary, that it was more consistent with the honour and dignity of the Government on whom we made those demands, that there should be placed before their eyes a force, which it would be vain to resist, and before which it would be no indignity to yield. If we had sent merely a frigate and a sloop of war, or any force with which it was possible their forces might have matched, we should have placed them in a more undignified position by asking them to yield to so small a demonstration. Therefore, so far from thinking that the amount of the force which happened to be on the spot was any aggravation of what is called the indignity of our demand, it seems to me that the Greek Government, on the contrary, ought rather to have considered it as diminishing the humiliation, whatever it might be, of being obliged to give at last to compulsion, that which had been so long refused to entreaty.

Well, then, however, did we, in the application of that force, either depart from established usage, or do anything that was unnecessarily pressing on the innocent and unoffending population of Greece? I say the innocent and unoffending population, because it was against the Government, and not against the nation, that our claim for redress was directed. The courses that may be pursued in cases where wrong is done by one Government towards the subjects of another, are various. One is, what is commonly called "reprisals;" that is, the seizing something of value, and holding it in deposit until your demands are complied with; or, if you fail in that, and don't choose to resort to other methods, applying that which you have seized, as a compensation for the wrong sustained. That is one method. Another is the modified application of war—

such as a blockade—a measure frequently adopted by the Governments of maritime States when they demand redress for injuries.
Last come actual hostilities. . . .

The right hon. Baronet [Sir James Graham] was justified in
taking that larger range into which he expatiated last night; but I
must be allowed to set him right as to the first point upon which he
touched. He stated what was quite true, that when he was a
Member of Earl Grey's Administration, he concurred with me in
many acts of foreign policy of which I was the organ, which
involved very active interposition in the affairs of other countries.
He instanced the negotiations in regard to Belgium, and its separation from Holland. He has done justice to the views which guided
the Government of that day, in their opinion that the independence
of Belgium would be a measure advantageous to the peace, present
and future, of Europe. But, then, he says, that case was different
from the acts of the present Government, because every step in
that affair was taken with the concurrence of all the five Powers
who were parties to the negotiation. The right hon. Baronet said
that there were, to be sure, some things which went beyond mere
negotiation: there was the siege of Antwerp, and the embargo laid
by us upon Dutch ships. He had concurred, he said, in both those
measures; but were those measures, steps taken with the full consent of all the five Powers? Were those acts measures of such a
description that they rendered it quite impossible that the friendly
relations of this country with other Powers could be disturbed
thereby? The right hon. Baronet must, I am sure, recollect that
Austria, Russia, and Prussia dissented from those measures; that
they protested against those measures; that in consequence thereof
they withdrew for a time from the conference, and that a Prussian
army was collected near the banks of the Meuse, the presence of
which rendered it necessary for the French to send a very large
force to Antwerp, much more than was required for the mere siege
of the citadel, and also to have a reserve ready in case of need. I
know very well that when people are out of office their memory is
not so quick and retentive as to things which happened while they
were in power as it would have been if they had remained in; but
on this point the right hon. Baronet made an important mistake,
especially as bearing upon the particular question now before the
House.

I agree with the right hon. Baronet that, in regard to the affairs of Belgium, the Government of England came to a wise determination. I think that the arrangement which in 1815 had been thought conducive to the peace of Europe, and by which, through the union of Belgium with Holland, a Power of some consideration was to be formed in that particular part of Europe, interposed between Germany on one side and France on the other—I think that that arrangement, which originally, by those who framed it, was, and not without reason, expected to prove advantageous to the peace of Europe, had, by the course of events, turned out to have a contrary tendency. The people of Belgium and of Holland evidently could not coalesce; and if certain Powers of Europe had combined at that moment to compel a reunion between these separated portions of the Kingdom of the Netherlands, I doubt whether that reunion could have been effected without the immediate explosion of a war in Europe of the greatest magnitude; and I am quite sure that if it had been effected, it could not have lasted, and the foundation must have been laid thereby of future and inevitable disturbance. We carried out our opinion upon that point to a practical result.

It is not to be disguised at this time of day, that our opinion on that matter was not shared by Austria, Russia, and Prussia. They would much rather have seen the two countries reunited; and if that reunion was at that time impossible, they would have been glad of any arrangement which might have tended to render a reunion thereafter more easy. This was no breach of faith on their part; they acted, I am bound to say, with great good faith and honour in the whole transaction; but they had that opinion which differed from the opinion of England and France. Nevertheless our arrangements prevailed; and was that, now, an instance of a policy which deserves the censure and condemnation of Parliament and of the country?

I remember being taunted in this House by being told of my "little experimental Belgian monarchy." It was predicted that the experiment would not succeed; it was said that there was no national feeling among the Belgians; that they would, on the first opportunity, throw themselves into the arms of their nearest neighbour; that we were only laying the foundation of another change; and that our arrangement was only "a transition state." Why, if ever there was an experiment—call it so if you will—that fully and completely succeeded, the erection of Belgium into an independent

State was that experiment. In times when almost all the other countries in Europe have been convulsed from top to bottom, Belgium has remained undisturbed. The people have shown the most admirable devotion and attachment to their Sovereign; the Sovereign the greatest confidence in, and love for, his people; the nation has made rapid advances in industry and in the arts, in everything which distinguishes a civilised State; all this reflects the greatest honour upon the Belgian people; and they have, moreover, acquired a spirit and sentiment of nationality which entitles them to the respect of every other country in the world. I say, then, that so far as we were concerned in effecting that arrangement, I think that is a case to which we can refer with pride and satisfaction, and in regard to which we can justly claim the approbation of Parliament and of the country. But it was not altogether without encountering difficulty, not only in other countries, but at home, that we were able to bring that long negotiation to a successful issue. . . .

Now, a question arose in Portugal between the claims of Donna Maria, represented by her father, Don Pedro, and those of Don Miguel, her uncle. Did it very much signify to England, in the abstract, whether this young queen was to be Sovereign of Portugal, or whether Don Miguel, who was actually in possession, should remain upon the throne? Not much certainly; but we looked upon the question, not as a simple choice between one sovereign and the other, but—what it was in reality—as a question between absolute government on the one hand, and constitutional government on the other. But what interest, you will say, had we in that? Why, we might have had a selfish interest in favour of despotism; because it is manifest that if you want to exercise influence over a country, you are more likely to have it where the Government rests in a Court and a Cabinet, than where it rests in an assembly representing the nation. But we scorned that sort of influence in Portugal. We knew, in espousing the cause of a constitution, that that particular kind of influence on our part would cease; but we felt that we should reap other advantages, which would more than counterbalance any disadvantage arising from that source. We knew that the prosperity of Portugal was concerned in the issue—that the best chance for the cessation of the manifold abuses, administrative and others, which had so long prevailed to keep down Portugal in the scale of nations—that the best chance of applying a remedy to those evils, and of giving full development to the natural resources of Portugal, would consist in securing to it the inestimable advantages of a free constitution; and, therefore, thinking as we did, that right was on the side of that party with whom waves the constitutional banner, we, and the right hon. Baronet with us, espoused that cause; and we concluded a treaty between England, France, Spain, and Portugal, by means of which, through the exertion of force, Donna Maria was seated upon the throne of Portugal. I think that course was wise—was perfectly defensible; and I think the right hon. Baronet is entitled to share with me in the merit of having been above all narrow-minded prejudices, and having concurred in that act of forcible interference, for the purpose of giving to Portugal the blessings of representative government.

But I shall be told that as late as 1847 there was another insurrection in Portugal, and another interference. Now, no man of common sense can suppose, that when you plant free institutions in a soil, in which none have hitherto grown, they are at once to attain their full maturity, and to bear their utmost fruit. It takes time to educate men for the well administration of representative government; it takes time to reconcile the governors to submitting themselves to the control of representative institutions; and in the early stages of constitutional experience you find, on the one hand, that the representatives of the people do not bring sufficient moderation and sense, and judgment, to the exercise of their functions; and, on the other, that the Members of the Government are too jealous of the restraints imposed upon them, and are constantly striving either to elude those restraints, or to break through them. The history of all constitutional countries, and especially of our own, will furnish abundant instances to exemplify this truth. But has Portugal derived no benefit from her constitution? Let any man compare her present condition with what she was under arbitrary government. There may now be abuses and misgovernment requiring correction; but the condition of Portugal is no more to be compared with what it formerly was, than is light with darkness.

Now, what did we do in 1847? . . . Portugal was then in a state of revolution; the Throne was in the utmost and imminent danger; the Government applied to this country for aid under the engagements of that Quadruple Treaty to which the right hon. Baronet was a party—and also applied to France and to Spain, the other parties to that treaty. . . . I am convinced that though for the moment we put down, or at least disarmed, the Liberal party, we saved that party, both individually and collectively, from great dangers and from serious evils.

My conviction is, that if we had declined, the other Powers, Spain especially, would have interfered. . . . My conviction is, that if we had not adopted the course we did, and by which the civil war was put an end to at once, without further effusion of blood, that civil war would have been put down by foreign interference, but not with the conditions which we attached to the termination of the contest.

The conditions we exacted were—ample and complete amnesty for all engaged in that civil war; a revocation of all illegal edicts which had been issued by the Government at variance with the constitution; the convocation of the Parliament as soon as the elections, which should immediately take place, were concluded; and the formation in the mean time of a Government consisting neither of members of the party of Cabral—the party then representing the arbitrary principle, the high Tory principle—nor of members of the Junta of Oporto. These terms were accepted; there was no further effusion of blood; the constitution continued in full force; and Portugal is now in the enjoyment of that constitution; and practically, it is working as well as under all circumstances, and considering how recently it has been established, could perhaps have been expected. . . .

[Palmerston turns next to the Spanish crisis generated by the Carlist rising.]

But in Spain, as in Portugal, the question was between arbitrary rule and constitutional and parliamentary government, and in relation to Spain, as well as to Portugal, we thought that the interests of England in every point of view, commercial and political, would be benefited by the establishment of constitutional government.

If England has any interest more than another with reference to Spain, it is that Spain should be independent, that Spain should be Spanish. Spain for the Spaniards, is the maxim upon which we proceed in our policy with regard to Spain. Much evil must ever come to this country from the fact of Spain being under the dictation of other Powers. It is eminently for our interest that when we have the misfortune to be in dispute or at war with any other Power, we should not, merely on that account, and without any

offence to or from Spain herself, be at war with Spain also. It is to
our advantage that so long as we have given no offence to Spain,
and she none to us, differences with other Powers should not
involve us in war with her; and we considered that the independence of Spain was more likely to be secured by a Government
controlled by a representative and national Assembly, than by a
Government purely arbitrary, and consisting merely of the Members who might form the Administration. Therefore, on grounds
of strict policy, independently of the general sympathy which
animated the people as well as the Government of this country
towards Spain at that time, we thought it our interest to take part
with Isabella, and against the pretensions of Don Carlos. That
policy was successful—the Carlist cause failed; the cause of the
constitution prevailed. . . .

However, Sir, the right hon. Baronet the Member for Ripon
says that these affairs of Spain were of long duration, and produced
disastrous consequences, because they were followed by events of
the greatest importance, as regards another country, namely,
France. He says, that out of those Spanish quarrels and Spanish
marriages, there arose differences between England and France,
which led to no slighter catastrophe than the overthrow of the
French monarchy. This is another instance of the fondness for
narrowing down a great and national question, to the smallness of
personal difference. It was my dislike to M. Guizot, forsooth,
arising out of these Spanish marriages, which overthrew his Administration, and with it the throne of France! Why, Sir, what will
the French nation say when they hear this? They are a highinded
and highspirited nation, full of a sense of their own dignity and
honour—what will they say, when they hear it stated that it was in
the power of a British Minister to overthrow their Government
and their monarchy? Why, Sir, it is a calumny on the French
nation to suppose that the personal hatred of any foreigner to their
Minister could have this effect. They are a brave, a generous, and a
noble-minded people; and if they had thought that a foreign
conspiracy had been formed against one of their Ministers—I say,
that if the French people had thought that a knot of foreign
conspirators were caballing against one of their Ministers, and
caballing for no other reason than that he had upheld, as he conceived, the dignity and interests of his own country; and if they
had thought that such a knot of foreign conspirators had co-

adjutors in their own land, why, I say that the French people, that
brave, noble, and spirited nation, would have scorned the intrigues
of such a cabal; and would have clung the closer to, and have
supported the more, the man against whom such a plot had been
made. . . .

Before I quit this subject, I must say that in my opinion the
policy which we have pursued in regard to France has been consistent with the interests of this country, and has been characterised
by an observance of the principles which the hon. and learned
Gentleman, whose resolution we are discussing, thinks ought to
govern our foreign policy, and which are calculated to preserve, as
they have preserved, the peace of Europe. Our prompt acknowl-
edgment in 1848 of the Government established in France, and the
kindly relations which we have maintained with the successive
chiefs of Administration in that country, sufficiently show that we
have been animated by a kindly feeling towards the French nation;
and that in our opinion the maintenance of friendly relations with
that country is not only consistent with our interests and our
dignity, but also forms a firm foundation for the peace of Europe.

Well, Sir, I leave the sunny plains of Castile and the gay
vineyards of France, and now I am taken to the mountains of
Switzerland, as the place where I am to render a stricter account.

[The question at issue here is that of the Sonderbund, the seven
strongly Catholic cantons, which came into conflict with the other
cantons in 1847 over a regulation for the expulsion of the Jesuits;
their difficulties soon blossomed into a complex diplomatic tangle
involving Britain, France, Spain, and the Papacy.]

It is said that Switzerland is an instance of the bad effects of our
interference. But Switzerland may be quoted as an instance of a
country, where the principles we have advocated have led to a
good result; for while almost all the surrounding nations of Europe
have been more or less convulsed, the people of Switzerland have
quietly effected changes which I believe to be improvements in
their internal organization; and those persons who were at one time
looked upon as being . . . "Red Republicans" . . . are now acknowledged to be, as in truth they always have been, lovers and
maintainers of good order; and, far from being revolutionists and
disturbers of the public peace, they have proved themselves not
only sincere supporters of good order in their own country, but

also discouragers of disorder in others; for they have gone great lengths in expelling from Switzerland persons who were justly supposed to have resorted there, for the purpose of disturbing the peace of neighbouring countries.

Now, travelling from the rugged Alps into the smiling plains of Lombardy, I find I have been accused of great injustice to the Austrian Government by withholding a certain despatch written by Prince Metternich to Count Dietrichstein.

[Palmerston discusses the charge and calls it ridiculous.]

With regard to our policy with respect to Italy, I utterly deny the charges that have been brought against us, of having been the advocates, supporters, and encouragers of revolution. It has always been the fate of advocates of temperate reform and of constitutional improvement to be run at as the fomentors of revolution. It is the easiest mode of putting them down; it is the received *formula*. It is the established practice of those who are the advocates of arbitrary government to say, "Never mind real revolutionists; we know how to deal with them; your dangerous man is the moderate reformer; he is such a plausible man; the only way of getting rid of him, is to set the world at him, by calling him a revolutionist."

Now, there are revolutionists of two kinds in this world. In the first place, there are those violent, hotheaded, and unthinking men, who fly to arms, who overthrow established Governments; and who recklessly, without regard to consequences, and without measuring difficulties and comparing strength, deluge their country with blood, and draw down the greatest calamities on their fellow-countrymen. These are the revolutionists of one class. But there are revolutionists of another kind; blind-minded men, who, animated by antiquated prejudices, and daunted by ignorant apprehensions, dam up the current of human improvement; until the irresistible pressure of accumulated discontent breaks down the opposing barriers, and overthrows and levels to the earth, those very institutions which a timely application of renovating means would have rendered strong and lasting. Such revolutionists as these are the men who call us revolutionists. It was not to make revolutions that the Earl of Minto went to Italy, or that we, at the request of the Governments of Austria and Naples, offered our mediation between contending parties.

Then, with respect to the war in Lombardy, it is said that we ought to have prevented Sardinia from making an attack on Lombardy. A perusal of the blue books will show, that we did apply those arguments which we thought most likely to have force with the Sardinian Government, to induce it not to take up arms against Austria; and it was not until after the revolution had broken out in Milan, and when the Austrians were for a time defeated, and expelled from the greater part of Lombardy, in a manner which can only be accounted for as being the result of a panic, it was not until after those events that the King of Sardinia, being invited by the people of Lombardy, moved and went to their assistance. I do not mean to say that there is in all this any justification—if you look to treaties or to international rights—for the invasion of the territory of a neighbouring Sovereign. As regards right, the King of Sardinia was entirely wrong, and there is nothing to be said for him on that score. But, at the same time, there are feelings and considerations which may at least explain conduct, which one cannot justify, and which one must condemn. He was appealed to by his Italian neighbours; the spirit of his own country was up; and he said, and not without some foundation, that if he had resisted the impulse which urged him on, that impulse might have been sufficient to overthrow his own throne. That was not a consideration which ought to weigh against the reasons and motives which should prevent the invasion of the territory of a neighbour. Nevertheless, man is man, and we ought not altogether to throw out of the account, circumstances of this kind.

Well, the Austrian Government sent a special envoy to London to ask our mediation between them and the people of Lombardy; and, in the course of the communications, we were told that Austria would consent to an arrangement, the basis of which should be, that Austria should relinquish all right and title to Lombardy. Now, if Austria contemplated that result, are we to be run down for thinking that such an arrangement would have been conducive to the well-understood interest of all parties concerned? . . .

[Palmerston goes into considerable detail on the Minto mission to Italy and the Italian revolutions of 1848.]

Under these circumstances, I am justified in denying that the policy which we pursued in Italy was that of exciting revolutions, and then abandoning the victims we had deluded. On the contrary, I maintain that we gave advice calculated to prevent revolutions, by reconciling opposite parties, and conflicting views. Ours was a policy of improvement and of peace; and therefore the Government deserves not condemnation, but praise.

We have been told, however, that if it had not been for the war in Lombardy, the indispensable interference of Russia in Hungary would not have taken place. What might have happened, if that which did happen, had not happened, I cannot undertake to say. But when I look at the deep-seated causes of contention between Hungary and the Austrian Government; when I look to the comparative resources and power of the conflicting parties; I cannot persuade myself that even if a part of Radetzki's army had been available for the war in Hungary, and the whole of it could not have been sent thither, the aid, the indispensable aid, as it has been termed, of Russia, would not still have been required. I, therefore, do not feel that the English Government is chargeable with any of the bloodshed which resulted from that Hungarian contest.

With respect to the questions which arose last autumn about Turkey, no blame has been imputed to Her Majesty's Government for the course which we pursued on that occasion, in answer to the appeal made by Turkey to this country and to France, for moral and material assistance. On that point all parties are agreed. It is a proud and honourable recollection which Englishmen may treasure up, that on an occasion like that, all party differences were merged in high and generous national feeling; and that men of all sides concurred in thinking, that the Government of the Queen would not have been justified in rejecting an appeal so made, on such a subject.

But it has been said that we ought to have confined our interference, at first, to sending a despatch, and that we should not have sent our fleet until we knew whether our despatches would produce the desired effect. That would have been a very imprudent and unwise course of proceeding. The agents of the two imperial Governments at Constantinople had used most menacing language to the Porte; had demanded the surrender of the refugees in the most peremptory manner; and had said, that if they did not receive a categorical answer within a limited time, they would suspend diplomatic relations. In short, they intimated that a refusal of their demands might lead to war. . . .

But it has been said that the sending of this fleet was a threat against Russia and Austria. I utterly deny that the sending of the fleet was a threat against either the one or the other. A fleet at the Dardanelles was not a threat against Austria. If it had been in the Adriatic, it might have been so regarded. A fleet in the Mediterranean was not a threat against Russia. Had it forced its way through the Dardanelles and Bosphorus, and had gone up to the Black Sea, and had anchored off Sebastopol, it might have been so considered. But a fleet at the mouth of the Dardanelles could be a threat against nobody; it must be manifest to the world that it could only be a symbol and source of support to the Sultan. It was a measure purely of defence, and not a measure of offence.

[Palmerston enters into an extended defense of British policy on this installment of the Eastern question, particularly the Besica Bay incident.]

I believe I have now gone through all the heads of the charges which have been brought against me in this debate. I think I have shown that the foreign policy of the Government, in all the transactions with respect to which its conduct has been impugned, has throughout been guided by those principles which, according to the resolution of the hon. and learned Gentleman the Member for Sheffield [John Arthur Roebuck, a leading Radical], ought to regulate the conduct of the Government of England in the management of our foreign affairs. I believe that the principles on which we have acted are those which are held by the great mass of the people of this country. I am convinced these principles are calculated, so far as the influence of England may properly be exercised with respect to the destinies of other countries, to conduce to the maintenance of peace, to the advancement of civilization, to the welfare and happiness of mankind.

I do not complain of the conduct of those who have made these matters the means of attack upon Her Majesty's Ministers. The government of a great country like this, is undoubtedly an object of fair and legitimate ambition to men of all shades of opinion. It is a noble thing to be allowed to guide the policy and to influence the destinies of such a country; and, if ever it was an object of honourable ambition, more than ever must it be so at the moment at which I am speaking. For while we have seen, as stated by the right [hon.] Baronet the Member for Ripon, the political earthquake rocking Europe from side to side—while we have seen thrones shaken, shattered, levelled; institutions overthrown and destroyed—while in almost every country of Europe the conflict of civil war has deluged the land with blood, from the Atlantic to the Black Sea, from the Baltic to the Mediterranean; this country has presented a spectacle honourable to the people of England, and worthy of the admiration of mankind.

We have shown that liberty is compatible with order; that individual freedom is reconcilable with obedience to the law. We have shown the example of a nation, in which every class of society accepts with cheerfulness the lot which Providence has assigned to it; while at the same time every individual of each class is constantly striving to raise himself in the social scale—not by injustice and wrong, not by violence and illegality—but by persevering good conduct, and by the steady and energetic exertion of the moral and intellectual faculties with which his Creator has endowed him. To govern such a people as this, is indeed an object worthy of the ambition of the noblest man who lives in the land; and therefore I find no fault with those who may think any opportunity a fair one, for endeavouring to place themselves in so distinguished and honourable a position. But I contend that we have not in our foreign policy done anything to forfeit the confidence of the country. We may not, perhaps, in this matter or in that, have acted precisely up to the opinions of one person or of another—and hard indeed it is, as we all know by our individual and private experience, to find any number of men agreeing entirely in any matter, on which they may not be equally possessed of the details of the facts, and circumstances, and reasons, and conditions which led to action. But, making allowance for those differences of opinion which may fairly and honourably arise among those who concur in general views, I maintain that the principles which can be traced through all our foreign transactions, as the guiding rule and directing spirit of our proceedings, are such as deserve approbation. I therefore fearlessly challenge the verdict which this House, as representing a political, a commercial, a constitutional country, is to give on the question now brought before it; whether the principles on which the foreign policy of Her Majesty's Government has been conducted, and the sense of duty which has led us to think ourselves bound to afford protection to our fellow subjects abroad, are proper and fitting guides for those who are charged with the Government of England; and whether, as the Roman, in

days of old, held himself free from indignity, when he could say
Civis Romanus sum; so also a British subject, in whatever land he
may be, shall feel confident that the watchful eye and the strong
arm of England, will protect him against injustice and wrong.

19. The Queen: Some Power and Much Influence

THE QUEEN's marriage to Albert in 1840 marked an important stage in
the revival of monarchy and the redefinition of British institutions.
Albert, counseled by Baron Stockmar, was a liberal by continental
standards and was prepared to learn and to adapt himself to new
conditions and circumstances. He was anxious to do right. Victoria
was anxious to have him accepted. Baron Stockmar recognized some of
the changes that had taken place, misread others. But the essence of his
message was that the monarch must not become a mandarin figure
under the reformed constitution. While Victoria never surrendered
control or initiative to Albert, his superior intelligence, his interest, and
their closeness in all things worked toward an Albertine or co-operative period of monarchy until the prince's death in 1861.

Victoria and Albert were moderators of British politics without ever
intruding on the constitutional rights of Parliament. They were careful
to take what they must, to adjust what they could, and to attempt to
maintain before Victoria's ministers a clear picture of the "national
interest" and the understanding that it must be served before any
partisan measures. Some ministers, as individuals, could be problems,
and no one more than Palmerston. He had all the Whig prejudices
without conventional Whig acreage. He ran the Foreign Office his
way with scant regard for the interests or the wishes of the Queen.
Victoria and Albert had their own channels of information—King
Leopold of Belgium, the innumerable royal cousins in almost every
capital of Europe—and their own opinions. Palmerston pressed a
breezy, superficial support of liberalism, while the court contended
that different countries might have other aspirations and prefer to
develop along their own lines.

Save for Palmerston who was never easy, the Victoria and Albert
method fitted English political life particularly well in the 1850's. After
the Conservative schism on the repeal of the Corn laws, Britain briefly
had three parties—more, some might argue. There were the Whigs,
the same cult of great-grandmotherhood dominated by the same families, but now suffering a conflict for leadership between Lord John

Russell and Palmerston. Under normal circumstances most Liberals and Radicals enrolled under the Whig banner. The Tories had a brief fling at office under Lord Derby, with Disraeli at the Exchequer, but could muster neither leaders, program, nor followers enough to carry an election. The Peelites, those Conservatives who remained loyal to Sir Robert, functioned independently through the decade. Although they had most of the talented leadership in the House, they had few followers.

The crown helped to negotiate the Aberdeen (Peelite) coalition government of 1852 after it was clear that neither Lord John with his Whig-Liberals nor Derby with the Tories could develop a majority. Palmerston was kept out of the Foreign Office in deference to royal sentiments and was given the Home Office instead. Lord John Russell started in the Foreign Office but gave it up because he was unwilling to indulge in continuous quarrels with Palmerston. But Palmerston, for his part, disliked the government's policy in the Eastern crisis and wanted nothing to do with Russell's plan for parliamentary reform—one of several proposals put forward in the mid-Victorian period in an effort to secure Radical support. Lord John was kept in line, if not at the Foreign Office. Palmerston defected. Victoria and Albert moved to maintain the government.

Recommended Reading

In addition to the studies cited for Document 19, see R. FULFORD, *The Prince Consort* (London, 1949); and F. EYCK, *The Prince Consort* (New York, 1959).

SOURCE: *The Letters of Queen Victoria: a Selection from Her Majesty's Correspondence between the Years 1837 and 1861,* Vol. II, *1844–1853* (New York, 1907), pp. 532–534, 567–569, 571.

Queen Victoria to Lord John Russell

Windsor Castle
February 13, 1853

The Queen has received Lord John Russell's letter of yesterday, and was very glad to hear that he considers the aspect of the House of Commons as favourable to the Government.

Lord John alludes for the first time in his letter to a Question on which the Queen has not hitherto expressed her opinion to him personally, viz., how far the proposed new arrangement of Lord

John's holding the leadership of the House of Commons without office was constitutional or not? Her opinion perfectly agrees with that expressed by Mr. Walpole to Lord John. If the intended arrangement were *undoubtedly illegal* it would clearly never have been contemplated at all; but it may prove a *dangerous precedent*.

The Queen would have been quite prepared to give the proposition of the Speaker "that the leadership of the House of Commons was so laborious, that an Office without other duties ought to be assigned to it," her fullest and fairest consideration, upon its merits and its constitutional bearings, which ought to have been distinctly set fourth before her by her constitutional advisers for her final and unfettered decision.

What the Queen complains of, and, as she believes with justice is, that so important an innovation in the construction of the executive Government should have been practically decided upon by an arrangement intended to meet personal wants under peculiar and accidental circumstances, leaving the Queen the embarrassing alternatives only, either to forego the exercise of her own prerogative, or to damage by her own act the *formation* or *stability* of the new Government, both of paramount importance to the welfare of the Country.

Lord John Russell to Queen Victoria

Chesham Place
February 13, 1853

Lord John Russell presents his humble duty to your Majesty. He cannot forbear from vindicating himself from the charge of forming or being a party to an arrangement "intended to meet personal wants under peculiar and accidental circumstances, leaving the Queen the embarrassing alternative only, either to forego the exercise of her own prerogative, or to damage by her own act the *formation* or *stability* of the new Government—both of paramount importance to the welfare of the Country."

Lord John Russell has done all in his power to contribute to the formation of a Ministry in which he himself holds a subordinate situation, from which nearly all his dearest political friends are excluded, and which is held by some to extinguish the party which for eighteen years he has led.

He has done all this in order that your Majesty and the Country

196

might not be exposed to the evil of a weak Ministry liable to be overthrown at any moment, formed whether by Lord Derby, or by himself at the head of one party only.

But in consenting to this arrangement he was desirous to maintain his honour intact, and for this purpose he asked before the Ministry was formed for the honour of an Audience of your Majesty, that he might explain all the circumstances of his position.

This Audience was not granted, and Lord John Russell has never been in a situation to explain to your Majesty why he believes that his leading the House of Commons without office is not liable to any constitutional objection.

The Speaker and Mr Walpole both concur that no constitutional objection to this arrangement exists, but should your Majesty wish to see the arrangements briefly stated, by which Lord John Russell has been convinced, he should be happy to be allowed to lay them before your Majesty.

The Earl of Aberdeen to Queen Victoria

London
December 6, 1853

As Lord John Russell will have the honour of seeing your Majesty to-morrow, he will be able to explain to your Majesty the present state of the discussions on [Parliamentary] Reform, and the progress of the Measure. Lord Aberdeen feels it to be his duty to inform your Majesty that on Saturday evening he received a visit from Lord Palmerston, who announced his decided objection to the greater part of the proposed plan. He did this in such positive terms that Lord Aberdeen should imagine he had made up his mind not to give the Measure his support; but Lord John entertains considerable doubt that such is the case.

Lord Aberdeen thinks it by no means improbable that Lord Palmerston may also desire to separate himself from the Government in consequence of their pacific policy [with Russia in the Crisis that would grow into the Crimean War], and in order to take the lead of the War Party and the Anti-Reformers in the House of Commons, who are essentially the same. Such a combination would undoubtedly be formidable; but Lord Aberdeen trusts that it would not prove dangerous. At all events, it would tend greatly to the improvement of Lord John's Foreign Policy.

Prince Albert to the Earl of Aberdeen

Osborne
December 9, 1853

My Dear Lord Aberdeen,—

The Queen has consulted with Lord John Russell upon the Reform plan, and on the question of Lord Palmerston's position with regard to it; and he will undoubtedly give you an account of what passed. She wishes me, however, to tell you likewise what strikes her with respect to Lord Palmerston. It appears to the Queen clear that the Reform Bill will have no chance of success unless prepared and introduced in Parliament by a *united* Cabinet; that, if Lord Palmerston has made up his mind to oppose it and to leave the Government, there will be no use in trying to keep him in it, and that there will be danger in allowing him to attend the discussions of the Cabinet, preparing all the time his line of attack; that if a successor to him would after all have to be found at the Home Office, it will be unfair not to give that important member of the Government full opportunity to take his share in the preparation and deliberation on the measure to which his consent would be asked. Under these circumstances it becomes of the highest importance to ascertain—

1. What the amount of objection is that Lord Palmerston entertain to the Measure;
2. What the object of the declaration was, which he seems to have made to you.

This should be obtained *in writing* so as to make all future misrepresentations impossible, and on this alone a decision can well be taken, and, in the Queen's opinion, even the Cabinet could alone deliberate.

Should Lord Palmerston have stated his objections with the view of having the Measure modified it will be right to consider how far that can safely be done, and for the Queen, also, to balance the probable value of the modification with the risk of allowing Lord Palmerston to put himself at the head of the Opposition Party, entailing as it does the possibility of his forcing himself back upon her as leader of that Party.

Should he on the other hand consider his declaration as a "notice

to quit," the ground upon which he does so should be clearly put
on record, and no attempt should be made to damage the character
of the Measure in the vain hope of propitiating him.

Ever yours truly,
ALBERT.

Queen Victoria to the Marquis of Lansdowne

Osborne
December 16, 1853

The Queen has been made very anxious by the Resignation of
Lord Palmerston, but still more so by hearing that Lord Lansdowne has not yet been able to reconcile himself to the Measure of
Reform as now proposed in the Cabinet, which has caused Lord
Palmerston's withdrawal. Lord Lansdowne is aware of the paramount importance which the Queen attached to a safe settlement
of that question, and to the maintenance of her present Government; and she would press upon Lord Lansdowne not to commit
himself to a final determination before she shall have an opportunity of seeing him. The Queen will go to Windsor on Thursday,
and hold a Council on Friday, at which it may perhaps be convenient to Lord Lansdowne to attend, and it will give the Queen the
greatest pleasure to find that Lord John Russell has succeeded in
removing Lord Lansdowne's objections.

20.   *The Middle-Class Franchise: A Mid-Victorian Election*

THE FRUITS of parliamentary reform were not all sweet. Although the
franchise had been extended and the constituencies remade, the old
problems remained. Corruption, intimidation, influence were seen as
necessary adjuncts to popular participation in politics—not desirable,
but inevitable. By the 1850's new proposals for franchise reform came
forth with stunning regularity. Until Disraeli's Act of 1867, which
accidentally democratized the towns, there were no breaks with the
traditional conception of representation. Even the Ballot Act of 1872,
which ended some of the more blatant forms of hustings intimidation
and violence, did not reduce other forms of corruption or cut the cost

of politics. The election of 1880 was the most expensive to that time in British history, and the Corrupt Practices Act of 1883 was an effort—partially successful—to come to grips with the insidious inroads of the purse to political control. *Punch*'s mid-Victorian election touched on many of the problems of power and influence. That guardian of middle-class values had great sport with the trivia that sustained the mansion of political life.

Recommended Reading

Beyond the conventional general narrative and analytical materials, the best study of the stuff of politics after the first Reform Act is N. GASH, *Politics in the Age of Peel* (London, 1953). For the second round on reform: F. B. SMITH, *The Making of the Second Reform Bill* (London, 1966); and M. COWLING, *1867: Disraeli, Gladstone and Revolution* (London, 1967). H. J. HANHAM, *Elections and Party Management* (London, 1959), is the equivalent to Gash in the later period. C. O'LEARY, *The Elimination of Corrupt Practices in British Elections* (Oxford, 1962), speaks directly to the problem in the last third of the century.

SOURCE: "Election Intelligence (From the Local Newspapers),"
    Punch, April 3, 1852, p. 143.

Punch's *"Election Intelligence"*

SNARLINGTON

We are greatly delighted, in this excitable borough, at the prospects of a new election, and preparations of exercising the great constitutional right of Englishmen are already on foot. The duck pond before the Town Hall has been filled, and the railings around it partially sawn through; and an eminent egg-merchant of High Street has sent to Leadenhall-market, to secure all the eggs which may be unavailing for any but electoral purposes. A sheaf of loaded bludgeons arrived last night at the Cracked Crown Hotel; and we believe that both BLACK JIM and the LIGHT-WEIGHT PET have received their retaining fees. In Snarlington, at least, the true old English spirit is not extinct. We add, at the last moment, that our respected townsman and Coroner, LARYNX FLEAM, Esquire, immediately on hearing that a dissolution was certain, gave some handsome orders to his wine-merchant and jeweller. This is as it should be. Live and let live.

GREAT GROWLSBY

The contest here will be severe, as the EARL OF CAMBERWELL, who owns one-half of the borough, has just obtained a good lump of money by mortgaging the parish of Quaggington; while the DOWAGER LADY PECKHAM (his lordship's cousin and particular enemy), who owns the other half, has given notice to every one of her tenants, that if the EARL's candidate be returned, she will raise all their rents twenty-five per cent. A spirited struggle is therefore, certain, but it is thought that the EARL's ready money will carry the day.

SQUASHBOROUGH

Politics here are curiously involved. The "Staggering Sparrows," a club which has hitherto carried the elections its own way, has met a sudden and well-organised rivalry in a new union called the "Downey Robin Redbreasts" (who took their name from the red waistcoat of a smart auctioneer, their Perpetual Grand), and who, it is said, have exchanged an electric message with the great MR. COPPERAS, of London. The Sparrows stand well with the Corporation, from using the Bung Tavern, kept by the Mayor; but there are two benefit societies, the "Heroes of Glory," and the "United Anti-Procrastinators," both in the Redbreast interest. Unless some arrangement can be made, the welfare of the Squashborough public will be sacrificed, and a candidate, who has notoriously nothing but a miserable eight hundred a-year, earned by his labours at the bar, will carry off the prize. We hope better things from the good sense of both parties.

THE FANTAIL BURGHS

There will be no battle this time. SIR PETER McGRAWLER, of Fishmaws, in whose hands the representation lies, had threatened ejection and ruin to any voter who should support young MR. BLEAK. But the latter having proposed for MISS MARGARETTA McGRAWLER (and his uncle, ALDERMAN TUNNIE, of The Loaches, having undertaken to see to the settlements), SIR PETER has sent a circular ordering the electors to return his intended son-in-law by acclamation.

BISHOP'S CROTCHET

This quiet little town will be disturbed by the bustle of election. The Honourable MISSES MUBLEPLUMB, the esteemed dowager heiresses, are so indignant that the townsfolk objected to the sermons at St. Sillery's being preached in Latin, as proposed by the Reverend ORIGEN ALTARFLOWERS (the ladies' Puseyite chaplain), that they have desired their nephew, CAPTAIN FITZDERBY, of the Guards, to come down and oppose the old Member, MR. JAMES BASKETWORK. The latter made his fortune in the town, and spends it there; and though not the wisest man in the world, is considered a better representative of the honest folk of Bishop's Crotchet than a "spangled officer." But the old ladies are on their mettle, and a costly struggle is commencing.

KILLCROCKERY

Again a Saxon insult! How long, O Nemesis of the West, how long? The new proprietor of Mount Target, a London merchant, a vile trader, has dared to issue an address asking the suffrages of the Killcrockery electors. And this because he has reclaimed an estate, once an Irish gentleman's from ruin, rebuilt the dilapidated mansion, and fed, with his wretched gold, some hundreds of starving peasants. On such grounds does the dastardly POPKINS (that is his plebian patronymic) presume to stand upon Hibernian hustings. Well has the glowing Pindar remarked in his Georgics, *Qui Deum vultus parcere prior demonstrat*, for POPKINS must be mad indeed. Irishmen, is this to be bourne? Catholics, will ye endure it? A thousand echoes from the green hills of Clonmuddle haughtily answer with a reverberating negative. POPKINS for Killcrockery! *Faugh-a-ballaboo!*

GOTHBURY

We await but the signal. The electors are ready—their souls in arms and eager for the pay. The original candidates meanly sought to avoid a contest, but our patriotic and wary rival agents, MESSRS. SAW and MOPUS, were alive to the interest of their friends and fellow-townsmen, and the disgraceful juggle was defeated. A third candidate was procured from London; a rising young barrister, FLUCKS DE SLACKJAW, ESQUIRE, and his soul-stirring speeches have been received with a double enthusiasm, from their merit, and from the noble purpose they were serving. MR. DE SLACKJAW will go to the poll, and we need hardly add that both his rivals will have to draw pretty largely upon their dearly-loved gold. We congratulate our townsmen that their cause is in good hands. Voters will command twenty-five per cent. More this time than ever before, and, besides, MR. DE SLACKJAW's speeches are oratorical treats of no common order.

BALLYWOBBLE

A difficulty has arisen in finding a second candidate, MAJOR SNAPSHOT, of Rifleton, having taken a solemn oath to wing anybody who comes down to canvass against him. This he calls taking a triggernometrical survey of his position. The Major attends a meeting of his constituents at the Bombshell Hotel every evening, and in the most affable manner answers all inquiries as to his political aims, by snuffing out candles with his pistols. He pledges himself not to miss his man; objects to the ballot because he likes to see where his ball goes, but is otherwise well disposed to the levellers. He is for popular education, thinking the young idea ought to be taught to shoot, and is very sarcastic on milder people, whom he calls Smooth Bores. Under the circumstances, his return seems probable.

21. Liberalism: Gladstone and Democracy

WILLIAM EWART GLADSTONE (1809–98) was the archetype of Victorian statesman, although he was unique and more important for what he was than for what he did. Such a contradiction (even though a truth) is a fitting introduction for a Briton who contained within himself a host of contradictions. Gladstone and Disraeli are inevitably paired in the mind of man (and this volume), and usefully so. For although Gladstone was to outlive his rival by almost two decades and to preside over two more administrations, his "Great Ministry" (1868–74) and Disraeli's second government (1874–80) are not paired simply for convenience. They focused on the principles of Liberal and Conservative politics in the later Victorian age. They recapitulated a political past and anticipated the future.

Gladstone's government represented the culmination of the Victorian liberal tradition, a triumph of modified utilitarian ideology, the ascendancy of Manchester school values. With the sole and significant exception of his Irish Land Act, which interfered with the rights of property, every crucial measure—education, civil service, abolition of vestigial privileges whether for a class in the army or Anglicans at the old universities, vote by ballot, and judicial reform—represented the fruition or the substantial realization of traditional liberal goals.

Some of these reforms are scrutinized more closely in other connections in this volume to reveal their own significance and the ideas and forces behind them; unfortunately they do not illuminate Gladstone, for his ideas owed little to conventional political doctrine. His views derived from Christianity and the classics, a circuitous route that often made his words as baffling to friend as to foe. He shifted ponderously from early toryism to Peelite free trade to conventional liberalism and finally to radicalism. But even his radicalism was not orthodox. He was no doctrinaire. He remained anti-imperialist and anti-collectivist to the end of his life. By the 1890's, Gladstone was obsolete. His longevity crippled his party. His moral values, the essence of his strength, no longer commanded even rhetorical support. Jingoism and modified socialism had come to dominate political life.

Gladstone is the moral liberal, and his franchise statements bring us closer to the involved workings of a great Victorian mind. Not only do his speeches on the subject represent a useful summary of the curious history of parliamentary reform, successful and unsuccessful; they suggest—culminating in the one given here—the stages through which the liberal Briton went as he hesitantly committed himself to democracy. It was, in the end, a moral choice.

Recommended Reading

Sir PHILIP MAGNUS's excellent biography (London, 1954) is the best beginning. I strongly recommend G. M. YOUNG's Romanes Lecture for 1944, "Mr. Gladstone," reprinted in *Victorian Essays*, edited by W. D. HANDCOCK (London, 1962), pp. 90–110.

SOURCE: William Ewart Gladstone, Speech on the Third Reform Bill, February 28, 1884. *Hansard's Parliamentary Debates*, Third Series, Vol. CCLXXXV, cols. 106–124, 132–134.

Motion

REPRESENTATION OF THE PEOPLE BILL
Motion for Leave

Mr. GLADSTONE, in rising to move for leave to introduce the Representation of the People Amendment Bill, said:—

. . . It commonly happens with regard to these large and Constitutional questions—and it is well that it should so happen—that, before they are proposed upon the responsibility of the Queen's Government, they have attained to an advanced stage of progress in the public mind through discussion out-of-doors; and, in consequence, it is not necessary very long to detain the House with the general arguments which, if they were entirely new, would undoubtedly be requisite in order to make a case for the introduction of a Bill. On that part of the subject, therefore, I shall be very brief; but a few words I must necessarily say.

I conceive that this Bill—this proposition—may be presented to the House under any one, and indeed under all, of three distinct and several aspects. In the first place, it is on our part a redemption of a pledge; because, although I do not use the word "pledge" in its more narrow and objectionable sense, there is no doubt, I think, as regards the persons prominently concerned in conducting the affairs of the country in conjunction with the Liberal Party, that at and before, as well as since, the last Election they have constantly assured the country that they regarded the work of Parliamentary Reform as a proper and vital part of the mission, so to speak, of the present Parliament. The proposition may be regarded, secondly, as intended to satisfy a desire, for our belief is that a desire for the extension of the household franchise to the counties is widely and generally entertained among the classes who are to be affected by that extension. But there is another aspect in which I, for one, should hope that it will still more pointedly and constantly be viewed: it is a proposal in satisfaction of a pledge; it is a proposal to meet a desire; but, above all, it is a proposal, in my view, and I think I may say in our view, to add strength to the State. I am not prepared to discuss admission to the franchise as it was discussed 50 years ago, when Lord John Russell had to state, with almost bated breath, that he expected to add in the Three Kingdoms 500,000 to the constituencies. It is not now a question of nicely calculated less or more. I take my stand on the broad principle that the enfranchisement of capable citizens, be they few or be they many—and if they be many so much the better—gives an addition of strength to the State. The strength of the modern State lies in the Representative system. I rejoice to think that in this happy country and under this happy Constitution we have other sources of strength in the respect paid to various orders of the State, and in the authority they enjoy, and in the unbroken course which has been allowed to most of our national traditions; but still, in the main, it is the Representative system which is the strength of the modern State in general, and of the State in this country in particular. Sir, I may say—it is an illustration which will not occupy more than a moment—that never has this great truth been so vividly illustrated as in the War of the American Republic. The convulsion of that country between 1861 and 1865 was, perhaps, the most frightful which ever assailed a national existence. The efforts which were made on both sides were marked. The exertions by which alone the movement was put down were not only extraordinary, they were what would antecedently have been called impossible; and they were only rendered possible by the fact that they proceeded from a nation where every capable citizen was enfranchised, and had a direct and an energetic interest in the well-being and the unity of the State. Sir, the only question that remains in the general argument is, who are capable citizens? and, fortunately, that is a question which, on the present occasion, need not be argued at length, for it has been already settled—in the first place by a solemn legislative judgment acquiesced in by both Parties in the State; and, in the second place, by the experience of the last more than 15 years. Who, Sir, are the capable citizens of the State, whom it is proposed to enfranchise? It is proposed, in the main, to enfranchise the county population on the footing, and according to the measure, that has already been administered to the population of the towns. What are the main constituents of the county population? First of all, they are the minor tradesmen of the country, and the skilled labourers and artizans in all the common arts of life, and especially in connection with our great mining industry. Is there any doubt that these are capable citizens? You hon. Gentlemen opposite have yourselves asserted it by enfranchising them in the

towns; and we can only say that we heartily subscribe to the assertion. But besides the artizans and the minor tradesmen scattered
throughout our rural towns, we have also to deal with the peasantry of the country. Is there any doubt that the peasantry of the
country are capable citizens, qualified for enfranchisement, qualified to make good use of their power as voters? This is a question
which has been solved for us by the first and second Reform Bills;
because many of the places which under the name of towns are
now represented in this House are really rural communities, based
upon a peasant constituency. For my part, I should be quite ready
to fight the battle of the peasant upon general and argumentative
grounds. I believe the peasant generally to be, not in the highest
sense, but in a very real sense, a skilled labourer. He is not a man
tied down to one mechanical exercise of his physical powers. He is
a man who must do many things, and many things which require in
him the exercise of active intelligence. But, as I say, it is not necessary to argue on that ground, first of all, because we have got his
friends here—on the opposite Benches—from whom we must
anticipate great zeal for his enfranchisement; and, secondly, because the question has been settled by legislative authority in the
towns, and by practical experience. If he has a defect, it is that he is
too ready, perhaps, to work with and to accept the influence of his
superiors—superiors, I mean, in worldly station. But that is the last
defect that hon. Gentlemen opposite will be disposed to plead
against him, and it is a defect that we do not feel ourselves entitled
to plead, and that we are not at all inclined to plead. We are ready
to take him as he is, and joyfully bring him within the reach of this
last and highest privilege of the Constitution. There is only one
other word, Sir, to add on this part of the subject. The present
position of the franchise is one of greater and grosser anomaly than
any in which it has been heretofore placed, because the exclusion
of persons of the same class and the same description is more
palpable and more pervading than before, being, in fact, spread
over the whole country, persons being excluded in one place, while
the same persons are admitted in another. I wish just to call the
attention of the House to an important fact connected with this
part of the question, which is of frequent occurrence. It is a thing
which the House detests, and which we in this Bill shall endeavour
to avoid—namely, the infliction of personal disfranchisement. Observe how the present state of the Franchise Law brings this about.

It is known, and well understood, that a labourer must follow his labour. Where his labour goes, where the works go in which he is employed, he must follow. He cannot remain at a great distance from them; and the instance I will give—and though I am not personally conversant with it, I believe there is no doubt about the fact—is an instance which I think singularly applicable. It is that of the ship-building works on the Clyde. Those works were within the precincts of the City of Glasgow, and the persons who laboured in them were able to remain within the city, being near their work, and at the same time to enjoy the franchise. But the marvellous enterprize of Glasgow, which has made that city the centre and crown of the ship-building business of the world, could not be confined within the limits of the City of Glasgow, and it moved down the river. As the trade moved down the river the artizans required to move down the river with it. That was a matter of necessity, and the obedience to that necessity involves, under the present law, wholesale disfranchisement. That is an argument which is sufficient for disposing of the general question. The whole population, I rejoice to think, have liberty of speech; they have liberty of writing; they have liberty of meeting in public; they have liberty of private association; they have liberty of petitioning Parliament. All these privileges are not privileges taking away from us, diminishing our power and security; they are all of them privileges on the existence of which our security depends. Without them we could not be secure. I ask you to confer upon the very same classes the crowning privilege of voting for a Representative in Parliament, and then I say we, who are strong now as a nation and a State, shall, by virtue of that change, be stronger still.

Sir, I think the House will now see that the Bill I am proposing to introduce is substantially, though not technically, confined to one main view, one great provision—to give unity and completeness to the household and occupation franchises throughout the United Kingdom. The principle upon which it proceeds is, that the head of every household, under the conditions of the law, shall vote; and we seek to go as far as we can to get the heads of households and enfranchise them. The lodger and service franchises we look upon simply as branches—I may call them enlargements—of the household franchise. It is, in point of fact, if it is to be described by a single phrase, a Household Franchise Bill for the United Kingdom; and the popular idea has not been far wrong which has seized upon the conception of it as a measure which is to extend to the counties what is now enjoyed by the towns, although in making that extension we endeavour to accompany it with some further provisions for giving greater completeness in practical application to the idea of household franchise. Now, let me say shortly, we leave the "ancient-right" franchises alone. Let me say that we disfranchise personally no one. Wherever there is a provision in the Bill which would operate against the creation of franchises hereafter, identical in principle with some that now exist, we do not interfere with the right already legally acquired, however illegitimate it may seem to be. We leave the property vote alone, and confine ourselves to the endeavour to stop the extension of fictitious votes.

Well, Sir, these are the matters which the Bill contains; but all will feel that it is impossible for me on this occasion to pass by what the Bill does not contain. I am prepared for the complaint that this is not a complete Bill, and for the question—"Why don't you introduce a complete Bill?" On that I have some things to say which appear to me to be of very considerable force; but, at any rate, I will state them; and the first thing I will state is, that there never has been a complete Bill presented to Parliament on this subject of Parliamentary Reform. Never one. I make that assertion in the broadest way. There never has been a complete Bill presented to Parliament. Parliament has never attempted a complete Bill; and, moreover, I will go a little further, and say that Governments and Parliaments would have committed a grievous error in judgment— I might almost say they would have been out of their senses—if they had attempted a complete Bill. . . .

Sir, there are three essential divisions of this great subject; and, if we intend to deal with the subject as practical men, if we are endeavouring to pass a measure, and not to overlay and smother it, we must recognize the limitation which is imposed, not upon our will and choice, but upon our power, by the nature of the case and by the conditions under which Parliamentary government is now carried on. The first of these three great divisions is to define the right of the individual—that is, to fix the franchise. To fix the franchise is of itself an enormous task; it is a question which may be led out, if you should think fit, into a score or scores of ramifications. But it is clearly one of principle—it is, to fix the right of the individual who shall be entitled to vote. The second branch of the question is to provide machinery for the exercise of that right, and that is the subject of registration. It has never been found, as far as I am aware, practicable to unite this vital subject of good registration with the subject of the franchise. The third is, to gather the persons whom Parliament judges to be capable of exercising the franchise with benefit to themselves and to the country into local communities; and that is the business of distribution of seats.

Now, Sir, what do we attempt? I am going, perhaps, to make a confession as to what you may think the nakedness of the land—of the stinted character of the measure; but, looking at these three divisions, we deal only with one, and we deal with that one, not upon exhaustive principles, but with a view to great practical ends, leaving much upon which the critic and the speculator may, if they think fit, exercise their ingenuity in the way of remark, or of complaint. And why is it we should not present a complete Bill? The faculty of authorship is getting very weak, I am afraid, in myself, although many of my Colleagues are not only in the vigour of life, but sufficiently fertile of mind and brain, and I have no doubt that, with our joint authorship, we could have produced a perfectly complete Bill. Why did we not do so? Because, if we had done so, we knew, as well as if the thing had happened, that the Bill must remain a Bill, and would never become an Act. I say this is not a perfect Bill with regard to the franchise. What are the questions we leave out? We do not aim at ideal perfection, and I hope Gentlemen will not force us upon that line; it would be the "Road to Ruin." I have heard that there have been artists and authors who never could satisfy themselves as to the perfection of their picture, or of their diction, as the case may be, and in consequence the picture and the diction have been wasted. . . . No, Sir; ideal perfection is not the true basis of English legislation. We look at the attainable; we look at the practicable; and we have too much of English sense to be drawn away by those sanguine delineations of what might possibly be attained in Utopia, from a path which promises to enable us to effect great good for the people of England. This is not an exhaustive list; but to aim at an ideal franchise might draw in the question of proportional representation, the question of women's suffrage—the question with regard to which my right hon. Friend (Mr. John Bright) has invented a wicked phrase, as he has invented a good many. I call a phrase a wicked phrase when it commits murder, and my right hon. Friend has had the fortune repeatedly to kill a proposal by a phrase. There was once a group of proposals made in a Reform Bill which he at once dubbed "fancy franchises," and by that phrase he killed them all. There is also the question of voting papers; the question of the franchises of the Universities, of the freeman's franchises, of the livery franchise and the burgage franchise; and there is again the principle of whether one man should have more than one vote. There is, in fact, no end to the proposals that might be raised even on the stage of the first of these three great divisions, without touching the other two. Our principle has been to inquire what was practicable; what were the conditions under which we had to move and to act in the present state of Parliament, and of Parliamentary Business. We have heard in former years, and possibly we may hear this year, something about the consequences of deck-loading a ship. We are determined, as far as depends upon us, not to deck-load our Franchise Bill. We consider that we have filled the hold with a good and a sufficient cargo, but the deck-loading of it would be a preliminary to its foundering; and were we with that impression—nay, not merely impression, but with that conviction and knowledge—to encumber our Bill with unnecessary weight, we should be traitors to the cause which we profess to have taken in hand, and we therefore will have nothing to do with giving encouragement to such a policy. As to registration, all I will say is this—that our Bill is framed with the intention of preparing a state of things in which the whole occupation franchise, which, I believe, will be about five-sixths of the franchise, shall be a self-acting franchise, and the labour, anxiety, and expense connected with proof of title, which is, after all, according to our view, the affair of the public and the State rather than of the individual, will, I trust, be got rid of. But, at the same time, our Bill is not a complete Bill in that vital respect, and we look to the introduction of another Bill for the purpose, with which we shall be prepared immediately when the House has supplied us with the basis on which it wishes us to proceed. [Gladstone continues with an extensive evasion on the subject of redistribution of seats, for which he declines to establish more than vague guidelines, holding the matter over until the next session.]

I entreat them [its friends] not to endanger the Bill by additions. This Bill is in no danger from direct opposition. It has some danger to encounter from indirect opposition; but of these dangers from indirect opposition, I for one am not afraid, unless they be aggravated by the addition of dangers which it may have to encounter from friendship. For I do not hesitate to say that it is just as possible for friends to destroy the measure by additions which it will not bear, as it is for enemies. If I may presume to tender advice, it is this—Ask yourselves whether the measure is worth having. What does it do, and what does it do in comparison with what has been done before? In 1832 there was passed what was considered a Magna Charta of British liberties; but that Magna Charta of British liberties added, according to the previous estimate of Lord John Russell, 500,000, while according to the results considerably less than 500,000 were added, to the entire constituency of the three countries. After 1832 we come to 1866. At that time the total constituency of the United Kingdom reached 1,364,000. By the Bills which were passed between 1867 and 1869 that number was raised to 2,448,000. And now, Sir, under the action of the present law the constituency has reached in round numbers what I would call 3,000,000. I will not enter into details; but what is the increase we are going to make? There is a basis of computation; but it is a basis which affords, I admit, ground for conjecture and opinion. That basis of computation is the present ratio in towns, between inhabited houses and the number of town electors. Of course, we have availed ourselves of that basis for the purpose of computation. I have gond into the matter as carefully as I can, and the best results I can attain are these. The Bill, if it passes as presented, will add to the English constituency over 1,300,000 persons. It will add to the Scotch constituency, Scotland being at present rather better provided for in this respect than either of the other countries, over 200,000, and to the Irish constituency over 400,000; or, in the main, to the present aggregate constituency of the United Kingdom taken at 3,000,000, it will add 2,000,000 more, nearly twice as much as was added since 1867, and more than four times as much as was added in 1832. Surely, I say, that is worth doing, that is worth not endangering. Surely that is worth some sacrifice.

This is a measure with results such as I have ventured to sketch them that ought to bring home to the mind of every man favourable to the extension of popular liberty, the solemn question what course he is to pursue in regard to it. I hope the House will look at it as the Liberal Party in 1831 looked at the Reform Bill of that date, and determined that they would waive criticism of minute details, that they would waive particular preferences and predilections, and would look at the broad scope and general effect of the measure. Do that upon this occasion. It is a Bill worth having; and if it is worth having, again I say it is a Bill worth your not endangering. Let us enter into no bye-ways which would lead us off the path marked out straight before us; let us not wander on the hill-tops of speculation; let us not wander into the morasses and fogs of doubt. We are firm in the faith that enfranchisement is a good, that the people may be trusted—that the voters under the Constitution are the strength of the Constitution. What we want in order to carry this Bill, considering as I fully believe that the very large majority of this country are favourable to its principle—what we want in order to carry it is union and union only. What will endanger it is disunion and disunion only. Let us hold firmly together and success will crown our effort. You will, as much as any former Parliament that has conferred great legislative benefits on the nation, have your reward, and "Read your history in a nation's eyes," for you will have deserved it by the benefits you will have conferred. You will have made this strong nation stronger still; stronger by its closer union without; stronger against its foes, if and when it has any foes without; stronger within by union between class and class, and by arraying all classes and all portions of the community in one solid compacted mass round the ancient Throne which it has loved so well, and round a Constitution now to be more than ever powerful, and more than ever free.

22. Conservatism: Disraeli's Platform

THE MORAL rhetoric of Gladstone sounds flat, even fatuous, to the sophisticated twentieth-century ear. His style is out of date, his party dead, his priorities devalued. Benjamin Disraeli, on the other hand, sounds refreshingly modern. His speeches are a trifle ornate, but you could listen to them today. His party survives—even his principles survive after a fashion, and not merely because they tend to be banal. Disraeli himself would still be marked off as odd. He might look high fashion in Carnaby Street but not in Westminster. His perfume and his affected lisp would be no more winning today than they were then. But these things were all aspects of Disraeli's capacity for self-dramatization, and publicity in politics, as for his novels, was the path of success.

Disraeli was not simply an opportunist. He just looked, sounded, and acted that way. He dabbled with an odd sort of radicalism, then with an even more eccentric feudal romanticism. Yet he was a Tory because he had made a simple calculation. That party offered better prospects for the political careerist than did the much more pedigree-conscious Whig connection. Peel's shift to free trade gave him his chance. He led the Tory backwoodsmen in revolt, defended the landed interest, and laid claims, grudgingly conceded, to leadership. The ease with which he dropped protection after the next general issue is some measure of his belief in principle. Lord Stanley, soon to be Earl of Derby, took Disraeli because he had no choice. The shadow of scandal, Dizzy's eccentric past (and present), and his Jewish background militated against his rise. How many novelist-dandies have become Chancellors of the Exchequer?

He displayed little capacity for administration and not much more for executive leadership. He was a political gambler, risking long odds and winning a surprising number of times, although not always in ways that he recognized or appreciated. He was a hustings and floor man, an impressive debater and speaker. He was not only brilliant; he was quick. Still he reacted rather than innovated. He proclaimed "Young England," the movement of enlightened aristocrats aspiring to reunite the two nations—the rich and the poor. But the divided land he found in the bluebooks—the reports of parliamentary committees and royal commissions—of the 1840's, and there is nothing profound about his analysis. Disraeli never accepted liberal, middle-class politics or values, although he practiced both at times. He had a dandy's contempt for the poor and scant respect for the aristocracy he flattered.

He gambled on an urban democratic electorate in 1867, confident that it would vote Tory in gratitude. That proved insufficient, and he was forced to develop a program. Disraeli set forth his party platform in the Crystal Palace speech and the speech at Free Trade Hall in Manchester. It was sound doctrine, calculated simultaneously to reassure restive Tories and to woo the new electorate. He stressed the attachment most Britons felt for the Queen, the Lords, the Church, the Empire. He ticked off the more vulnerable radical criticisms and answered them. These institutions were sound and good and should be sustained. He proposed minimal measures of social welfare as bait for the new mass electorate—artisans' housing, control of food adulteration, public health, and a trade union measure to capture those annoyed by Gladstone's failure to legalize peaceful picketing. Thanks in part to John Gorst's constituency organization and to Richard Cross's herculean labors at the Home Office, Disraeli won his election in 1874 and redeemed most of his election pledges.

Power, in his own phrase, came too late to please him. For he did have beliefs, not terribly encouraging ones. Metternich impressed him in 1848. Disraeli felt his world was spinning toward catastrophe. His mission was to fight a rearguard action against the collapse of civilization. As in his own life, he could always assert appearances against the facts—and occasionally even make them come true. Proclaiming Victoria Empress of India somehow confirmed Britain's primacy in the world. Peace with honor at Berlin was Bismarck's doing and Disraeli's fête.

Recommended Reading

Fortunately ROBERT BLAKE's *Disraeli* (London, 1966), makes it unnecessary to bewail the shortage of sensible studies. D. C. SOMERVELL, *Disraeli and Gladstone* (New York, 1926), did a masterful job of condensing and balancing the old tombstone biographies: three volumes by MORLEY on Gladstone and six by MONEYPENNY and BOUCKLE on Disraeli. A. J. P. TAYLOR has an incisive essay on Disraeli in *Englishmen and Others* (London, 1956), reprinted in N. CANTOR and M. WERTHMAN, *The English Tradition;* and CLYDE J. LEWIS takes Disraeli's ideas and beliefs quite seriously in "Theory and Expediency in the Policy of Disraeli," *Victorian Studies*, Vol. IV (1961), pp. 237–258.

SOURCE: Benjamin Disraeli, "Speech at Manchester, Free Trade Hall, 3 April 1872," *The Times*, April 4, 1872.

Gentlemen, . . . Our opponents assure us that the Conservative party have no political programme; and, therefore, they must look with much satisfaction to one whom you honour tonight by considering him the leader and representative of your opinions when he comes forward, at your invitation, to express to you what that programme is. The Conservative party are accused of having no programme of policy. If by a programme is meant a plan to despoil Churches and plunder landlords, I admit we have no programme. If by a programme is meant a policy which assails or menaces every institution and every interest, every class and every calling in the country, I admit we have no programme. But if to have a policy with distinct ends, and these such as most deeply interest the great body of the nation, be a becoming programme for a political party, then, I contend, we have an adequate programme, and one which, here or elsewhere, I shall always be prepared to assert and to vindicate.

Gentlemen, the programme of the Conservative party is to maintain the Constitution of the country. I have not come down to Manchester to deliver an essay on the English Constitution; but when the banner of Republicanism is unfurled—when the fundamental principles of our institutions are controverted—I think, perhaps, it may not be inconvenient that I should make some few practical remarks upon the character of our Constitution—upon that monarchy, limited by the co-ordinate authority of Estates of the realm, which, under the title of Queen, Lords and Commons, has contributed so greatly to the prosperity of this country, and with the maintenance of which I believe that prosperity is bound up.

Gentlemen, since the settlement of that Constitution, now nearly two centuries ago, England has never experienced a revolution, though there is no country in which there has been so continuous and such considerable change. How is this? Because the wisdom of your forefathers placed the prize of supreme power without the sphere of human passions. Whatever the struggle of parties, whatever the strife of factions, whatever the excitement and exultation of the public mind, there has always been something in this country round which all classes and parties could rally, representing the majesty of the law, the administration of justice, and involving, at the same time, the security for every man's rights, and the fountain of honour.

Now, gentlemen, it is well clearly to comprehend what is meant by a country not having a revolution for two centuries. It means, for that space, the unbroken exercise and enjoyment of the ingenuity of man. It means, for that space, the continuous application of the discoveries of science to his comfort and convenience. It means the accumulation of capital, the elevation of labour, the establishment of those admirable factories which cover your district, the unwearied improvement of the cultivation of the land, which has extracted from a somewhat churlish soil harvests more exuberant than those furnished by lands nearer to the sun. It means the continuous order which is the only parent of personal liberty and political right.

And you owe all these, gentlemen, to the Throne. There is another powerful and most beneficial influence which is also exercised by the Crown. Gentlemen, I am a party man. I believe that, without party, Parliamentary government is impossible. I look upon Parliamentary government as the noblest government in the world, and certainly the one most suited to England. But without the discipline of political connexion, animated by the principle of private honour, I feel certain that a popular Assembly would sink before the power of the corruption of a Minister. Yet, gentlemen, I am not blind to the faults of party government. It has one great defect. Party has a tendency to warp the intelligence, and there is no Minister, however resolved he may be in treating a great public question, who does not find some difficulty in emancipating himself from the traditional prejudice on which he has long acted. It is, therefore, a great merit in our Constitution that before a Minister introduces a measure to Parliament, he must submit it to an intelligence superior to all party, and entirely free from influence of that character. I know it will be said, gentlemen, that, however beautiful in theory, the personal influence of the Sovereign is now absorbed in the responsibility of the Minister. Gentlemen, I think you will find there is great fallacy in this view. The principles of the English Constitution do not contemplate the absence of personal influence on the part of the Sovereign; and if they did, the principles of human nature would prevent the fulfilment of such a theory.

Gentlemen, I need not tell you that I am now making on this subject abstract observations of general application to our institutions and our history. But take the case of a Sovereign of England who enjoys a long reign—take an instance like that of George III. From the earliest moment of his accession that Sovereign is placed in constant communication with the most able statesmen of the period, and of all parties. Even with average ability it is impossible not to perceive that such a Sovereign must soon attain a great mass of political information and political experience. Information and experience, gentlemen, whether they are possessed by a Sovereign or by the humblest of his subjects, are irresistible in life. No man with the vast responsibility that devolves upon an English Minister can afford to treat with indifference a suggestion that has not occurred to him, or information with which he had not been previously supplied. But, gentlemen, pursue this view of the subject. The longer the reign, the influence of that Sovereign must proportionately increase. All the illustrious statesmen who served his youth disappear. A new generation of public servants rises up. There is a critical conjuncture in affairs—a moment of perplexities and peril. Then it is that the Sovereign can appeal to a similar state of affairs that occurred perhaps 30 years before. When all are in doubt among his servants he can quote the advice that was given by the illustrious men of his early years, and though he may maintain himself within the strictest limits of the Constitution, who can suppose when such information and such suggestions are made by the most exalted person in the country that they can be without effect? No, gentlemen; a Minister who could venture to treat such influence with indifference would not be a Constitutional Minister, but an arrogant idiot.

Gentlemen, the influence of the Crown is not confined merely to political affairs. England is a domestic country. Here the home is revered, and the hearth is sacred. The nation is represented by a family—the Royal Family; and if that family is educated with a sense of responsibility and a sentiment of public duty, it is difficult to exaggerate the salutary influence they may exercise over a nation. It is not merely an influence upon manners; it is not merely that they are a model for refinement and for good taste—they affect the heart as well as the intelligence of the people; and in the hour of public adversity, or in the anxious conjuncture of public affairs, the nation rallies round the Family and the Throne, and its spirit is animated and sustained by the expression of public affection.

Gentlemen, there is yet one other remark that I would make upon our Monarchy, though, had it not been for recent circumstances, I should have refrained from doing so. An attack has recently been made upon the Throne on account of the costliness of the institution. Gentlemen, I shall not dwell upon the fact that if the people of England appreciate the Monarchy, as I believe they do, it would be painful to them that their Royal and representative family should not be maintained with becoming dignity, or fill in the public eye a position inferior to some of the nobles of the land. Nor will I insist upon what is unquestionably the fact, that the revenues of the Crown estates, on which our Sovereign might live with as much right as the Duke of Bedford or the Duke of Northumberland has to his estates, are now paid into the public Exchequer. All this, upon the present occasion, I am not going to insist upon. What I now say is this, that there is no Sovereignty of any first-rate state which costs so little to the people as the Sovereignty of England.

[After observing that the Prime Minister and the President of the United States draw approximately the same salary, "the income of a second-class professional man," Disraeli develops the case that the United States equivalent to the Civil List is between £700,000 and £800,000, while the British Civil List is merely £300,000.]

Gentlemen, I have not time to pursue this interesting theme, otherwise I could show you that you have still but imperfectly ascertained the cost of Sovereignty in a Republic. But, gentlemen, I cannot resist giving you one further illustration. The government of this country is considerably carried on by the aid of Royal Commissions. So great is the increase of public business that it would be probably impossible for a Minister to carry on affairs without this assistance. The Queen of England can command for these objects the services of the most experienced statesmen, and men of the highest position in society. If necessary, she can summon to them distinguished scholars or men most celebrated in science and in art; and she receives from them services that are unpaid. They are only too proud to be described in the Commission as her Majesty's "trusty Councillors"; and if any member of these Commissions performs some transcendent services, both of thought and of labour, he is munificently rewarded by a public distinction conferred upon him by the Fountain of Honour. Gentlemen, the Government of the United States has, I believe, not less availed itself of the services of Commissions than the Government of the United Kingdom, but, in a country where there is no Fountain of Honour, every member of these Commissions is paid.

Gentlemen, I trust I have now made some suggestions to you respecting the Monarchy of England which at least may be so far serviceable that when we are separated they may not be altogether without advantage; and now, gentlemen, I would say something on the subject of the House of Lords. It is not merely the authority of the Throne that is now disputed, but the character and influence of the House of Lords that are held up by some to public disregard. Gentlemen, I shall not stop for a moment to offer you any proof of the advantage of a Second Chamber; and for this reason. That subject has been discussed now for a century, ever since the establishment of the Government of the United States, and all great authorities, American, German, French, Italian, have agreed in this, that a Representative Government is impossible without a Second Chamber. And it has been, especially of late, maintained by great political writers in all countries that the repeated failure of what is called the French Republic is mainly to be ascribed to its not having a Second Chamber. But, gentlemen, however anxious foreign countries have been to enjoy this advantage, that anxiety has only been equalled by the difficulty which they have found in fulfilling their object. How is a Second Chamber to be constituted? By nominees of the Sovereign power? What influence can be exercised by a Chamber of nominees? Are they to be bound by popular election? In what manner are they to be elected? If by the same constituency as the popular body, what claim have they, under such circumstances, to criticize or control the decisions of that body? If they are to be elected by a more select body, qualified by a higher franchise, there immediately occurs the objection, why should the majority be governed by the minority? The United States of America were fortunate in having a solution of this difficulty; but the United States of America had elements to deal with which never occurred before, and never probably will occur again, because they formed their illustrious Senate from the materials that were offered them by the 37 States.

We, gentlemen, have the House of Lords, an assembly which has historically developed and periodically adapted itself to the wants and necessities of the times. What, gentlemen, is the first quality which is required in a Second Chamber? Without doubt, independence. What is the basic foundation of independence? Without doubt, property. The Prime Minister of England has only recently told you, and I believe he spoke quite accurately, that the average income of the members of the House of Lords is 20,000 *l.* a year. Of course there are some who have more and some who have less; but the influence of a public assembly, so far as property is concerned, depends upon its aggregate property, which, in the present case, is a revenue of 9,000,000 *l.* a year. But, gentlemen, you must look to the nature of this property. It is visible property, and therefore it is responsible property, which every ratepayer in the room knows to his cost. But, gentlemen, it is not only visible property; it is, generally speaking, territorial property; and one of the elements of territorial property is that it is representative. . . .

But, gentlemen, the charge against the House of Lords is that the dignities are hereditary, and we are told that if we have a House of Peers they should be peers for life. There are great authorities in favour of this. . . . The question arises, who is most responsible—a peer for life whose dignities are not descendible, or a peer for life whose dignities are hereditary? Now, gentlemen, a peer for life is in a very strong position. He says, "Here I am; I have got power and I will exercise it." I have no doubt that, on the whole, a peer for life would exercise it for what he deemed was the public good. Let us hope that. But, after all, he might and could exercise it according to his own will. Nobody can call him to account; he is independent of everybody. But a peer for life whose dignities descend is in a very different position. He has every inducement to study public opinion, and, when he believes it just, to yield; because he naturally feels that, if the order to which he belongs is in constant collision with public opinion the chances are that his dignities will not descend to his posterity.

Therefore, gentlemen, I am not prepared myself to believe that a solution of any difficulties in the public mind on this subject is to be found by creating peers for life. . . . Whether it be the recollection of that performance or not, I confess I am inclined to believe that an English gentleman, born to business, managing his own estate, administering the affairs of his county, mixing with all classes of his fellow-men, now in the hunting field, now in the Railway Direction, unaffected, unostentatious, proud of his ancestors, if they have contributed to the greatness of our common country—on the whole more likely to form a senator agreeable to English opinion and English taste than any substitute that has yet been produced.

Gentlemen, let me make one observation more, on the subject of the House of Lords, before I conclude. There is some advantage in political experience. I remember the time when there was a similar outcry against the House of Lords, but much more intense and powerful; and, gentlemen, it arose from the same cause. A Liberal Government had been installed in office, with an immense Liberal majority. They proposed some violent measures. The House of Lords modified some, delayed others, and some they threw out. Instantly there was a cry to abolish or to reform the House of Lords, and the greatest popular orator that probably ever existed was sent on a pilgrimage over England to excite the people in favour of this opinion. What happened? That happened, gentle-

men, which may happen to-morrow. There was a dissolution of
Parliament. The great Liberal majority vanished. The balance of
parties was restored. It was discovered that the House of Lords had
behind them at least half of the English people. We heard no more
cries for their abolition or their reform, and before two years more
passed England was really governed by the House of Lords under
the wise influence of the Duke of Wellington and the commanding
eloquence of Lyndhurst: and such was the enthusiasm of the
nation in favour of the Second Chamber that at every public
meeting its health was drunk, with the additional sentiment for
which we are indebted to one of the most distinguished members
that ever represented the House of Commons, "Thank God, there
is the House of Lords."

Gentlemen, you will perhaps not be surprised that, having made
some remarks upon the Monarchy and the House of Lords, I
should say something respecting that House in which I have liter-
ally passed the greater part of my life and to which I am devotedly
attached. It is not likely, therefore, that I should say anything to
depreciate the legitimate position and influence of the House of
Commons. Gentlemen, it is said that the diminished power of the
Throne and the assailed authority of the House of Lords are owing
to the increased power of the House of Commons, and the new
position which of late years, and especially during the last 40 years,
it has assumed in the English Constitution. Gentlemen, the main
power of the House of Commons depends upon its command over
the public purse and its control of the public expenditure; and if
that power is possessed by a party which has a large majority in the
House of Commons, the influence of the House of Commons is
proportionately increased, and, under some circumstances, becomes more predominant. But, gentlemen, this power of the House
of Commons is not a power which has been created by any Reform
Act, from the days of Lord Grey in 1832 to 1867. It is the power
which the House of Commons has enjoyed for centuries—which
it has frequently asserted and sometimes even tyrannically asserted.

Gentlemen, the House of Commons represents the constituencies
of England, and I am here to show you that no addition to the
elements of that constituency has placed the House of Commons in
a different position with regard to the Throne and the House of
Lords from that it has always constitutionally occupied. Gentlemen, we speak now on this subject with great advantage. We

recently have had published authentic documents upon this matter which are highly instructive. We have, for example, just published the Census of Great Britain, and we are now in possession of the last registration of voters for the United Kingdom. Gentlemen, it appears that by the Census the population at this time is about 32,000,000. It is shown by the last registration that, after making the usual deductions for deaths, removals, double entries, and so on, the constituency of the United Kingdom may be put at 2,300,000. So, gentlemen, it at once appears that there are 30,000,000 people in this country who are as much represented by the House of Lords as by the House of Commons, and who, for the protection of their rights, must depend upon them and the majesty of the Throne.

[Disraeli then proceeds to contrast Grey's Reform Act of 1832 unfavorably with his own of 1867. Grey "fortified the legitimate influence of the aristocracy, and accorded to the middle classes great and salutary franchises" but cut the working classes out entirely, even abolishing the ancient franchises under which some workingmen voted in a few constituencies. This was the origin of Chartism. England trembled in 1848; but with Disraeli's reform of 1867, not a handful of men would have risen for the Commune of 1871.]

But, gentlemen, the Constitution of England is not merely a Constitution in State, it is a Constitution in Church and State. The wisest Sovereigns and statesmen have ever been anxious to connect authority with religion—some to increase their power, some, perhaps, to mitigate its exercise. But the same difficulty has been experienced in effecting this union which has been experienced in forming a Second Chamber—either the spiritual power has usurped upon the civil and established a sacerdotal society, or the civil power has invaded successfully the rights of the spiritual and the ministers of religion have been degraded into stipendaries of the State and instruments of the Government. In England we accomplish this great result by an alliance between Church and State, between two originally independent parties. I will not go into the history of that alliance, which is rather a question for those archaeological societies which occasionally amuse and instruct the people of this city. Enough for me that the union was made and has contributed for centuries to the civilization of this country.

Gentlemen, there is the same assault against the Church of

England and the union between the State and the Church as there is against the Monarchy and against the House of Lords. It is said that the existence of Nonconformity proves that the Church is a failure. I draw from these premises an exactly contrary conclusion; and I maintain that to have secured a national profession of faith with the unlimited enjoyment of private judgment in matters spiritual is the solution of the most difficult problem and one of the triumphs of civilization. It is said that the existence of parties in the Church also proves its incompetence. On that matter, too, I entertain a contrary opinion. Parties have always existed in the Church, and some have appealed to them as arguments in favour of its Divine institution, because, in the services and doctrines of the Church have been found representatives of every mood in the human mind. Those who are influenced by ceremonies and consolation in forms which secure to them "the beauty of holiness." Those who are not satisfied except with enthusiasm and in its ministrations the exultations they require while others who believe that the "anchor of faith" can never be safely moored except in the dry sands of reason find a religion within the pale of the Church which can boast of its irrefragable logic and its irresistible evidence.

Gentlemen, I am inclined sometimes to believe that those who advocate the abolition of the union between Church and State have not carefully considered the consequences of such a course. The Church is a powerful corporation of many millions of Her Majesty's subjects, with a consumate organization and wealth which in the aggregate is vast. Restricted and controlled by the State, so powerful a corporation may be only fruitful of public advantage, but it becomes a great question what might be the consequence of the severing of the controlling ties between these two bodies. The State would be enfeebled, but the Church would probably be strengthened. Whether that is a result to be desired is a grave question for all men. For my own part, I am bound to say that I doubt whether it would be favourable to the cause of civil and religious liberty. I know that there is a common idea that if the union between Church and State was severed, the wealth of the Church would revert to the State; but it would be well to remember that the great proportion of ecclesiastical property is the property of individuals. Take, for example, the fact that the great mass of Church patronage is patronage in the hands of private persons. That you could not touch without compensation to the patrons. And in the present state of the public mind on the subject, there is very little doubt that there would be scarcely a patron in England—irrespective of other aid the Church would receive—who would not dedicate his compensation to the spiritual wants of his neighbours. . . .

Gentlemen, you are well acquainted in this city with this controversy [the Anglican Church role in national education]. It was in this city—I don't know whether it was not in this hall—that that remarkable meeting was held of the Nonconformists to effect important alterations in the Education Act, and you are acquainted with the discussion in Parliament which arose in consequence of that meeting. Gentlemen, I have due and great respect for the Nonconformist body. I acknowledge their services to their country, and though I believe that the political reasons which mainly called them into existence have entirely ceased, it is impossible not to treat with consideration a body which has been so eminent for its conscience, its learning, and its patriotism; but I must express my mortification that, from a feeling of envy or of pique, the Nonconformist body, rather than assist the Church in their great enterprise, should absolutely have become the partisans of a merely secular education. I believe myself, gentlemen, that without the recognition of a superintending Providence in the affairs of this world all national education will be disastrous, and I feel confident that it is impossible to stop at that mere recognition. Religious education is demanded by the nation generally and by the instincts of human nature. I should like to see the Church and Nonconformists work together; but I trust, whatever may be the result, the country will stand by the Church in its efforts to maintain the religious education of the people.

Gentlemen, I foresee yet trials for the Church of England; but I am confident in its future. I am confident in its future because I believe there is now a very general feeling that to be national it must be comprehensive. I will not use the word "broad," because it is an epithet applied to a system with which I have no sympathy. But I would wish Churchmen, and especially the clergy, always to remember that in our "Father's Home there are many mansions," and I believe that the comprehensive spirit is perfectly consistent with the maintenance of formularies and the belief in dogmas without which I hold no practical religion can exist.

Gentlemen, I have now endeavoured to express to you my general views upon the most important subjects that can interest Englishmen. They are subjects upon which, in my mind, a man should speak with frankness and clearness to his countrymen, and although I do not come down here to make a party speech, I am compelled to say that the manner in which these subjects are treated by the leading subject of this realm is to me most unsatisfactory. Although the Prime Minister of England is always writing letters and making speeches, and particularly on these topics, he seems to me ever to send forth an "uncertain sound." If a member of Parliament announced himself to be a Republican, Mr. Gladstone takes the earliest opportunity of describing him as "a fellow worker" in public life. If an inconsiderate multitude calls for the abolition or reform of the House of Lords, Mr. Gladstone says that is no easy task, and that he must think once or twice, or perhaps even thrice, before he can undertake it. If your neighbour the member for Bradford, Mr. [Edward] Miall, brings forward a motion in the House of Commons for the severance of Church and State, Mr. Gladstone assures Mr. Miall with the utmost courtesy that he believes the opinion of the House of Commons to be against him; but that if Mr. Miall wishes to influence the House of Commons he must address the people out of doors; whereupon Mr. Miall immediately calls a public meeting, and alleges as its cause the advice he has just received from the Prime Minister.

But, gentlemen, after all, the test of political institutions is the condition of the country whose fortunes they regulate; and I do not mean to evade that test. You are inhabitants of an island of no colossal size; which, geographically speaking, was intended by nature as the appendage of some Continental Empire—either of the Gauls and Franks on the other side of the Channel, or of Teutons and Scandinavians beyond the German Sea. Such indeed, and for a long period, was your early history. You were invaded, you were pillaged and you were conquered; yet among all these disgraces and vicissitudes there was gradually formed that English race which has brought about a very different state of affairs. Instead of being invaded, your land is proverbially and the only "inviolate land"—"the inviolate land of the sage and free." Instead of being plundered, you have attracted to your shores all the capital of the world. Instead of being conquered, your flag floats on many waters, and your standard waves in either zone. It may be said that these achievements are due to the race that inhabited the land, and not to its institutions.

Gentlemen, in political institutions are the embodied experiences of a race. You have established a society of classes which give vigour and variety to life. But no class possesses a single privilege, and all are equal before the law. You possess a real aristocracy, open to all who deserve to enter it. You have not merely a middle class, but a hierarchy of middle classes, in which every degree of wealth, refinement, industry, energy, and enterprise is duly represented.

And now, gentlemen, what is the condition of the great body of the people? In the first place, gentlemen, they have for centuries been in the full enjoyment of that which no other country in Europe has ever completely attained—complete rights of personal freedom. In the second place, there has been a gradual, and therefore a wise, distribution on a large scale of political rights. Speaking with reference to the industries of this great part of the country, I can personally contrast it with the condition of the working classes 40 years ago. In that period they have attained two results—the raising of their wages and the diminution of their toil. Increased means and increased leisure are the two civilizers of man. That the working classes of Lancashire and Yorkshire have proved not unworthy of these boons may be easily maintained; but their progress and elevation have been during this interval wonderfully aided and assisted by three causes, which are not so distinctly attributable to their own energies. The first is the revolution in locomotion, which has opened the world to the working man, which has enlarged the horizon of his experience, increased his knowledge of nature and of art, and added immensely to the salutary recreation, amusement, and pleasure of his existence. The second cause is the cheap postage, the moral benefits of which cannot be exaggerated. And the third is that unshackled press which has furnished him with endless sources of instruction, information, and amusement.

Gentlemen, if you would permit me, I would now make an observation upon another class of the labouring population. This is not a civic assembly, although we meet in a city. That was for convenience, but the invitation which I received was to meet the county and all the borough[s] of Lancashire; and I wish to make a few observations upon the condition of the agricultural labourer.

That is a subject which now greatly attracts public attention. And, in the first place, to prevent any misconception, I beg to express my opinion that an agricultural labourer has as much right to combine for the bettering of his condition as a manufacturing labourer or worker in metals. If the causes of his combination are natural—that is to say, if they arise from his own feelings and from the necessities of his own condition, the combination will end in results mutually beneficial to employers and employed. If, on the other hand, it is factitious and he is acted upon by extraneous influences and extraneous ideas, the combination will produce, I fear, much loss and misery both to employers and employed; and after a time he will find himself in a similar or a worse position.

Gentlemen, in my opinion the farmers of England, as a body, cannot afford to pay higher wages than they do, and those who will answer me by saying that they must find their ability by the deduction of rents are, I think, involving themselves with economic laws which may prove too difficult for them to cope with. The profits of a farmer are very moderate. The interest upon capital invested in the land is the smallest that any property furnishes. The farmer will have his profits and the investor in land will have his interest, even though they may be obtained at the cost of changing the mode of the cultivation of the country.

Gentlemen, I should deeply regret to see the tillage of this country reduced, and a recurrence to pasture take place. I should regret it principally on account of the agricultural labourers themselves. Their new friends call them Hodge, and describe them as a solid race. I must say that, from my experience of them, they are sufficiently shrewd and open to reason. I would say to them with confidence, as the great Athenian said to the Spartan who rudely assailed him, "Strike, but hear me." First, a change in the cultivation of the soil of this country would be very injurious to the labouring class, and, secondly, I am of opinion that that class instead of being stationary have made, if not as much progress as the manufacturing class, very considerable progress during the last 40 years. Many persons write and speak about the agricultural labourer with not so perfect a knowledge of his condition as is desirable. They treat him always as a human being who in every part of the country finds himself in an identical condition. Now, on the contrary, there is no class of labourers in which there is greater variety of condition than that of the agricultural labourers.

It changes from north to south, from east to west, and from county to county, where there is an alteration of soil and of configuration. . . .

Gentlemen, I would not dare to maintain that there is nothing to be done to increase the wellbeing of the working classes of this country. . . . There is not a single class in the country which is not susceptible of improvement, and that makes the life and animation of our society. But in all we do we must remember . . . that much depends upon the working classes themselves; and what I know of the working classes in Lancashire makes me sure that they will respond to this appeal. Much also may be expected from that sympathy between classes which is a distinctive feature of the present day; and, in the last place, no inconsiderable results may be obtained by judicious and prudent legislation. But, gentlemen, in attempting to legislate upon social matters the great object is to be practical—to have before us some distinct aims and some distinct means by which they can be accomplished.

Gentlemen, I think public attention as regards these matters ought to be concentrated upon sanitary legislation. That is a wide subject, and, if properly treated, comprises almost every consideration which has a just claim upon legislative interference. Pure air, pure water, the inspection of unhealthy habitations, the adulteration of food, these and many kindred matters may be legitimately dealt with by the Legislature; and I am bound to say the Legislature is not idle upon them; for we have at this time two important measures before Parliament on the subject. One—by a late colleague of mine, Sir Charles Adderley—is a large and comprehensive measure, founded upon a sure basis, for it consolidates all existing public Acts and improves them. A prejudice has been raised against that proposal, by stating that it interferes with the private Acts of the great towns. I take this opportunity of contradicting that. The Bill of Sir Charles Adderley does not touch the Acts of the great towns. It only allows them if they think fit to avail themselves of its new provisions. The other measure, by the Government, is of a partial character. What it comprises is good, so far as it goes, but it shrinks from that bold consolidation of existing Acts which I think one of the great merits of Sir Charles Adderley's Bill, which permits us to become acquainted with how much may be done in favour of sanitary improvement by existing provisions. Gentlemen,

I cannot impress upon you too strongly my conviction of the importance of the Legislature and society uniting together in favour of these important results. A great scholar and a great wit 300 years ago said that, in his opinion, there was a great mistake in the Vulgate, which, as you all know, is the Latin translation of the Holy Scriptures, and that, instead of saying "Vanity of vanities, all is vanity—Vanitas vanitatum, omnia vanitas"—the wise and witty King really said "Sanitas sanitatum, omnia sanitas." Gentlemen, it is impossible to overrate the importance of the subject. After all, the first consideration of a Minister should be the health of the people. A land may be covered with historic trophies, with museums of science and galleries of art, with Universities and with libraries; the people may be civilized and ingenious; the country may be even famous in the annals and action of the world, but, gentlemen, if the population every ten years decreases, and the stature of the race every ten years diminishes, the history of that country will soon be the history of the past.

Gentlemen, it will not do for me—considering the time I have already occupied, and there are still some subjects of importance that must be touched—to dwell upon any of the other similar topics of which there is a rich abundance. I doubt not there is in this hall more than one farmer who has been alarmed by the suggestion that his agricultural machinery should be taxed. I doubt not there is in this hall more than one publican who remembers that last year an Act of Parliament was introduced to denounce him as a "sinner." I doubt not there are in this hall a widow and an orphan who remember the profligate proposition to plunder their lonely heritage. But, gentlemen, as time advanced it was not difficult to perceive that extravagance was being substituted for energy by the Government. The unnatural stimulus was subsiding. Their paroxysms ended in prostration. Some took refuge in melancholy, and their eminent chief alternated between a menace and a sigh. As I sat opposite the Treasury Bench the Ministers reminded me of one of those marine landscapes not very unusual on the coasts of South America. You behold a range of exhausted volcanoes. Not a flame flickers on a single pallid crest. But the situation is still dangerous. There are occasional earthquakes, and ever and anon the dark rumbling of the sea.

But, gentlemen, there is one other topic on which I must touch.

If the management of our domestic affairs has been founded upon a principle of violence, that certainly cannot be alleged against the management of our external relations. I know the difficulty of addressing a body of Englishmen on these topics. The very phrase "foreign affairs" makes the Englishman convinced that I am about to treat of subjects with which he has no concern. Unhappily, the relations of England to the rest of the world, which are "foreign affairs," are the matters which most influence his lot. Upon them depends the increase or reduction of taxation. Upon them depends the enjoyment or the embarrassment of his industry. And yet, though so momentous are the consequences of the mismanagement of our foreign relations, no one thinks of them till the mischief occurs, and then it is found how the most vital consequences have been occasioned by mere inadvertence.

I will illustrate this point by two anecdotes. Since I have been in public life there has been for this country a great calamity and there is a great danger, and both might have been avoided. The calamity was the Crimean War. You know what were the consequences of the Crimean War—a great addition to your debt, an enormous addition to your taxation, a cost more precious than your treasure,—the best blood of England. Half a million of men, I believe, perished in that great undertaking. Nor are the evil consequences of that war adequately described by what I have said. All the disorders and disturbances of Europe, those immense armaments that are an incubus on national industry and the great obstacle to progressive civilization, may be traced and justly attributed to the Crimean War. And yet the Crimean War need never have occurred. . . .

The great danger is the present state of our relations with the United States. When I acceded to office, I did so, so far as regarded the United States of America, with some advantage. During the whole of the Civil War in America both my noble friend near me and I had maintained a strict and fair neutrality. This was fully appreciated by the Government of the United States, and they expressed their wish that with our aid the settlement of all differences between the two Governments should be accomplished. . . . There is before us every prospect of the same incompetence that distinguished our negotiations respecting the independence of the Black Sea; and I fear that there is every chance that that incompetence will be sealed by our ultimately acknowledging those indirect claims of the United States, which, both as regards principle and practical results, are fraught with the utmost danger to this country.

Gentlemen, don't suppose, because I counsel firmness and decision at the right moment, that I am of that school of statesmen who are favourable to a turbulent and oppressive diplomacy. I have resisted it during a great part of my life. I am not unaware that the relations of England to Europe have undergone a vast change during the century that has just elapsed. The relations of England to Europe are not the same as they were in the days of Lord Chatham or Frederick the Great. The Queen of England has become the Sovereign of the most powerful of Oriental States. On the other side of the globe there are now establishments belonging to her, teeming with wealth and population, which will, in due time, exercise their influence over the distribution of power. The old establishments of this country, now the United States of America, throw their lengthening shades over the Atlantic, and mix with European waters. These are vast and novel elements in the distribution of power. I acknowledge that the policy of England with respect to Europe should be a policy of reserve, but a proud reserve; and, in answer to those statesmen—those mistaken statesmen who have intimated the decay of the power of England and the decline of its resources, I express here my confident conviction that there never was a moment in our history when the power of England was so great and her resources so vast and inexhaustible. And yet, gentlemen, it is not merely our fleets and armies, our powerful artillery, our accumulated capital, and our unlimited credit on which I so much depend, as upon that unbroken spirit of her people, which I believe was never prouder of the Imperial country to which they belong.

Gentlemen, it is to that spirit that I above all things trust. I look upon the people of Lancashire as a fair representative of the people of England, I think the manner in which they have invited me here, locally a stranger, to receive the expression of their cordial sympathy, and only because they recognize some effort on my part to maintain the greatness of their country, is evidence of the spirit of the land. I must express to you again my deep sense of the generous manner in which you have welcomed me, and in which you have permitted me to express to you my views upon public affairs.

Proud of your confidence and encouraged by your sympathy, I
now deliver to you, as my last words, the cause of the Tory Party,
of the English Constitution, and of the British Empire.

23.   The Limitations of Liberalism:
John Bright

THERE is no representative Victorian liberal just as there is no precise
body of doctrine that can be called Liberal. Victorian liberalism was an
ad hoc mixture of ideology, morality, and self-interest. John Bright
(1811–89) was atypical but representative. He was the second generation of successful new men. Bright knew the Rochdale world of
industry and commerce, but his ambitions lay far beyond. Like many
contemporaries of advanced views, Bright was propelled into politics
by religion. From his opposition to church rates in the 1830's to his
support of the atheist Charles Bradlaugh in the 1880's, this distinguished Quaker was found in the vanguard of the campaign for religious liberty and disestablishment. Bright was a pacifist, and his
principles cost him dearly during the Crimean War. He was a paragon
of respectability; but his role in the campaign to repeal the corn laws
in the 1830's and 1840's, and his leadership of the Reform League to
democratize the urban franchise in 1866–67, show a man much involved in class war.

Class war—if one can use the term without Marxian overtones—was
a Jacobin legacy to the politics of the emerging Victorian middle
classes. The respectable and substantial gained the franchise in 1832,
but they discovered that they had the trappings rather than the substance of political power. Thus the campaign against the corn laws, the
protective tariff on English agriculture. Economic self-interest was less
important than the middle-class sense of social inferiority. John Bright
partook of this sense of grievance. He believed that the middle and the
lower classes should make common claims against the traditional ruling
orders. But the lower classes had their own claims and pretensions,
which did not square with middle-class interests or ambitions. Bright,
in his letter to the workingmen of Rochdale, addresses himself directly
to the question. He argues that the differences between masters and
men are more apparent than real, that the actual conflict in society is
between those who work for their living and those who do not, the
latter maintaining their privileges by a tax on workingmen's bread.

George Jacob Holyoake, one of the more impressive and articulate
artisan radicals, saw a different John Bright from the perspective of

later years. Bright had always been a champion of the elimination of privilege; he demanded equality of opportunity. But although he believed in political democracy, he abhorred social democracy. He became a Conservative ostensibly on the issue of Irish home rule—in fact in reaction to the growing collectivism of liberalism. Holyoake understood this shift and tension much better than many who remained staunch Liberals—Gladstone and Morley, for example. And Holyoake addressed himself to what he called the limitations of liberalism, its insufficiency in the coming age of mass politics.

Recommended Reading

Among other titles, consult H. AUSUBEL, *John Bright* (New York, 1966); G. M. TREVELYAN, *John Bright* (Boston, 1913); M. R. D. FOOT, *Gladstone and Liberalism* (London, 1952).

SOURCES: Document A; John Bright, "To the Working Men of Rochdale [August 1842]," *The Public Letters of John Bright* London, 1855), pp. 334–340. Document B: George Jacob Holyoake, "Quite a New View of John Bright (1850–1889)," *Sixty Years of an Agitator's Life* (London, 1893), Vol. II, pp. 577–583.

A. John Bright to the Workingmen of Rochdale, August 1842

A deep sympathy with you in your present circumstances induces me to address you. Listen and reflect, even though you may not approve. You are suffering—you have long suffered. Your wages have for many years declined, and your position has gradually and steadily become worse. Your sufferings have naturally produced discontent, and you have turned eagerly to almost any scheme which gave hope of relief.

Your fellow-workmen in Ashton and Oldham turned out for an advance of wages; they invaded your town, and compelled you to turn out. Some of you, doubtless, were willing, but many of you were reluctant to join them. They urged you to treat the men of Bacup and Todmorden as they had treated you. They told you that you had no courage, and that you would be unworthy the good opinion of your fellow-workmen if you refused to act towards others as they had acted towards you. You became an invading force. You visited the peaceful villages of Bacup and Todmorden, and compelled your fellow-workmen to cease their labour. You were regardless of the sufferings you were bringing on

their wives and children; you relentlessly, and contrary to every
principle of justice and freedom, deprived them of bread! You
have had many meetings to deliberate on your position and prospects. An advance of wages to the rate paid in 1840 and ten hours
per day were the demands you were urged to make. But when the
turning-out in this district was completed, and you had become
evicted, these demands were abandoned, and you were urged to
refuse to work until the charter became law.

Many of you know full well that neither Act of Parliament nor
act of a multitude can keep up wages. You know that trade has
long been bad, and with a bad trade wages cannot rise. If you are
resolved to compel an advance of wages, you cannot compel
manufacturers to give you employment. Trade must yield a profit,
or it will not long be carried on; and an advance of wages now
would destroy profit. You have a strong case now in the condition
of the colliers and calico-printers. The wages of the colliers are not
so low as those in many other trades, but they suffer because they
are only employed two or three days per week. The wages of
calico-printers have only been reduced *once* during twenty or
thirty years, and yet they are now earning as little as any class of
workmen, having not more than two or three days' work per
week. If they combined to double the rate of wages, they would
gain nothing, unless they could secure increased regular employment. Your attempt to raise wages cannot succeed. Such attempts
have always failed in the end; and yours must fail.

To diminish the hours of labour at this time is equally impossible; it is, in effect, a rise of wages, and must also fail. You can
have no rise of wages without a greater demand for labour; and
you cannot dictate what hours you will work until workmen are
scarce.

Your speakers and self-constituted leaders urge you to give up
the question of wages, and stand upon the Charter. Against the
obtaining the charter the laws of nature offer no impediment, as
they do against a forcible advance of wages; but to obtain the
charter *now* is just as impossible as to raise wages by force.

The aristocracy are powerful and determined; and, unhappily,
the middle classes are not yet intelligent enough to see the safety of
extending political power to the whole people. The working classes
can never gain it of themselves. Physical force you wisely repudi-
ate. It is immoral, and you have no arms, and little organization.

Moral force can only succeed through the electors, and these are not yet convinced. The principles of the charter will one day be established; but years *may* pass over, months *must* pass over before that day arrives. You cannot stand idle till it comes. Your only means of living are from the produce of your own labour. Unhappily, you have wives and children, and all of you have the cravings of hunger, and you must live, and, in order to live, you must work.

Your speakers talk loudly. They tell you of your numbers and your power, and they promise marvellous results *if you will but be firm*. They deceive you; perhaps they are themselves deceived. Some of them contrive to live on this deception, and some are content with the glory of their leadership. They flatter you grossly, and they as grossly calumniate your employers. They pretend to be working out your political freedom; they know that *that* freedom can only be obtained through the electoral body and the middle classes, and yet they incessantly abuse the parties whom it is your interest to conciliate and convince. For four years past they have held before your eyes an object *at present* unattainable, and they have urged you to pursue it; they have laboured incessantly to prevent you from following any practical object. They have vilified the substance and extolled the shadow. They have striven continually to exasperate you against those who alone will or can aid you to overturn the usurpations of the aristocracy. They have succeeded in creating suspicion and dissension, and upon that dissension many of them have lived. They have done their utmost to perpetuate *your* seven or eight shillings per week, and by their labours in that cause *they* have enjoyed an income of three or four times that amount.

My fellow-townsmen, you have been in a fever during this week. Your conduct, unopposed as you have been, has been peaceable and such as my intimate knowledge of you led me to expect from you. We are all liable to err; you have committed an error, but it is not a fatal one—it may be retrieved. I believe you to be intelligent men, or I would not address you. As intelligent men you cannot remain out; you cannot permanently raise wages by force; you cannot get the charter *now*. What are you to do then? RETURN TO YOUR EMPLOYMENT. It is more noble to confess your error than to persist in it, and the giving up of an error brings you nearer the truth. When you resume your labour, do not give up the hope of political improvement—that would be even more to be deplored than your present movement. Cherish it still—a brighter day will come—and you and your children will yet enjoy it. Your first step to entire freedom must be *commercial* freedom—freedom of industry. We must put an end to the partial famine which is destroying trade, the demand for your labour, your wages, your comforts, and your independence. The aristocracy regard the Anti-Corn-Law League as their greatest enemy. That which is the greatest enemy of the remorseless aristocracy of Britain must almost of necessity be your firmest friend. Every man who tells you to support the Corn Law is your enemy—every man who hastens, by a single hour, the abolition of the Corn Law, shortens by so much the duration of your sufferings. Whilst that inhuman law exists your wages must decline. When it is abolished, and not till then, they will rise.

If every employer and workman in the kingdom were to swear on his bended knees that wages should not fall, they would assuredly fall if the Corn Law continues. No power on earth can maintain your wages at their present rate if the Corn Law be not repealed. You may doubt this now, but consider the past, I beseech you—what the past tells you the future will confirm. You may not thank me for thus addressing you, but, nevertheless, I am your friend. Your own class does not include a man more sincerely anxious than I am to obtain for you both industrial and political freedom. You have found me on all occasions, if a feeble, yet an honest and zealous defender; and I trust in *this*, time will work no change in me. My heart sympathizes deeply in your sufferings. I believe I know whence they mainly spring, and would gladly relieve them. I would willingly become poor if that would make you comfortable and happy.

I now conclude. I ask only the exercise of your reason. If possible lay aside prejudices, and you will decide wisely.

To such of you as have been employed at the mills with which I am connected, I may add that, as soon as you are disposed to resume work, the doors shall be open to you. I invite you to come, and you shall be treated as, I trust, you have ever been—as I would ever wish you to treat me.

I am, with all sincerity, your friend,

JOHN BRIGHT

B. George Jacob Holyoake on John Bright

Mr. Bright resembled a Company Limited. Compared with average men he was a company in himself, but, not being registered under the Companies Act, few noticed that his trading capital of convictions (if his noble qualities may be so spoken of) was limited. No other simile I can think of so well describes what was not understood about him.

In politics there is more eagerness than observation. Public men are not adequately regarded for what they do, and are often praised for what they do not intend to do. Champions of a popular question are taken to be champions of all that the people desire. Those who have long observed public men know where and on what questions they will fail the people. Hardly ten leaders in a hundred are thorough and can be trusted all round—not so much because they are base, as because they are limited in knowledge or sympathy, and are for a question without knowing or caring for the principle of it. The safe rule is to accord leaders full credit for the service they do render, and not count on more, unless they give reason for such expectation.

The Tory hatred of Mr. Bright which long prevailed was without foundation, and the eulogies passed upon him since his death for merits but lately discerned, have given the public no consistent or complete idea what manner of man he was politically. Not being under youthful illusions as to public men is an advantage. I may do them more justice for the service they do render, and not defame them, nor feel disappointment at their not doing what is not and never was, in their nature to do.

Mr. Bright was not a political tribune of the people, though his fame was political. He was a social tribune—though he was against Socialism. Working men distrusted Mr. Bright when he first became known to them, because he was against the Factory Acts, which he regarded as opposed to free trade between employer and workman, and did not see that where humanity comes in, humanity is to be respected, and is not to be subjected to laws of barter. Mr. Bright was for Free Trade before everything, and the Chartists were of the same mind, being for political freedom before everything. We have lived to see men of higher position than Chartists persist in their own views to the peril of every other interest. Mr. Bright professed no sympathy with Chartist aims, and they knew he was not with them; but when Free Trade brought them better wages and fuller employment they respected Mr. Bright for his defence of it, and when he advocated the suffrage they thought he was with them in their political theories, not seeing that Mr. Bright was still Conservative, and moving in a plane apart from them. He never expressed sympathy for struggling nationalities. The patriots of Poland—of Hungary, of Italy, of France—never had help from his voice. He was silent on Neapolitan and Austrian oppression which moved the heart of Mr. Gladstone. He was incapable of approving the perjury and usurpation of Louis Napoleon, but no protest came from him. He was for the extension of the suffrage, because it was a necessity—not because it was a right. With him the franchise was a means to an end, and that end was the creation of a popular force for the maintenance of Free Trade, international peace, and public economy. Politically, he regarded the voter not as a man, but as an elector—nor did he think it necessary that all men should be electors. He was content if the majority of the people had a determining power, and whatever franchise gave this was sufficient in his eyes. He had no sympathy with manhood suffrage, and less for womanhood suffrage. He believed in the aristocracy of sex, and thought the political equality of women unnecessary, a perplexing and disturbing element in electoral calculations. That manhood suffrage gave dignity to the individual, by investing him with power and responsibility, was not much in his mind. Womanhood suffrage, enabling half the human race to bring their quicker, gentler, and juster influence to bear on public affairs in which their welfare and that of their children are concerned, was outside Mr. Bright's sympathies.

There are two sorts of Tories—those who seek power for ends of personal supremacy; and the better sort, who seek to retain power in order to do good, but the good is to be good they give the people—the Tory belief being that the people cannot be trusted to determine what is good for themselves. Mr. Bright was better than the better sort of Tories. He believed a majority of the people were to be trusted. So far he was for Liberalism—but he was for Liberalism Limited. The Whigs of 1832 put down boroughmongering and entrusted the franchise to a "worshipful company of ten-pound householders." Mr. Bright was for enlarging that company by the admission of six-pound householders. When the Duke of Wellington heard new prayers read which were not to be found in the old, crude prayer book of the Established Church, he refused to join in them, as being "fancy prayers." Following in the Duke's steps Mr. Bright contemptuously called any new scheme of enfranchisement, which increased the number of electors indefinitely, "fancy franchises."[1] The Duke was for addressing Heaven by regulation prayers, and in the same spirit Mr. Bright was for "standing on the old lines." He was against working-class representation just as the Tories were against middle-class representation. Those in possession always think they sufficiently represent those excluded. Mr. Bright was of this way of thinking. He had this defence: he meant to be just to all outsiders, and did not deem it necessary that they should be able to enforce their own claim in person. Later he applied this doctrine to the whole Irish nation.

He was against the ascendency of the Church as allied to the State, not because its ascendency was an offence against equality, but because it was contrary to the simplicity of Christ's teaching as he read it, and because a State Church gave religious sanction to State war. As a man Mr. Bright put Christianity in the first place as a personal influence—as a politician he regarded it chiefly as a public force to be appealed to on behalf of social welfare. What he hated was injustice; what he abhorred was cruelty, whether of war or slavery; what he cared for was the comfort and prosperity of common people. Whatever stood in the way of these things he would withstand, whether the opposing forces were spiritual principalities, or peers, or thrones. If they fell, it would be their own fault—the forces of humanity must triumph. He would not set up privilege, nor would he put it down—provided it behaved itself. He was no leveller, he envied no rank, he coveted no distinction; but he was for the honest, industrious people, whether manufacturers or workmen, having control over their own interests—come what would.

It was to this end that he opposed the Corn Laws and advocated Free Trade and the repeal of the taxes on knowledge. He desired that the people might learn what their social interests were. He was for the extension of the suffrage, that those who came to under-

---

[1] He applied this phrase to my proposal, that proof of intelligence, such as a workman could give and which I defined, should be a certificate of enfranchisement.

stand their commercial and industrial interests should be able to insist upon attention, and not have to supplicate for it. If the governing classes had given heed to social interests, Mr. Bright would never have invoked the power of the people. Like Canning, he was for calling in a "new world" [of power] to redress the persistent injustice of "the old." He would no more have sought the suffrage than Robert Owen would the support of the people, if his aims could have been realised without them. Owen went from court to court; he waited in the ante-chamber of Sidmouth and Liverpool in vain; and when courts and Ministers gave no heed he appealed to the people. Because he did so, Liberals and Radicals thought he was with them, but all the while he was a Tory. Bright, like Owen, cared for the people more than for theories; and the people, whose principles were opposed to thrones, thought the great social tribune was with them all through. This was the mistake which they, and wiser men than they, have made. Bright aided the extinction of slavery because it shocked his sense of justice and humanity; but had the slave been well treated, and not bought and sold and flogged, he might, like Owen, have seen no such harm in it as to warrant the disturbance of States to put it down. But when its immorality and cruelty became authentically known to Bright, his noble sense of humanity was outraged, and his splendid eloquence, like O'Connell's, was exerted on behalf of the slave.

He was friendly to co-operators—he spoke for their protection, but never in favour of their principle. Like Bastiat, he believed in the divinity of competition. He was at once the advocate of Peace and Competition—the principle of sleepless and pitiless resistance to the interests of others. With him adulteration was but a form of competition. This is true. But if adulteration be its concomitant, that is the condemnation of both. Mr. Bright thought this reasoning Utopian.

Mr. Bright, like Mr. Disraeli, had little respect for philosophers. He did not dread them like Lord Beaconsfield, but he mistrusted them in politics. The region of the philosopher is the region of the possible. Bright's mind ran always in the region of the practical. His tendency was to regard new rights as "fads." The philosophers laid down new lines—he was content with the old. He, as I have said, ridiculed a franchise founded upon intelligence, as a "fancy franchise." Yet he sat in the House himself under a "fancy franchise." The concession which enabled the Quaker to affirm was a "fancy franchise;" the Jews were brought into the House by a "fanciful" alteration of the oath to meet their tribal but honourable fastidiousness. It was not well that he should have contempt for new paths discovered by thought; but he was not without merit in his preference for established roads, since many men give all their time to searching for new precepts who would be the better for practising the good ones they already have.

If, however, the great Tribune had the characteristics herein described, the reader will ask, "How is it that he was so widely mistaken for an aggressive and uncompromising Liberal?" Most men think that because a man goes down the same street with them he is going to the same place. Bright accepted the aid of the men of right, without sympathy with the passion for right, beyond the helpfulness of its advocates in the attainment of the public ends he cared for. Cobden did the same, but he owned it, and sought such aid. Bright did neither, but did not decline alien aid when it came. He was the terror of the Tories, and they never discerned that he was their friend. He opposed them for what they did, not for what they were.

When riotous Radicals of 1832 had became fat and contented middle-class manufacturers, and were shrieking as dismally as Conservatives against a transfer of power to workmen, Mr. Bright, deserted by his compeers in Parliament, appeared alone on provincial platforms, pleading for larger enfranchisement. Members of Parliament, themselves Liberals, thought the question of the suffrage hopeless for years to come, and said to me, "Why does Bright go about flogging a dead horse?" Tories expressed contemptuous scorn for his enthusiasm. Had he been silent or supine, working men would be without substantial enfranchisement now. What Ebenezer Elliott wrote of Cobbett they may, with a change of name, say of Bright:—

> Our friend when other friend we'd none,
> Our champion when we had but one;
> Cursed by all knaves, beneath this sod
> Brave John Bright lies—a man by God.

Yet he had limits in his mind beyond which he would not, and did not, go. In 1870, he deprecated the admission of working men in Parliament as likely to increase the evils of class legislation, yet all the while the House of Commons is, and always has been, full of class interests. Mr. Bright and his friend Cobden were the great representatives of the middle class, yet he did not propose that middle-class representation should cease so that the evils of class representation might cease or diminish. If any class at all ought to be represented in the House of Commons, surely it is the working class, who exceed all other classes in numbers and usefulness in the State. But the idea of democracy was not in his mind, and women, as part of the human race, having political interests was simply abhorrent to him. He was always for the Crown, the Bible, and the Constitution as much as any Conservative. He was against the Tories—when they put passion in the place of principle and their interests in the place of duty—but not otherwise.

It is quite a vulgar error to suppose that the democracy are more undiscerning than patricians. They made as many mistakes about Mr. Bright as the people did. An illustrious poet could write of him as:—

> This broad-brimmed brawler of holy things,
> Whose ear is cramm'd with his cotton, and sings
> Even in dreams, to the chink of his pence.

True, this was said long ago. But no one who personally knew Bright, at his advent in public affairs, could think this. Bright was no "bawler of holy things." Sincerity and reverence were always deep in his heart. There was no "cotton in his ears." He knew Free Trade and peace would benefit the manufacturer, but would benefit the people more. No politician of his day was less influenced by the "chink of his pence" than John Bright. Carlyle, with all his clamorous philosophy, made the same mistake as the poet, in his contemptuous remark upon the "cock-nosed Rochdale Radical," who had as fair a nose as the scornful "Sage of Chelsea."

All the while Mr. Bright's eloquence was directed to the maintenance of an honest garrison in the fortress of authority. He was the one platform warder of the constitution, but it must minister to freedom and justice. He spoke no word against the throne from his first speech until his last. Quakers ask protection from power; they never seek to subvert power. Their doctrine of non-resistance makes them the natural allies of monarchs. Penn had the ear of Charles II. Edmundson had ready audience of King James. Shillitoe prayed with the Emperor of Russia, who knelt by Shillitoe's side.

Quakers were not spies against freedom, but honest reporters of wrong done, whose honest impartial word kings could trust. Mr. Bright was always of the Quaker mind. He regarded authority as of God, but he held that authority was responsible for righteous rule. He was a courtier with an honest conscience. He was for the perpetuity of the Crown, and also, and more so, for the welfare of the people. In one of his great speeches he avowed:—

> There is a yet auguster thing,
> Veiled though it be, than Parliament or King.

Mr. Bright was always for freedom of conscience, and equally for freedom of action, at the dictate of conscience. "Are mankind to stand still?" he asked in one of his earlier speeches. He was for order, but with order there must be progress. It was this conviction which made him insurgent against the policy of doing nothing. Now he is gone, there is no great popular Conservative force left, save Mr. Gladstone.

24. The Rationalization of Institutions: The Fog of Chancery and Judicial Reform

THESE two selections concern a problem and its resolution. The judicial system is no less important than the law in articulating the relationship between man and his political authorities. And the judicial system had come under repeated attack through the first two-thirds of the nineteenth century. Minor attempts had been made to answer specific needs. The Metropolitan Criminal Court ("Old Bailey") was established as a permanent "assize" court in 1834. County Courts were established in 1846 to handle small civil cases, most often actions for debt, and to avoid cluttering regular court dockets with trivial business. A cumbersome appeal apparatus developed.

The basic institutional problems remained. A series of common law courts and the Court of Chancery had overlapping jurisdiction and different procedures. The Supreme Court of Judicature Act of 1873 established one Supreme Court of Judicature, with common law and equity procedure in all courts. All judges were members of the High Court of Justice and attended, as occasion dictated, to cases in the Court of Queen's Bench, the Court of Chancery, and the Court of Probate, Divorce, and Admiralty. Three judges sat as a court of appeal.

The House of Lords formally retrieved its right in 1876 as the highest court of appeal, but in form only. Specific judges, nominated as life peers, sat as the House of Lords in judicial matters. English legal institutions remained cumbersome, complex, and confusing, but they began to acquire some rationality.

Recommended Reading

Like the institution, the literature is cumbersome. W. S. HOLDS-WORTH, *A History of English Law*—the first fifteen of sixteen volumes published from 1903 to 1965—is being posthumously completed. The makers of the fog are best studied in the last volumes of Lord CAMP-BELL's *Lives of the Chancellors*, 8 vols. (London, 1848–69); and J. B. ATLAY, *The Victorian Chancellors*, 2 vols. (London, 1906–1908). R. M. JACKSON, *The Machinery of Justice*, 4th ed. (London, 1964), is a complete guide.

SOURCES: Document A: Charles Dickens, *Bleak House* (London, 1853), ch. 1. Document B: Sir John Coleridge, Speech on the Second Reading of the Supreme Court of Judicature Bill, June 9, 1873, *Hansard's Parliamentary Debates*, Third Series, Vol. CCXVI, cols. 640–646, 648–654.

A. The Fog of Chancery

Charles Dickens (1812–70) has perhaps been the most widely read English novelist. For thirty-five years literate Britons eagerly awaited each installment and pondered the fate of Little Nell or Tom Dombey. Cruelty, thoughtlessness, inhumanity, insensitivity were pilloried by this outspoken champion of the humane tradition. Whether it was the workhouse in *Oliver Twist*, debtors' prison in *Pickwick*, or education in *Nicholas Nickleby*, Dickens caricatured institutions and values that he believed warped the quality of British life. The brilliantly savage assault on the majesty of the law in *Bleak House* proved an almost unique union of the best political satire and a masterpiece of art.

The English legal system, barricaded behind centuries of tortuous growth and precedent, seemed to defy human comprehension. Law was obfuscation developed as a fine art. The law functioned at two levels. On the one hand, the average man confronted it, insofar as he ever did, through the magistrate, the often unsalaried gentleman justice-of-the-peace. The law could be stern or benevolent, but even though the limits of authority were small, there remained this somewhat *ad hoc* area of summary jurisdiction. On the other hand, there was the elaborate system of courts, sustained by an extensive body of lawyers and fortified by intricate procedures. As W. S. Gilbert's Lord Chancellor put it,

The law is the true embodiment
Of everything that's excellent.
It has no kind of fault or flaw,
And I, my lords, embody the law.

CHAPTER I. IN CHANCERY

LONDON. Michaelmas Term lately over, and the Lord Chancellor sitting in Lincoln's Inn Hall. Implacable November weather. As much mud in the streets, as if the waters had but newly retired from the face of the earth, and it would not be wonderful to meet a Megalosaurus, forty feet long or so, waddling like an elephantine lizard up Holborn Hill. Smoke lowering down from chimney-pots, making a soft black drizzle, with flakes of soot in it as big as full-grown snow-flakes—gone into mourning, one might imagine, for the death of the sun. Dogs, undistinguishable in mire. Horses, scarcely better; splashed to their very blinkers. Foot passengers, jostling one another's umbrellas, in a general infection of ill-temper, and losing their foot-hold at street-corners, where tens of thousands of other foot passengers have been slipping and sliding since the day broke (if the day ever broke), adding new deposits to the crust upon crust of mud, sticking at those points tenaciously to the pavement, and accumulating at compound interest.

Fog everywhere. Fog up the river, where it flows among green aits and meadows; fog down the river, where it rolls defiled among the tiers of shipping, and the waterside pollutions of a great (and dirty) city. Fog on the Essex marshes, fog on the Kentish heights. Fog creeping into the cabooses of collier-brigs; fog lying out on the yards, and hovering in the rigging of great ships; fog drooping on the gunwales of barges and small boats. Fog in the eyes and throats of ancient Greenwich pensioners, wheezing by the firesides of their wards; fog in the stem and bowl of the afternoon pipe of the wrathful skipper, down in his close cabin; fog cruelly pinching the toes and fingers of his shivering little 'prentice boy on deck. Chance people on the bridges peeping over the parapets into a nether sky of fog, with fog all round them, as if they were up in a balloon, and hanging in the misty clouds.

Gas looming through the fog in divers places in the streets, much as the sun may, from the spongey fields, be seen to loom by husbandman and ploughboy. Most of the shops lighted two hours before their time—as the gas seems to know, for it has a haggard and unwilling look.

The raw afternoon is rawest, and the dense fog is densest, and the muddy streets are muddiest, near that leaden-headed old obstruction, appropriate ornament for the threshold of a leaden-headed old corporation: Temple Bar. And hard by Temple Bar, in Lincoln's Inn Hall, at the very heart of the fog, sits the Lord High Chancellor in his High Court of Chancery.

Never can there come fog too thick, never can there come mud and mire too deep, to assort with the groping and floundering condition which this High Court of Chancery, most pestilent of hoary sinners, holds, this day, in the sight of heaven and earth.

On such an afternoon, if ever, the Lord High Chancellor ought to be sitting here—as here he is—with a foggy glory round his head, softly fenced in with crimson cloth and curtains, addressed by a large advocate with great whiskers, a little voice, and an interminable brief, and outwardly directing his contemplation to the lantern in the roof, where he can see nothing but fog. On such an afternoon, some score of members of the High Court of Chancery bar ought to be—as here they are—mistily engaged in one of the ten thousand stages of an endless cause, tripping one another up on slippery precedents, groping knee-deep in technicalities, running their goat-hair and horse-hair warded heads against walls of words, and making a pretence of equity with serious faces, as players might. On such an afternoon, the various solicitors in the cause, some two or three of whom have inherited it from their fathers, who made a fortune by it, ought to be—as are they not?—ranged in a line, in a long matted well (but you might look in vain for Truth at the bottom of it), between the registrar's red table and the silk gowns, with bills, cross-bills, answers, rejoinders, injunctions, affidavits, issues, references to masters, masters' reports, mountains of costly nonsense, piled before them. Well may the court be dim, with wasting candles here and there; well may the fog hang heavy in it, as if it would never get out; well may the stained glass windows lose their colour, and admit no light of day into the place; well may the uninitiated from the streets, who peep in through the glass panes in the door, be deterred from entrance by its owlish aspect, and by the drawl languidly echoing to the roof from the padded dais where the Lord High Chancellor looks into the lantern that has no light in it, and where the

attendant wigs are all stuck in a fog-bank! This is the Court of
Chancery; which has its decaying houses and its blighted lands in
every shire; which has its worn-out lunatic in every madhouse, and
its dead in every churchyard; which has its ruined suitor, with his
slipshod heels and threadbare dress, borrowing and begging
through the round of every man's acquaintance; which gives to
monied might the means abundantly of wearying out the right;
which so exhausts finances, patience, courage, hope; so overthrows
the brain and breaks the heart; that there is not an honourable man
among its practitioners who would not give—who does not often
give—the warning, "Suffer any wrong that can be done you,
rather than come here!"

Who happen to be in the Lord Chancellor's court this murky
afternoon besides the Lord Chancellor, the counsel in the cause,
two or three counsel who are never in any cause, and the well of
solicitors before mentioned? There is the registrar below the
Judge, in wig and gown; and there are two or three maces, or petty-
bags, or privy-purses, or whatever they may be, in legal court suits.
These are all yawning; for no crumb of amusement ever falls from
JARNDYCE AND JARNDYCE (the cause in hand), which was squeezed
dry years upon years ago. The short-hand writers, the reporters of
the court, and the reporters of the newspapers, invariably decamp
with the rest of the regulars when Jarndyce and Jarndyce comes
on. Their places are a blank. Standing on a seat at the side of the
hall, the better to peer into the curtained sanctuary, is a little mad
old woman in a squeezed bonnet, who is always in court, from its
sitting to its rising, and always expecting some incomprehensible
judgment to be given in her favour. Some say she really is, or was,
a party to a suit; but no one knows for certain, because no one
cares. She carries some small litter in a reticule which she calls her
documents; principally consisting of paper matches and dry laven-
der. A sallow prisoner has come up, in custody, for the half-
dozenth time, to make a personal application "to purge himself of
his contempt;" which, being a solitary surviving executor who has
fallen into a state of conglomeration about accounts of which it is
not pretended that he had ever any knowledge, he is not at all
likely ever to do. In the meantime his prospects in life are ended.
Another ruined suitor, who periodically appears from Shropshire,
and breaks out into efforts to address the Chancellor at the close of
the day's business, and who can by no means be made to under-

stand that the Chancellor is legally ignorant of his existence after making it desolate for a quarter of a century, plants himself in a good place and keeps an eye on the Judge, ready to call out "My Lord!" in a voice of sonorous complaint, on the instant of his rising. A few lawyers' clerks and others who know this suitor by sight, linger, on the chance of his furnishing some fun, and enlivening the dismal weather a little.

Jarndyce and Jarndyce drones on. This scarecrow of a suit has, in course of time, become so complicated, that no man alive knows what it means. The parties to it understand it least; but it has been observed that no two Chancery lawyers can talk about it for five minutes, without coming to a total disagreement as to all the premises. Innumerable children have been born into the cause; innumerable young people have married into it; innumerable old people have died out of it. Scores of persons have deliriously found themselves made parties in Jarndyce and Jarndyce, without knowing how or why; whole families have inherited legendary hatreds with the suit. The little plaintiff or defendant, who was promised a new rocking-horse when Jarndyce and Jarndyce should be settled, has grown up, possessed himself of a real horse, and trotted away into the other world. Fair wards of court have faded into mothers and grandmothers; a long procession of Chancellors has come in and gone out; the legion of bills in the suit have been transformed into mere bills of mortality; there are not three Jarndyces left upon the earth perhaps, since old Tom Jarndyce in despair blew his brains out at a coffee-house in Chancery Lane; but Jarndyce and Jarndyce still drags its dreary length before the Court, perennially hopeless.

Jarndyce and Jarndyce has passed into a joke. That is the only good that has ever come of it. It has been death to many, but it is a joke in the profession. Every master in Chancery has had a reference out of it. Every Chancellor was "in it," for somebody or other, when he was counsel at the bar. Good things have been said about it by blue-nosed, bulbous-shoed old benchers, in select port-wine committee after dinner in hall. Articled clerks have been in the habit of fleshing their legal wit upon it. The last Lord Chancellor handled it neatly, when, correcting Mr. Blowers the eminent silk gown who said that such a thing might happen when the sky rained potatoes, he observed, "or when we get through Jarndyce and Jarndyce, Mr. Blowers;"—a pleasantry that particularly tickled the maces, bags, and purses.

How many people out of the suit, Jarndyce and Jarndyce has stretched forth its unwholesome hand to spoil and corrupt, would be a very wide question. From the master, upon whose impaling files reams of dusty warrants in Jarndyce and Jarndyce have grimly writhed into many shapes; down to the copying-clerk in the Six Clerks' Office, who has copied his tens of thousands of Chancery-folio-pages under that eternal heading; no man's nature has been made the better by it. In trickery, evasion, procrastination, spoliation, botheration, under false pretences of all sorts, there are influences that can never come to good. The very solicitors' boys who have kept the wretched suitors at bay, by protesting time out of mind that Mr. Chizzle, Mizzle, or otherwise, was particularly engaged and had appointments until dinner, may have got an extra moral twist and shuffle into themselves out of Jarndyce and Jarndyce. The receiver in the cause has acquired a goodly sum of money by it, but has acquired too a distrust of his own mother, and a contempt for his own kind. Chizzle, Mizzle, and otherwise, have lapsed into a habit of vaguely promising themselves that they will look into that outstanding little matter, and see what can be done for Drizzle—who was not well used—when Jarndyce and Jarndyce shall be got out of the office. Shirking and sharking, in all their many varieties, have been sown broadcast by the ill-fated cause; and even those who have contemplated its history from the outermost circle of such evil, have been insensibly tempted into a loose way of letting bad things alone to take their own bad course, and a loose belief that if the world go wrong, it was, in some off-hand manner, never meant to go right.

Thus, in the midst of the mud and at the heart of the fog, sits the Lord High Chancellor in his High Court of Chancery.

"Mr. Tangle," says the Lord High Chancellor, latterly something restless under the eloquence of that learned gentleman.

"Mlud," says Mr. Tangle. Mr. Tangle knows more of Jarndyce and Jarndyce than anybody. He is famous for it—supposed never to have read anything else since he left school.

"Have you nearly concluded your argument?"

"Mlud, no—variety of points—feel it my duty tsubmit—ludship," is the reply that slides out of Mr. Tangle.

"Several members of the bar are still to be heard, I believe?" says the Chancellor, with a slight smile.

Eighteen of Mr. Tangle's learned friends, each armed with a little summary of eighteen hundred sheets, bob up like eighteen hammers in a piano-forte, make eighteen bows, and drop into their eighteen places of obscurity.

"We will proceed with the hearing on Wednesday fortnight," says the Chancellor. For, the question at issue is only a question of costs, a mere bud on the forest tree of the parent suit, and really will come to a settlement one of these days.

The Chancellor rises; the bar rises; the prisoner is brought forward in a hurry; the man from Shropshire cries, "My lord!" Maces, bags, and purses, indignantly proclaim silence, and frown at the man from Shropshire.

"In reference," proceeds the Chancellor, still on Jarndyce and Jarndyce, "to the young girl——"

"Begludship's pardon—boy," says Mr. Tangle, prematurely.

"In reference," proceeds the Chancellor, with extra distinctness, "to the young girl and boy, the two young people,"

(Mr. Tangle crushed.)

"Whom I directed to be in attendance to-day, and who are now in my private room, I will see them and satisfy myself as to the expediency of making the order for their residing with their uncle."

Mr. Tangle on his legs again.

"Begludship's pardon—dead."

"With their," Chancellor looking through his double eye-glass at the papers on his desk, "grandfather."

"Begludship's pardon—victim of rash action—brains."

Suddenly a very little counsel, with a terrific bass voice, arises, fully inflated, in the back settlements of the fog, and says, "Will your lordship allow me? I appear for him. He is a cousin, several times removed. I am not at the moment prepared to inform the Court in what exact remove he is a cousin; but he *is* a cousin."

Leaving this address (delivered like a sepulchral message) ringing in the rafters of the roof, the very little counsel drops, and the fog knows him no more. Everybody looks for him. Nobody can see him.

"I will speak with both the young people," says the Chancellor anew, "and satisfy myself on the subject of their residing with their cousin. I will mention the matter to-morrow morning when I take my seat."

The Chancellor is about to bow to the bar, when the prisoner is presented. Nothing can possibly come of the prisoner's conglomeration, but his being sent back to prison; which is soon done. The man from Shropshire ventures another remonstrative "My lord!" but the Chancellor, being aware of him, has dexterously vanished. Everybody else quickly vanishes too. A battery of blue bags is loaded with heavy charges of papers and carried off by clerks; the little mad old woman marches off with her documents; the empty court is locked up. If all the injustice it has committed, and all the misery it has caused, could only be locked up with it, and the whole burnt away in a great funeral pyre,—why, so much the better for other parties than the parties in Jarndyce and Jarndyce!

B. Judicial Reform

THE LIBERAL reform of British institutions reached its zenith with Gladstone's "Great Ministry" from 1868 to 1874. While other governments might add more social legislation (as Disraeli did), Gladstone's first administration represented something close to the fruition of the Liberal ideal. Special privilege fell. The government abolished the purchase of army commissions, disestablished the Anglican Church in Ireland, and opened civil service to competitive examination. Democracy was protected by the secret ballot. The first Education Act (1870), while less than many had hoped, provided state-supported national elementary education. With that Liberal respect for freedom, compulsory attendance remained, for the moment, a question of local option.

After an exhaustive investigation, a comprehensive plan for the reform of the judicature emanated from a royal commission. A reforming Lord Chancellor, Selhorne, guided the crucial bill through the House of Lords. Trouble still waited in the House of Commons. Sir John Coleridge (1820-94), the Attorney General, effectively guided it past many reefs. In this speech moving the second reading, (approval in principle) is future Lord Chief Justice of England animadverted on many of the problems in structure and practice. He emphasized the need to make a realistic, sensible, and intelligent reform of one of Britain's most cumbersome institutions. Dickens' prayer in *Bleak House* would soon be answered, at least in part.

THE ATTORNEY GENERAL, in moving that the Bill be now read a second time, said, it would be his duty to state as shortly and as clearly as possible the general principles of the measure to which he was about to ask the House to give its assent. So far as the drafting of the measure was concerned, his noble and learned Friend the

Lord Chancellor—taking, in some degree, the Law Officers of the
Crown into his counsel—was responsible; but the noble and
learned Lord would, no doubt, admit that the Bill itself was, to a
large extent, an embodiment of the recommendations of the Judicature Commission, which was itself the result of a considerable
amount of Parliamentary discussion which had been had on the
subject, and which had created an opinion out-of-doors on the
question. No doubt, the matter had first taken tangible form in the
memorable speech which had been delivered by the noble and
learned Lord in that House in 1867, and the influence and authority of the noble and learned Lord had doubtless given to the
question an impulse which it might otherwise have wanted. The
subject was fortunately one entirely removed from the ordinary
regions of party politics; but while labouring under that disadvantage, every candid person must admit, at the same time, that it was
one on which it was necessary that a competent opinion should be
created out-of-doors before the attention of Parliament could be
successfully directed towards it. He hoped that by that time there
had been sufficient discussion in and out of that House to enable
them to deal with it once for all, and that the Bill would be found,
he would not say so perfect as to shut out all future legislation, but
a large and valuable contribution to that portion of law reform.

Without entering into a lengthened history of the subject, or a
defence of the law of England as at present administered, or of the
tribunals which administered that law, he might say, as one who
had passed a large portion of his life in its study, that he had
formed a strong opinion that, whatever might be the defects in the
law, they were to be attributed, not to the learned Judges who
administered it, but to the fact that the system on which it was
founded, having grown up during the Middle Ages, was incapable
of being adapted to the requirements of modern times. While
saying, on the whole, that whatever might be its defects, it was
founded on substantial justice and common sense, yet it was
beyond controversy, that in many instances our procedure was
impracticable and inconvenient, for no one practically conversant
with its details could deny that there were certain great defects in
them which ought to be remedied.

First of all, there was the broad distinction which had become
inveterate between what was called in this country Law and Equity.
In other countries, the distinction existed, and must always exist;

but in this country alone, Law and Equity were made the subject of separate and even conflicting jurisdiction.

A second defect of their system had been a great waste of judicial power. Many questions which came before the Common Law Courts were questions rather for the determination of a single Judge than a Court of four persons, highly paid, and generally men of first-rate ability. It was no answer to the statement that there had been a great waste of judicial power, to say that as the business of the country had increased more Judges had been made, because so long as we went on making more Judges and occupied them in the same Courts, we really only intensified the mischief, and did not to any appreciable extent diminish the evil of a waste of judicial power.

Another great defect of the present system had been the Terms and Vacations of the legal year. The Terms had been altered in some respects, that was to say the beginning and the end of Terms had been fixed by Act of Parliament, but, practically speaking, and without going into antiquarian discussion, the Terms and the Vacations remained what they were in the Middle Ages. Many things could be done in Term only, and the singular practical inconvenience which arose from that cause must have struck everyone having any knowledge of the subject. . . .

Another great defect of our present system had been the exceedingly imperfect constitution, and the still more imperfect working, at any rate, on the Common Law side, of our Courts of Appeal. The operation of their intermediate Court of Appeal was bad and intermittent; and no man, whatever might be his view of the constitutional position of the House of Lords, who had had any knowledge of its practical working, could deny, that a more indefensible institution as a judicial institution it was hardly possible to conceive. Although lawyers had been able to maintain a poor sort of living, still everyone knew that the people who went into a Court of Law were greatly the exception. Very few persons, comparatively speaking, ever went to law, and very few who had gone once would ever go again; and those people who had enjoyed the luxury of an appeal to the House of Lords must be very few indeed. When they had got a great appeal decided by that august tribunal, and when they had the satisfaction of paying the highly deserving recipients whom they must pay for that luxury, both sides probably went away with a thankful feeling of relief, and with a hope that they would never hear of the House of Lords again in its judicial capacity. These were matters which lay upon the surface, and which he hoped it would be found this Bill satisfactorily dealt with. . . .

The great defect in the system was the conflict of jurisdiction that existed between the Courts of Law and the Courts of Equity. Most descriptions which were epigrammatic and antithetical were sure to be incorrect; and it was not correct to say, as he had heard it stated, that they had established one set of Courts for correcting the intolerable injustice which another set of Courts had committed. At the same time, that description contained truth. No doubt, the Courts of Common Law, without the ameliorating and softening hand of Equity, would have administered a system under which this country, with its various complicated relations, would have found it impossible to live. There had been an inconvenient contest between the Courts of Law and the Courts of Equity, and that would be put an end to at once if the Bill passed. There were Courts of Law and Courts of Equity, each of them separate and distinct, with co-ordinate jurisdiction, unable to interfere with each other, except as the Court of Chancery interfered with suits at Common Law. These defects were known both to lawyers and suitors; but the public at large were not interested in them, and therefore let things go on as they were.

The first and main principle of the Bill was that there should be one Queen's Court—the Queen's Court of Supreme Jurisdiction; and in that Court perfect Law and perfect Equity should together be administered. That Supreme Court, into which all the existing Courts would be merged, would itself be divided into a High Court of Justice and an Appellate Court, of which the various Courts of Appeal and of First Instance would respectively form part. The Bill was not one for the fusion of Law and Equity. Law and Equity would remain, and for this reason—they were not the creatures of statute; an inherent distinction existed between them, and the subject-matter of Law and of Equity was not the same, and could not be made the same by Act of Parliament. The defect of our legal system was, not that Law and Equity existed, but that if a man went for relief to a Court of Law, and an equitable claim or an equitable defence arose, he must go to some other Court and begin afresh. Law and Equity, therefore, would remain if the Bill passed, but they would be administered concurrently, and no one would be sent to get in one Court the relief which another Court had refused to give. It seemed to him that that was the only intelligible way of dealing with the question. Great authorities had no doubt declared that Law and Equity might be fused by enactment; but in his opinion, to do so would be to decline to grapple with the real difficulty of the case. If an Act were passed doing no more than fuse Law and Equity, it would take 20 years of decisions and hecatombs of suitors to make out what Parliament meant and had not taken the trouble to define. It was more philosophical to admit the innate distinction between Law and Equity, which you could not get rid of by Act of Parliament, and to say, not that the distinction should not exist, but that the Courts should administer relief according to legal principles when these applied, or else according to equitable principles. That was what the Bill proposed, with the addition that, whenever the principles of Law and Equity conflicted, equitable principles should prevail. Few Common lawyers would deny that where the two principles differed Equity was right and Common Law wrong; and the Bill, therefore, did homage in such cases to the superior breadth and wisdom of Equity.

Though the separate jurisdiction of the Courts would be merged in the one Supreme Court, it was more philosophical to recognize facts, and as for the general convenience, as it was impossible you could have 31 or 32 Judges all sitting together, there must be Divisions of the Court, the question arose—what shall they be called? Now, he thought it very important to preserve historical associations wherever you could do so. England was not the least great in its legal history and associations, and to destroy all those associations in the nomenclature of the Law Courts would be unwise. As the things remained it was well that the names also should remain. Instead, therefore, of calling these different Courts by names which were not only new but new-fangled, it was proposed to call them by the old names—the Chancery, Queen's Bench, Common Pleas, Exchequer, Bankruptcy Divisions, and so on. Further, as there must be a division of labour, and the Courts must consider criminal informations, election petitions, registration appeals, questions of real property, specific performance, winding-up cases, questions between husband and wife, the enforcement of trusts, and so on, it was far more convenient, while getting rid of any conflict of jurisdiction, that the work which the Courts now did they should continue to do, at all events in the first instance. Every Division of a Court would have the jurisdiction to hear any class of business; but if it were found that some kinds of business could be better decided by one Division than another, this business might be transferred, without cost or inconvenience to the suitor. He hoped that we should thus get rid of the scandals of our present procedure, and that, while preserving necessary and inevitable distinctions, we should not allow them to obstruct the process of substantial relief to suitors. . . .

So much for the High Court of Justice, but the Bill would be imperfect without the creation also of a Court of Appeal. What could be more anomalous than the present state of the Courts of Appeal? As far as Common Law cases were concerned, there were two Courts of Appeal—first, the Exchequer Chamber, and then the House of Lords. In the Court of Chancery, speaking under correction, he would say there was not always a reference to an intermediate Court of Appeal; in certain cases there might be an appeal to the House of Lords, without the intermediate appeal to the Lords Justices. Then there was the Judicial Committee of the Privy Council for appeals from the Colonies, Ecclesiastical and Admiralty cases. The Exchequer Chamber had almost every fault that a Court of Appeal could have. . . . [The Judges] were men who had feelings, and he had known cases when a judgment of a particular Court, if there were any means of overruling it, was pretty sure to be overruled in the Exchequer Chamber. Then, there was no absolute necessity that the Exchequer Chamber should have a larger number of Judges than the Court which it overruled, and it had often happened that where the two Courts were divided, it was the opinion held by the minority of Judges which had prevailed. The Court sat, too, but for a very limited time, and that time was uncertain. The Lords Justices formed a much better Court of Appeal, and for a very long time had given satisfaction. The Privy Council, too, for something like 25 or 26 years was about as good a Court as this Empire contained; but it became exceedingly difficult to maintain it in that high state of efficiency, because, as it was until lately an entirely unpaid Court, it was almost entirely dependent on the services of unpaid Judges. At last it became almost impossible for it to continue its sittings. . . .

As for the House of Lords, it was his duty, whatever hon. Gentlemen opposite might think, to say what he thought of it as a judicial institution. For his part, he would say that if this Bill did nothing else but get rid of the House of Lords as a judicial tribunal it would be worth while to pass it. He could not believe that if suitors had any power of combination the House of Lords would have lasted as a judicial institution to the present time, such were the expenses and delays of it. He was himself in a case which had been pending in the House of Lords for six or seven years. The utter irresponsibility of the Judges who composed it made it a perfectly indefensible institution. He did not know what would be said now of Chancery Appeals, but he did know that some time ago they used to be decided by a single Peer, and a caustic Lord Justice used to say that the way they were decided made him hold up his hands in a respectful amazement. Practically, at present the Common Law Appeals were decided by a single Judge, for there was not a single Common Law Lord but one who attended the sittings of the House of Lords. Lord Penzance was too ill at present to attend, and before he generally was too busy. He recollected cases in which the unanimous opinion of the Court of Common Pleas and of the Court of Exchequer was overruled by this single Common Law Lord, the Judges not being summoned. Besides, the House of Lords now was not what it used to be in former times. Everyone knew that it was to the House of Lords, as a co-ordinate branch of the Legislature, and to the whole Peerage that the Constitution wisely, or unwisely, intrusted the declaration upon appeal of what was the law of England; the Judges were in those days habitually summoned as their advisers, and the House of Lords, in 99 cases out of 100, or even in a still larger proportion, followed the advice given by the Judges.

It was perfectly true that Lord Eldon said he had the right to overrule all the Judges in England, but that was a right which neither that noble and learned Lord nor the House of Lords itself had ever yet exercised. The House of Lords was at that time a convenient medium through which to ascertain the judgment of all the Judges; but that was not the case now. The whole character of the House of Lords was definitely changed in the famous cases of The Queen v. O'Connell. The lay Members of the House attended in large numbers on that occasion, as they had done in former days; but the Duke of Wellington earnestly advised them to take no part in the decision. They acted upon his advice and abstained from voting, and the Law Lords divided according to their political sentiments. He had no doubt that they were perfectly honest in what they did, but the fact was that the noble and learned Lords who were opposed in opinion to O'Connell voted against him, and those who were in favour of his views voted for him. From that day to this an appeal to the House of Lords had really been an appeal to two or three Law Lords who happened to attend, for the rule of the House now was, that the Judges were not summoned unless both parties desired it. . . . Practically the Appellate Jurisdiction of the House of Lords was in different hands from what it used to be, and from what the constitution intended it should be, and he saw no reason for maintaining the new state of things for which there was no precedent, and which was found extremely inconvenient. That, indeed, might be said to be the opinion of the House of Lords itself, which had passed that Bill and sent it down to them with those provisions.

Now, the Court of Appeal which it was proposed to create would consist of 12 or 14 persons. There would be five *ex officio* Members—the Lord Chancellor, the three Chief Judges of the Common Law Courts, the Master of the Rolls; the four paid Judges of the Privy Council—who took office with the understanding that they should be available for any reconstruction of the Court of Supreme Appeal—and three others—an ex-Lord Chancellor or Judge, and certain Scotch and Irish Judges, if they thought fit to come. The Court of Appeal would sit in two divisions all the year round, according to rules to be drawn up, and the present unintelligible and inconvenient distinction between Terms and Vacations would be abolished. Except an increase to the salary of the Judges of the Admiralty Court, as proposed by the House of Lords, and an increase of £1,000 a-year to the salaries of the paid Members of the Court of Appeal other than the *ex officio* Members, the Bill did not create any additional charge to the country—or, at least, certainly no permanent additional charge.

He had always thought the defect of the Judicial Committee of the Privy Council, if it had a defect, was in ecclesiastical matters, and that the presence of Bishops on that tribunal contributed nothing whatever to the weight of its decisions as legal decisions, while it affected to give them a sort of factitious spiritual influence which three Bishops who happened to be Privy Councillors could not possibly confer. He thought that questions of property and

law, even as far as the interests of the Church herself were concerned, ought to be decided by lawyers. However, they had to
deal with questions which were not strictly legal questions, and
therefore the Judicial Committee would remain for the purpose of
ecclesiastical appeals.

As he had stated, there would be two Divisions of the Supreme
Court, to one of which would be entrusted the cases now dealt
with by the Judicial Committee. In that case, the whole jurisdiction
and process being thus transferred to the Supreme Court, the decisions would still remain as the decisions of the Queen herself, Her
Majesty being advised by the Judges of that Court, as she was now
advised by the Judicial Committee. They would sit continuously
all the year round, and as he had said before, the present inconvenient distinction between Terms and Vacations would be abolished.
There would also be sittings in London and Middlesex. Another
important provision in the Bill was the power of appointing official
and regularly constituted referees. It was proposed that the Judge
in Chambers or the Court should be able at any stage of the case, if
it clearly appeared not to be a case fit for trial in Court or for
adjudication by a Judge and jury, to refer it by an Order. There
would be attached to the Courts certain official referees, who
would take those references as part of their regular duty. He hoped
that portion of the Bill would be found satisfactory, and get rid, in
working, of one of the justest causes of complaint that existed, at
all events, on the Common Law side of the question.

Such in outline was this measure which he had introduced—he
knew how imperfectly—to the attention of the House. There were
two subjects connected with the question of Law Reform—the
Reform of the Law itself and the reform of the procedure by
which the Law was administered; and they were very distinct. In
some respects this Bill, in different portions of it, dealt with both
these subjects; and he trusted it would be found to deal with them
satisfactorily. At any rate, such as it was, he begged leave to
recommend it to the attention of the House of Commons. So far as
the Government were concerned, they did not aspire or pretend to
any greater responsibility or merit in the question than having
recognized the position of public opinion, and striven, as far as
they could, to give effect to it. He asked the House to recollect
that the Bill came to them with the sanction of the House of Lords

—it came to them from the House of Lords, which had shown both great wisdom and patriotism in declining any longer to stand in the way of a great public advantage, for which there was a great public demand. The Government proposed to do no more than accept the will of Parliament, to become, in this respect, the ministers of its will and interpreters, as far as they understood them, of the wishes of the people—perfectly content, if they could conduct the Bill to a successful issue, to give credit when they found it was due to others for having by intelligent discussion brought about that state of public opinion and feeling which rendered that or any other measure possible. . . . He would, therefore, say no more than this—Here was a large, important, and valuable contribution to Law Reform; they had waited for it long enough, too long—and he would be no party to any proceeding that had any tendency to imperil its success, or even, in any appreciable manner to delay its progress.

25. The Career Open to Talents: Civil Service

RADICAL and conservative interests were both served by civil service reforms. Economy and efficiency, as well as equal opportunity based upon objective criteria, lay behind the drive for administrative reform and reorganization. While professional qualifications were increasingly in demand, the element of political jobbery remained. Ministers feared a loss of party control if government patronage were wrested from their hands, and members of Parliament expected to have some say about government appointments within their constituencies. But there were insufficient places to meet demand, and continued use of executive patronage was likely to create more problems than it was worth. The record of some government departments, moreover, was not altogether bad. But the investigation by John Arthur Roebuck, a Radical M.P., into the scandals of administration during the Crimean War raised questions on the civilian side that the conduct of the war raised about the army itself.

Gladstone, who was busy with the problem of university reform, had Sir Stafford Northcote and Sir Charles Trevelyan prepare a report that gradually became the basis of civil service selection and recruiting. George Cornewall Lewis, editor of the *Edinburgh Review* and Liberal

M.P., secured the Order in Council of 1855 establishing civil service commissioners. The commissioners had the power to check on the qualifications of entrants, but the qualifications continued to be defined by individual departments. An Order in Council of 1870 finally made competitive examination mandatory except in the Foreign Office. It, too, was included after 1919.

The relationship of these proposals and university reform was more than casual. Benjamin Jowett of Balliol, the most influential university figure of the day, proposed a model examination to select promising careerists to start not as junior clerks but at the policy level. Social stratification of a peculiarly mid-Victorian kind was built into civil service recruitment. Executives and upper-echelon administrators would be generalists, not men highly trained in specific areas or fields. There were to be administrative civil servants and clerical civil servants. A barrier based upon educational opportunity would be constructed against excessive social mobility. Since the liberal arts curriculum of the university was the basis for the civil service examinations, the university's function was increasingly to provide bright young men to serve the state. This reinforced the function of public school and university as a vehicle for middle-class social mobility. Civil service examinations and board interviews guaranteed a conservative transition in the management of the state.

Recommended Reading

E. W. COHEN, *The Growth of the British Civil Service, 1780–1939* London, 1941); and H. FINER, *The British Civil Service* (London, 1927).

SOURCE: Stafford H. Northcote and Charles E. Trevelyan, "The Organisation of the Permanent Civil Service," November 23, 1853, Report on Inquiries into Civil Service Establishments, *Parliamentary Papers*, 1854, Vol. XXVII, pp. 335–355.

On the Organisation of the Permanent Civil Service

We now proceed to comply with that part of our instructions which states that, in connection with the inquiries which we were directed to make into each particular office, it is highly necessary that the conditions which are common to all the public establishments, such as the preliminary testimonials of character and bodily health to be required from candidates for public employment, the examination into their intellectual attainments, and the regulation of the promotions, should be carefully considered, so as to obtain full security for the public that none but qualified persons will be appointed, and that they will afterwards have every practicable inducement to the active discharge of their duties.

It cannot be necessary to enter into any lengthened argument for the purpose of showing the high importance of the Permanent Civil Service of the country in the present day. The great and increasing accumulation of public business, and the consequent pressure upon the Government, need only to be alluded to; and the inconveniences which are inseparable from the frequent changes which take place in the responsible administration are matter of sufficient notoriety. It may safely be asserted that, as matters now stand, the Government of the country could not be carried on without the aid of an efficient body of permanent officers, occupying a position duly subordinate to that of the Ministers who are directly responsible to the Crown and to Parliament, yet possessing sufficient independence, character, ability, and experience to be able to advise, assist, and, to some extent, influence, those who are from time to time set over them.

That the Permanent Civil Service, with all its defects, essentially contributes to the proper discharge of the functions of Government, has been repeatedly admitted by those who have successively been responsible for the conduct of our affairs. All, however, who have had occasion to examine its constitution with care, have felt that its organisation is far from perfect, and that its amendment is deserving of the most careful attention.

It would be natural to expect that so important a profession would attract into its ranks the ablest and the most ambitious of the youth of the country; that the keenest emulation would prevail among those who had entered it; and that such as were endowed with superior qualifications would rapidly rise to distinction and public eminence. Such, however, is by no means the case. Admission into the Civil Service is indeed eagerly sought after, but it is for the unambitious, and the indolent or incapable, that it is chiefly desired. Those whose abilities do not warrant an expectation that they will succeed in the open professions, where they must encounter the competition of their contemporaries, and those whom indolence of temperament or physical infirmities unfit for active exertions, are placed in the Civil Service, where they may obtain an honourable livelihood with little labour, and with no risk; where their success depends upon their simply avoiding any flagrant misconduct, and attending with moderate regularity to routine duties; and in which they are secured against the ordinary consequences of old age, or failing health, by an arrangement which provides them with the means of supporting themselves after they have become incapacitated.

It may be noticed in particular that the comparative lightness of the work, and the certainty of provision in case of retirement owing to bodily incapacity, furnish strong inducements to the parents and friends of sickly youths to endeavour to obtain for them employment in the service of the Government; and the extent to which the public are consequently burdened, first with the salaries of officers who are obliged to absent themselves from their duties on account of ill health, and afterwards with their pensions when they retire on the same plea, would hardly be credited by those who have not had opportunities of observing the operation of the system.

It is not our intention to suggest that all public servants entered the employment of the Government with such views as these; but we apprehend that as regards a large proportion of them, these motives more or less influenced those who acted for them in the choice of a profession; while, on the other hand, there are probably very few who have chosen this line of life with a view to raising themselves to public eminence.

The result naturally is, that the public service suffers both in internal efficiency and in public estimation. The character of the individuals influences the mass, and it is thus that we often hear complaints of official delays, official evasions of difficulty, and official indisposition to improvement.

There are, however, numerous honourable exceptions to these observations, and the trustworthiness of the entire body is unimpeached. They are much better than we have any right to expect from the system under which they are appointed and promoted.

The peculiar difficulties under which the Permanent Civil Service labours, in obtaining a good supply of men, as compared with other professions, are partly natural and partly artificial.

Its natural difficulties are such as these:—

Those who enter it generally do so at an early age, when there has been no opportunity of trying their fitness for business, or forming a trustworthy estimate of their characters and abilities.

This to a great extent is the case in other professions also, but those professions supply a corrective which is wanting in the Civil Service, for as a man's success in them depends upon his obtaining and retaining the confidence of the public, and as he is exposed to a sharp competition on the part of his contemporaries, those only can maintain a fair position who possess the requisite amount of ability and industry for the proper discharge of their duties. The able and energetic rise to the top; the dull and inefficient remain at the bottom. In the public establishments, on the contrary, the general rule is that all rise together. After a young man has been once appointed, the public have him for life; and if he is idle or inefficient, provided he does not grossly misconduct himself, we must either submit to have a portion of the public business inefficiently and discreditably performed, or must place the incompetent person on the retired list, with a pension, for the rest of his life. The feeling of security which this state of things necessarily engenders tends to encourage indolence, and thereby to depress the character of the Service. Again, those who are admitted into it at an early age are thereby relieved from the necessity of those struggles which for the most part fall to the lot of such as enter upon the open professions; their course is one of quiet, and generally of secluded, performance of routine duties, and they consequently have but limited opportunities of acquiring that varied experience of life which is so important to the development of character.

To these natural difficulties may be added others arising from what may be called artificial causes.

The character of the young men admitted to the public service depends chiefly upon the discretion with which the heads of departments, and others who are entrusted with the distribution of patronage, exercise that privilege. In those cases in which the patronage of departments belongs to their chief for the time being, the appointments which it commonly falls to his lot to make are either those of junior clerks, to whom no very important duties are in the first instance to be assigned, or of persons who are to fill responsible and highly paid situations above the rank of the ordinary clerkships. In the first case, as the character and abilities of the new junior clerk will produce but little immediate effect upon the office, the chief of the department is naturally led to regard the selection as a matter of small moment, and will probably bestow the office upon the son or dependant of some one having personal or political claims upon him, or perhaps upon the son of some meritorious public servant, without instituting any very minute inquiry into the merits of the young man himself. It is true that in many offices some kind of examination is prescribed, and that in almost all the person appointed is in the first instance nominated on probation; but, as will presently be pointed out, neither of these tests are at present very efficacious. The young man thus admitted is commonly employed upon duties of the merest routine. Many of the first years of his service are spent in copying papers, and other work of an almost mechanical character. In two or three years he is as good as he can be at such an employment. The remainder of his official life can only exercise a depressing influence on him, and renders the work of the office distasteful to him. Unlike the pupil in a conveyancer's or special pleader's office, he not only begins with mechanical labour as an introduction to labour of a higher kind, but often also ends with it. In the meantime his salary is gradually advancing till he reaches, by seniority, the top of his class, and on the occurrence of a vacancy in the class above him he is promoted to fill it, as a matter of course, and without any regard to his previous services or his qualifications. Thus, while no pains have been taken in the first instance to secure a good man for the office, nothing has been done after the clerk's appointment to turn his abilities, whatever they may be, to the best account. The result naturally is, that when the chief of the office has to make an appointment of visible and immediate importance to the efficiency of his department, he sometimes has difficulty in finding a clerk capable of filling it, and he is not unfrequently obliged to go out of the office, and to appoint some one of high standing in an open profession, or some one distinguished in other walks of life, over the heads of men who have been for many years in the public service. This is necessarily discouraging to the Civil Servants, and tends to strengthen in them the injurious conviction, that their success does not depend upon their own exertions, and that if they work hard, it will not advance them,—if they waste their time in idleness, it will not keep them back.

It is of course essential to the public service that men of the highest abilities should be selected for the highest posts; and it cannot be denied that there are a few situations in which such varied talent and such an amount of experience are required, that it is probable that under any circumstances it will occasionally be found necessary to fill them with persons who have distinguished themselves elsewhere than in the Civil Service. But the system of appointing strangers to the higher offices has been carried far beyond this. In several departments the clerks are regarded as having no claim whatever to what are called the staff appointments; and numerous instances might be given in which personal or political considerations have led to the appointment of men of very slender ability, and perhaps of questionable character, to situations of considerable emolument, over the heads of public servants of long standing and undoubted merit. Few public servants would feel the appointment of a barrister of known eminence and ability to some important position, like that of Under Secretary of State, as a slight, or a discouragement to themselves; but the case is otherwise when some one who has failed in other professions, and who has no recommendation but that of family or political interest, is appointed to a Librarianship, or some other such office, the duties of which would have been far better discharged by one who had been long in the department, and to whom the increased salary attached to the appointment would have been a fair reward for years of faithful service.

One more peculiarity in the Civil Service remains to be noticed. It is what may be called its fragmentary character.

Unlike the Military and Naval, the Medical, and the Commissariat Services, and unlike even the Indian Civil Service, the public establishments of this country, though comprising a body of not less than 16,000 persons, are regulated upon the principle of merely departmental promotion. Each man's experience, interests, hopes, and fears are limited to the special branch of service in which he is himself engaged. The effect naturally is, to cramp the energies of the whole body, to encourage the growth of narrow views and departmental prejudices, to limit the acquisition of experience, and to repress and almost extinguish the spirit of emulation and competition; besides which, considerable inconvenience results from the want of facilities for transferring strength from an office where the work is becoming slack to one in which it is increasing, and from the consequent necessity of sometimes keeping up particular departments on a scale beyond their actual requirements.

Having thus touched upon some of the difficulties with which the public service is beset, we come to the consideration of the problem, what is the best method of providing it with a supply of good men, and of making the most of them after they have been admitted?

The first question which here presents itself is, Whether it is better to train young men for the discharge of the duties which they will afterwards have to perform, or to take men of mature age, who have already acquired experience in other walks of life?

Our opinion is, that, as a general rule, it is decidedly best to train young men. Without laying too much stress on the experience which a long official life necessarily brings with it, we cannot but regard it as an advantage of some importance. In many offices, moreover, it is found that the superior docility of young men renders it much easier to make valuable public servants of them, than of those more advanced in life. This may not be the case in the higher class of offices, but is unquestionably so in those where the work consists chiefly of account business. The maintenance of discipline is also easier under such circumstances, and regular habits may be enforced, which it would be difficult to impose for the first time upon older men. To these advantages must be added the important one of being able, by proper regulations, to secure the services of fit persons on much more economical terms. A young man who has not made trial of any other profession will be induced to enter that of the Civil Service by a much more moderate remuneration than would suffice to attract him a few years later from the pursuit of one in which he had overcome the first difficulties and begun to achieve success; while to attempt to fill the ranks of the Civil Service with those who had failed elsewhere, and were on that account willing to accept a moderate salary, would be simply to bring it into discredit. It cannot be doubted that, even in the absence of proper precautions for securing good appointments, it is more probable that a fair proportion of eligible men will be found among a number taken at their entrance into life, particularly if pains be bestowed upon them after their appointment, than among an equal number taken after some years of unsuccessful efforts to open another line for themselves. The temptation to jobbing, and the danger of decidedly improper appointments being made, is also considerably less in the case of the selection of young men than in that of persons more advanced in life.

The general principle, then, which we advocate is, that the public service should be carried on by the admission into its lower ranks of a carefully selected body of young men, who should be employed from the first upon work suited to their capacities and their education, and should be made constantly to feel that their promotion and future prospects depend entirely on the industry and ability with which they discharge their duties, that with average abilities and reasonable application they may look forward confidently to a certain provision for their lives, that with superior powers they may rationally hope to attain to the highest prizes in the Service, while if they prove decidedly incompetent, or incurably indolent, they must expect to be removed from it.

The first step towards carrying this principle into effect should be, the establishment of a proper system of examination before appointment, which should be followed, as at present, by a short period of probation. The necessity of this has been so far admitted that some kind of examination does now take place before clerks are admitted into any of the following offices:—The Treasury, the Colonial Office, the Board of Trade, the Privy Council Office, the Poor Law Board, the War Office, the Ordnance Office, the Audit Office, the Paymaster General's Office, the Inland Revenue Office, the Emigration Office, and some others. These examinations vary in their character; in some offices more is required than in others, and in some cases what is required will be more rigidly enforced by one set of Examiners than by another.

The preliminary examination of candidates for civil employment, however, cannot be conducted in an effective and consistent manner throughout the Service, while it is left to each department to determine the nature of the examination and to examine the candidates. Some on whom the duty of examining devolves feel no interest in the subject; others, although disposed to do their best, are likely to entertain erroneous or imperfect conceptions of the standard of examination which ought to be fixed, and to be unable to apply it properly after it has been settled. The time and attention of the superior officers are fully occupied in disposing of the current business of their respective departments. To do this in a creditable manner will always be their primary object; and as the bearing of the subject under consideration upon the efficiency of their departments, although very important, is not of a direct or immediate kind, and is not likely to have much effect during their own tenure of office, what has to be done in reference to it will either be done by themselves in a hurried and imperfect manner, or will be left by them to their subordinate officers to be dealt with at their discretion. In a large department, in which numerous candidates have to be examined, want of time will prevent the superior officers from giving the subject the attention it deserves; and other matters, although of infinitely less real consequence, will have the precedence, because they press, and must be disposed of at the moment. Moreover, a large proportion of the persons appointed to a public department usually consists of young men in whose success the heads of the office or the principal clerks take a lively personal interest, owing to relationship or some other motive connected with their public or private position; and an independent opinion is hardly to be expected from an examiner who is acting under the orders of the one, and is in habits of daily intercourse with the other. A public officer ought not to be placed in a situation in which duty might require him to make an unfavourable report under such circumstances. Lastly, even supposing every other circumstance to be favourable, it is impossible that each department, acting for itself, can come to such just conclusions in regard to the nature of the preliminary examination, or can conduct it in such a fair, and effective, and consistent manner, as would persons having the advantage of a general view of the subject as it affects every public department, and who should have been selected for the duty on account of their experience in matters of this description.

We accordingly recommend that a central Board should be constituted for conducting the examination of all candidates for the public service whom it may be thought right to subject to such a test. Such board should be composed of men holding an independent position, and capable of commanding general confidence; it should have at its head an officer of the rank of Privy Councillor; and should either include, or have the means of obtaining the assistance of, persons experienced in the education of the youth of the upper and middle classes, and persons who are familiar with the conduct of official business. It should be made imperative upon candidates for admission to any appointment, (except in certain special cases which will presently be noticed,) to pass a proper examination before this Board, and obtain from them a certificate of having done so.

We are of opinion that this examination should be in all cases a competing literary examination. This ought not to exclude careful previous inquiry into the age, health, and moral fitness of the candidates. Where character and bodily activity are chiefly required, more, comparatively, will depend upon the testimony of those to whom the candidate is well known; but the selection from among the candidates who have satisfied these preliminary inquiries should still be made by a competing examination. This may be so conducted as to test the intelligence, as well as the mere attainments of the candidates. We see no other mode by which (in the case of inferior no less than of superior offices) the double object can be attained of selecting the fittest person, and of avoiding the evils of patronage.

For the superior situations endeavours should be made to secure the services of the most promising young men of the day, by a competing examination on a level with the highest description of education in this country. In this class of situations there is no limit to the demands which may ultimately be made upon the abilities of those who, entering them simply as junior clerks, gradually rise to the highest posts in them. To obtain first-rate men, it is obvious that recourse should be had to competition. It would be impossible to impose upon each candidate for a clerkship, as a positive test of his fitness for the appointment, the necessity of passing an examination equal to that of first-class men at the universities; but if, on the occurrence of a vacancy, it is found that a number of candidates present themselves, of whom some are capable of passing such an examination, there can be no reason why the public should not have the benefit of such men's services, in preference to those of persons of inferior merit. It may be repeated that no other means can be devised of avoiding the evils of patronage, which, if, in this case, less objectionable because of the comparatively small number of superior appointments, is much more objectionable in its effects on the public business of the country.

Our proposal is not inconsistent with the appropriation of special talents or attainments to special departments of the public service. In the case, for example, of the subordinate grades from which collectors, surveyors, secretaries, junior commissioners, and other superior officers of the Revenue departments are usually selected, the nature of the examination should be adapted to the object of securing the scientific and other attainments which are so important to the efficiency of these great national establishments. In the same way provision might be made for securing the peculiar attainments to be required of persons to be employed in the Foreign

Office, and in the diplomatic and consular services; and in respect to offices of account, arithmetic and book-keeping will be principally insisted on.

It next becomes a question, whether the competition which we have proposed should take place on the occasion of each vacancy, or whether there should be periodical examinations. We are of opinion that it would be desirable to adopt the latter alternative. There are peculiar advantages in a system of periodical examinations. It economizes the number, and also the time of the examiners, who, instead of being overworked half the year, have their employment regularly distributed. It is also more convenient to the candidates themselves. We propose, therefore, that examinations should be held at stated times; that an average having been taken of the number of situations of the class contended for, which periodically fall vacant, it should be announced, before the commencement of each trial, how many gentlemen were to be elected for admission into the public service on that occasion. The election having taken place, those who have succeeded should be distributed among the offices to which appointments are to be made, on the footing of probationers. The precise mode in which the successful candidates should be allotted to the several departments will require some consideration; but there will be no difficulty in it which may not easily be overcome. One obvious course of proceeding would be to send to each department a list of those who are selected for appointments, leaving to the head of each office to choose from among them as vacancies occur. Or it might be thought desirable that the Board of Examiners should recommend particular men to particular departments, according to their capacities, the head of the department in each case exercising his discretion in accepting them or not; or the choice might be given to the candidates themselves, some restriction being imposed to prevent any from choosing offices for which their peculiar education had not fitted them. If more have been elected (in order to maintain the average) than there is immediate demand for, they should be sent as supernumerary clerks to the offices in which the work happens to be the heaviest, unless there is any special service upon which they can with advantage be temporarily employed, or they might wait to take their turn. As vacancies occur from time to time before the next general examination, the supernumeraries should be appointed to them, and, if the whole have not been placed before that time, it will only be necessary to make the next batch the smaller. It would be desirable to retain the probation as at present, rendering it more efficient by precise reports of the conduct of the probationers.

In the examinations which we have recommended, we consider that the right of competing should be open to all persons, of a given age, subject only, as before suggested, to the necessity of their giving satisfactory references to persons able to speak to their moral conduct and character, and of producing medical certificates to the effect that they have no bodily infirmity likely to incapacitate them for the public service. It is only by throwing the examinations entirely open that we can hope to attract the proper class of candidates.

The choice of the subjects to be comprehended in the examination, as well as the mode in which the examination should be conducted, so as to diminish the labour by eliminating such candidates as have obviously no chance of success, should, of course, be left to the Board of Examiners. We will therefore only indicate the advantage of making the subjects as numerous as may be found practicable, so as to secure the greatest and most varied amount of talent for the public service. Men whose services would be highly valuable to the country might easily be beaten by some who were their inferiors, if the examination were confined to a few subjects to which the latter had devoted their exclusive attention; but if an extensive range were given, the superiority of the best would become evident. Besides, an opportunity would be afforded for judging in what kind of situation each is likely to be most useful; and we need hardly allude to the important effect which would be produced upon the general education of the country, if proficiency in history, jurisprudence, political economy, modern languages, political and physical geography, and other matters, besides the staple of classics and mathematics, were made directly conducive to the success of young men desirous of entering into the public service. Such an inducement would probably do more to quicken the progress of our Universities, for instance, than any legislative measures that could be adopted.

It would probably be right to include in the examination some exercises directly bearing upon official business; to require a preçis to be made of a set of papers, or a letter to be written under given circumstances; but the great advantage to be expected from the examinations would be, that they would elicit young men of general ability, which is a matter of more moment than their being possessed of any special acquirements. Men capable of distinguishing themselves in any of the subjects we have named, and thereby affording a proof that their education has not been lost upon them, would probably make themselves useful wherever they might be placed. . . .

We must remark that there will be some cases in which examination will not be applicable. It would be absurd to impose this test upon persons selected to fill the appointments which have been previously spoken of under the name of staff appointments, on account of their acknowledged eminence in one of the liberal professions, or in some other walk of life. We think, however, that the circumstances under which any person is appointed to such an office should always be placed on record by an official correspondence between the department to which he is assigned and the Board of Examiners; and we would also suggest for consideration the expediency of making an annual return to Parliament of the names of persons who may be so appointed.

In dealing with the lower class of appointments, it will be necessary to make provision against the difficulty that if the examinations were all held at one place, a large proportion of those who might reasonably become candidates would be deterred from presenting themselves by the expense of the journey. If the scheme of examinations were more favourable to one locality than another, there can be no doubt that it would soon be set aside as unjust. We propose, therefore, that an arrangement should be made for holding examinations in various parts of the United Kingdom. . . .

With regard to the age of admission, we are of opinion that in the case of candidates for superior situations the limits should, as a general rule, be 19 and 25; in the case of candidates for inferior offices, 17 and 21.

Having thus completed our suggestions as to the best mode of obtaining a proper supply of public servants in the first instance, we have next to offer some remarks on what appears to us to be the best mode of regulating their employment, and their promotion, so as to maintain the efficiency of the office at the highest point.

As we have already spoken of the importance of establishing a proper distinction between intellectual and mechanical labour, we need offer no further observations on this most vital point. The

proper maintenance of such distinction depends more upon the
discretion and management of the chiefs of offices and those
immediately below them, than upon any general regulations that
could be made by a central authority. We consider that a great step
has been taken by the appointment in several offices of a class of
supplementary clerks, receiving uniform salaries in each department, and capable therefore of being transferred, without inconvenience, from one to another, according as the demand for their
services may be greater or less at any particular time; and we
expect that the moveable character of this class of officers, and the
superior standard of examination which we have proposed for the
higher class, will together have the effect of marking the distinction between them in a proper manner.

The theory of the public service is, that the annual increase of
salary from the minimum to the maximum of the class, is given as
matter of course as the reward of service, and with no reference to
the comparative merits of the individuals; but that promotion from
class to class is the reward of merit, or rather that it is regulated by
a consideration of the public interests, and that those only are to be
transferred from one class to a higher who have shown themselves
capable of rendering valuable services in it. This salutary principle
is, however, in practice often overlooked, and promotion from
class to class, as well as the annual rise within the class, is more
commonly regulated by seniority than by merit. The evil consequences of this are too obvious to require lengthened comment: it
is, perhaps, more important to point out some of the difficulties
which lie in the way of amendment.

If the opinions of the gentlemen engaged in the Civil Service
could be taken on the subject of promotion, it would probably be
found that a very large majority of them would object strongly to
what is called promotion by merit. The reason they would assign
would be, that promotion by (so called) merit would usually
become promotion by favouritism. . . . Now, setting aside cases
of actual favouritism, there must be many instances in which the
chief permanent officers fail to perceive, and properly to bring into
notice, the valuable qualities of those beneath them. A man may be
timid and hesitating in manner, and on that account may be passed
over as dull, in favour of some one by no means his superior in real

worth, but having more address in recommending himself; or, on the other hand, the chief officer may have taken a particular fancy to some young man on his first entrance into the department, and may have thrown in his way special opportunities of advancing himself, which others have not had. All such cases are watched with jealousy even now, and if promotion by seniority were wholly set aside, without the introduction of proper safeguards, they would be the cause of still more discomfort.

It ought, therefore, to be a leading object with the Government so to regulate promotion by merit as to provide every possible security against its abuse. . . .

With regard to the annual increase of salary, we are of opinion that it would be right to require that each clerk, before becoming entitled to receive the addition, should produce a certificate from his immediate superior, that he has been punctual in his attendance, and has given satisfaction in the discharge of his duties, during the preceding year. Such certificates are required from the heads of rooms in the Ordnance Department, and from each Inspector in the Audit Office. They would ordinarily be given as a matter of course, but the knowledge that they might be withheld would be useful in maintaining discipline, and in enforcing regularity of attendance, which in some cases is a matter of difficulty, the only penalties which can at present be imposed for irregularity being those of suspension and dismissal, which are too severe to be applied unless in aggravated instances.

The subject of pensions and retired allowances is one intimately connected with the matters treated of in this paper. . . . We desire . . . to call attention to the importance of establishing an uniform and consistent system of regulating the amounts to be granted to superannuated public servants, with reference to the character of their service. . . .

It is obvious that the proposed Board of Examiners might be turned to good account in supplying these defects. Duplicates of the books [with regular efficiency reports on each civil servant] which we have recommended to be kept in the separate Offices should be transmitted to the Department of Examination, which should also be furnished with all information relating to promotions and other matters bearing on the services of the officers in each department. No grant of superannuation allowance or good service pension should be made by the Treasury without a previ-

ous report from the Board of Examiners embodying this information.

By this system, not only would greater certainty be introduced
into the superannuation business, but a degree of consistency
would be given to the whole scheme of promotion by merit, which
would, we think, ensure its success. It would also have this further
advantage, that it would serve to direct the attention of the
Government to the merits of individual clerks,—now seldom
known beyond the sphere of their own offices,—and would thus
enable it to select deserving persons from the ranks of the public
service to fill important situations which might become vacant. It is
to be hoped that in future, if any staff appointment falls vacant in
an office in which there is a deserving clerk well qualified to fill it,
his claims will not be passed over in favour of a stranger; but this
principle might advantageously be carried further, by filling the
appointment with a person from another office, if there is no one in
the department itself qualified to take it; and there might often be
occasions in which the advantages of encouraging public servants,
and at the same time introducing fresh blood into an office, might
be combined; as, for instance, by filling a staff appointment in
office A by the transfer to it of a meritorious staff officer from
office B, and then supplying the vacancy caused in office B by
the appointment to it of one of the most deserving clerks in office A. . . .

Upon a review of the recommendations contained in this paper it
will be seen that the objects which we have principally in view are
these:—

1. To provide, by a proper system of examination, for the
supply of the public service with a thoroughly efficient class of
men.

2. To encourage industry and foster merit, by teaching all
public servants to look forward to promotion according to their
deserts, and to expect the highest prizes in the service if they can
qualify themselves for them.

3. To mitigate the evils which result from the fragmentary
character of the Service, and to introduce into it some elements of
unity, by placing the first appointments upon an uniform footing,
opening the way to the promotion of public officers to staff
appointments in other departments than their own, and introduc-

ing into the lower ranks a body of men (the supplementary clerks) whose services may be made available at any time in any office whatever.

It remains for us to express our conviction that if any change of the importance of those which we have recommended is to be carried into effect, it can only be successfully done through the medium of an Act of Parliament. The existing system is supported by long usage and powerful interests; and were any Government to introduce material alterations into it, in consequence of their own convictions, without taking the precaution to give those alterations the force of law, it is almost certain that they would be imperceptibly, or perhaps avowedly, abandoned by their successors, if they were not even allowed to fall into disuse by the very Government which had originated them. A few clauses would accomplish all that is proposed in this paper, and it is our firm belief that a candid statement of the grounds of the measure would insure its success and popularity in the country, and would remove many misconceptions which are now prejudicial to the public service.

November 23, 1853   STAFFORD H. NORTHCOTE
                                                 C. E. TREVELYAN

26. Irish Nationalism: Problems in the Devolution of Power

THE SIMPLEST way to explain the Irish problem is to say that it was unsolvable; and it was badly handled at that. The root of the problem was nationality, but there were always other elements to confuse the issue. There was, initially, the problem of religion. So long as legislation excluded Roman Catholics from a share in central or local government, so long did religion appear to be the source of Irish difficulties. But as Daniel O'Connell warned in 1828–29 during the Catholic Association agitation to which Lord Eldon and many Englishmen reacted so violently, Catholic emancipation was but the beginning of the drive for repeal of the union of Ireland with the United Kingdom.

Then there was the question of land. Ireland had been repeatedly "conquered" from the twelfth to the nineteenth century, and most Irish land was owned by absentee landlords who were usually, although not always, English. Their sole interest in their estates was a maximum yield. Rack rents were easily secured, for Ireland had insufficient land and insecure tenure. Agrarian disorder, almost always brutal, was endemic outside of Ulster through the eighteenth and nineteenth centuries. It provided ample excuse, if such were needed, for English coercion.

Irish separatism and Irish nationalism developed through the nineteenth century. The romantic "Young Ireland" movement inspired good poetry but ineffective politics among a limited elite in the 1840's. For most Irish, famine was the reality. One million died; another million emigrated. The liveliest Irish spirits were gone, and the English found suppression of the rest deceptively easy. At the close of the American civil war, the Irish Republican Brotherhood, spurred on by U.S. money and Irish veterans of the Union army, opened a new phase of Irish violence. Counterforce prevailed, and the Fenians were suppressed. Sinn Fein had the dual misfortune of being few in numbers and anathema to the Roman Catholic Church hierarchy. Subversive overtones of violence continued to ring, but nationalist agitation shifted back to constitutional themes.

Protestants, who provided much Irish nationalist leadership in the nineteenth century, recaptured church support and national backing by mobilizing the Irish Nationalist party in Parliament and combining its agitation with that of the Irish Land League. The conception was inspired and effective, but circumstances militated against success. The lengthening shadows of the agricultural depression after 1873 worked against any quick solution of the land question, and the increasingly racist tone of British imperialism boded ill for political reason. But against this background the last attempts were made to find some constitutional answer short of Irish separation.

Gladstone was one of the first Englishmen to appreciate the problem as one of nationality. He sought to provide concessions for religion—disestablishment of the Irish Church and support for a Catholic university—and to guarantee agrarian security through two land acts (1870, 1881), which represented sharp breaks with English doctrines of property and contract. Gladstone also grappled for some answer to the key issue. One could not kill home rule with kindness, but he hoped to arrange for the orderly devolution of authority and responsibility.

On the other hand, Charles Stewart Parnell (1846–91), leader of the Irish Nationalist party in the House of Commons, got caught in a web of his own spinning. By uniting the parliamentary party and the Land League under his control, he secured the necessary power base for effective political action; but these were means, not ends. Given his position, this dour, unlovable Protestant found himself incapable of compromise, even when he saw a measure was good. He always had to ask for more—again, because the problem was one of nationality, not land. Irish Americans, his principal financial backers, would permit no compromise either. Nor would many groups within Ireland itself: the omnipresent terrorist minorities which later fell to slaughtering each other after there were no English left to fight. Parnell's commitment to moderation was, in fact, self-defeating. But he tried.

The home rule controversy ran from 1886 past the First World War. It raised the political temperature to impossible heights, almost destroyed the Liberal party, brought out the worst in Irishmen, and capped a record for consistent English misrule. But there were exceptions—the men like Gladstone, a convert to home rule in 1886, who believed that right was right and incurred martyrdom to prove it.

Recommended Reading

Irish history is provocative and provoking. Only recently have we been so fortunate as to have sound monographic work. One exciting study is C. C. O'BRIEN, *Parnell and His Party, 1880–90* (Oxford, 1957). J. L. HAMMOND, *Gladstone and the Irish Nation* (London, 1938), is very useful; as is R. D. COLLISON BLACK, *Economic Thought and the Irish Question* (Cambridge, 1960).

SOURCES: Document A: Public Record Office, Granville Papers 30/29/29A; also printed in entirety with editorial correction in Agatha Ramm (ed.), *The Political Correspondence of Mr. Gladstone and Lord Granville 1876–1886*, Vol. II, *1883–1886* (Oxford, 1962), pp. 9–11. Document B: Charles Stewart Parnell, "Speech in Answer to the Address from the Throne, January 21, 1886," *Hansard's Parliamentary Debates*, Third Series, Vol. CCCII, cols. 152–160.

A. William Gladstone to Lord Granville

[Secret]

Château Scott, Cannes
Jan. 22, [18]83

[Gladstone opens the letter by worrying about the effect of the Marquis of Hartington's speech to his constituents on January 19, which could be, and was, interpreted as suggesting a government retreat on the issue of extending more freedom in local government to Ireland.]

I console myself with thinking it is hardly possible that Hartington *can* have meant to say what nevertheless both Times and Daily News make him seem to say, namely that we recede from, or throw into abeyance the declarations we have constantly made about our desire to extend local Government, properly so called, to Ireland on the first opportunity, which the state of business in Parliament would permit.

We announced our intention to do this at the very moment when we were preparing to suspend the *Habeaus Corpus* Act.

Since that time we have seen our position in Ireland immensely strengthened, and the leader of the agitation has even thought it wise, and has dared, to pursue a somewhat conciliatory course.

Many of his coadjutors are still as vicious, it may be, as ever, but how can we say (for instance) to the Ulster men, you shall remain with shortened liberties & without local Government because Biggar[1] and Co are hostile to British connection?

There has also come prominently into view a new and powerful set of motives which, in my deliberate judgment, require us, for the sake of the United Kingdom even *more* than for the sake of Ireland, to push forward this question.

Under the present highly centralised system of Government, every demand, which can be started on behalf of a poor and ill-organised country, comes directly on the British Government and Treasury; if refused it becomes at once a head of grievance, if granted not only a new drain but a certain source of political complication and embarassment, the peasant proprietary—the winter's distress—and state of the labourers—the loans to farmers —the promotion of public works—the encouragement of fisheries—the promotion of emigration—each and every one of these questions has a sting, and the sting can only be taken out of it by our treating it in correspondence with a popular and responsible *Irish* body—competent to act for its own portion of the country.

Every consideration, which prompted our pledges, prompts the recognition of them & their extension rather than curtailment.

The Irish Government have in preparation a Local Government Bill.

Such a bill may even be an economy of time. By no other means that I can see shall we be able to ward off most critical and questionable discussions on questions of the class I have mentioned.

The argument that we cannot yet trust Irishmen with popular local institutions is the mischievous argument by which the Con-

[1] Joseph Gillis Biggar (1828–90), a leading pioneer of obstructionist tactics in the Irish Parliamentary party.

servative opposition to the Melbourne Government resisted, and finally crippled, the reform of municipal Corporations in Ireland.

By acting on principles diametrically opposite, we have broken down to 35 or 40 what would have been a party, in this Parliament, of 65 Home Rulers, and have thus averted (or at the very least postponed) the perilous crisis, which no man has as yet looked in the face: the crisis which will arise when a large & united majority of Irish Members demand some fundamental changes in the legislative relations of the two countries.

I can ill convey to you how clear are my thoughts, or how earnest my convictions, on this important subject. Do not hurry any reply, if you find the reply difficult.

One word on another matter, less arduous. I am puzzled about these prosecutions [of twenty Irishmen for plotting to assassinate members of the government] in Ireland, for speeches: on none of which have we, I believe, been consulted. I wrote to Spencer [Lord Lieutenant of Ireland] to express my misgivings in the case of the wretched Biggar; but he was already committed. I do not mean to condemn, but am not able at present to express satisfaction.

Should there prove to be a radical difference of opinion, which God forbid, among us as to the propriety of putting forward an Irish local Government Bill, I see no other advisable course for the moment than the use of general terms in the Speech from the Throne, and the adjournment of the final interpretation at any rate until Easter.

B. Charles Stewart Parnell in Answer to Address from the Throne, January 21, 1886

For the present, I can only say I have little doubt that if the House at large, or even a majority, approach the question of the government of Ireland, or the alterations to be made in it, in the same spirit and with the same largeness of views as have characterized the speech of the right hon. Gentleman the Member for Mid Lothian [Gladstone], such a solution would be found as would enable Ireland to be entrusted with the right of self-government, and secure those guarantees, regarding the integrity of the Empire, the supremacy of the Crown, and the protection of the minority—

of what is called the loyal minority—in Ireland which have been required by the Leaders of both the political Parties in the House. I have always believed that if we could come to a discussion—if we could agree upon the principle that the Irish people are entitled to some self-government, that Parliament has to a very large extent failed to impose conditions for governing Ireland during the 85 years that have elapsed since the Union—we should not find the details so very formidable, or such great difficulties in the way of securing the Empire against the chances of separation, which seem to oppress the public mind in England at the present moment.

My own candid opinion is this—that so far from increasing the chances of separation the concession of autonomy to Ireland would undoubtedly very largely diminish them. I believe that the feeling in this country upon the matter—a feeling which I believe to be a genuine one and really to exist—the feeling that the entrusting of Ireland with self-government might result in danger to the Empire, simply arises from the want of knowledge, which must befall Englishmen, with reference to any Irish question; and from the very industrious attempts which have been set on foot by some gentlemen, who assume to represent the landlords of Ireland, with the view of throwing the public opinion of this country on the wrong scent, and diverting attention from the real issue to a question about danger to the integrity of the Empire, with reference to which I believe there is really no apprehension at all. Indeed, the very persons who are loudest in their talk about the risk run by the loyal minority in Ireland, and the integrity of the Empire, secretly and in their own hearts know perfectly well that the statement has no foundation.

No, Mr. Speaker; this question is really a question of the amount of rent which the landlords of Ireland shall receive; and when hon. Members, representing the landowners of the country, talk about the integrity of the Empire they are thinking rather about the integrity of their breeches pockets. The Land Question is, undoubtedly, a very difficult question, and to my mind presents the real point of difficulty in arriving at a solution of the question of Irish autonomy; and the House will find that if that question be once settled on a basis satisfactory to the Irish landlords and tenants, if such a basis could be arrived at, you would hear nothing more from Irish Representatives on the opposite Benches about the integrity of the Empire and the risk of separation.

We have been spoken to to-night about the necessity of protecting the loyal minority. Now, I myself was born, a Protestant; I have always lived a Protestant, and I hope to die a Protestant; and if in the future, after the concession of the Irish claims, any danger were to arise to my Protestant fellow-countrymen, I would be the first to stand up for liberty of speech, liberty of conscience, and liberty to live and thrive for every section of the community, whether they be Protestants or whether they be Catholics; and perhaps I might be a more effectual aid, in times of real danger, than some of those hon. Gentlemen who talk so loudly and who boast so much. But I have no such apprehension. I am convinced that the Catholics of Ireland would not attempt to oppress their fellow countrymen. They would desire, and it would be their object, in view of the history of the past, to give the Protestants of Ireland more than fair play; they would endeavour to bring them to the front, and give them the fullest share in the government of Ireland. Look at the considerable proportion of Protestants which the Irish national constituencies have willingly and freely returned. If they have not returned more Protestants it is not on account of any prejudice against their creed, but because it has been difficult to find more from that class with the necessary leisure and with a desire sufficient to induce them to come to Westminster in order to represent Irish constituencies. No, Sir; I have no belief at all in the talk either of the danger of separation or the danger to the Protestant minority. The allegation is brought forward for interested motives by the landlord class in Ireland in order that they may, for a few years longer, retain the power of exacting from their tenants exorbitant rents which the soil has not produced. If there was no Land Question in Ireland there would be no opposition from any influential or considerable section in the country to the concession of a full measure of autonomy for Ireland. But in any case the Catholics of Ireland are perfectly willing that any guarantees that the ingenuity of man can frame for the protection of the minority shall be framed and shall be put in force; and it would be found that the Catholics would treat much more justly and much more generously the 1,000,000 Protestants of Ireland in regard to their future representation in the Irish Parliament than the Protestants of England and Scotland have treated the 2,000,000 of Catholics in regard to their just representation in this Imperial Parliament.

Allusion, Sir, has been made in the Queen's Speech, and also by

the right hon. Gentleman the Chancellor of the Exchequer—I
admit a most moderate allusion has been made by him—to the
difficulties in connection with what is called "Boycotting," and also
the difficulties in the way of obtaining of rents. The right hon.
Gentleman certainly did not appear to me, speaking from his point
of view, to attempt to magnify these difficulties. The right hon.
Gentleman admitted that convictions had been obtained in almost
every instance under the ordinary law, and that more serious crime
had not increased since the Government allowed the more stringent provisions of the Coercion Act to drop. He also admitted that
while, what he terms, and justly terms, minor offences, such as
threatening letters, have somewhat increased, yet, in regard to
"Boycotting" offences, the Government have obtained about 150
convictions out of 400 prosecutions, and that in other cases prosecutions are still pending and have yet to come off. I regard that
testimony as most important, for it shows that at the termination of
the Crimes Act there was not that relapse into serious crime which
many people had apprehended; and it is a somewhat remarkable
result in the case of a people of such an elastic nature as that which
unhappily belongs to the Irish. It is much to their credit that they
should have abstained from crime, and set their faces resolutely
against crime as they have done. I think it is a matter which ought
to be better known and admitted more by the public feeling in
England than it appears to be. Nevertheless, I admit that, unhappily, in regard to the question of land, affairs in Ireland are at
present very serious. That result is one which I myself have
deprecated very much.

Neither the organization of which I am the head in Ireland [the
Land League] nor I myself can charge ourselves with having done
anything to foment that state of things. On the contrary, so far as
my influence and that of my friends has been available it has distinctly been used to prevent "Boycotting" in as many cases as we
could possibly interfere; and it has also been distinctly used in the
direction of repressing and restraining the movement which sprung
up in a spontaneous manner among the people themselves. These
matters are on record, and, of course, it will not be denied that
these have been the efforts of nearly all of the important leaders of
the National Party in Ireland. I do not deny that some extravagant
speeches have been made by one or two gentlemen—speeches
which I have been the first to deprecate—but we all know that it is

very difficult at times to put an old head on young shoulders, and young men are sometimes very much carried away when making speeches into saying things which in their sober moments they would undoubtedly regret. But as regards the movement itself, it is a very remarkable and a noteworthy fact that the present movement was a spontaneous one, and in that it differs from the Land League movement of 1879. Upon that movement £250,000 sterling was spent in organizing the tenantry and in persuading them to resist the payment of rents which were admittedly, at the time, rack rents. That movement resulted in the passing of the Land Act of 1881. But upon the present movement not one single penny has been spent. In addition to the repressing and restraining influences we have exercised, we have refrained from making any expenditure whatever in aid of the movement for the reduction of rents, to which the right hon. Gentleman the Chancellor of the Exchequer has referred. Therefore, it cannot be said that it has been a movement which has been encouraged and fomented by the National League.

I think the spontaneous character of the movement is a matter well worthy the attention and consideration of the House and of the Government. The Irish tenantry have, for a very great number of years, paid large sums of money in the shape of rent. They are represented as persons desirous of evading their obligations. That is not my experience. My experience, on the contrary, has been that they have been rather too willing to pay excessive rents; and so long as they could keep body and soul together, even at the risk of starvation to their families and themselves, they have attempted to keep the roofs over their heads at any cost. But now their condition is so desperate, and brought as it has been to its present pitch by such a reduction in the prices of agricultural produce as we have not had any experience of for 30 years—in the prices of all the agricultural produce which their farms yield—that they have been forced into the present movement in order to claim from certain landlords—not all landlords, because I believe the majority of the Irish landlords at the present moment are giving fair reductions, and are, in that way, preventing the tenants from going to extremities, and also saving the remains of their own property—but in the case of a minority of the Irish landlords who have stubbornly refused all reduction of rent there does unhappily exist on a certain number of estates in Ireland a combination for the

286   HEYDAY OF VICTORIANISM

purpose of obtaining a reduction of these rack rents. If the matter
be inquired into, I think it will be found that that is the whole
dimension to which the complaint is capable of being stretched.
The House, composed, as it is, largely of Representatives from
agricultural districts, must know that that agricultural depression
does exist, and has sprung up since rents were fixed under the Land
Act of 1881. The rents were then fixed for a term of 15 years; but
owing to the depreciation in the prices of agricultural produce,
amounting to 50 per cent, it has now become in many cases absolutely impossible to collect these rents. I think that it is no discredit
to the exertions of the right hon. Gentleman the Member for Mid
Lothian (Mr. Gladstone) to say that the rents fixed under his Act,
owing to this great fall in the prices of agricultural produce, have
become impossible rents, and that the purpose of that Act has been
defeated. . . .

Well, Sir, the situation is undoubtedly a serious one; but if the
Government step in and support that small minority of landlords
who are refusing all reasonable concessions to their tenants, like
that which I have cited, the result will be that these landowners
and many others will be strengthened in their unjust demands, and
great suffering and misery would befall the unfortunate and
wretched people. The weight of authority and power which must
always exist will weigh down the scale unjustly and cruelly towards the tenant. I shall be glad if some proposition can be made
for dealing with the land difficulty in Ireland, because I look upon
it as the real difficulty in that country, which overshadows every
other. I do not think that there is any real disposition on the part of
the Irish tenants to refuse just and fair concessions; and I am sure
the great majority of the people are most anxious that the landlords
should receive such fair terms and fair treatment as the extremity
of the times renders at all possible. Some scheme of purchase might
be devised . . . under which the bulk of the land in the occupation of agricultural tenants might be purchased. . . .

The question demands the careful attention of the House and
the Government; and I believe, and all those who are not influenced by Party motives in Ireland are of opinion, that there should
be some fair settlement, and if such fair settlement were arrived at
and agreed upon by all parties, and if it were really a fair one, I am
convinced that the payments would be made by the Irish tenants to
the last penny. I hope, Sir, that we may have a further opportunity

of reverting to this matter. We are bound to stand by our people. When it comes to be a struggle between the Irish landowners, aided by the Government, and the Irish tenants, whom I and my Friends represent, and the Irish labourers, we can have no doubt as to which side we should cast our lot with. But we wish that the "still small voice of reason" should prevail. We do not desire to go into any contest. We see in the present position a desire and a wish on the part of Englishmen to study and understand, with a view to its final settlement, this great Irish question; and we are resolved that no extravagance on our part of action or language shall mar the chance which we believe our country possesses now for the first time in her history.

IV

Toward Collectivism

Introduction

In July 1914, Andrew Bonar Law, the leader of the Conservative party, repeated his pledge to back Ulster to civil war if necessary and to disrupt the workings of the British Parliament to prevent the implementation of Irish home rule. Sir Henry Wilson, the chief of military operations, publicly sided with mutinous army officers on the same issue. One month before the fighting broke out in the First World War, British parliamentary government was collapsing, and civil war seemed imminent, and not merely in Ireland. Increasingly bitter class war in England reached a peak as ever more workers turned to strikes instead of seeking parliamentary redress. Feminism reached its most frenzied stage with incendiarism in post boxes, suicide under the hoofs of the King's horse at the Derby, "Votes for Women" etched with acid on golf-course putting greens, and an attempt to blow up the coronation chair in Westminster Abbey.

Germany, when deciding to make war in 1914, counted Britain out. The nation appeared to be on the verge of disintegration. The Germans also did their bit to help by providing arms for both Ulster and South Irish Volunteers. Britain did not count in the world balance that July. She could not manage her own affairs let alone intervene in those of anyone else. But Germany made a fatal miscalculation by deciding that, if war must come—as she believed it would—time and circumstances dictated that it must come now. The British suddenly discovered what Winston Churchill called "a higher principle of hatred." Britain then buried her nineteenth century in Flanders. She also squandered the husbanded economic assets of a century and the youth that might have spared her the disasters of the twentieth century.

The legacy of British politics in the nineteenth century seemed to be chaos and ruin. An age of humanity appeared to end in an unparalleled outburst of hatred. A century of extraordinary intellectual and cultural achievement culminated in nihilism and despair. Having discovered how to end poverty, Britain made war. These were bitter fruits of revolutions averted and cynical plaudits for the tireless labors of those who sought betterment for all mankind.

The Great Depression (1873–96) cast a pall on the late Victorian years. It was ushered in by the first great international financial collapse and hit agriculture hardest; it was neither consistent nor unrelieved. It was, as Alfred Marshall, the distinguished contemporary economist, put it, a depression of "profits, interest, and prices."[1] There were defective sectors of the economy, areas that were old, obsolete, overcapitalized, and unimaginative. There were hard pockets of unemployment, and there was great industrial tension both between and within labor and management. Real wages moved up, often substantially, during the depression. For workingmen the recovery (1896–1914) was economically more difficult. After bitter strikes, hard-won wage increases evaporated in rising prices as quickly as they had been gained. Real wages fell slightly in the years leading up to the First World War, generating acute social tension. The British economy was ageing, and not passing gracefully from its profitable years.

Social adjustments were often more cumbersome than in previous decades and were almost invariably fraught with great political significance. The underworld of labor made its voice heard through trade unions. Drawing upon a sense of grievance, neglect, and the support of humanitarian idealists (the well-to-do who turned increasingly to social work), match girls struck in 1888, London dockworkers in 1889. A new concept of mass organized labor threatened the more complacent, conservative, established craft unions. All unions, moreover, faced the threat of larger industrial units and combinations and increasingly hostile attitudes toward the labor movement. Technological innovation created new skills and displaced others, making older workers more insecure. Much of the new leadership was avowedly socialist, although many would not have been able to give their socialism a coherent definition. The new leadership was militant and politically engaged. It fostered a change in the style and the tone of industrial relations.[2]

[1] See *VS&C*, Document 5, "The Great Depression."
[2] See *VS&C*, Document 14, "Trade Unions."

The labor movement both progressed and retrogressed in the last quarter of the century. Lower middle-class groups enrolled in their own trade unions; office help, shop assistants, and junior clerks were organized with varying degrees of success. Robert Owen's dream of a massive, irresistible labor movement seemed deceptively close to reality seventy years after he had proposed it. By 1900 something between one-fifth and one-quarter of the English labor force belonged to trade unions.

The upper classes, like the working classes, went through considerable readjustments during these years. The steady merging of the aristocracy and the plutocracy was characteristic of the late nineteenth century. The collapse of agriculture proved crucial here. Dairy farming and livestock were not seriously affected, but grain prices fell by 50 per cent and stayed down. With a substantial decline of rents, the landed classes were thrown increasingly upon non-landed resources. The increasing overlap of economic function led to the sharing of attitudes and politics. The upper middle classes moved closer to the aristocracy; the lower middle classes moved closer to labor. The great social gulf came increasingly to be somewhere within the middle classes themselves.[3]

The alarms and excursions of late Victorian politics were overseas. Political torpor prevailed at home. This was implicit in the failure of the second Gladstone government (1880–85) and was guaranteed after the defeat of home rule (1886). The formal structure of politics was remade. The old Whigs joined the Tories in the House of Lords with fearful political results. The Liberal Unionists, blocked from their old party by the Irish problem, gravitated to the Tories and raised the intellectual capacity of that party just as it captured business and professional groups. The result was a colorful, if domestically uneventful, twenty years of Conservative domination.

There had been serious attempts to adapt politics to the new democracy. Joseph Chamberlain, who sported a stunning record of success in business and was a reforming Lord Mayor of Birmingham, attempted to remake the Liberal party in the image of respectable radical dissent and preclude the evolution of a proletarian party by a program of social reform. He framed a radical program and sought to force it on his party,[4] but he could not get

---

[3] See *VS&C*, Part III, "Social Organization."
[4] See Document 27.

it past Gladstone. After the home rule dispute Chamberlain turned his considerable talents to imperialism, forgetting most of his domestic program and leaving his national party organization to Liberal party hacks. Chamberlain's Conservative *alter ego*, Lord Randolph Churchill, stormed his party's bastions by leaping from the back benches to the Exchequer, but he proved unable to formulate a program. "Tory Democracy" was a slogan, a public relations device. It was effective as such things often are, but "Tory Democracy" meant little more than masses voting Conservative. Lord Randolph attempted unsuccessfully to impose something like the American nominating convention system on his party. He anticipated the future when politicians could appeal beyond their colleagues to the people—the modern age in which the public relations image is all.

Neither Joseph Chamberlain nor Lord Randolph Churchill recruited the people. Liberal failures and Tory gains gave the problem of mass democracy a remote air. Something must surely be done, but meanwhile there was an empire to be federated and extended, a world position to define, and British interests to secure. Lord Randolph had his "Orange card," Ulster resistance to home rule, to play. Nevertheless, there were significant institutional advances and political accomplishments, almost all of which were complementary to measures already passed or to steps already taken. Elementary education was provided free in 1891; secondary state-supported education was finally provided in 1902. The Small Holdings Act of 1892 was a token gesture in the direction of land reform; and Joseph Chamberlain secured a Workingman's Compensation Act in 1897. Salisbury's government provided the Local Government Act of 1888,[5] the logical corollary of the Reform Act of 1884, and established the system of elective county councils.

In one instance there was a significant new departure, although its implications were unclear at the time. Sir William Harcourt brought in his famous Death Duties Budget (1894) during the brief Liberal interregnum (1892–95). His proposal was not new. Lord Randolph Churchill had toyed with the idea eight years before, and estate taxes already had some standing. Harcourt added the principle of graduated taxation beginning at 1 per cent on £100 and soaring to 8 per cent on £1,000,000. These tariffs hit hard, for they were assessed on personal and real property and had to be

[5] See Document 30.

paid in cash. With declining land values and heavily encumbered estates, the landed classes felt much aggrieved. As budget needs increased, death duties rose, and the revenues worked to redistribute the wealth. Like municipal improvement—"gas and water socialism"—inheritance taxes were part of the inexorable march toward collectivism.[6]

One cardinal fact of late Victorian domestic political history was the gradual evolution of a working-class political party. The Labor party was little more than a pressure group until after the First World War when, thanks to another Liberal schism, it discovered itself to be the opposition party. The Labor party, like the evolving Conservative party, was constructed upon a class basis and appealed, overtly or covertly, to class prejudices. Tories had their workingmen, and Labor had its middle-class intellectuals, but both depended upon their social-class foundations. The Liberals found themselves increasingly—and after the war, fatally—at a disadvantage as domestic politics came to be more often defined in class terms.

Evolving British socialism colored, but neither shaped nor controlled, the rise of the Labor party. British socialism had a great deal of difficulty finding out what it was and where it might be going. H. M. Hyndman, a public school boy and a Cambridge graduate, spent much of his time making money dealing in stocks and bonds. He had less success in his persistent efforts to merchandise Marx to the British public through his Democratic Federation (1881). But he did find enough enthusiasts to proclaim their Marxism in the Socialist Democratic Federation (the S.D.F., founded in 1884). The S. D. F. had a checkered, occasionally violent, history. The aesthetic socialists, led by William Morris, defected in 1885 to found the Socialist League. Animated by John Ruskin,[7] the Socialist League proclaimed the gospel of fellowship, sponsored group activities like hiking and cycling clubs, and found itself strangely drawn toward continental anarchism. Both the S.D.F. and the Socialist League were a doctrinal nursery school for several leaders of the new unionism and were champions of the need for developing a working-class political party.

The best-known socialist organization was the Fabian Society, founded in 1884. The *Fabian Essays* (1889) articulated their

[6] See Document 29.
[7] See *VS&C*, Document 23, "Ruskin Questions the System."

critique of economic, social, and political organization and set forth the Fabian proposal for the gradual, peaceful march to public ownership.[8] The Fabians were part of the revisionist movement that loomed so large in Western Europe toward the turn of the century—Jean Jaurès in France, Eduard Bernstein in Germany, the Fabian Society in England: all were concerned with educating themselves and others out of the socialist addiction for violent revolution. The liberal state, they argued, provided a vehicle to achieve socialist ends. The Fabians were champions of gradualism and permeation. They lobbied among civil servants and members of Parliament. They worked extensively and successfully in disseminating their doctrines. The impact of the Fabians in the rise of the Labor party is easily overestimated, and there is little that they did not borrow from the Progressives in their work on the London County Council. The most significant achievement of the Fabians was to condition the middle classes to accept collectivism.

Workingmen first sat in Parliament in 1874, but it was not until 1892 that Keir Hardie showed his fellow laborers just what it might mean to have independent representation. The emancipated workingman was not gentle with parliamentary traditions or decorum.[9] Keir Hardie sought to consolidate his success by organizing the Independent Labor party (I.L.P.) at Bradford in 1893. It enjoyed little success as a party but much as a propagandist for a working-class party. The I.L.P. helped to change the attitude of labor men, both the leaders and the rank and file. But the need for a labor party was not driven home by agitation; it came from the law courts. As class antagonism sharpened at the turn of the century, trade unions confronted a series of adverse legal decisions. The most famous was the Taff Vale case (1901). This Welsh railroad, with a history of bad labor relations, sued the Amalgamated Society of Railway Servants for loss of business during a strike. The suit was upheld by the House of Lords sitting as the highest court of appeal. Damages of £23,000 were the least important loss; court costs ran far higher. The decision struck down unionists' principal weapon. Any employer could sue a union for the civil damages of a strike. Disraeli's act of 1871, which legalized peaceful picketing, was, in the union view, voided. A series of compromises and conferences produced the Labor Representation Committee

[8] See Document 28.
[9] See Document 33.

(L.R.C.) of the Trades Union Congress, organized to secure the election of more labor members to Parliament. The L.R.C. returned two in 1900. Confronting the heavy hand of the law, the unions and the L.R.C. went to work, bargained with the Liberals on constituencies, and secured the election of twenty-nine members of Parliament in 1906. The Trade Disputes Act of that year undid the Taff Vale decision.

If the rise of the masses distressed many Britons, the challenge to the nation from Europe and the world upset them more. Britain chronically collided with Russia—in the Ottoman Empire, Persia, Afghanistan, Tibet, and China. And the British feared the French for their instability and their obvious desire for revenge against Germany. But British interests had little influence upon European affairs, which up to 1890 were firmly in the hands of Bismarck. The constant display of German political power coupled with German competitive economic success raised bitter feelings and some fears.[10] Every European power had some grievance, real or imaginary, against the British, and Salisbury's position as the independent threatened to become the position of the isolated victim.

The African scramble and the Chinese railroad concession gambits were afforts to play the game of European politics in areas of the world where every move did not threaten a holocaust. There was no slack in Europe, and the steady diet of prestige that best suited the newly enfranchised nationalistic masses came from the competition for empire. Collisions in this contest were dangerous—France and England in Egypt in 1898, for example. And the results could be embarrassing, as when the Ethiopians defeated the Italians in 1896. But the classic case of British jingoism was the Boer War (1899–1902).[11] This was fought neither for Rand gold nor for Uitlander (European foreigner) rights in the Transvaal: it was fought as an unresolved problem in national security, that is, to secure the route to India and to preserve the British African position. It was one installment in the reorientation of British foreign policy against Germany, and British policy would have been no different had there been no gold, although the war might have been won more easily. And the war answered domestic needs—not economic but psychological. The relief of Mafeking compensated for the dullness, the psychological depression of late Victorian England.

[10] See Document 31.
[11] See Document 34.

"Queen dead!" shouted the newsboys on January 22, 1901. The tinsel of Jubilee tarnished[12] in the Edwardian epilogue to the nineteenth century. Collectivism and imperialism were increasingly the guidelines of the age; social disintegration was the background. Peers and laborers, Ulstermen and suffragettes turned to stronger and stronger measures to resist the reality they lived in. The governments of Henry Campbell-Bannerman and H. H. Asquith (1905–14) presided over an unparalleled degree of statute and administrative reform. They laid the foundations of the welfare state, modernized the navy, reformed the army, developed the system of labor conciliation that persists little changed to the present, righted the wrongs of trade unions, and finally reformed the House of Lords.[13] The days of graceful retreat and political bargaining were over; they passed away with the Queen. The political temperature rose, civil war threatened, an Austrian archduke was shot, and the nineteenth century was over.

Recommended Reading

W. ARNSTEIN, *The Bradlaugh Case* (London, 1964).

W. ASHWORTH, *An Economic History of Modern Britain* (London, 1960).

———, *The Genesis of Modern British Town Planning* (London, 1954).

H. AUSUBEL, *In Hard Times* (New York, 1960).

R. BLAKE, *Unrepentant Tory* (New York, 1954).

A. BRIGGS, *Seebohm Rowntree* (London, 1961).

B. H. BROWN, *The Tariff Reform Movement in Great Britain* (London, 1943).

E. H. PHELPS BROWN, *The Growth of British Industrial Relations* (London, 1959).

O. CHADWICK, *Mackenzie's Grave* (London, 1954).

R. CHURCHILL, *Winston Churchill*, Vols. I–II (London, 1966–1967).

H. A. CLEGG, A. FOX, and A. F. THOMPSON, *History of British Trade Unionism since 1889*, Vol. I, *1889–1910* (London 1964).

M. COLE, *The Story of Fabian Socialism* (London, 1961).

I. COLVIN, *Carson*, 3 vols. (New York, 1932–1937).

[12] See Document 32.
[13] See Document 35.

L. P. Curtis, *Coercion and Conciliation in Ireland 1880–92* (New Haven, 1963).

G. Dangerfield, *The Strange Death of Liberal England* (London, 1936).

H. J. Dyos, *Victorian Suburb* (London, 1961).

R. Fulford, *Votes for Women* (London, 1957).

W. B. Gwyn, *Democracy and the Cost of Politics in Britain* (London, 1962).

R. R. James, *Lord Randolph Churchill* (London, 1959).

———, *Rosebery* (London, 1963).

R. Jenkins, *Asquith* (London, 1964).

———, *Sir Charles Dilke* (London, 1958).

T. Jones, *Lloyd George* (Cambridge, Mass., 1951).

A. L. Kennedy, *Salisbury* (London, 1953).

E. Larkin, *James Larkin* (London, 1965).

J. G. Lockhart and C. M. Woodhouse, *Cecil Rhodes* (New York, 1963).

H. M. Lynd, *England in the Eighteen Eighties* (New York, 1946).

A. M. McBriar, *Fabian Socialism and English Politics* (London, 1962).

P. Magnus, *Edward VII* (London, 1964).

J. S. Marais, *The Fall of Kruger's Republic* (Oxford, 1961).

J. Morris, *Pax Britannica* (London, 1968).

S. Nowell-Smith, *Edwardian England* (London, 1965).

C. O'Leary, *The Elimination of Corrupt Practices in British Elections* (London, 1962).

H. Pelling, *Origins of the Labour Party* (London, 1954).

H. Pelling and F. Bealey, *Labour and Politics* (London, 1958).

P. P. Poirier, *Advent of the Labour Party* (New York, 1958).

M. Richter, *The Politics of Conscience* (Cambridge, Mass., 1964).

B. Semmel, *Imperialism and Social Reform* (London, 1960).

T. S. and M. Simey, *Charles Booth* (London, 1960).

P. Stansky, *Ambitions and Strategies* (Cambridge, Mass., 1964).

A. P. Thornton, *Doctrines of Imperialism* (New York, 1965).

———, *The Habit of Authority* (Toronto, 1966).

———, *The Imperial Idea and Its Enemies* (London, 1959).

C. Tsuzuki, *H. M. Hyndman and British Socialism* (London, 1961).

B. Webb, *My Apprenticeship* (New York, 1926).

———, *Our Partnership* (New York, 1948).

K. Young, *Arthur James Balfour* (London, 1963).

27. The New Radicalism:
The Intrusion of Collectivism

MANCHESTER-SCHOOL radicalism, however amorphic its content, did not survive the coming of the Great Depression (1873–95). John Bright— free trader, pacifist, and democrat—had become a Conservative. He rejected the notion that political democracy had to imply some measure of social democracy. The traditional radical conceived of society as so many individuals: each to be permitted the opportunity to develop unfettered by social restraint, political disability, and economic privilege. The depression, the first great modern crash, demonstrated, or appeared to demonstrate, that economic forces could overwhelm wise and able men. Many individuals could not help themselves and became less capable of doing so with the passage of time.

A new generation of respectable revolutionaries turned cautiously to state intervention. Liberal values sustained heavy fire from political critics. The democratization of the suffrage threatened to produce a working-class party bent on social revolution. Liberals like Robert Lowe, even radicals like John Stuart Mill, became uneasy when confronted directly with the conflict between quantity and quality in society. The liberal option demanded restraint and involved risk. It was by no means clear that democracy would elect liberty in preference to security. The new radicalism was an effort to provide a measure of both as the price for continued upper- and middle-class domination of British political life. Joseph Chamberlain (1836–1914) was one of the leading spokesmen for this new departure. He offered a political program that would answer the legitimate needs of society and retain lower-class support for upper-class parties and politicians.

Chamberlain, who had built an industrial empire on an American screw patent, turned to politics in the partially successful fight for a national system of state-supported secular education. As Lord Mayor of Birmingham he pioneered "gas and water socialism," urbanizing basic public utilities and coupling this profitable development to an urban-renewal campaign. Chamberlain had a social conscience and shrewd political instincts. He saw the potential appeal of collectivism and understood that the attraction of socialism as a mass movement lay in social and economic deprivation, not in political ideology. He believed that the working classes shared most middle-class assumptions, and he demonstrated that his theory could be put to direct political use. The Chamberlain family dominated Birmingham for two generations.

Both the Tory country squire and William Gladstone believed that

Chamberlain was preaching class war. Shrewd critics observed that Chamberlain spent most of his time talking about revolutionary land reform rather than about a reconstitution of urban-industrial relationships. The Conservative party, not the Liberal, depended upon the support of the landed interests. The criticism is partially valid but unfair. There was no self-interest in his equally strong push for tax reform and free national secular education. Ironically Chamberlain had his great success in the Conservative, not the Liberal, party. Gladstone would have nothing to do with Chamberlain's radicalism, and the Grand Old Man still dominated his party. But the schism did not come of social welfare; Gladstone and Chamberlain broke on imperialism, on the issue of Irish home rule. Imperialism and economic protection came to monopolize Chamberlain's attention, although he never wholly abandoned his radicalism. He championed a program of workingmen's compensation and succeeded, with a judicious mixture of imperialism and social reform, in retaining much working-class support for the continued rule of the established social orders.

Chamberlain's defection to the Conservative party, Sir Charles Dilke's innocent involvement in a divorce case, and the radical split on imperialism debilitated but did not exhaust the new radicalism. It was revitalized by such firebrands as David Lloyd George in the years before the First World War in the Liberal government of Henry Campbell–Bannerman and Herbert Asquith, which swept into office in 1906. The legacy of the new radicalism was bequeathed to both of the older parties and to the future parliamentary Labor party.

Recommended Reading

In addition to the standard studies, the student can profitably consult: J. L. GARVIN and J. AMERY, *The Life of Joseph Chamberlain*, 6 vols. with more to come (1935–1969); B. SEMMEL, *Imperialism and Social Reform* (London, 1960); and P. STANSKY, *Ambitions and Strategies* (Cambridge, Mass., 1964).

SOURCE: Joseph Chamberlain, Speech at Hull, August 5, 1885, *The Radical Platform* (Edinburgh, 1885), pp. 1–13.

In the Liberal army there must be pioneers to clear the way, and there must be men who watch the rear. Some may always be in advance; others may occasionally lag behind; but the only thing we have a right to demand is that no one shall stand still, and that all shall be willing to follow the main line of Liberal progress to which the whole party are committed. I do not conceal from you my own opinion that the pace will be a little faster in the future than it has been in the past. Everywhere the reforms to which the resolution has made reference are casting their shadows before; everywhere in the country I see a quickening of political life; everywhere there is discussion and hope and expectation. Gentlemen, it will be dangerous to disappoint that hope. It will be impossible to stifle that discussion; and if there are any people who imagine that the enfranchisement of two millions of citizens can have taken place, and that these men intend to make no use of the privilege which has been conferred upon them, they will have a rude awakening. They are not wise men, believe me—they are not the true friends of the institutions of this country, who will not bring impartial minds to the consideration of the new problems that are calling for solution.

I am not altogether surprised, under these circumstances, that there has recently been a demand in some quarters that the leaders of the two great parties should frame a definite programme; that they should discard empty platitudes and generalities, and put a clear issue before the electors. I can say for myself personally that I have done my best in that direction; and although in the speeches I have recently made I have expressly disclaimed any right to speak for the party as a whole, I have been soundly rated for my presumption in daring to speak at all, and I have been solemnly excommunicated by some of the great authorities who claim a monopoly of the orthodox Liberal faith and doctrine. Gentlemen, I am not discouraged, I am not repentant. I am told that if I pursue this course I shall break up the party, and that I shall altogether destroy any chance which I might otherwise have had of office. I do not believe it. But if it were true, I say that I care little for party, and nothing at all for office, except so far as these things may be made instrumental in promoting the objects which I publicly avowed when I first entered Parliament, and which I will prosecute as long as I remain in public life. The Liberal party has always seemed to me the great agency of progress and reform, and by the changes which have recently taken place it has secured a vantage ground which I myself had hardly dared to anticipate. I had looked forward with hope to the future, but I had not supposed in my time so great a change could have been successfully effected.

But now that my wildest expectations have been surpassed, I am not willing to be silent as to the uses to which, I believe, the people ought to put the new power and the privileges which have been conferred upon them. I have always had a deep conviction that when the people came to govern themselves, and when the clamour of vested interests and class privileges was overborne by the powerful voice of the whole nation, that then the social evils which disgrace our civilisation, and the wrongs which have cried vainly for redress, would at last find a hearing and a remedy. And if that be not so, it will be no longer statesmen or Governments that you will have to blame. It will not be the fault of parties or of individuals—it will be the apathy or the ignorance, the indifference or the folly, of the people themselves, which alone can hinder their progress and their prosperity.

One of the speakers has said, and said truly, that this is a critical time—it is the turning-point in our political history, and if the people are content with the old formulae, and with the watch-words which satisfied a limited electorate, then, I think, some of us might have been better employed than we were when we joined the agitation of last autumn, and the enfranchisement of two millions of men will have been a barren and an unprofitable business. We shall have perfected the machinery, but we shall have done nothing at all to improve the manufacture.

I do not want you to think that I suggest to you that legislation can accomplish all that we desire, and, above all, I would not lead you into wild and revolutionary projects which would upset unnecessarily the existing order of things. But, on the other hand, I want you not to accept as final or as perfect, arrangements under which hundreds of thousands, nay millions, of your fellow-countrymen are subjected to untold privations and misery, with the evidence all around them of accumulated wealth and un-bounded luxury. The extremes of wealth and of poverty are alike the sources of great temptation. I believe that the great evil with which we have to deal is the excessive inequality in the distribution of riches. Ignorance, intemperance, immorality, and disease—these things are all inter-dependent and closely connected; and although they are often the cause of poverty they are still more frequently the consequence of destitution; and if we can do anything to raise the whole condition of the poor in this country, to elevate the masses of the people, and give them means of enjoyment and recreation, to afford to them opportunities of improvement, we should do more for the prosperity, aye, and for the morality of this country than anything we can do by laws, however stringent, for the prevention of excess or the punishment of crime.

I want you to make this the first object in the Liberal programme for the reformed Parliament. It is not our duty, it is not
our wish, to pull down and abase the rich, although I do not think
that the excessive aggregation of wealth in a few hands is any
advantage to anybody. But our object is to elevate the poor, to
raise the general condition of the people. . . .

Gentlemen, believe me, the question of the poor labourer cannot
be put aside. Our ideal, I think, should be that in this rich country,
where everything seems to be in profusion, an honest, a decent, and
an industrious man should be able to earn a livelihood for himself
and his family, should have access to some means of self-improve-
ment and enjoyment, and should be able to lay aside something for
sickness and old age. Is that unreasonable? Is it impossible? It is a
condition of things which already exists under the British rule in
certain communities, and in certain favoured districts of the country. . . . Why should it be impossible for modern statesmanship to
secure for the whole of the United Kingdom the advantages
which, by a different system of law and custom, the Channel
Islands have been able to secure for their population, and which
certain generous and wise landlords have been able to provide for
the benefit of those who are dependent upon them?
Let us consider what are the practical means by which we can
accomplish such an object. I am not a Communist, although some
people will have it that I am. Considering the difference in the
character and the capacity of men, I do not believe that there can
ever be an absolute equality of conditions, and I think that nothing
would be more undesirable than that we should remove the stimulus to industry and thrift and exertion which is afforded by the
security given to every man in the enjoyment of the fruits of his
own individual exertions. I am opposed to confiscation in every
shape or form, because I believe that it would destroy that security
and lessen that stimulus. But, on the other hand, I am in favour of
accompanying the protection which is afforded to property with a
large and stringent interpretation of the obligations of property. It
seems to me that there are three main directions in which we may
seek for help in the task which I think we ought to set to ourselves.
In the first place, I look for great results from the development
of local government amongst us. The experience of the great
towns is very encouraging in this respect. By their wise and liberal

use of the powers entrusted to them they have in the majority of cases protected the health of the community; they have provided means of recreation and enjoyment and instruction, and they have done a great deal to equalize social advantages, and to secure for all the members of the community the enjoyments which, without their aid and assistance, would have been monopolized by the rich alone.

You have in connection with the great municipal corporations, hospitals, schools, museums, free libraries, art galleries, baths, parks. All these things which a generation ago could only have been obtained by the well-to-do are now, in many large towns, placed at the service of every citizen by the action of the municipalities. I desire that this opportunity should be afforded to the whole country, and I think that, having regard to what has been done in the past, we may show great confidence in the work of popular representative bodies, and be contented to extend their functions and increase their powers and authority.

Closely connected with this subject there is another question which I think of urgent importance. I have spoken of education. I think the time has come when education ought to be free. I have always held that the exaction of fees in our primary schools was unjust and uneconomical, and prejudicial to the best interests of education. It is a system which long ago has been abolished in the United States. It has recently disappeared in France; it does not exist in the majority of Continental countries, or in the majority of the self-governing colonies of the British Empire; and I hope that working men will insist that in this country also the system shall cease, which is only defended in deference to false and pedantic notions of political economy, and to the supposed interest of denominational schools. Just consider for a moment the objections to this system. Look, in the first place, at the heavy burdens which it inflicts on the teachers. Their time is too valuable to be taken up in the collection of pence and in the preparation of the voluminous returns which the present system demands. Then it tends to irregularity of attendance. Poor people who cannot find the pence at the beginning of the week, keep their children away until, perhaps, they are forced to send them under the pressure of the compulsory law, and in that way what ought to be a boon, and what ought to be recognised as such by the whole population, becomes an irritating and exacting obligation. I believe that nothing has done more to tend to the unpopularity of our educational system than the exaction of these miserable fees. Then it is uneconomical, because the cost of collection is in excessive proportion to the amount collected; and it is unjust, because it lays upon the shoulders of the poor man a burden which is proportioned, not to his means, but to his necessities and his wants. Well, what is to be said in its favour? If you have paid any attention to the subject, you will find that the chief argument is that it is necessary in order to secure the independence of the parents. There are two answers which strike one at once to such an argument. In the first place, the fees only pay for one-fourth of the education—the independence of the parents has been three-fourths destroyed already. Is it worth while to protect this small fraction at the cost of the efficiency of the schools themselves? But, I think, there is a better answer than that. Why should working men feel themselves degraded, or their independence gone, if they send their children to free schools, to which every one contributes his share, either through the local rates or through the imperial taxation, any more than he does when he uses the free libraries, which I wish you had in Hull, or the free roads or the free bridges, or any other of the benefits of civilisation, which are provided by the whole community at the cost of every member of the community? I do not attach much importance to these arguments. I think little of the arguments, and I think still less of them because of the quarter from whence they come. Who are the people who are so anxious for the independence of the working classes? The nobility, the gentry, the professors, the editors of newspapers—every one who has owed more or less to free education, by scholarships, or other endowments, in connection with our public schools or universities, and to the cost of which they have not contributed a single farthing. Let them look at home; let them take care of their own independence before they look after yours. I hope that one of the first acts of the new Parliament will be to see that this anomaly shall cease, and that education, suited to the capacity of every child, which is the indispensable instrument for any progress in life, shall be conferred on all, for the benefit of all at the cost of all.

In the second place, we have to consider the question of taxation. Now I have been criticised a good deal for saying that the rich pay too little and the poor pay too much. Well, I have given the matter further and careful consideration, and I maintain the statement. On

the occasion of previous speeches I have endeavoured to compare
the proportion of taxation paid by families in the different classes,
and I admit that that may fairly be objected to, because the condition of families vary so much that, unless you take them over a
large area, you might make a mistake. I will take, however, a few
statistics bearing upon the whole of the country and upon the
different classes of the population. I take for my purpose the year
1883–84, because that was a year of normal expenditure, although
it included a grant of £1,000,000 for the Afghan War, and very
large naval and military expenditure. In that year the revenue was
£87,200,000. From that I deduct £21,800,000, as being the product
of the Post Office and telegraph service, and also some other
sources of taxation, which it is impossible to distribute between
different classes. Well, that leaves £65,400,000 as the sum with
which we have to deal. Now I have assumed that the upper and
middle classes pay the whole of the assessed taxes, the whole of the
land tax, the whole of the income tax, the whole of the death
duties, the whole of the wine duties, the whole of the game li-
cences, and some other small taxes. I have assumed that they pay
one-third of the duties on spirits, beer, and tobacco, and three-
fifths of the duty upon tea and coffee. I think you will agree with
me that I have made a very liberal estimate of what the upper and
middle classes pay. In the first place, I believe I ought to have
excluded the land tax. It is not a tax in the proper sense of the
word, but it is a State rent, and a very inadequate one. Then I do
not believe that the consumption by the upper and middle classes
of dutiable articles is anything like so great as I have taken it at, and
I suppose that working men occasionally receive a legacy, although
I am afraid not so often as I could wish. But still, taking the calculation upon the basis I have stated, I find that the upper and middle
classes pay £38,200,000 on an income which has been reckoned
. . . at £750,000,000. That is, upon the whole of this amount they
pay a little more than 5 per cent. The working classes pay
£27,200,000 upon an income estimated by the same authority at
£520,000,000, so that they also pay a little over 5 per cent. But that
does not exhaust the considerations you have to take into account.
All political economists are agreed that the true principle of taxation
is equality of sacrifice, and it is perfectly absurd to talk of "equality
of sacrifice" when a great duke with £300,000 or £400,000 a year,
or a capitalist with £10,000 a year, pays in the same proportion as a
working man with twenty shillings a week. You must deduct, at

least, from the incomes of these working classes what is absolutely necessary for existence. Mr. Giffen, the most eminent of living statisticians, has calculated that £12 a head ought to be deducted on this ground, and if you will make that correction you will get then the net result of the whole matter. Twenty-six and a half millions of working people have between them incomes available for taxation of £203,000,000. Upon that the taxation which they pay amounts to 13½ per cent. On the other hand, nine and a half millions, belonging to the upper and middle classes, have an income available for taxation of £639,000,000, upon which the taxation which they actually pay amounts to 6 per cent, so that, to put the matter in another way, at the present time the working classes are paying upon their available incomes more than double the rate which is paid by the upper and the middle classes. Now, in my opinion, there is only one way in which this injustice can properly be remedied, and that is by some scheme of graduated taxation—of taxation which increases in proportion to the amount of the property taxed. It need not necessarily be a graduated income tax. It might be more convenient to levy it in the shape of a graduated death tax or house tax. I care nothing at all about the method—all I want to bring before you, for your earnest and serious consideration, is the principle of such taxation. . . .

Now I will go on to what is the last, but also the most important, of the reforms to which I wish to call your attention, and that is the reform of the land laws. This is a question which lies at the root of the whole matter that we have been discussing. Agriculture is the greatest of all our industries. When it is depressed every employment follows suit, and when work is scant in the counties and the wages are low the agricultural labourers are driven into the towns to compete with you for employment and to reduce the rate of your remuneration. Anything which could bring about a revival of prosperity in agriculture, anything which would increase the production of the land and give better prospects to the agricultural labourer, would do an immense deal towards raising the general condition of the whole country, and would procure a market for our manufacturers for surpassing any that can possibly be expected from foreign countries, and even from our own colonies. The evils of the present land system are apparent to everybody. They are greater than accompany the land system of any other country in the world. Our laws and practice seem to have been designed over a long course of years in order to build up and maintain vast estates, until at the present moment something less than 1000 persons hold one-third of the land of the United Kingdom. In the meantime the rights of property have been so much extended that the rights of the community have almost altogether disappeared, and it is hardly too much to say that the prosperity and the comfort and the liberties of a great proportion of the population have been laid at the feet of a small number of proprietors, who "neither toil nor spin." The soil of every country originally belonged to its inhabitants, and if it has been thought expedient to create private ownership in place of common rights, at least that private ownership must be considered as a trust, and subject to the conditions of a trust. Land must be owned so as to give the greatest employment to the largest number of persons and so as to secure the greatest possible return in the produce of the soil. The land was not created—and it must not be used as a mere machine for exacting the highest possible rent from the cultivators of the soil—for the benefit of those who own it. I have not time for anything like an exhaustive treatment of this vast subject. . . .

I am in favour of free trade in land. That includes the registration of title, the cheapening of transfer, the abolition of settlements and entails, and of the custom of primogeniture in cases of intestacy. Upon all that, I think, we are pretty well agreed. It would do something. It would tend no doubt to the dispersion of those great estates. It would bring more landed property into the market, but I do not think it would do much for the labourers of Wiltshire or for the crofters of the Highland of Scotland. We must go further if we want to go to the root of the matter.

. . . There is only one thing that can benefit the farmer, and that is a fair rent, fixed by an impartial tribunal, with the right of free sale of the goodwill of his undertaking just the same as any other trader. He would be required, of course, to provide a fit and proper person, and his landlord might object if the person provided was not satisfactory in character or means. Subject to that, the farmer should have the same liberty of sale which is enjoyed by other persons. I am told that the farmers do not care about "fair rent" or "free sale." All that I can say is, that so long as that is their position they are not likely to get it. Nobody will impose upon them a benefit that they do not want, and that was only conferred on Irish tenants after many years of bitter and almost savage agitation.

But when we come to the labourers the task is easier. They know what they want, which is the first condition for getting it. They want that facilities shall be afforded to them for having decent cottages and fair allotments at reasonable rents and with security of tenure. Why should they not have it? Who would be injured if they did have it? The produce of the land would be increased, the respectability and character of the labourers would be raised, the happiness of their families would be secured. Who would be injured? For my part, I confess I see no injustice at all in the case of great landlords, many of whom have driven the labourers off their properties, and have pulled down their cottages, partly in order to escape responsibilities in connection with them, partly in order to throw the land into immense farms, and partly for other reasons—I see no objection in such cases as these to compelling these landlords to repair the wrong they have done. I do not see why you should not enforce upon them the duty of providing in every case a sufficient number of decent cottages, with land attached, for all the men who are required for the cultivation of the particular estate. I would leave the supervision of this duty to the local authority, and in order to meet every case which may arise I would give to local authorities power to acquire land on their own behalf and to let it out in allotments for labourers and small farms. I believe that this would meet the cases to which I have called your attention. Where the landlord will not do his duty to the land the local authority would have power to step in and restore it to production. . . . All these things could be done, and only one other condition is absolutely necessary, and that is that when the local authority acquires land for this or any other public purpose, it should not be called upon to pay an extravagant or unnatural price; that it should be able to obtain it at the fair market value—at the value which the willing purchaser would pay to the willing seller, without any addition for compulsory sale. I believe that if these additional powers were conferred upon local authorities, if these additional obligations were enforced upon landlords, that, at all events, so far as the labourers are concerned, the land difficulty will disappear. Then, I would go a step further, and I would revise the taxation upon land. I would equalize the death-duties, as the Government recently proposed to do. To that extent, at all events, I would invade the sanctity of landed property, and in addition I would tax all unoccupied and sporting land at its full value. I believe that that would put an end to much of the abuse of

which we now complain. And, lastly, gentlemen, I would insist
upon the restitution of the property of the community where it has
been wrongfully appropriated. I would insist upon the restitution
of the endowments which have been diverted to improper uses, of
enclosures which have been illegally made, of rights which have
been improperly disregarded and ignored. I cannot allow that there
should be a prescription for such arbitrary acts as these, or why a
man should be able to allege a long enjoyment of the profits
of wrongdoing as a reason for immunity and a bar to all redress on
the part of the people who have suffered. I do not pretend that this
constitutes an exhaustive programme. It is perhaps enough for
tonight. If objection is taken to it in any quarter, I ask my opponents, what are their proposals? If they have an alternative
which is more effective than the suggestions I have made, I have no
pride in the matter, and I will gladly accept it; but something must
be done. We have been suffering from a depression in trade unex-
ampled in its intensity and duration. The privations which it has
imposed have been borne with resignation and courage by those
upon whose shoulders they have most heavily fallen, but these men
have a right to demand that the depression shall not be intensified
or fostered by bad legislation, and that there shall be no obstacle or
hindrance to the fullest development of the resources of the country. The sanctity of private property is no doubt, an important
principle, but the public good is a greater and higher object than
any private interest, and the comfort and the happiness of the
people and the prosperity of the country must not be sacrificed to
the exaggerated claim of a privileged class who are now the exclusive possessors of the great gift of the Almighty to the human
race.

28.   The Fabians:
Toward Socialism—as Slowly as Possible

THE FABIAN SOCIETY, always its own best press agent, was a purveyor
of propaganda and collectivist notions. Always small, rather aloof, but
usually exciting, the Fabians were the English version of revisionary
socialism. Bernard Shaw sketched the Fabian claims in the original

preface to *Fabian Essays*. "There are at present no authoritative teachers of Socialism. The essayists make no claim to be more than communicative learners." And so seven of the more exciting minds of the late nineteenth century—Shaw, Sidney Webb, William Clarke, Sydney Olivier, Graham Wallas, Annie Besant, and Hubert Bland—sorted through historical, economic, social, and moral questions in eight essays (Shaw, naturally, wrote two).

The Fabians were endlessly practical. They conceived of socialism as the logical outgrowth of the liberal state. Bit by bit Britain was to steer a more collectivist course. Any effort to turn off it would founder on the reef of revolution. In his essay Shaw does not argue that this gradualism is good—it is the "sordid, slow, reluctant, cowardly path to justice"—but it is inevitable. Given this belief, the Fabians were of mixed minds about the utility of a working-class political party. If the Liberals, and the Conservatives for that matter, were accomplishing the ends of a socialist party, why confuse the issue and perhaps jeopardize gains? Why not continue to bore from within?

Although Robert Applegarth, the leader of the moderate trade union junta of mid-century, had attended the First International, Marx and revolutionary socialism met a cool reception in Britain. H. M. Hyndman, a gentleman of impeccably upper-middle-class origins, was the moving spirit in the Democratic Federation founded in 1881. Never more than a tiny pressure group, the Democratic Federation became in 1884 the Social Democratic Federation. H. H. Champion and artist-poet William Morris were among the leaders of this body patterned upon the French and German Social Democratic parties. The S.D.F. was short on members and long on factionalism. William Morris split away to found the Socialist League. Hyndman, his parliamentary ambitions thwarted, temporarily turned to investments in imperialism. But the socialist organizations fulfilled an educational function. Many of the leaders of the new unionism—John Burns, Ben Tillet, and Tom Mann, among others—served an ideological apprenticeship under the banner.

The prospects for British socialism were very poor. The success of the liberal state and the adaptability of capitalism combined with the habitual deference of the lower classes to produce low returns on a heavy investment in ideological capital. Socialism made its impact at a different level—that of sentimental morality. The fuzzy ethical socialism of Keir Hardie or of the publicist Robert Blatchford did touch a responsive note, just as William Morris had with his socialist hymns, cycling or hiking clubs, and preaching the gospel of fellowship.

The Fabians were concerned to translate socialism into terms acceptable to the governing classes without losing the mass support potentially available to a working-class party. They were as concerned about socialism as a moral issue as they were about socialism as economic or social policy. They were cautious, avoiding the shibboleths of class war, and anxious to adjust their creed to what they conceived to be the

realities of the situation. They, like other European revisionary socialists, presumed that they would eventually assume the management of a
successful economic enterprise. If they educated themselves out of
revolution, surely capitalism would cooperate by avoiding economic
catastrophe. Some tinkering here and there, a little planning, a lot of
education, and the general recognition that the Fabians really understood and had the right answers for Britain: these notions lay behind
Fabian doctrines of success by permeation. Fabian rhetoric was democratic, but the Fabians themselves were elitists with tidy bureaucratic
minds. They liked Joe Chamberlain's "gas and water socialism." They
admired the continued extension of civil service activity. They shared
the assumption of the older governing classes that government should
be left to people who knew what they were doing.

The Fabian Society, for all of its weaknesses, was a peculiarly English organization and a logical development from Victorian culture.
Few propaganda groups have been able to claim such well merited
success.

Recommended Reading

The literature on the Fabians is vast, but the following titles are
particularly useful: M. Cole, *History of the Fabian Society* (London,
1961); *Fabian Essays in Socialism* (London, 1889, and countless subsequent editions); E. Hobsbawm, "The Fabians," *Labouring Men* (London, 1964); and A. M. McBriar, *Fabian Socialism and British Politics*
(London, 1962). Mary P. Mack traces the Fabian imitation of and
intellectual debt to the philosophic radicals in "The Fabians and
Utilitarianism," *Journal of the History of Ideas* (1955), pp. 76–88.

Source: George Bernard Shaw, "Transition," *Fabian Essays in
Socialism* (London, 1889), pp. 171–187.

First, then, as to the consummation of Democracy. Since 1885
every man who pays four shillings a week rent can only be
hindered from voting by anomalous conditions of registration
which are likely to be swept away very shortly. This is all but
manhood suffrage; and it will soon complete itself as adult suffrage.
However, I may leave adult suffrage out of the question, because
the outlawry of women, monstrous as it is, is not a question of class
privilege, but of sex privilege. To complete the foundation of the
democratic State, then, we need manhood suffrage, abolition of all
poverty disqualifications, abolition of the House of Lords, public
payment of candidature expenses, public payment of representa-

tives, and annual elections. These changes are now inevitable, however unacceptable they may appear to those of us who are Conservatives. They have been for half a century the common-places of Radicalism. We have next to consider that the State is not merely an abstraction: it is a machine to do certain work; and if that work be increased and altered in its character, the machinery must be multiplied and altered too. Now, the extension of the franchise does increase and alter the work very considerably; but it has no direct effect on the machinery. At present the State machine has practically broken down under the strain of spreading democracy, the work being mainly local, and the machinery mainly central. Without efficient local machinery the replacing of private enterprise by State enterprise is out of the question; and we shall presently see that such replacement is one of the inevitable consequences of Democracy. A democratic State cannot become a *Social-Democratic* State unless it has in every centre of population a local governing body as thoroughly democratic in its constitution as the central Parliament. This matter is also well in train. In 1888 a Government avowedly reactionary passed a Local Government Bill which effected a distinct advance towards the democratic municipality.[1] It was furthermore a Bill with no single aspect of finality anywhere about it. Local self-Government remains prominent within the sphere of practical politics. When it is achieved, the democratic State will have the machinery for Socialism.

And now, how is the raw material of Socialism—otherwise the Proletarian man—to be brought to the Democratic State machinery? Here again the path is easily found. Politicians who have no suspicion that they are Socialists, are advocating further instalments of Socialism with a recklessness of indirect results which scandalizes the conscious Social Democrat. The phenomenon of economic rent has assumed prodigious proportions in our great cities. The injustice of its private appropriation is glaring, flagrant, almost ridiculous. In the long suburban roads about London, where rows of exactly similar houses stretch for miles countrywards, the rent changes at every few thousand yards by exactly the amount saved or incurred annually in travelling to and from the house-

[1] This same Government, beginning to realize what it has unintentionally done for Social Democracy, is already (1889) doing what it can to render the new County Councils socialistically impotent by urgently reminding them of the restrictions which hamper their action.

holder's place of business. The seeker after lodgings, hesitating
between Bloomsbury and Tottenham, finds every advantage of
situation skimmed off by the landlord with scientific precision. As
lease after lease falls in, houses, shops, goodwills of businesses
which are the fruits of the labor of lifetimes, fall into the maw of
the ground landlord. Confiscation of capital, spoliation of households, annihilation of incentive, everything that the most ignorant
and credulous fundholder ever charged against the Socialists, rages
openly in London, which begins to ask itself whether it exists and
toils only for the typical duke and his celebrated jockey and his
famous racehorse. Lord Hobhouse and his unimpeachably respectable committee for the taxation of ground values are already in the
field claiming the value of the site of London for London collectively; and their agitation receives additional momentum from
every lease that falls in. Their case is unassailable; and the evil they
attack is one that presses on the ratepaying and leaseholding classes
as well as upon humbler sufferers. This economic pressure is reinforced formidably by political opinion in the workmen's associations. Here the moderate members are content to demand a progressive Income Tax, which is virtually Lord Hobhouse's proposal;
and the extremists are all for Land Nationalization, which is again
Lord Hobhouse's principle. The cry for such taxation cannot
permanently be resisted. And it is very worthy of remark that
there is a new note in the cry. Foremerly taxes were proposed with
a specific object—as to pay for a war, for education, or the like.
Now the proposal is to tax the landlords in order to get some of
our money back from them—take it from them first and find a use
for it afterwards. Ever since Mr. Henry George's book reached the
English Radicals, there has been a growing disposition to impose a
tax of twenty shillings in the pound on obviously unearned incomes: that is, to dump four hundred and fifty millions a year
down on the Exchequer counter; and then retire with three cheers
for the restoration of the land to the people.

The results of such a proceeding, if it actually came off, would
considerably take its advocates aback. The streets would presently
be filled with starving workers of all grades, domestic servants,
coach builders, decorators, jewellers, lacemakers, fashionable professional men, and numberless others whose livelihood is at present
gained by ministering to the wants of these and of the proprietary
class. "This," they would cry, "is what your theories have brought

to us! Back with the good old times, when we received our wages, which were at least better than nothing." Evidently the Chancellor of the Exchequer would have three courses open to him. (1) He could give the money back again to the landlords and capitalists with an apology. (2) He could attempt to start State industries with it for the employment of the people. (3) Or he could simply distribute it among the unemployed. The last is not to be thought of: anything is better than *panem et circenses*. The second (starting State industries) would be far too vast an undertaking to get on foot soon enough to meet the urgent difficulty. The first (the return with an apology) would be a *reductio ad absurdum* of the whole affair—a confession that the private proprietor, for all his idleness and his voracity, is indeed performing an indispensable economic function—the function of capitalizing, however wastefully and viciously, the wealth which surpasses his necessarily limited power of immediate personal consumption. And here we have checkmate to mere Henry Georgism, or State appropriation of rent without Socialism. It is easy to shew that the State is entitled to the whole income of the Duke of Westminster, and to argue therefrom that he should straightway be taxed twenty shillings in the pound. But in practical earnest the State has no right to take five farthings of capital from the Duke or anybody else until it is ready to invest them in productive enterprise. The consequences of withdrawing capital from private hands merely to lock it up unproductively in the treasury would be so swift and ruinous, that no statesman, however fortified with the destructive resources of abstract economics, could persist in it. It will be found in the future as in the past that governments will raise money only because they want it for specific purposes, and not on *a priori* demonstrations that they have a right to it. But it must be added that when they *do* want it for a specific purpose, then, also in the future as in the past, they will raise it without the slightest regard to *a priori* demonstrations that they have no right to it.

Here then we have got to a deadlock. In spite of democrats and land nationalizers, rent cannot be touched unless some pressure from quite another quarter forces productive enterprise on the State. Such pressure is already forthcoming. The quick starvation of the unemployed, the slow starvation of the employed who have no relatively scarce special skill, the unbearable anxiety or dangerous recklessness of those who are employed to-day and unem-

ployed to-morrow, the rise in urban rents, the screwing down of
wages by pauper immigration and home multiplication, the hand-in-
hand advance of education and discontent, are all working up to
explosion point. It is useless to prove by statistics that most of the
people are better off than before, true as that probably is, thanks to
instalments of Social Democracy. Yet even that is questionable; for
it is idle to claim authority for statistics of things that have never
been recorded. Chaos has no statistics: it has only statisticians; and
the ablest of them prefaces his remarks on the increased consumption of rice by the admission that "no one can contemplate the
present condition of the masses without desiring something like a
revolution for the better." The masses themselves are being converted so rapidly to that view of the situation, that we have Pan-
Anglican Synods, bewildered by a revival of Christianity, pleading
that though Socialism is eminently Christian, yet "the Church must
act safely as well as sublimely." During the agitation made by the
unemployed last winter (1887–8), the Chief Commissioner of
Police in London started at his own shadow, and mistook Mr. John
Burns for the French Revolution, to the great delight of that genial
and courageous champion of his class.[2] The existence of the
pressure is further shewn by the number and variety of safety
valves proposed to relieve it—monetization of silver, import duties,
"leaseholds enfranchisement," extension of joint stock capitalism
masquerading as co-operation,[3] and other irrelevancies. My own
sudden promotion from the street corner to this platform is in its
way a sign of the times. But whilst we are pointing the moral and
adorning the tale according to our various opinions, an actual
struggle is beginning between the unemployed who demand work
and the local authorities appointed to deal with the poor. In the
winter, the unemployed collect round red flags, and listen to
speeches for want of anything else to do. They welcome Socialism,
insurrectionism, currency craze—anything that passes the time and
seems to express the fact that they are hungry. The local authori-

[2] Finally, the Commissioner was superseded; and Mr. Burns was elected a
member of the first London County Council by a large majority.
[3] It is due to the leaders of the Co-operative movement to say here that
they are no parties to the substitution of dividend-hunting by petty capitalists for the pursuit of the ideal of Robert Owen, the Socialist founder
of Co-operation; and that they are fully aware that Co-operation must be
a political as well as a commercial movement if it is to achieve a final solution of the labor question.

ties, equally innocent of studied economic views, deny that there is
any misery; send leaders of deputations to the Local Government
Board, who promptly send them back to the guardians; try bully-
ing; try stoneyards; try bludgeoning; and finally sit down help-
lessly and wish it were summer again or the unemployed at the
bottom of the sea. Meanwhile the charity fund, which is much less
elastic than the wages fund, overflows at the Mansion House only
to run dry at the permanent institutions. So unstable a state of
things cannot last. The bludgeoning, and the shocking clamor for
bloodshed from the anti-popular newspapers, will create a revul-
sion among the humane section of the middle class. The section
which is blinded by class prejudice to all sense of social responsibility, dreads personal violence from the working class with a
superstitious terror that defies enlightenment or control. Municipal
employment must be offered at last. This cannot be done in one
place alone: the rush from other parts of the country would
swamp an isolated experiment. Wherever the pressure is, the relief
must be given on the spot. And since public decency, as well as
consideration for its higher officials, will prevent the County Council from instituting a working day of sixteen hours at a wage of a
penny an hour or less, it will soon have on its hands not only the
unemployed, but also the white slaves of the sweater, who will
escape from their dens and appeal to the municipality for work the
moment they become aware that municipal employment is better
than private sweating. Nay, the sweater himself, a mere slave
driver paid "by the piece," will in many instances be as anxious as
his victims to escape from his hideous trade. But the municipal
organization of the industry of these people will require capital.
Where is the municipality to get it? Raising the rates is out of the
question: the ordinary tradesmen and householders are already
rated and rented to the limit of endurance: further burdens would
almost bring them into the street with a red flag. Dreadful
dilemma! in which the County Council, between the devil and the
deep sea, will hear Lord Hobhouse singing a song of deliverance,
telling a golden tale of ground values to be municipalized by
taxation. The land nationalizers will swell the chorus: the Radical
progressive income taxers singing together, and the ratepaying
tenants shouting for joy. The capital difficulty thus solved—for we
need not seriously anticipate that the landlords will actually fight,

as our President[4] once threatened—the question of acquiring land will arise. The nationalizers will declare for its annexation by the municipality without compensation; but that will be rejected as spoliation, worthy only of revolutionary Socialists. The no-compensation cry is indeed a piece of unpractical catastrophic insurrectionism; for whilst compensation would be unnecessary and absurd if every proprietor were expropriated simultaneously, and the proprietary system at once replaced by full blown Social-ism, yet when it is necessary to proceed by degrees, the denial of compensation would have the effect of singling out individual proprietors for expropriation whilst the others remained unmo-lested, and depriving them of their private means long before there was suitable municipal employment ready for them. The land, as it is required, will therefore be honestly purchased; and the purchase money, or the interest thereon, will be procured, like the capital, by taking rent. Of course this will be at bottom an act of expro-priation just as much as the collection of Income Tax to-day is an act of expropriation. As such, it will be denounced by the landlords as merely a committing of the newest sin the oldest kind of way. In effect, they will be compelled at each purchase to buy out one of their body and present his land to the municipality, thereby dis-tributing the loss fairly over their whole class, instead of placing it on one man who is no more responsible than the rest. But they will be compelled to do this in a manner that will satisfy the moral sense of the ordinary citizen as effectively as that of the skilled economist.

We now foresee our municipality equipped with land and capi-tal for industrial purposes. At first they will naturally extend the industries they already carry on, road making, gas works, tram-ways, building, and the like. It is probable that they will for the most part regard their action as a mere device to meet a passing emergency. The Manchester School will urge its Protectionist theories as to the exemption of private enterprise from the competi-tion of public enterprise, in one supreme effort to practise for the last time on popular ignorance of the science which it has consis-tently striven to debase and stultify. For a while the proprietary party will succeed in hampering and restricting municipal enter-prise; in attaching the stigma of pauperism to its service; in keeping the lot of its laborers as nearly as possible down to private competi-

---

[4] Lord Bramwell, President of the Economic Section of the British Associa-tion in 1888.

tion level in point of hard work and low wages. But its power will be broken by the disappearance of that general necessity for keeping down the rates which now hardens local authority to humane appeals. The luxury of being generous at someone else's expense will be irresistible. The ground landlord will be the municipal milch cow; and the ordinary ratepayers will feel the advantage of sleeping in peace, relieved at once from the fear of increased burdens and of having their windows broken and their premises looted by hungry mobs, nuclei of all the socialism and scoundrelism of the city. They will have just as much remorse in making the landlord pay as the landlord has had in making them pay—just as much and no more. And as the municipality becomes more democratic, it will find landlordism losing power, not only relatively to democracy, but absolutely.

The ordinary ratepayer, however, will not remain unaffected for long. At the very outset of the new extension of municipal industries, the question of wage will arise. A minimum wage must be fixed; and though at first, to avoid an overwhelming rush of applicants for employment, it must be made too small to tempt any decently employed laborer to forsake his place and run to the municipality, still, it will not be the frankly infernal competition wage. It will be, like mediaeval wages, fixed with at least some reference to public opinion as to a becoming standard of comfort. Over and above this, the municipality will have to pay to its organizers, managers, and incidentally necessary skilled workers the full market price of their ability, minus only what the superior prestige and permanence of public employment may induce them to accept. But whilst these high salaries will make no more disturbance in the labor market than the establishment of a new joint stock company would, the minimum wage for laborers will affect that market perceptibly. The worst sort of sweaters will find that if they are to keep their "hands," they must treat them at least as well as the municipality. The consequent advance in wage will swallow up the sweater's narrow margin of profit. Hence the sweater must raise the price per piece against the shops and wholesale houses for which he sweats. This again will diminish the profits of the wholesale dealers and shopkeepers, who will not be able to recover this loss by raising the price of their wares against the public, since, had any such step been possible, they would have taken it before. But fortunately for them, the market value of their ability as men of business is fixed by the same laws that govern the prices of commodities. Just as the sweater is worth his profit, so they are worth their profit; and just as the sweater will be able to exact from them his old remuneration in spite of the advance in wages, so they will be able to exact their old remuneration in spite of the advance in sweaters' terms. But from whom, it will be asked, if not from the public by raising the price of the wares? Evidently from the landlord upon whose land they are organizing production. In other words, they will demand and obtain a reduction of rent. Thus the organizer of industry, the employer pure and simple, the *entrepreneur*, as he is often called in economic treatises nowadays, will not suffer. In the division of the product his share will remain constant; whilst the industrious wage worker's share will be increased, and the idle proprietor's share diminished. This will not adjust itself without friction and clamor; but such friction is constantly going on under the present system in the opposite direction, *i.e.*, by the raising of the proprietor's share at the expense of the worker's.

The contraction of landlords' incomes will necessarily diminish the revenue from taxation on such incomes. Let us suppose that the municipality, to maintain its revenue, puts on an additional penny in the pound. The effect will be to burn the landlord's candle at both ends—obviously not a process that can be continued to infinity. But long before taxation fails as a source of municipal capital, the municipalities will have begun to save capital out of the product of their own industries. In the market the competition of those industries with the private concerns will be irresistible. Unsaddled with a single idle person, and having, therefore, nothing to provide for after paying their employees except extension of capital, they will be able to offer wages that no business burdened with the unproductive consumption of an idle landlord or shareholder could afford, unless it yielded a heavy rent in consequence of some marked advantage of site. But even rents, when they are town rents, are at the mercy of a municipality in the long run. The masters of the streets and the traffic can nurse one site and neglect another. The rent of a shop depends on the number of persons passing its windows per hour. A skilfully timed series of experiments in paving, a new bridge, a tramway service, a barracks, or a small-pox hospital are only a few of the circumstances of which city rents are the creatures. The power of the municipality to control these circumstances is as obvious as the impotence of competing private individuals. Again, competing private individuals are compelled to sell their produce at a price equivalent to the full cost of production at the margin of cultivation. The municipality could compete against them by reducing prices to the average cost of production over the whole area of municipal cultivation. The more favorably situated private concerns could only meet this by ceasing to pay rent: the less favorably situated would succumb without remedy. It would be either stalemate or checkmate. Private property would either become barren, or it would yield to the actual cultivator of average ability no better an income than could be obtained more securely in municipal employment. To the mere proprietor it would yield nothing. Eventually the land and industry of the whole town would pass by the spontaneous action of economic forces into the hands of the municipality; and, so far, the problem of socializing industry would be solved.

Private property, by cheapening the laborer to the utmost in order to get the greater surplus out of him, lowers the margin of human cultivation, and so raises the "rent of ability." The most important form of that rent is the profit of industrial management. The gains of a great portrait painter or fashionable physician are much less significant, since these depend entirely on the existence of a very rich class of patrons subject to acute vanity and hypochondriasis. But the industrial organizer is independent of patrons; instead of merely attracting a larger share of the product of industry to himself, he increases the product by his management. The market price of such ability depends upon the relation of the supply to the demand: the more there is of it the cheaper it is: the less, the dearer. Any cause that increases the supply lowers the price. Now it is evident that since a manager must be a man of education and address, it is useless to look ordinarily to the laboring class for a supply of managerial skill. Not one laborer in a million succeeds in raising himself on the shoulders of his fellows by extraordinary gifts, or extraordinary luck, or both. The managers must be drawn from the classes which enjoy education and social culture; and their price, rapidly as it is falling with the spread of education and the consequent growth of the "intellectual proletariat," is still high. It is true that a very able and highly trained manager can now be obtained for about £800 a year, provided his post does not compel him to spend two-thirds of his income on what is called "keeping up his position," instead of on his own gratification. Still, when it is considered that laborers receive less than £50 a year, and that the demand for laborers is necessarily vast in proportion to the demand for able managers—nay, that there is an inverse ratio between them, since the manager's talent is valuable in proportion to the quantity of labor he can organize—it will be admitted that £800 a year represents an immense rent of ability. But if the education and culture which are a practically indispensable part of the equipment of competitors for such posts were enjoyed by millions instead of thousands, that rent would fall considerably. Now the tendency of private property is to keep the masses mere beasts of burden. The tendency of Social Democracy is to educate them—to make men of them. Social Democracy would not long be saddled with the rents of ability which have during the last century made our born captains of industry our masters and tyrants instead of our servants and leaders. It is even conceivable that rent of managerial ability might in course of time become negative,[5] astonishing as that may seem to the many persons who are by this time so hopelessly confused amid existing anomalies, that the proposition that "whosoever of you will be the chiefest, shall be servant of all" strikes them rather as a Utopian paradox than as the most obvious and inevitable of social arrangements. The fall in the rent of ability will, however, benefit not only the municipality, but also its remaining private competitors. Nevertheless, as the prestige of the municipality grows, and as men see more and more clearly that the future is to it, able organizers will take lower salaries for municipal than for private employment; whilst those who can beat even the municipality at organizing, or who, as professional men, can deal personally with the public without the intervention of industrial organization, will pay the rent of their places of business either directly to the municipality, or to the private landlord whose income the municipality will absorb by taxation. Finally, when rents of ability had reached their irreducible natural level, they could be dealt with by a progressive Income Tax in the very improbable case of their proving a serious social inconvenience.

[5] That is, the manager would receive less for his work than the artisan. Cases in which the profits of the employer are smaller than the wages of the employee are by no means uncommon in certain grades of industry where small traders have occasion to employ skilled workmen.

It is not necessary to go further into the economic detail of the process of the extinction of private property. Much of that process as sketched here may be anticipated by sections of the proprietary class successively capitulating, as the net closes about their special interests, on such terms as they may be able to stand out for before their power is entirely broken.[6]

We may also safely neglect for the moment the question of the development of the House of Commons into the central government which will be the organ for federating the municipalities, and nationalizing inter-municipal rents by an adjustment of the municipal contributions to imperial taxation: in short, for discharging national as distinct from local business. One can see that the Local Government Board of the future will be a tremendous affair; that foreign States will be deeply affected by the reaction of English progress; that international trade, always the really dominant factor in foreign policy, will have to be reconsidered from a new point of view when profit comes to be calculated in terms of net social welfare instead of individual pecuniary gain; that our present system of imperial aggression, in which, under pretext of exploration and colonization, the flag follows the filibuster and trade follows the flag, with the missionary bringing up the rear, must collapse when the control of our military forces passes from the capitalist class to the people; that the disappearance of a variety of classes with a variety of what are now ridiculously called "public opinions" will be accompanied by the welding of society into one class with a public opinion of inconceivable weight; that this public opinion will make it for the first time possible effectively to control

[6] Such capitulations occur already when the Chancellor of the Exchequer takes advantage of the fall in the current rate of interest . . . to reduce Consols. This he does by simply threatening to pay off the stockholders with money freshly borrowed at the current rate. They, knowing that they could not reinvest the money on any better terms than the reduced ones offered by the Chancellor, have to submit. There is no reason why the municipalities should not secure the same advantage for their constituents. For example, the inhabitants of London now pay the shareholders of the gas companies a million and a half annually, or 11 per cent. on the £13,-650,000 which the gas works cost. The London County Council could raise that sum for about £400,000 a year. By threatening to do this and start municipal gas works, it could obviously compel the shareholders to hand over their works for £400,000 a year, and sacrifice the extra 8 per cent. now enjoyed by them. The saving to the citizens of London would be £1,100,000 a year, sufficient to defray the net cost of the London School Board . . .

the population; that the economic independence of women, and the supplanting of the head of the household by the individual as the recognized unit of the State, will materially alter the status of children and the utility of the institution of the family; and that the inevitable reconstitution of the State Church on a democratic basis may, for example, open up the possibility of the election of an avowed Freethinker like Mr. John Morley or Mr. Bradlaugh to the deanery of Westminster. All these things are mentioned only for the sake of a glimpse of the fertile fields of thought and action which await us when the settlement of our bread and butter question leaves us free to use and develop our higher faculties.

This, then, is the humdrum programme of the practical Social Democrat to-day. There is not one new item in it. All are applications of principles already admitted, and extensions of practices already in full activity. All have on them that stamp of the vestry which is so congenial to the British mind. None of them compel the use of the words Socialism or Revolution: at no point do they involve guillotining, declaring the Rights of Man, swearing on the altar of the country, or anything else that is supposed to be essentially un-English. And they are all sure to come—landmarks on our course already visible to far-sighted politicians even of the party which dreads them.

Let me, in conclusion, disavow all admiration for this inevitable, but sordid, slow, reluctant, cowardly path to justice. I venture to claim your respect for those enthusiasts who still refuse to believe that millions of their fellow creatures must be left to sweat and suffer in hopeless toil and degradation, whilst parliaments and vestries grudgingly muddle and grope towards paltry installments of betterment. The right is so clear, the wrong so intolerable, the gospel so convincing, that it seems to them that it *must* be possible to enlist the whole body of workers—soldiers, policemen, and all—under the banner of brotherhood and equality; and at one great stroke to set Justice on her rightful throne. Unfortunately, such an army of light is no more to be gathered from the human product of nineteenth century civilization than grapes are to be gathered from thistles. But if we feel glad of that impossibility: if we feel relieved that the change is to be slow enough to avert personal risk to ourselves; if we feel anything less than acute disappointment and bitter humiliation at the discovery that there is yet between us and the promised land a wilderness in which many must perish miserably of want and despair: then I submit to you that our institutions have corrupted us to the most dastardly degree of selfishness. The Socialists need not be ashamed of beginning as they did by proposing militant organization of the working classes and general insurrection. The proposal proved impracticable; and it has now been abandoned—not without some outspoken regrets—by English Socialists. But it still remains as the only finally possible alternative to the Social Democratic programme which I have sketched to-day.

29. The Logic of Socialism: The Unconscious Conversion

SOURCE: Interview with Sidney Webb, 1890, George Eastgate to the Editor, August 20, 1902, *The Times*, August 23, 1902.

The practical man, oblivious or contemptuous of any theory of the social organism or general principles of social organization, has been forced, by the necessities of the time, into an ever-deepening collectivist channel. Socialism, of course, he still rejects and despises. The individualist town councillor will walk along the municipal pavement, lit by municipal gas and cleansed by municipal brooms with municipal water, and seeing, by the municipal clock in the municipal market, that he is too early to meet his children coming from the municipal school hard by the county lunatic asylum and municipal hospital will use the national telegraph system to tell them not to walk through the municipal park but to come by the municipal tramway, to meet him in the municipal reading-room, by the municipal art gallery, museum, and library, where he intends to consult some of the national publications in order to prepare his next speech in the municipal town-hall in favour of the nationalization of canals and the increase of Government control over the railway system. "Socialism, Sir," he will say, "don't waste the time of a practical man by your fantastic absurdities. Self-help, Sir, individual self-help, that's what's made our city what it is."

30.   The Revolution in Local Government:
London

THE OLIGARCHICAL structure of English politics and society rested upon economic control and local political power. The aristocracy and gentry in the country, merchants and industrialists (less consistently) in some towns, rested their power upon both bases. Social deference might become habit, but it derived from respect for power. Little had changed in the form or the content of local government since the days of Elizabeth. Justices of the peace were collectively responsible, in quarter sessions, for the management of counties and as individuals for the affairs of the parish. Before 1835 approximately 250 chartered boroughs were in the hands of oligarchies—often, although not invariably, the mercantile element. Procedures were medieval. Even statutory authorities for special purposes, established by special acts of Parliament, tended to augment rather than to limit oligarchic authority. Some police commissioners or turnpike commissioners or lighting and paving commissioners could boast of great success, but the powers of statutory authorities were always circumscribed in scope. Nevertheless these various local improvement commissions were responsible for what little adaptations were made to modernize England in the face of a demographic and industrial revolution.

Radicals knew what the problem was and were anxious to strike at its root. The Poor Law Amendment Act of 1834 (Document 12), the Municipal Corporations Act of 1835, and the County Constables Act of 1839 were three thrusts at oligarchy. The new poor law was the most important both in what it was and in its implications. The Municipal Corporations Act began a process of standardizing and civilizing municipal government, but the great era of municipal improvement symbolized by Joseph Chamberlain's administration in Birmingham lay well in the future. The act, like the Reform Act of 1832, enfranchised a new elite. Fewer people could vote for the Manchester town council than voted for members of Parliament. The "shopocracy" of Manchester proved little improvement over the city's old guard of parish and court leet. The County Constables Act contained a provision for local option; and only half of England's counties adopted it. The others preferred to risk crime and chartist outrage rather than suffer an invasion of their liberty.

There was much officious centralization in those early years of reform. Edwin Chadwick, while by no means the sole offender, became the object of criticism which reached its peak with the Local

Government Act of 1858. The act granted local authorities a considerable range of autonomy without reference to a central board. Yet ironically the act worked, as Royston Lambert has demonstrated, in precisely the opposite way.[1] Voluntary centralization worked wonders in transforming attitudes. Local authorities were dependent upon London expertise. Lacking it themselves, they came to see that local interests and prejudices must give way. This was a surrender in fact before it was a surrender in form. Bureaucracy and democracy eroded the local sources of oligarchic power.

The County Councils Act of 1888 was a logical outgrowth of the democratization of the parliamentary franchise. While there were no revolutionary changes in local command, the erosion of control continued and could not be checked. In London, 1888 was the last full year for the Metropolitan Board of Works; the London County Council would begin operation on April 1 in the following year. The L.C.C., a test tube for collectivist experimentation, would move dramatically in areas as little touched as education. But its predecessor was proud of its record since 1855. The board reviewed its history and in doing so touched upon problems still unresolved in modern urban society.

Recommended Reading

K. B. SMELLIE, *A History of Local Government in England* (London, 1946); and J. REDLICH and H. W. HIRST, *Local Government in England*, 2 vols. (London, 1903). P. THOMPSON, *Socialists, Liberals and Labour: The Struggle for London 1885–1914* (Toronto, 1967), shows how London works out.

SOURCE: Report of the Metropolitan Board of Works, December 31, 1888, *Parliamentary Papers*, 1889, Vol. LXVI, pp. 5–10.

Report—1888

Spring Gardens
December 31, 1888

Thirty-three years have elapsed since the Metropolitan Board of Works was called into existence by Sir Benjamin Hall's "Act for the better Local Management of the Metropolis," and the year just closed is the last during which the Board will have jurisdiction, or be able to give an account of the way in which it has performed the duties and discharged the responsibilities cast upon it by the

[1] R. Lambert, "Central and Local Relations in Mid-Victorian England," *Victorian Studies*, Vol. VI (1962), pp. 121–150, and *Sir John Simon and English Social Administration* (London, 1963).

Legislature. The Board, it is true, remains in existence three months longer, that is to say, until 31st March 1889; but, as its annual Reports and accounts are required to be made up to the end of December in each year, there will be no further opportunity of giving to the Legislature and to the inhabitants of London an account of its stewardship. On 1st April next, according to the Local Government Act passed in the last Session of Parliament, all the powers, duties, and liabilities of the Board will (unless the Local Government Board shall previously fix some other date) pass to the County Council of London to be constituted under the provisions of that Act, and the Board will no longer exist.

In view of the impending change, it seems desirable that the Board, in its last annual Report, should not confine itself to a simple record of the year's proceedings, but by briefly describing the condition of London in 1855, and by tracing the alterations and improvements effected since that date, endeavour to bring home to the mind of the Londoner of 1888 how much more favourable are the conditions under which he lives, in point of health, comfort and convenience of every kind, than were those of the generation which witnessed the passing of the Metropolis Management Act. The better state of things is due, no doubt, in part to the social, political, and financial reforms of the last 30 or 40 years; but, after making full allowance for these, it will be seen to how great an extent the improved conditions of life in London are to be attributed to the works of the Board and of the subsidiary local bodies created by the Act of 1855.

The Londoner of to-day, accustomed to the unity of management which he sees continually exemplified in the great drainage system, the fire brigade, the embankments of the Thames, the new main thoroughfares running through different districts and connecting one part of the town with another, finds it difficult, if indeed he ever make the attempt, to realise that so recently as the beginning of the second half of this century such unity of management was altogether unknown, and that there was no single representative body to care for or attend to those important branches of municipal administration which concerns the great city as a whole, and which can only be efficiently dealt with by treating it as a whole. At that time the only part of the metropolis which had a complete organisation for even local purposes was the City of London proper, containing an area of little more than one square mile. This, no doubt, had been for several centuries the extent of the urban area, and, as buildings and population extended beyond these limits, there had been no adjustment or extension of the boundaries so as to include within the City the whole of the urban population. The consequence was that until the passing of the Metropolis Management Act in 1855 the large and populous districts of London outside the City had no general system of local government, and were for the most part wholly unconnected with each other. Each parish had its own method of parochial administration, some having a representative constitution, others being under the control of self-elected bodies to a great extent irresponsible to the ratepayers, and many of them being governed by local statutes presenting great diversity in their objects and provisions.

The "Times," writing on the subject on 20th March 1855, used these words:

> We may really say that there is no such place as London at all, the huge city passing under this title being rent into an infinity of divisions, districts, and areas. . . . Within the metropolitan limits the local administration is carried on by no fewer than 300 different bodies, deriving powers from about 250 different local Acts, independent of general Acts. The number of Commissioners employed, though not precisely ascertainable, Sir Benjamin Hall estimates by his own computation at about 15,000.

The necessary consequence of this want of connection between the different districts was, there was no co-operation or conjoint action, and that the needs of London as a whole, needs common to every great city, received very little attention.

Of all the evils from which London suffered, the most manifest and the most detrimental to the health and well being of the inhabitants was the extremely defective sewerage, and with this was the accompanying evil that all the filth of the vast metropolitan population was poured into the river in the very midst of the most populous quarters. The sewers, which were under the control of Commissioners appointed for the purpose by the Brown, were originally intended to carry off only rain water from the streets, the open ground and the roofs of houses. But upon the compulsory abolition of cesspools, which was effected by the Metropolitan Commissioners of Sewers under the provisions of an Act of the year 1848, the sewers became the vehicle for carrying into the river all the excreta and waste water of the population. Most of the sewers having to pass under the low grounds on the margin of the river, discharged their contents at or about the low-water level, and at the time of low water only. As the tide rose it closed the outlets, and thus the sewage flowing from the high grounds accumulated in the low-lying portion of the sewers, where it remained stagnant in many cases for 18 out of every 24 hours. During stagnation the heavier ingredients fell to the bottom, and from day to day accumulated in the sewers; besides which, in times of heavy and long-continued rain, and more particularly when much rain fell at the time of high-water in the river, the closed sewers were unable to store the increased volume of sewage water, which then rose through the house drains and flooded the basements of the houses.

The mischief caused by emptying the sewers into the Thames in the middle of London was of course intensified by the circumstance of the discharge taking place at the time of low water only. The sewage was carried by the rising tide up the river, to be brought back to London by the following ebb tide, there to mix with each day's additional supply, the progress of many days' accumulation towards the sea being almost imperceptible. Moreover, the small volume of water in the river at low tide was quite incapable of effectually diluting and neutralising the offensiveness of the vast quantities of sewage poured into it. Thus were the Thames and its tributaries turned into veritable open sewers, and the broader reaches of the river as it then was, such as that between Westminster and Waterloo Bridges, had their banks covered with vast accumulations of foul and offensive mud, which were exposed at low tide, and in warm weather and under the influence of the sun gave forth exhalations almost pestiferous in character.

An article in a leading medical newspaper, "The Lancet," in July 1855, thus describes the state of the river:

> The waters of the Thames are swollen with the feculence of the myriads of living beings that dwell upon the banks, and with the waste of every manufacture that is too foul for utilisation. Wheresoever we go, whatsoever we eat or drink within the circle of London we find tainted with the Thames. . . . No one having eyes, nose, or taste, can look upon the Thames and not be convinced that its waters are year by year, and day by day, getting fouler and more pestilential. The Thames water is already so turbid that the lower part of a bit of card, sinking edgeways, is invisible before the upper part has become immersed. The abomina-

tions, the corruptions we pour into the Thames are not, as some falsely say, carried away into the sea. The sea rejects the loathsome tribute, and heaves it back again with every flow. Here, in the heart of the doomed city, it accumulates and destroys.

The philanthropic Earl of Shaftesbury, whose efforts to alleviate the hardships and to improve the lot of the poorer class of workers in London will never be forgotten, gave to the Royal Commissioners on the Housing of the Working Classes, in 1884, some striking testimony as to the bad sanitary conditions amid which the poor in some quarters of the town were compelled to live in the earlier days of his labours among them. The following are a few extracts from the official report of his evidence:

Formerly there were a great many long alleys, and when I used to go into them if I stretched out my arms I struck the walls on both sides. They were very long, like a tobacco pipe. In those alleys lived from 200 to 300 people, and there was but one accommodation for the whole of that number, and that at the end; and I do not hesitate to say that it was so tremendously horrible, that one could not even approach that end. . . . The air was dreadfully foul. The sun could not penetrate, and there never was any ventilation.

There was the famous Frying-pan-alley, near Holborn, now swept away. I inspected the whole of Frying-pan-alley, and I am happy to say that such a thing does not exist now in London, and could not exist, because the attention of the officer of health and others would be called to it, and it would be abolished. Frying-pan-alley was a very famous alley in Holborn, like one of those I have described to you; it was very narrow, the only necessary accommodation being at the end; in the first house that I turned into there was a single room, the window was very small, and the light came through the door. I saw a young woman there, and I asked her if she had been there some little time. "Yes," she said, "her husband went out to work, and was obliged to come there to be near his work." She said, "I am miserable!" "What is it?" I asked. "Look there," said she, "at that great hole; the landlord will not mend it. I have every night to sit up and watch, or my husband sits up to watch, because that hole is over a common sewer, and the rats come up, sometimes twenty at a time, and if we did not watch them they would eat the baby up." I am giving you that as a typical instance of what went on in London at that time. That could not exist now.

Such a thing as occurred in Tyndall's-buildings could not exist now, but it will show you what I believe occurred in a great number of instances. I was sitting in this very room, in the Board of

Health, and a person came to me and said that he had discovered
something in Tyndall's-buildings which he thought I ought to see.
This was before we got possession of the court. I went off directly
with Dr. Southwood Smith; I went into a low cellar, and there I
saw what your Lordship will hardly believe. There was not so
much wood in it as would make a faggot. There were a woman
and two children there, but the striking part of it is this: from a
hole in the ceiling there came a long open wooden tube supported
by props, and from that flowed all the filth of the house above,
right through the place where this woman was living, into the
common sewer. Nobody paid the least attention to it. There were
no health officers, and no people looking after the matter; and I
believe much of that sort of thing occurred in London which
could not occur now.

There was a famous place called Bermondsey Island, in Bermondsey. You should know something about that, because I do
not think that such a thing could occur again, it is hardly credible.
It was a large swamp; a number of people lived there, as they do
in Holland, in houses built upon piles. Only two days ago I met
a gentleman, with whom I had inspected that place 20 years before. He put me in mind of it, and he said that it was now completely drained and houses built upon it. So bad was the supply of
water there that I have positively seen the women drop their
buckets into the water over which they were living, and in which
was deposited all the filth of the place, that being the only water
that they had for every purpose, washing, drinking, and so on.

Whilst the condition of the Thames and the sewerage and
sanitary arrangements of London were as here described, other
necessities of a great city and a vast population were equally
unsatisfied and neglected. Districts which are now connected by
broad and well-paved highways, affording ample accommodation
for the traffic, were hindered by labyrinths of narrow and tortuous
streets and lanes from easy and direct communication with each
other. Of all the bridges over the Thames only three were free
from toll, and consequently nearly all traffic between the Middlesex and Surrey sides of the river passed over London, Blackfriars,
and Westminster Bridges. There were no orderly and well-kept
flower-gardens, diversifying the scene and relieving the eye
wearied and dulled with the monotonous rows of dingy brick
houses; for, be it remembered, the London of 1855 was not the city
of palatial structures which, so far at least as its central portions are
concerned, it now is. The sites of the Thames Embankments, with
their broad and handsome thoroughfares, flourishing trees and

gardens, and striking architectural features, were occupied by unsightly and offensive mudbanks, and by wharves and buildings of mean appearance, altogether unworthy of so prominent a position in a great city. On the Surrey side of the river, the low-lying ground, particularly in Lambeth and Southwark, was subject to periodical inundations during high spring-tides, whereby great misery, distress, and illness were caused to the poor inhabitants of the river-side streets.

In the suburban districts, even in what may be called the first zone, that nearest the centre, comparatively few of the footpaths in the streets were paved. In wet weather the side walks in most of the thoroughfares were almost as muddy as the carriage-ways, and it was only after a great outlay of money that the new authorities under the Act of 1855 succeeded in bringing the footpaths into the convenient state to which people are now accustomed.

And what were the means available for preventing the ravages of fire, that terrible enemy in the midst of a crowded population? The only provision made by public authority was that the church-wardens and overseers of every parish were bound to keep a fire-engine for putting out fires in their own parish. The engine, which was worked by hand and was generally of an antiquated type, was in many parishes kept in the churchyard; sometimes, however, a separate building was provided. These arrangements being miserably inadequate, the fire insurance companies had, in the absence of a metropolitan authority, joined together for the purpose of suppressing outbreaks of fire, and preventing the destruction of property in which they were themselves interested. The insurance companies' establishment, which in 1855 consisted of not much more than a hundred men, with engines worked by hand-power, was always ready to do battle with fire, wherever it showed itself, without inquiring what interest the fire offices had in the particular property in danger. Effectual service was thus often rendered. But the utmost that such a force could do, what was it in comparison with the needs of a population even then numbering more than two millions and a half of people? For the saving of life from fire the inhabitants of London were entirely dependent upon the exertions of a society supported by voluntary contributions, which kept by night a number of fire-escapes at prominent points in the public thoroughfares.

The great increase of London since the passing of the Metropolis

Management Act is shown by the many miles of new streets and sewers which have been laid out and constructed; but it may be well to further illustrate this fact by mentioning that at the beginning of the present century the rateable value of the whole of what now constitutes the metropolitan area was, as far as can be ascertained, no more than 3,416,153*l.*, while the population was but 958,863 occupying 136,196 houses. In the period which elapsed between the first year of the century and the establishment of the Board in 1855, the rateable value had risen to 11,283,663*l.*, the population to 2,543,292, and the number of houses to 329,467. In the 33 years which have elapsed since the Board came into existence the progress has been much greater than in the previous 55 years, the rateable value for the year 1889 being no less than 31,033,786*l.*, whilst the population has increased to 4,306,380, and the number of inhabited houses to 549,283.

The London death-rate which, according to the Registrar General's Annual Summary, has during the last few years been less than 20 in the 1,000 (the actual figures of the last three years being for 1885, 19.8; for 1886, 19.9; and for 1887, 19.6), was in the year 1855, which saw the passing of the Metropolis Management Act, 24.3 in the thousand. The difference between this figure and that of the average of the last three years above-mentioned is equivalent in a population of four millions to a saving of not less than 18,000 lives per annum. In 1854, the year before the passing of the Act, when there was an outbreak of cholera, the deaths among each thousand persons numbered 29.4. It was the visitation of cholera in the year 1854 which helped to rouse the people of London and the Legislature to the necessity for some sort of effective municipal government, which should introduce order and harmonious administration where at that time there was nothing but confusion, and should set itself to remedy the accumulated evils and defects resulting from the neglect of many generations.

Sir Benjamin Hall, speaking in the summer of 1855 on the subject of the Act for the better local management of the metropolis, which, as First Commissioner of Works, &c., in Lord Palmerston's Administration, he had just succeeded in passing through Parliament, said: "I was determined, on the merciful abatement of the epidemic that ravaged the metropolis, to turn my attention to the state of this vast city. I knew that unless great and speedy radical changes in the constitution of its local affairs were effected it was utterly hopeless to expect that those affairs would be well conducted." The great and pressing needs which the cholera had forced on public attention were, as has already been indicated, a thorough reform of the sewerage system, and the freeing of the Thames from pollution by the vast quantities of filth daily poured into it as it flowed through London. But other needs, though not so closely affecting the lives and health of the people, were urgently felt. In the year of Sir Benjamin Hall's Act, a Select Committee had been appointed by the House of Commons to consider the subject of metropolitan communications, and the Report contained the following expression of opinion: "Until some authority is established in the 'metropolis sufficiently comprehensive' to effect improvements on a scale adequate to the existing and prospective wants of the traffic, little can be done by the interposition of the Legislature in this matter." The Committee, therefore, expressed "satisfaction at the prospect of a Metropolitan Board of Works being shortly established, with power to carry out those changes which the existing state of London renders it impossible much longer to postpone."

A Royal Commission, which had been appointed in the year 1853 to inquire into the state of the Corporation of the City of London, had considered whether it was practicable to give a municipal organization to the whole of London by means of an extension of the boundaries of the City. This method did not commend inself to the commissioners, and it was they who first recommended a division of the metropolis into municipal districts, and the creation of a Metropolitan Board of Works as a central body, the members of which should be elected by the boards or councils of the several districts, including the City. This central body, they thought, should be entrusted with the management of public works in which all parts of the metropolis had a common interest.

From what has been said it will be seen that the Act of 1855 for the better local management of the metropolis was not passed before there was urgent need. The Act, which is the principal statute under which all the great London improvements of the last 30 years have been effected, created a number of local boards for the governance of their respective areas; that is to say, the maintenance of the local sewers as distinct from the main sewers, the paving, lighting, and cleansing of the thoroughfares, and the general sanitary arrangements; each body being empowered to raise money by means of rates for these various purposes. The areas of administration consisted for the most part of the existing parishes, each of the large parishes forming a separate area under the management of a vestry, and the smaller parishes being grouped into districts under the management of district boards. The part of London known as the City retained its constitution unaltered, the functions which in other parts of London were discharged by vestries and district boards being in the City exercised by the Commissioners of Sewers, a body which had been in existence many years, and whose members were nominated by the Court of Common Council. The number of local management areas, including the City, was originally 39, a number which has in recent years been increased by subdivision of two districts to 41. The Metropolitan Board of Works was at the same time constituted as a central authority to exercise jurisdiction over matters which concerned London as a whole. The Board was composed of representatives of all the parishes and districts (including the City). These representatives were elected not by the ratepayers direct, but by the local governing bodies, each of which returned one, two, or three members, according to the population and rateable value of the area represented. By a Statute passed so recently as the year 1885, the number of representatives of some of the parishes and districts was increased to satisfy the claims of a largely augmented population and higher rateable value.

Since the Act of 1855 many other Acts of Parliament have been passed, conferring powers and imposing obligations upon the Board as the central municipal authority of the metropolis. Indeed, as the necessity has arisen from time to time for the performance of some municipal duty concerning London as a whole, the Legislature has looked to the Board as the body to which the duty must necessarily be entrusted.

The functions which at the present date devolve upon the Board, and which under the recent Act are about to pass, with others, to the new County Council of London, may be shortly stated as follows:—

(1) The maintenance of the main sewers, the interception of sewage from the Thames, its conveyance to a distance from London, and its purification before being discharged into the river.

(2) The prevention of floods from the Thames.

(3) The formation of new main thoroughfares through crowded districts, and the carrying out of other great improvements.

(4) The control over the formation of new streets, and over the erection of buildings, and the construction of local sewers. The naming of streets and numbering of houses.

(5) The construction and maintenance of highways across the Thames, whether in the form of bridges, tunnels, or ferries.

(6) The formation and maintenance of parks and gardens, and the preservation of commons and open spaces.

(7) The demolition of houses in areas condemned as unhealthy under the Artizans' and Labourers' Dwellings Improvement Acts, and the sale or letting of the land for the erection of improved habitations.

(8) The maintenance of a fire brigade for the extinction of fires and the saving of life and property in case of fire.

(9) The supervision of the structural arrangements of theatres and music-halls, with special reference to the safety of persons frequenting them.

(10) The sanctioning of tramways.

(11) The control over the construction of railway bridges.

(12) The supervision to a limited extent of the gas and water supply.

(13) The control over the sale and storage of explosives, petroleum, and other inflammable substances.

(14) The supervision of slaughter-houses and various offensive businesses; also of cowsheds, dairies, and milk-shops; and the prevention of the spread of contagious diseases among cattle, horses. and dogs.

(15) The supervision and control of what is known as baby-farming; and other matters of detail incidental to municipal government.

31. Power and Fear: "Made in Germany"

MOST VICTORIAN affirmations were simple; many were ill conceived. Victorian self-confidence rested upon, among other things, Britain's secure place in the world. The promised era of peace and free trade did not materialize in the mid-Victorian years. Violence and war punctuated the unification of the United States, of Italy, and of Germany. The world that emerged after 1871 was not calculated to gladden the British heart. What happened seemed right, but the results were all wrong. Central Europe was unified, so one object of British foreign policy for two hundred years had been secured. France could not dominate Europe—nor, for that matter, could Russia. But at what cost? Bismarck's Reich was a refutation of British liberal values. German strength and resources threatened Britain's world economic position. So did the United States, but the republic was not perceived as a political threat.

Proximity and political power coincided with economic dangers to raise British fears about Germany. Had it not been for continued sharp disputes with France and Russia, the German problem would have been clear cut in British eyes. Instead British policy zigged this way, zagged that. Economic nationalism proved a concomitant of political nationalism. Britain found herself isolated in values and politics as she gravitated closer to war in South Africa. In the end, Britain was not drawn toward France; she was repelled by Germany. The naval race with Germany, that little cloud no larger than a man's hand at the time, would prove crucial in the reorientation of British policy.

Through the 1890's, however, an important psychological change took place. The traditional stereotype of the happy, harmless German in his *Biergarten* was trampled under the boots of the Prussian army in Paris. An act of 1887 requiring all imported commodities to Britain to be labeled by country of origin provided a new symbol—a threat "Made in Germany." Edwin Ernest Williams, a skillful propagandist, proposed to slaughter a mid-Victorian sacred cow—free trade. To gain support for imperial preference and modest tariffs to establish the principle of reciprocity, Williams wrote his startling, alarmist tract. It hit just the right note to shake wobbly confidence. Williams argued that Britain could never regain her absolute economic supremacy of mid-century; but that she could, by resolute and dramatic action, arrest her decline and recover some measure of departed glory.

Joseph Chamberlain, among others, was a convert. His move to "Fair Trade" in 1903 proved disastrous for the short-term interests of the Conservatives and the Unionists by permitting the Liberals their smashing election triumph in 1906 on a tired slogan dating back two generations. But symbols have potent staying power. The alarms and excursions of "Made in Germany" shook British confidence and probably helped to whet British aggressions, but free trade remained a durable myth.

Recommended Reading

A. L. KENNEDY, *Salisbury* (London, 1953); W. L. LANGER, *The Diplomacy of Imperialism* (2nd ed. New York, 1956), and *European Alliances and Alignments* (New York, 1931); R. SONTAG, *Germany*

and England (New York, 1938); and A. J. P. TAYLOR, *The Struggle
for the Mastery in Europe* (Oxford, 1954).

SOURCE: Edwin Ernest Williams, *Made in Germany* (4th ed., London 1896), pp. 7–10.

As It Was

There was a time when our industrial Empire was unchallenged. It was England which first emerged from the Small-Industry stage. She produced the Industrial Revolution about the middle of the last century, and well-nigh until the middle of this she developed her multitude of mills, and factories, and mines, and warehouses, undisturbed by war at home, and profiting by wars abroad. The great struggles which drained the energies of the Continental nations, sealed her industrial supremacy, and made her absolute mistress of the world-market. Thanks to them, she became the Universal Provider. English machinery, English pottery, English hardware, guns, and cutlery, English rails and bridge-work, English manufacturers of well-nigh every kind formed the material of civilisation all over the globe. She covered the dry land with a network of railways, and the seas were alive with her own ships freighted with her own merchandise. Between 1793 and 1815 the value of her exports had risen from £17,000,000 to £58,000,000. Her industrial dominion was immense, unquestioned, unprecedented in the history of the human race; and not unnaturally we have come to regard her rule as eternal. But careless self-confidence makes not for Empire. While she was throwing wide her gates to the world at large, her sisters were building barriers of protection against her; and behind those barriers, and aided often by State subventions, during the middle and later years of the century, they have developed industries of their own. Of course, this was to a certain extent inevitable. England could not hope for an eternal monopoly of the world's manufacturs; and industrial growths abroad do not of necessity sound the knell of her greatness. But she must discriminate in her equanimity. And most certainly she must discriminate against Germany. For Germany has entered into a deliberate and deadly rivalry with her, and is battling with might and main for the extinction of her supremacy.

In estimating England's industrial position, regard must also be had to her function as the world's middleman. Not only is she a manufacturer for other peoples: she is likewise their agent for distribution. There is scarce a nation—certainly not one of any importance—which does not come to England to buy goods sent in for sale from elsewhere. She sells those nations hams from her Colonies, coffee from Arabia, gloves from France, currants from Greece, cotton from America—in fact it would be hard to name an article produced abroad which is not on sale in those universal market-places, the Mersey and the Thames. In this retail business, also, the Germans are setting themselves to beat us; and South Americans are already buying their Irish linen from Hamburg houses. If there be an advance in this form of competition on the part of Germany, we shall lose the little benefit accruing from the German export trade; for in all other respects it is wholly baneful to us.

The German Revolution

Up to a couple of decades ago, Germany was an agricultural State. Her manufacturers were few and unimportant; her industrial capital was small; her export trade was too insignificant to merit the attention of the official statistician; she imported largely for her own consumption. Now she has changed all that. Her youth has crowded into English houses, has wormed its way into English manufacturing secrets, and has enriched her establishments with the knowledge thus purloined. She has educated her people in a fashion which has made it in some branches of industry the superior, and in most the equal of the English. Her capitalists have been content with a simple style, which has enabled them to dispense with big immediate profits, and to feed their capital. They have toiled at their desks, and made their sons do likewise; they have kept a strict controlling hand on all the strings of their businesses; they have obtained State aid in several ways—as special rates to shipping ports; they have insinuated themselves into every part of the world—civilised, barbarian, savage—learning the languages, and patiently studying the wants and tastes of the several peoples. Not content with reaping the advantages of British colonisation—this was accomplished with alarming facility—Germany has "protected" the simple savage floats on the breezes of the South Sea Islands, and drops in the thick air of the African littoral. Her diplomats have negotiated innumerable commercial treaties. The population of her cities has been increasing in a manner not unworthy of England in the Thirties and Forties. Like England, too, she is draining her rural districts for the massing of her children in huge factory towns. Her yards (as well as those of England) too, are ringing with the sound of hammers upon ships being builded for the transport of German merchandise. Her agents and travellers swarm through Russia, and wherever else there is a chance of trade on any terms—are even supplying the foreigner with German goods *at a loss*, that they may achieve their purpose in the end. In a word, an industrial development, unparalleled, save in England a century ago, is now her portion. A gigantic commercial State is arising to menace our prosperity, and contend with us for the trade of the world. It is true that this mad rush towards industrialism does not meet with universal approval; and the Agrarian Party is energetic in its denunciation of the ruin wrought thereby to German as an agricultural State. But its protests have nothing availed it yet, nor are ever likely to avail it anything.

Made in Germany

The phrase is fluent in the mouth: how universally appropriate it is, probably no one who has not made a special study of the matter is aware. Take observations, Gentle Reader, in your own surroundings: the mental exercise is recommended as an antidote to that form of self-sufficiency which our candid friends regard as indigenous to the British climate. Your investigations will work out somewhat in this fashion. You will find that the material of some of your own clothes was probably woven in Germany. Still more probable is it that some of your wife's garments are German importations; while it is practically beyond a doubt that the magnificent mantles and jackets wherein her maids array themselves on their Sundays out are German-made and German-sold, for only so could they be done at the figure. Your governess's *fiancé* is a clerk in the City; but he also was made in Germany. The toys, and the dolls, and the fairy books which your children maltreat in the nursery are made in Germany: nay, the material of your favourite (patriotic) newspaper had the same birthplace as like as not. Roam the house over, and the fateful mark will greet you at every turn, from the piano in your drawing-room to the mug on your kitchen dresser, blazoned though it be with a legend, *A present from*

Margate. Descend to your domestic depths, and you shall find your very drain-pipes German made. You pick out of the grate the paper wrappings from a book consignment, and they also are "Made in Germany." You stuff them into the fire, and reflect that the poker in your hand was forged in Germany. As you rise from your hearthrug you knock over an ornament on your mantelpiece; picking up the pieces you read, on the bit that formed the bace, "Manufactured in Germany." And you jot your dismal reflections down with a pencil that was made in Germany. At midnight your wife comes home from an opera which was made in Germany, has been here enacted by singers and conductor and players made in Germany, with the aid of instruments and sheets of music made in Germany. You go to bed, and glare wrathfully at a text on the wall; it is illuminated with an English village church, and it was "Printed in Germany." If you are imaginative and dyspeptic, you drop off to sleep only to a dream that St. Peter (with a duly stamped halo round his head and a bunch of keys from the Rhineland) has refused you admission into Paradise, because you bear not the Mark of the Beast upon your forehead, and are not of German make. But you console yourself with the thought that it was only a Bierhaus Paradise any way; and you are awakened in the morning by the sonorous brass of a German band.

32. Jubilee:
"The Captains and the Kings Depart . . ."

ON JUNE 21, 1887 the old Queen had reigned fifty years. She was related to almost every crowned head in Europe. Her eldest son, Edward ("Bertie"), led a very different life with very different people. His Marlborough House set would never have done at Balmoral or at Windsor Castle. "Tum Tum," as he was known to intimates who felt certain he could not hear them—the name tells all—ran with a fast, plutocratic set. His was the new society. The younger sons—those whose social life brought them to the West End, whose careers tended increasingly to be connected with the City—were more in tune with this environment.

The world was ceasing to be Victorian before the good Queen died. But she had her moment—or rather, two moments. The first Jubilee, in

1887, saw her surrounded by Europe's royalty and linked to mid-, even to early Victorian years. People admired the same art, read the same books, conceived of politics and society in essentially similar ways. Of course there was cultural continuity. The age of self-help did not die in 1887—it never has. But both England and the world of the 1890's were different. The second Jubilee in 1897 was almost an anticlimax. The changes, if subtle, were important. The year 1887 had seen the greatest assemblage of European royalty in history. A generation later there would be a shortage of crowned heads. In 1897, with several charming exceptions like Franz Ferdinand, the boy whose assassination would set in motion the war of 1914, the Jubilee was much more an imperial fête. Indian princes, Canadian Indians, colorful representatives from every corner of the world—the living proof that the sun never sets on the British Empire—marched for her just two years before the Boer War.

She enjoyed it, this woman who had given her name to the age. There were other days and other things, but everything thereafter was epilogue. Until at last there were the interviews with Lord Roberts, home, so he thought, from winning the South African war. She reminisced briefly about another general talking to her about his wars nearly a century before. And then she died.

SOURCE: Extracts from the Queen's Journal, *The Letters of Queen Victoria*, Third Series, *1886–1901:* June 21, 1887, Vol. I (London, 1930), pp. 322–325; June 21, 1897, Vol. III (London, 1932), pp. 172–177.

Buckingham Palace June 21, 1887

This very eventful day has come and is passed. It will be very difficult to describe it, but all went off admirably. This day, fifty years ago, I had to go with a full Sovereign's escort to St. James's Palace, to appear at my proclamation, which was very painful to me, and is no longer to take place.

The morning was beautiful and bright with a fresh air. Troops began passing early with bands playing, and one heard constant cheering. . . . The scene outside was most animated, and reminded me of the opening of the Great Exhibition, which also took place on a very fine day. Received many beautiful nosegays and presents. . . .

At half-past eleven we left the Palace, I driving in a handsomely gilt landau drawn by six of the Creams, with dear Vicky and Alix, who sat on the back seat. Just in front of my carriage rode the 12

Indian officers, and in front of them my 3 sons, 5 sons-in-law, 9 grandsons, and grandsons-in-law. Then came the carriages containing my 3 other daughters, 3 daughters-in-law, granddaughters, one granddaughter-in-law, and some of the suite. All the other Royalties went in a separate procession. . . . The route was up Constitution Hill, through the Arch, down Picadilly, past Trafalgar Square, along the new Northumberland Avenue, the Embankment, and then turned to the right to the Abbey. At the door I was received by the clergy, with the Archbishop of Canterbury and Dean at their head, in the copes of rich velvet and gold, which had been worn at the Coronation. The Royal family and suite had all got out before. We Princesses went into a little waiting-room. The crowds from the Palace gates up to the Abbey were enormous, and there was such an extraordinary outburst of enthusiasm as I had hardly ever seen in London before; all the people seemed to be in such good humour. The old Chelsea Pensioners were in a stand near the Arch. The decorations along Picadilly were quite beautiful, and there were most touching inscriptions. Seats and platforms were arranged up to the tops of the houses, and such waving of hands. Picadilly, Regent Street, and Pall Mall were all alike most festively decorated. Many schools out, and many well-known faces were seen.

When all was ready, the procession was formed, my grandsons and grandsons-in-law, sons and sons-in-law, preceding me in the order in which they rode, the Lord Chamberlain, Lord Steward and Garter walking immediately before me, and followed by my daughters, daughters-in-law, granddaughters and granddaughter-in-law, all the ladies (beginning with the Mistress of the Robes, dear Louisa Buccleuch), the Master of the Horse, and other gentlemen. *God Save the Queen* was played, and then changed to Handel's *Occasional Overture*, as I walked slowly up the Nave and Choir, which looked beautiful, all filled with people. The Royalties of highest rank were seated within the altar rails. The House of Commons was below us to the left, and I recognised several persons amongst them, but did not see Mr. Gladstone, though he was there. The Ambassadors and the Household were to the right.

I sat *alone* (oh! without my beloved husband, for whom this would have been such a proud day!) where I sat forty-nine years ago and received the homage of the Princes and Peers, but in the old Coronation Chair of Edward III, with the old stone brought from Scotland, on which the old Kings of Scotland used to be crowned. My robes were beautifully draped on the chair. The service was very well done and arranged. The *Te Deum*, by my darling Albert, sounded beautiful, and the anthem, by Dr. Bridge, was fine, especially the way in which the National Anthem and dear Albert's Chorale were worked in. Dr. Stainer's beautiful *Amen* at the end of the service was most impressive. When the service was concluded, each of my sons, sons-in-law, grandsons (including little Alfred), and grandsons-in-law, stepped forward, bowed, and in succession kissed my hand, I kissing each; and the same with the daughters, daughters-in-law . . . granddaughters, and granddaughter-in-law. They curtsied as they came up and I embraced them warmly. It was a very moving moment, and tears were in some of their eyes.

The procession then reformed, and we went out as we came in, resting a moment in the waiting-room, whilst the Princes were all getting on their horses. The whole ceremony, particularly the outside procession and progress, took twenty minutes longer than was expected. The Sovereigns' procession started too late, which made us, who had waited, later in leaving the Palace, and there were many stoppages, which is almost unavoidable in long processions. Came back another way until we got into Picadilly. The heat of the sun was very great, but there was a good deal of wind, which was a great relief. . . . On a stand, just at the gate of Marlborough House, I descried good old Lord Sydney and Lady Sydney (who have given me a beautiful bust of him [Albert] by Boehm). We only got back at a quarter to three. . . .

Buckingham Palace June 21, 1897

The 10th anniversary of the celebration of my fifty years Jubilee. Breakfasted with my three daughters at the Cottage at Frogmore. A fine warm morning.

At quarter to twelve we drove to the station to start for London. The town was very prettily decorated, and there were great crowds, who cheered very much. At Paddington I was received by Lord Cork, Lord Emlyn, Sir N. Kingscote, Mr. Murdoch, and the other Directors of the G[reat] W[estern] R[ailway]. Drove with Vicky, Lenchen, and Beatrice, going at a fast pace to the Paddington Vestry platform, where an address was presented by the Vicar of Paddington. Then we proceeded at a slow trot, with a Sovereign's escort of the 1st Life Guards. Passed through dense crowds, who gave me a most enthusiastic reception. It was like a triumphal entry. We passed down Cambridge Terrace, under a lovely arch, bearing the motto, "Our hearts thy Throne." The streets were beautifully decorated, also the balconies of the houses with flowers, flags, and draperies of every hue. At Edgware Road there were two more very fine arches. The streets, the windows, the roofs of the houses, were one mass of beaming faces, and the cheers never ceased. On entering the park, through the Marble Arch, the crowd was even greater, carriages were drawn up amongst the people on foot, even on the pretty little lodges well-dressed people were perched. Hyde Park Corner and Constitution Hill were densely crowded. All vied with one another to give me a heartfelt, loyal, and affectionate welcome. I was deeply touched and gratified. The day had become very fine and very hot. . . .

June 22

A never-to-be-forgotten day. No one ever, I believe, has met with such an ovation as was given to me, passing through those six miles of streets, including Constitution Hill. The crowds were quite indescribable, and their enthusiasm truly marvellous and deeply touching. The cheering was quite deafening, and every face seemed to be filled with real joy. I was much moved and gratified.

The night had been very hot, and I was rather restless. There was such a noise going on the whole time, but it did not keep me from getting some sleep. Dull early and close. . . . The head of the procession, including the Colonial troops, had unfortunately already passed the Palace before I got to breakfast, but there were still a great many, chiefly British, passing. I watched them for a little while. At a quarter-past eleven, the others being seated in their carriages long before, and having preceded me a short distance, I started from the State entrance in an open State landau, drawn by eight creams, dear Alix, looking very pretty in lilac, and Lenchen sitting opposite me. I felt a good deal agitated, and had been so all these days, for fear anything might be forgotten or go wrong. Bertie and George C. rode one on each side of the carriage, Arthur (who had charge of the whole military arrangements) a little in the rear. . . .

Before leaving I touched an electric button, by which I started a message which was telegraphed throughout the whole Empire. It was the following: "From my heart I thank my beloved people, May God bless them!" At this time the sun burst out. . . . We went up Constitution Hill and Piccadilly, and there were seats right along the former, where my own servants and personal attendants, and members of the other Royal Households, the Chelsea Pensioners, and the children of the Duke of York's and Greenwich schools had seats. St. James's Street was beautifully decorated with festoons of flowers across the road and many loyal inscriptions. Trafalgar Square was very striking, and outside the National Gallery stands were erected for the House of Lords. The denseness of the crowds was immense, but the order maintained wonderful. The streets in the Strand are now quite wide, but one misses Temple Bar. Here the Lord Mayor received me and presented the sword, which I touched. He then immediately mounted his horse in his robes, and galloped past bare-headed, carrying the sword, preceding my carriage, accompanied by his Sheriffs. As we neared St. Paul's the procession was often stopped, and the crowds broke out into singing *God Save the Queen*. In one house were assembled the survivors of the Charge of Balaclava.

In front of the Cathedral the scene was most impressive. All the Colonial troops, on foot, were drawn up round the Square. My carriage, surrounded by all the Royal Princes, was drawn up close to the steps, where the Clergy were assembled, the Bishops in rich copes, with their croziers, the Archbishop of Canterbury and the Bishop of London each holding a very fine one. A *Te Deum* was sung, specially composed by Dr. Martin; the Lord's Prayer, most beautifully chanted, a special Jubilee prayer, and the benediction concluded the short service, preceded by the singing of the *old* 100*th*, in which everyone joined. *God Save the Queen* was also sung. I then spoke to the Archbishop and Bishop of London. As I drove off, the former gave out, "Three cheers for the Queen."

I stopped in front of the Mansion House, where the Lady Mayoress presented me with a beautiful silver basket full of orchids. Here I took leave of the Lord Mayor. Both he and the Lady Mayoress were quite *émus*. We proceeded over London Bridge, where no spectators were allowed, only troops, and then along the Borough Road, where there is a very poor population, but just as enthusiastic and orderly as elsewhere. The decorations there were very pretty, consisting chiefly of festoons of flowers on either side of the street. Crossed the river again over Westminster Bridge, past the Houses of Parliament, through Whitehall, Parliament Street, which has been much enlarged, through the Horse Guards and down the Mall. The heat during the last hour was very great. . . .

33.   The Masses Emerge:
Keir Hardie

BRITAIN's traditional governors viewed the coming of democracy with varying degrees of alarm. Some sought to minimize its effect; others to capture the masses. Most feared the emergence of a full-fledged proletarian political party backed by the massive numbers of the working classes. Some hoped that public education might teach the people to know their place. Where Gladstone hoped that the masses would prove a thoughtful court of appeal on matters of moral statesmanship, Disraeli argued more crudely that they would reward their benefactors. The new political tacticians of the late Victorian age agreed with Disraeli. Joseph Chamberlain attempted to formulate a radical program and constituency organization to capture and regiment the electorate. His failure contributed to his growing interest in the glories of empire rather than the virtues of the social service state. Lord Randolph Churchill attempted to substitute sloganeering for political ideas—an effective touch—while appealing to the conceit and the subservience of the working classes.

The laboring men of Britain, seldom articulate or coherent, had their self-appointed champions. One was James Keir Hardie, a Scottish coal miner. Workingmen had a long list of champions in Parliament. William Cobbett and Thomas Hughes, even Feargus O'Connor, the mad gentleman-Chartist, had their day and many words. Other workingmen sat in Parliament before Keir Hardie: two miners in 1874, Henry Broadhurst of the Trades Union Congress elected in 1880 and serving briefly as under secretary of the Home Office in 1886; but every previous workingclass member of Parliament had been returned as a Liberal.

Both the political liberalism and the craft union exclusiveness of the leaders of organized labor came under sharp attack in the late 1880's. The "New Unionism"—semiskilled and unskilled workers in mass organizations—challenged the prosperous and orderly world of labor's junta. Simultaneously Keir Hardie and his associates launched a campaign for the election of independent labor members of Parliament. Having seen Parnell in action, they felt labor could share his success. Keir Hardie and two colleagues won seats as independents in the election of 1892. The following year he established the Independent Labor party at Bradford; it was a failure as a party but was a very successful pressure group. Gladstone's retirement in 1894 brought a brief, totally misleading impression of support. Affable Lord Rosebery, who could not govern even if his horses did win the Derby, held few attractions for the workingman. But I.L.P. ranks emptied again in the jingoistic orgy of the Boer War.

James Keir Hardie was the political workingman released. A Scottish miner from boyhood, he nursed a sense of grievance against a world of callous exploitation. He believed in and practiced self-help. He was a temperance man, quick to denounce drink as a fatal temptation for the laborer, and he was a devout Methodist lay preacher. Keir Hardie was also a socialist, but a very strange one, deriving his views from John Ruskin and Henry George. Keir Hardie looked in on the Socialist Democratic Federation and, with his usually sound instincts, found it wanting. If his ideology was short, his sense of working-class values and grievances was long.

The birth of yet another royal great-grandchild (most Britons had long ago lost count, but this one was the future Edward VIII and Duke of Windsor) coincided with the loss of 260 miners in a Welsh disaster. Sir William Harcourt and Arthur Balfour, the leaders of the House and the Opposition, entered the usual flowery congratulations to the Royal Family. Keir Hardie challenged the scale of priorities. The masses emerged with a vengeance, and the Commons never fully recovered.

Recommended Reading

Labor literature is extensive, and much of it is good. Three particularly useful studies are: G. D. H. COLE, *British Working Class Politics 1832–1914* (London, 1941); H. PELLING, *Origins of the Labor Party* (London, 1954); and P. P. POIRIER, *Advent of the Labor Party* (London, 1958).

SOURCE: James Keir Hardie, "Speech on a Motion for an Address to T. R. H. the Duke and Duchess of York, 28 June 1894," *Hansard's Parliamentary Debates*, Fourth Series, Vol. XXVI, cols. 462–464.

MR. KEIR-HARDIE (West Ham, S.): Mr. Speaker, on my own behalf and those whom I represent, I am unable to join in this public address. I owe no allegiance to any hereditary ruler—[*inter-*

ruption]—and I will expect those who do to allow me the ordinary courtesies of debate. The Resolution, Sir, proposes to congratulate Her Majesty on the birth of a son to the Duke and Duchess of York. It seeks to elevate to an importance which it does not deserve an event of everyday occurrence. I have been delighted to learn that the child is a fairly healthy one, and had I had the opportunity of meeting its parents I should have been pleased indeed to join in the ordinary congratulations of the occasion, but when we are asked as the House of Commons representing the nation to join in these congratulations then in the interests of the dignity of the House I take leave to protest. There is one aspect of this question which concerns the House of Commons. A Minister of the Government is required to be present on this interesting occasion. I submit, Sir, that such a proceeding is not calculated to enhance the dignity of this House in the eyes of the nation. [*Interruption, and a* VOICE: "Rot!"] Hon. Gentlemen may say "rot." If those hon. Gentlemen mixed as freely as I do with the common people they would know their opinions on this question. From that point of view it seems to me that a protest of some kind ought to be made by this House. It is a matter of small concern to me whether the future ruler of the nation be the genuine article or a spurious imitation. Now, Sir, this proposal has been made because a child has been born into the Royal Family. We have a right to ask what particular blessing the Royal Family has conferred upon the nation that we should be asked to take part in this proceeding to-day. We have just heard it said that Her Majesty had ruled for over half a century. I would correct that, Sir, by saying that Her Majesty has reigned, but has not ruled. I remember in reading the proceedings in connection with the Jubilee that the one point made was that during the 50 years of Her Majesty's reign the Queen had not interfered in the affairs of the nation. That may be reigning, but it certainly is not ruling. Then there is the Prince of Wales. What special advantage has His Royal Highness conferred upon the nation?

COLONEL SAUNDERSON (Armagh, N.): I rise, Sir, for the purpose of moving that the hon. Member be no longer heard.

SIR W. HARCOURT: I hope that the hon. and gallant Member will not press his Motion. I do not think it would tend to produce the result which he desires, and which, I think, we all desire—namely, the prevention of disorder.

MR. KEIR-HARDIE: I was about to observe that I do not know anything in the career or the life of the Prince of Wales which commends him especially to me. The "fierce white light" which we are told "beats upon the Throne" sometimes reveals things in his career it would be better to keep covered. Sometimes we get glimpses of the Prince at the gaming tables, sometimes on the racecourse. His Royal Highness is Duke of Cornwall, and as such he draws £60,000 a year from the Duchy property in London, which is made up of some of the vilest slums——[*Cries of* "Question!"]

MR. SPEAKER: The hon. Gentleman is not now speaking to the Resolution before the House.

MR. KEIR-HARDIE: I will bow to your ruling, Sir, and proceed to the subject of the Resolution. We are asked to rejoice because this child has been born, and that one day he will be called to rule over this great Empire. Up to the present time we have no means of knowing what his qualification or fitness for that task may be. It certainly strikes me—I do not know how it strikes others—as rather strange that those who have so much to say about the hereditary element in another place should be so willing to endorse it in this particular instance. It seems to me that if it is a good argument to say that the hereditary element is bad in one case, it is an equally good argument to say that it is bad in the other. From his childhood onward this boy will be surrounded by sycophants and flatterers by the score—[*Cries of* "Oh, oh!"]—and will be taught to believe himself as of a superior creation [*Cries of* "Oh, oh!"] A line will be drawn between him and the people whom he is to be called upon some day to reign over. In due course, following the precedent which has already been set, he will be sent on a tour round the world and probably rumours of a morganistic alliance will follow—[*Loud cries of* "Oh, oh!" *and* "Order!" *and* "Question!"]—and the end of it all will be that the country will be called upon to pay the bill. [*Cries of* "Divide!"] As a matter of principle, I protest against this Motion being passed, and if there is another Member of the House who shares the principles I hold I will carry my protest the length of a Division. The Government will not find an opportunity for a Vote of Condolence with the relatives of those who are lying stiff and stark in a Welsh valley, and, if that cannot be done, the Motion before the House ought never to have been proposed either. If it be for rank and title only that time and occasion can be found in this House, then the sooner that truth is known outside the better for the House itself. I will challenge a Division on the Motion, and if the Forms of the House will permit, I will go to a Division in the hope that some Members at least will enter their protest against the mummery implied in a Resolution of this kind.

34. Jingoism:
The Boer War

BRITAIN led the imperialist ball of the late nineteenth century. That raucous party and the world war that followed marked the end of European domination. For three hundred years Europe ruled most of the accessible world through a combination of technology and zeal. But competitive flag-raising over meaningless tracts of real estate—the Kalahari desert or an inhospitable, uninhabited Pacific atoll—was the last installment of a neurotic quest for power. Europeans and quasi-Europeans asserted themselves in what are now fashionably described as underdeveloped areas, because the real game of power politics was too dangerous to play at home.

Britain was a veteran of the assertion of overseas power. Sir Stamford Raffles suffered no fit of absence of mind when he founded Singapore in 1819 and entrenched the British on the trade routes to the South China Sea. Spoils from the Napoleonic wars like the Cape Colony and Ceylon fitted well into evolving British economic and strategic needs. The new world that Canning called in to redress the balance of the old came to be more, not less, attractive with the passage of time—even in an era of Gladstonian anti-imperialistic morality and Manchester school anti-imperialistic political economy. Palmerston proclaimed Britain's strength to the world in his Don Pacifico speech, and asserted it in the Opium and the Crimean wars.

Empire was also the darling of many radicals. Two of the chief spokesmen of the imperial revival, Sir Charles Dilke and Joseph Chamberlain, were viewed as subversives; but both had an almost mystic sense of Britain's imperial destiny. So did Cecil Rhodes who began making wills in 1877 bequeathing his fortune

> To and for the establishment, promotion and development of a Secret Society, the true aim and object whereof shall be for the extension of British rule throughout the world, the perfecting of a system of emigration from the United Kingdom, and of

colonisation by British subjects of all lands where the means of livelihood are attainable by energy, labour and enterprise, and especially the occupation by British settlers of the entire Continent of Africa, the Holy Land, the Valley of the Euphrates, the Islands of Cyprus and Candia, the whole of South America, the Islands of the Pacific not heretofore possessed by Great Britain, the whole of the Maylay Archipelago, the seaboard of China and Japan, the ultimate recovery of the United States of America as an integral part of the British Empire, the inauguration of a system of Colonial representation in the Imperial Parliament which may tend to weld together the disjointed members of the Empire and, finally, the foundation of so great a Power as to render wars impossible and promote the best interests of humanity.

Empire was the practical application of power. Fewer than two thousand Britons administered the affairs of India. The Christian myth of mission could be secularized as bringing order to the disordered, culture to the savage, opportunity to the oppressed. That great Whig-Liberal, Thomas Babington Macaulay, felt that Shakespeare and English constitutional history could save India from the misery and oppression of native culture. The Indians could not explain why they did not agree, and their more violent effort, the Sepoy rebellion of 1857, was ruthlessly suppressed.

Britain had its white dominions and its non-white empire. White colonies of settlement usually, although not invariably, developed lives and cultures of their own, were encouraged by the implementation of the Durham report to refine their own institutions on the English model, and evolved relatively smoothly into a confederate empire in which the components might, and eventually did, pursue policies at variance with those of the mother country. Yet some of the most dramatic conflicts of imperial policy took place in precisely these areas. Throughout the century in Ireland, in Canada in the 1830's and 1860's, in New Zealand during Gladstone's great ministry, and in South Africa episodically through the second half of the century, something approximating battle lines were drawn between white and white.

The South African war had its roots in Boer (Dutch) withdrawal from contact with the British on the Cape, their collision with Bantu tribesmen and appeal for English help, the overly successful British campaign in the Zulu War, and a confused set of relationships and policies between Britain and the Dutch republics in the 1870's and 1880's. The expansionism of Cecil Rhodes was complicated, not eased, by the gold strikes of 1886 in the Transvaal. Paul Kruger, President of the Transvaal, was enabled to launch his own expansionist program. Jameson's Raid, a brawl scarcely meriting the name of a military action in 1895, was an utter failure. Alfred Milner, Britain's commissioner on the spot, saw force as the only answer. The real and fancied grievances of Britons in the Transvaal, their Uitlander status, proved emotional dynamite. A century that had grown stale and bored wanted excitement. The imperial jag culminated, with all its racism, emotion, and violence, in a sharp, tough series of actions. The British, after indulging in their usual early incompetence, which was exceeded only by that of the Boers, won the conventional war, only to find they had won nothing at all. There remained a dirty war—wiring off and sweeping squares of land for guerrillas, concentration camps, and the rest—which no one could win.

Balfour's speech was made in the early glow of adventure, although the First Lord of the Treasury already entertained doubts about just how easy the job would be. Nonetheless—there were all the racist alarms and excursions, the vulgar appeals to jingo, the mindless bounce of "Ta-ra-ra-boom-de-ay." It is to Britain's eternal credit that there were many who resisted the appeal.

Recommended Reading

D. JUDD, *Balfour and the British Empire* (London, 1968); W. L. LANGER, *The Diplomacy of Imperialism,* 2d ed. (New York, 1956); J. MORRIS, *Pax Britannica* (London, 1968); R. ROBINSON, J. GALLAGHER, and A. DENNY, *Africa and the Victorians* (London, 1961); A. P. THORNTON, *The Habit of Authority* (Toronto, 1966); A. P. THORNTON, *The Imperial Idea and Its Enemies* (London, 1959); A. J. P. TAYLOR, *The Struggle for the Mastery in Europe* (Oxford, 1954); and R. WINKS, *British Imperialism: God, Gold, Glory* (New York, 1961).

SOURCE: Arthur Balfour, "Address to the National Union of Conservative Associations, Dewsbury, November 28, 1899," *The Times*, November 29, 1899.

It is our lot to be spectators rather than actors, to be commentators and observers rather than assistants in these great deeds; and from that point of view I think it desirable both as a justification of the past and as a guide to the future—for the future is one which after the war is over is not without its difficulties and perplexities—I say as a justification of the past and as a guide to the future, to make some answer to the accusations that have been hurled, not against the Government alone, but against the people that is behind the Government, and to give some account, some explanation of the facts and the truths and the realities of South African politics as I, at all events, understand them.

It is hardly, perhaps, worth my while, or worth your while, to spend any time over an accusation freely levelled against us, against this country I mean, by the foreign Press, nor to reply to the relatively faint echo of those accusations by the Irish Home Rule members in the House of Commons. Those members are not usually supposed to suffer under any difficulty in expressing themselves in tolerably violent language, even on subjects on which perhaps their feelings are not quite as violent as the terms in which they express them; but they have been completely outdone on the occasion, and I note it with pride—they have been completely outdone by the foreign critics of whom, as I have said just now, they are, after all, but the pale and feeble reflection. Now, what is the fundamental charge which this particular class of critics, animated by whatsoever motive, have thought fit to bring against us? It is that the Government in the first instance, and the country through its complicity with the Government, have been moved by corrupt motives to adopt a policy having for its object to destroy the independence of free and self-governing Republics. Money, they tell us, the acquisition of goldfields, they tell us, it was that have been the moving springs of our action, the ground and the ultimate goal of our iniquitous and selfish policy. Well, in so far as the charge proceeds from envy, hatred, malice, and all uncharitableness, I leave it alone, but in so far as it proceeds from ignorance, very gross and very unjustifiable, let me say one word in reply to it. Those who make that charge have never made themselves acquainted with the colonial system of this country. It is quite true that we have a great, though indirect, interest in the good government of every part of the civilised glove. It is true that we have a great, though an indirect, interest in seeing that in no part of the world is commerce strangled by tyranny, corruption, or maladministration. In that sense, no doubt, it is for our interest to see that some better form of government should be adopted in the Transvaal. But as to the direct pecuniary interest which these critics see, to assume, what is it? What penny of direct profit is it our habit to extract from our colonies? Has it ever occured to the mind of an English statesman for over 100 years that taxes should be imposed on colonies for the benefit of the mother country? If it be true, as it is true, that we have no pecuniary advantage to gain of this direct and corrupt kind from any conquests or any territorial acquisitions, are we not, on the other hand, sacrificing the lives of those dearest to us, risking the death, as each one can probably say, as I myself and most of us can say, of those who by blood or by friendship are most closely bound to us, in a contest from which we have nothing to gain except the security and the honour of the Empire?

I am told by the same class of critics as those on whom I have already animadverted that we have been moved to adopt this military and aggressive policy by the influence of South African capitalists. I do not understand this distinction between capitalists and workmen. If anything we are doing is for the interest of the South African capitalists, it is also for the benefit of the South African workmen, chiefly men of English blood, English descent, English language, and English nationality. But with regard to those who make these charges, whether it be that we are influenced by the employers or the employed, have they reflected how serious is the charge against the Transvaal Government which this accusation against us implies? For please mark this. The critics tell us that we are making this war to please the owners of the South African goldfields. Those owners, by the very fact that there is war, have seen their property threatened, their mines shut up for an indefinite period, and they have been told in language as plain as one of the greatest masters of plain language could speak—I mean the Chancellor of the Exchequer—they have been told in perfectly plain language by him that, when the war is concluded, the mines, in common with other forms of property in the Transvaal State will undoubtedly be burdened with some of the charges connected with the war. Therefore the accusation against the Transvaal Government, not against us, comes to this, that the Government is so bad, it has so iniquitously used its powers to strangle a legitimate industry, that it pays the industry and is for the advantage of the industry that for the time being its workers should be swept to the four winds of Heaven, that the mines should be shut up, and that it should be finally saddled with a heavy charge in consequence of the war; and, after submitting to all those charges, it pays them because there is some chance of their being put under a good administration instead of the administration under which they have so long groaned. I cannot imagine a more severe commentary upon the Transvaal Government than this argument which is entirely used, so far as I know, by those whose boast it is that they support that Government.

Then we are told that the Uitlanders' grievances, about which so much as been said, are, after all, nothing in particular, nothing

really serious, and the persons who most ardently urge that contention are again the Irish members. Now, according to the Irish
members, there is no more oppressed country than Ireland. I
should suppose, therefore, that, if the Uitlander grievances are
nothing, they must be less than the grievances under which poor
Ireland suffers. Now, just consider how the case stands. One of the
most fundamental and important foundations of free government is
the right of public meeting, whenever public meeting does not
degenerate, as in Ireland it has too often degenerated, into the
means for promoting crime. So far as I know, and I speak in the
presence of our chairman [the Marquis of Zetland], who was
associated with me for many years in the government of Ireland—
so far as I know there never has been any check of any sort placed
upon a public meeting in Ireland called together for the purpose of
discussing public grievances, real or imagined, and which confined
itself to that legitimate purpose. In the Transvaal the right of
public meeting was practically non-existent. A single policeman
was, by law, entitled to dissolve any assembly consisting of more
than seven persons at his own good will. I take it, therefore, that, so
far as the right of public meeting is concerned, the comparison is
altogether in favour of oppressed Ireland. I then ask how the
matter stands in regard to religious freedom? In the Transvaal no
Roman Catholic can hold any office of any kind whatsoever. In
Ireland, as you know, for more than two generations practically
every office has been open to all Irishmen. The majority of Irish
members in the House of Commons are Roman Catholics. Many of
the Judges on the Bench are Roman Catholics and, as far as I know
anything about the government of Ireland, there has always been a
desire to see that competent Roman Catholics should have their fair
share of all administrative posts. Well, then, as to taxation, the
Irish, I believe, allege that they are overtaxed compared with the
English. Personally, I think just the reverse, and I have given my
reasons for that opinion in a very elaborate form open to anybody
to discuss and to criticize, and, if they can, to answer; but, at all
events, even the Irishmen who most believe in Ireland's financial
grievances will hardly maintain that the Irish are taxed at the rate
of £16 a head, which is what the Uitlanders are taxed at, that
England lives upon Ireland's industry, and, living upon Ireland's
industry, does not allow Ireland any voice in the distribution of the
money thus illegitimately acquired. Again I think "oppressed Ire-

land" has no advantage. Then we come to representation. The Uitlanders are not represented at all. They bear all the taxation. They have none of the representation. It has never, I think, been maintained that Ireland is under-represented. Even the most eloquent Irishman, in his moments of highest flight, has never, so far as I know, mentioned in the catalogue of Ireland's woes the fact that Ireland sent too few representatives to the House of Commons; and, without going into the question of education at length, let me remind you that in Ireland everything has been done to make elementary education and secondary as harmonious, not merely to the interests but to the prejudices of the people, as possible, and that that system of education is largely kept up at English expense. Then compare it with the case of the Transvaal, where the Uitlanders are practically not allowed to educate their own children in their own language or in their own way, while they have to contribute vast sums towards a system of education of which they utterly disapprove. Finally, to complete the comparison, President Kruger rejected with scorn the suggestion that when the Uitlanders were represented in the Transvaal representative Assembly they should be allowed to use their own tongue. Unlike the Orange Free State, unlike the Cape Parliament, unlike the Canadian Parliament, unlike every Parliament where free institutions are really understood, these Uitlanders when they did get representation were not to be allowed to use the privilege thus accorded to them of attending debates of which they should be able to understand the language and in which they could take part. In regard to Ireland, fortunately, the Irish speak the same language as the rest of their compatriots. No one, I think, will contend that they have found any difficulty in expressing at the utmost length, with the utmost vigour, and with a fluency which no Englishman can hope to emulate all that their heart moved them to say about the wrongs inflicted by the united Parliament upon the Irish minority. At all events, in their mouth—and they are the people who have chiefly used the argument—it is one that is shattered at the first touch. You have only got to consider the condition of the Uitlanders—mark you, the superior section of the population in numbers, in culture, in civilisation, in all that goes to make industrial progress—and no comparison can be made between their condition and the condition of any other subject population in the world. It was not possible for England to tolerate that, in the very middle of one of her own dependencies, her own sons should be treated as inferior creatures. It was not consistent with our honour or our dignity, still less was it consistent with the ultimate interests of either men of our own blood and language in South Africa, or even of the white races taken as a whole.

Now one other point, one other attack, and only this one other, will I notice, and that very briefly. It is that had negotiations been carried on with greater dexterity by the Government in general, by Mr. [Joseph] Chamberlain [now Unionist Colonial Secretary] in particular, the calamities of war would have been avoided and all our legitimate desires could have been peacefully obtained. That is the argument chiefly used in the somewhat petty and querulous commentaries used by one or two—I am glad to think not the majority, but by one or two—of the leading members of the Opposition. But, after all, do not believe that great events can spring out of petty causes like that, do not believe that two States like the Orange Free State and the South African Republic are going to risk their very existence because a dispatch was couched in one set of formulae rather than another, or was sent on one day of the week rather than on another day of the week. All those are petty details, which you may well sweep from your recollection and need never, in my judgment, give a thought to at all. But if you want, in order to meet your enemies in the gate, a plain and simple argument which must appeal to all I will give it you. It would have been in the power of the South African Republic at any moment, up to that fatal Wednesday when they declared war—it would have been in their power undoubtedly to checkmate English diplomacy, if English diplomacy had for its object to provoke a war, by any measure which gave immediate and substantial representation to the Uitlanders; and they could at the same time have claimed, if they had liked, that we should guarantee their independence in, I think it was, the year 1896 or 1897, and the offer made was scornfully rejected. Now, it is folly to say that people who could have avoided war by this simple procedure were driven into war itself by the wiles of unscrupulous diplomatists or by the follies of foolish diplomatists. They had their fate in their own hands. They could have chosen peace and permanent independence had they preferred to do so, but they elected for the opposite policy. They plunged themselves and their neighbours of the Orange Free State and us into a war of which the end is not yet, and which, whatever blessings it may ultimately produce for South Africa, will certainly not tend to carry out the policy which these Transvaal statesmen most desire to see carried out. People say "Oh well, but the Government had a majority of 140 behind them and, if they desired war, they could, whatever the Transvaal had done, have made war a necessity." I speak in the presence of many of our most loyal supporters in the House of Commons, and I appeal to them whether, if the Transvaal Government had offered immediate and substantial representation to the Uitlanders and we had refused to accept the offer, that 140 majority would not have melted like a summer snow. Our power is as nothing and we cannot command a single vote if we once persuade the House of Commons, and the country which is behind the House of Commons, that there is some sinister object at which we are aiming, some object neither recommended by national honour nor approved by the national conscience.

I ask myself, then, if it be true, as it certainly is true, that the Transvaal Government deliberate elected for war rather than make any concession about the franchise, what is the explanation of the fact which seems at first so astonishing? For, mark you, all that was asked of the Transvaal Government was to do something for the Uitlanders, far less than is done for the Uitlanders in the Orange Free State, and far less than is done for the Dutch-speaking colonists in Natal or in Cape Colony. What can have been the influence which prevented them adopting a policy so obvious, so just, and recommended to them by the nearest examples among men of their own faith and men of their own language? I am afraid we cannot shut our eyes to the fact that one reason was a reason of corruption. You have heard a great deal of the corruption of the Transvaal Government, and I fear that nothing you have heard is exaggerated. I only bring it in now, not to make unnecessary attacks upon those with whom we are at war, still less to throw discredit upon this or that individual Boer politician; but because my argument requires me to point out to you that when you have a system in which you use a subject as a kind of a milch cow—from which vast sums are drawn and distributed among a comparatively small governing class—when you have that system it is not charity, but common sense, that points out to you that the whole forces of corrupt interest are on the side of maintaining that system intact. It is evident that if they had given this immediate and substantial representation to the Uitlanders the very first results would have been that public criticism before which corruption flies terrified, and that impartial investigation into the finances which would have made impossible the illegitimate distribution of public wealth amongst the few who contribute not at all, or scarcely at all, to its production. I therefore fear that we cannot hide from ourselves that one of the reasons of the present situation is the corruption of the Transvaal Government and the vast numbers of the Transvaal leaders who were bound either by their own interest or the interest of their *entourage* to see that their interests were not touched in any essential particular.

Formerly I was of opinion that that motive, combined with the more honourable motive of reluctance to see a change, a reluctance to admit to the Government those who did not share either the privileges or the language of the oligarchy who held power—I was formerly of opinion that those motives and those motives alone were sufficient to account for the absolute refusal of the Transvaal Government to adopt those necessary reforms. But I have changed my opinion. I have been reluctantly brought to the conclusion that there was another motive, at least as strong, which would have made, either now or hereafter, war an absolute and inevitable necessity. I now believe this—that the declaration of war by the Transvaal Government and the Orange Free State was not any despairing struggle for liberty, but a bid for Empire. I now believe that it was not to preserve what they had, but to get what they had not, that they went to war. I now believe that nothing less than to make themselves—these two Republics as a nucleus and what additions they could obtain to them—the centre of a Dutch-speaking paramount power in South Africa, and to exclude for ever the hated Britisher from any dominating influence in the future of that part of the world—that is the only explanation which fits the facts; that is the only explanation which, amongst other things, makes the policy of the Orange Free State credible. We never had any quarrel with the Orange Free State; we never did interfere, or desired to interfere, with their internal affairs. If I had been asked two months ago whether it was likely we should be at war with the Orange Free State, I should have said "You might as well expect us to be at war with Switzerland." They were local friends from whom we had nothing to fear and who had nothing to fear from us. These people have risked their all upon the stake of war, and I say that it is incredible that that risk should be run merely to prevent the Uitlanders getting the vote, and that you have to regard this transaction as part of a larger policy, a deeper and darker design, which aimed at nothing less than to substitute a Boer for a British rule. But you will ask me "How is such madness possible? How could the responsible statesmen of these two Republics ever have entertained the dream that they could oust the power of Britain from South Africa?" Well, I agree with the objector into whose mouth I have put these words. I agree it was madness, but if you will go over all the circumstances of the case it was a very intelligible madness. To begin with, you must not measure the relative strength of the two Powers in South Africa, or the wealth of the two alone—that is, ours and that of the Transvaal and the Orange Free State taken together—and balance one against the other.

The leaders of the two Republics know the military difficulties which would necessarily beset us in carrying out a campaign in South Africa. They knew, in the first place, that it would involve a military expedition without parallel in the history of the world. There has never been in the whole history of the world such a spectacle as the transport of our Army 7,000 miles across the sea, to a country which is incapable of supporting an army, where fodder for the horses, food for the soldiers, ammunition, weapons, everything, down, I believe, to horseshoes, has to be taken from a base 7,000 miles away by sea and 300 miles by rail. They knew also that they had an immense advantage in strategical position—I will not go into the technicalities, but every soldier will tell you how great that is—they knew they had an immense advantage in strategical position from which they could strike in any direction they pleased, while we had to scatter our forces round a large circumference for the purpose of resisting aggression or making an attack. They knew also that they possessed in the irregular militia which makes up their army a military force admirably suited to the country in which the warfare had to be carried on, a military force in which every man by his training was individually qualified for the species of warfare in which he is engaged. They knew, therefore, that we had a very serious job on hand, a difficult military operation to carry through. They also knew what we did not know at the time—what I certainly did not realize until a very short period before the breaking out of the war—that the Orange Free State would throw all their forces into line with the Transvaal

Republic. They conjectured—a false conjecture happily—that there would be European intervention upon their behalf. They counted, as gamblers will, on the improbable, not necessarily the impossible, but the improbable, and they counted last of all (*a voice*, "Upon the Little Englanders," . . .) my friend has put in more concise words the very thought that I was about to express. I was going to say they counted upon the English party system under which any Government has always got to reckon with a certain number, a very large number, of persons who look at their policy with a not unnatural suspicion, and from the habit of constantly criticizing are apt to criticize where criticism had better be silent. They counted on our party system in vain. They did not realize that, however divided we may be about the relatively unimportant questions which divide the great parties in the State, we should come together, if not as one man, still with a practical unanimity, whenever the great interests of the Empire were threatened. And let me say on this point, how very fortunate I count the country which has among its statesmen men like those who, not agreeing with us in politics, have spoken in patriotic and statesman-like language. We here, the Conservative Union, are essentially a party organization, but it is our business, our pleasure, and, as we think, our duty to support and promote the interests of the party to which we belong, but we know of course that in the fluctuation of free institutions now one party is entrusted with the responsibilities of Government, now another, and I am sure all of you rejoice with me that when we end our term—I trust not soon and not dishonourably—when we end our term of office, there are men among our political opponents not less imbued than us with the tradition of an Imperial people, not less worthy to carry on the Imperial policy, or to protect the great interest of the Empire.

Slowly but surely the indignation caused by the treatment of our fellow-countrymen in South Africa has been mounting up in the breasts of the people of this country. They have had relations in the Transvaal; they have known that this is no capitalist question, but that Englishmen, accustomed at home to have a voice in municipal and imperial affairs and to be treated as free men, have been subject, in a country within our sphere of influence, to treatment that should be resented if meted out to an inferior race; and though the unhappy incident of the [Jameson] raid deferred for a period any action that we took in this matter, as soon as it became clear to the country that nothing but force would put this right, then, I am certain, was formed that resolution from which nothing will now turn us, that force should be used rather than that wrong should be endured. We have learned our lesson.

This is not the time to forecast the future or to discuss the arrangements that may be necessary when the war has been brought to a successful termination. But some things we can say. Never again shall we allow to grow up within our midst communities of our own creation in a position to use the liberties that we have granted them to turn their country into a place of arms to be used against us. Never again shall we see the spectre of an English colony being invaded, of English farmers being raided, of the Queen's dominions being annexed by these insolent Republics. Whatever else be done, whatever other arrangements are come to, however the future policy be worked out, the people of this country are unalterably determined that the paramount Power in South Africa shall be the paramount Power indeed, and that the *Pax Britannica* shall be supreme over all the regions in which the Queen now has territorial rights or paramount rights arising from her position. I know not how long this contest may continue, but I know what its conclusion will be; and when the time comes for deciding what policy the victors are to pursue I trust we shall not, on the one hand, forget the generosity which befits us as conquerors, but that, on the other hand, we shall remember that the incidents of the last few months are never to be repeated, that once and for all we must not only show that we mean to have our way but must take our precautions that that way shall never be interfered with.

War is an unhappy necessity—always unhappy, not always necessary indeed, but in this case, as I believe, looking back to what has occurred, inevitable from the first. It must produce much suffering; it has produced, and it will yet produce, sorrow in this country for those that have been lost, and pain and suffering among our soldiers abroad; but war—this war, at all events—has its compensation. It has brought out great virtues in almost every class of the community at home and in our colonies. . . .

The future of South Africa is at present involved in darkness, and I have no title to attempt to lift the veil; but surely I am safe in saying that with all these good results, this exhibition of admirable

qualities which this war has elicited, with the determination of this
country to see the power of Great Britain paramount where it
ought to be paramount, we may look forward to that not distant
peace, which may have for its results, in the first place, the permanent quietening of all those hostile elements in South Africa, and
may in the long run bring in their train the freedom, the justice,
the equality which has never in any other part of the globe failed
to follow the English flag, which has never in any other part of the
globe failed to carry in its train industrial development—development of all the arts of peace, of business, of commerce—and that
we may look forward to these blessings, not as being wrung from
us by the mixture of generosity and fear, but as granted under
conditions which make them safe for all purposes to those who,
however much they may now hate our name, however much they
may now desire the destruction of our power, may yet live (or
their children may yet live), to regard this war as the beginning of
an era of prosperity to South Africa, and to look back to the great
war of 1899, not as the end of their liberties, but as the beginning
of that new era in which true liberty, understood as equality for all
men of the white races and as a liberty under which there shall be
secured everything that the Boers have valued in the shape of
independence, personal independence, shall be guaranteed to them
with as much security, nay, more security, tha[n] they could ever
have hoped for under the scarce civilized rule which they desire to
keep up. If these results follow this war, the heavy sacrifices in men
and money which we have made, and which we are still, I fear, to
make, will not have been made in vain. It is in that firm hope—it is
in that confident faith—that I venture to look forward to the
future.

35. The New Liberalism:
Lloyd George, the Budget, and the Peers

THE EDWARDIAN epilogue to the nineteenth century usually evokes a
pleasant, nostalgic sense of "the good old days" before our century of
modern war. For contemporaries, even for those who wrote retrospectively about the Edwardian days of twenty shillings in the pound,

conflict characterized every aspect of life. The allegedly weaker sex exploded in a demoralizing display of suffragette frenzy, adding a colorful, tawdry last note to the great Victorian feminist movement. The civil, deferential workingman seemed to have disappeared. Labor was no longer the domesticated force wielded by Robert Applegarth half a century before. New men and new notions, political frustration, economic unrest, and general emotional *malaise* found expression in mushrooming strikes for the sake of striking—Britain's brief brush with syndicalism. Privy councilors and ultra conservatives were drilling Ulstermen to resist the anticipated coming of Irish home rule. There was revolt in the arts and chaos in the world. Small wonder that German observers filing extensive reports at home completely misread Britain's capacity or will to resist Germany's thrust for world power.

The Liberal government returned to office in the first twentieth-century landslide in 1906 drew many, perhaps most, of its votes on the old cry of free trade, but there was nothing outdated in the government's performance. Had it not sundered on the reefs of war and the personal ambitions of Lloyd George, the Liberals would probably have remained a principal party in the nation. They were on the way up, not down, in 1914. The Liberals drew the outlines of the modern welfare state. They questioned proconsular imperial policies but found themselves swept into the vortex of war. Armament and domestic reform, the features of the modern state, proved more expensive than predicted.

But political calculation played a greater role than revenue needs in the budget of 1909. The Unionists (essentially the Conservatives) were stunned by the Tory slaughter in the election of 1906. They fell back upon an expedient used with great success since the home rule dispute of 1886—using the House of Lords to destroy Liberal legislation. This required some skill, for the only safe issues were those on which the country was divided. Liquor licensing and secular education, both dear to the Liberal heart, were safe places to use the veto. But the Trade Disputes Act, Workingmen's Compensation, and the vital Old-Age Pension Law of 1909 had to go through. So clever was the Balfour-Lansdowne campaign against liberal legislation that Lloyd George exploded with his famous remark, "The House of Lords is not the watchdog of the constitution; it is Mr. Balfour's poodle." Lloyd George's counterattack was the budget of 1909. It was a Henry George, landlord-baiting budget deliberately calculated to infuriate the peers. It did. Whenever a compromise seemed possible, Lloyd George went out and made another speech. Dukes took a terrible drubbing. They responded by leading the Lords in the rejection of the budget. In return they got everything they feared: two electoral defeats, the budget, Irish home rule, far more sweeping radical social reform, and their own powers trimmed to a suspensory veto. The House of Lords, representative of one class and one party, had outreached themselves and had been beaten.

The "Welsh Wizard" was one of the most striking political figures of the century. Here at Newcastle he displayed his capacity to whip up and move masses of people. In spite of repeated suffragette interruptions (which I have excised), "his lively, boldly suggestive speech," *The Times'* special correspondent glumly observed, "with its colloquialism about revolution and other everyday topics, evoked a very enthusiastic response from men who have the crude taste for ginger in their politics." Lloyd George was the new man who "made it" in politics—very different from the John Brights of the previous century. David Lloyd George liquidated the past and pointed to the future.

Recommended Reading

Biographies of Lloyd George leave much to be desired. That by TOM JONES (1951) is the best, although A. J. P. TAYLOR, "Lloyd George: Rise and Fall," *Politics in Wartime* (London, 1954), pp. 123–149, is more critically perceptive. There is a wealth of general and specific Edwardiana, but the spirit of the time is cleverly evoked by GEORGE DANGERFIELD, *The Strange Death of Liberal England* (London, 1935, and subsequent paperback editions). R. S. CHURCHILL, *Winston S. Churchill*, Vol. II, *The Young Statesman, 1901–1914* (London, 1967), is the best recent study of the controversy and of one of its principal participants.

SOURCE: David Lloyd George, "Speech at Newcastle-on-Tyne, October 9, 1909," *The Times*, October 11, 1909.

A Minister in charge of a great Bill has no time to prepare speeches, and I have not come here to deliver a speech. I have just come here for a plain straight talk about the Budget, the opposition to it, and the prospects of both. It is six years since I had the privilege of addressing a gathering in this theatre, and I have some recollection that then I dwelt upon the great burden imposed upon industry by ground landlords and royalty owners, and I then mildly suggested that it was about time they should contribute something out of their wealth towards the necessities of the State. I come here to-day, six years afterwards, to tell you it will be done, and in a few years. The Bill is through all its most troublesome stages, and it has emerged out of its 40 days and 40 nights in the wilderness rather strengthened and improved. We have made alterations and modifications. You cannot apply any great principle or set of principles without necessary hardships. We have done our best to meet every hard case that was presented to us, done our

best, and done it amidst the taunts of the very people who pressed
those cases upon us. I have had to listen to them for five months. I
have done five months' hard labour. . . .

Although we have made alterations and modifications, the Bill in
its main structure remains. All the taxes are there. The Land Taxes
are there and the Super Tax is there. The poor fellows who are
receiving only £5,000 a year and £10,000 and £20,000 a year will
have to contribute just a little towards the expenses of the country,
and then the poor man to whom somebody has left a fortune will
have to contribute a little more. All these taxes remain, as they
necessarily must, because after all when you order Dreadnoughts a
respectable country like this must pay for them. Now I have told
you that all the taxes remain. There has been one alteration in the
form of one tax. I refer to mineral rights. When we taxed mineral
rights they said—We do not object to pay the tax; all we object to
is the form of the tax.

They said it was uncertain. Well, I said, it was not the form I
cared for so much as the substance. So I said I was quite prepared
to accommodate them. I did not want an uncertain tax, and they
said that so long as the tax was a certain one they preferred paying
more. Well, I said, I was prepared to meet them. I said the present
uncertain tax will produce £175,000; so I altered it to a tax on
mining royalties, which was certain and produced £350,000. They
are not a bit better pleased. You cannot satisfy some people,
although I made that substantial concession to them. We are
through the Committee stage, we are through the last stage where
the substance of the Bill can be modified. The Committee stage is
the stage for the axe and the chisel and the plane; the report stage is
the stage for the sandpaper, just to alter the drafting, but the substance remains. So you see the Bill practically in the form in which
it is going to become an Act of Parliament.

What is the chief charge against the Budget by its opponents?
That it is an attack on industry and an attack on property. I am
going to demonstrate to you that it is neither. It is very remarkable
that since this attack on industry was first promulgated in the
House of Commons trade has improved. It is beginning to recover
from the great crash which first of all came from America, the
country of high tariffs, and it has improved steadily. It has not

quite recovered—the operation will take some time—but it is better. Industries which were having losses last year are beginning to make profits this year. The imports and the exports have gone up during the last few months by millions. Industrial investments have been steady, and there has been on the whole an improvement even in Brewery shares. Only one stock has gone down badly; there has been a great slump in dukes. They used to stand rather high in the market, especially in the Tory market, but the Tory Press has discovered that they are of no value. They have been making speeches recently. One especially expensive duke made a speech, and all the Tory Press said:—Well now, really, is that the sort of thing we are spending £250,000 a year upon?—because a fully-equipped duke costs as much to keep up as two Dread-noughts; and the dukes are just as great a terror and they last longer. . . . As long as they were contented to be mere idols on their pedestals, preserving that stately silence which became their rank and their intelligence, all went well, and the average British citizen rather looked up to them and said to himself, "Well, if the worst came to the worst for this old country we have always the dukes to fall back on." But then came the Budget, they stepped off their perch, they have been scolding like omnibus-drivers, purely because the Budget cart has knocked a little of the gilt off their old stage coach. Well, we cannot put them back again. That is the only property that has gone down badly in the market; all the rest has improved. The prospects of trade are better. Why should Liberal-ism be supposed to be ready to attack property? After all they forget this—I lay it down as a proposition that most of the people who work hard for a living in the country belong to the Liberal party. I would say and think, without offence, that most of the people who never worked for a living at all belong to the Tory party. Whenever you go across country you see men building up trade and businesses, some small, some great, by their industry, by their skill, by their energy, by their enterprise, not merely main-taining themselves and their families, but putting something by for evil days. Not all of them, but hundreds of thousands of them belong to the Liberal party. . . .

If you came to the House of Commons you might imagine that all the men who had anything to lose were on the Tory side of the House, and that the men who had nothing to lose all sit on the Liberal side, whilst as a matter of fact the richest men in the House

of Commons—I only mention the fact—happen to sit on the
Liberal side of the House. Yet we are told that they are all engaged
at the present moment in destroying property and industry and
riches. Why are they engaged in the operation? And let me say this
about these men—my friend Mr. [Winston] Churchill mentioned
it last night in his speech—you will find these rich men in the
House of Commons sitting up night after night, risking health,
some of them most advanced in years—and what for? To pass a
measure which taxes them to the extent of hundreds, maybe
thousands of pounds a year. All honour to them. That is the kind
of rich man one honours, who is prepared to make sacrifices.
Therefore you may take it from me that the Liberal party is not a
party that is likely to engage in a mere wanton war upon industry,
and upon property in this country. All we ask for is that wealth
shall pay its fair share. We are simply seeking to establish in an Act
of Parliament a very old friend and honoured fiscal principle, that
men should contribute to the needs of the State as God has pros-
pered them. But why should there be all this anger, all this fury
against the Budget? I will tell you. There are two classes who
really object to the Budget. The first are those who are seeking to
establish a complete change in the fiscal system of this country, to
tax food, and they know that once this Budget is through there is
an end to their desired opportunity. The tax will be on the right
shoulders, and they cannot shift it.

There is a second and I think a most powerful class, who are the
great landlords of this country. Why do they object? Why are
they angrier about the land taxes than about any part of the
Budget? We are raising this year 11 or 12 millions of money out of
the taxation. We shall probably raise next year something approaching 20 millions by the same taxation. And yet the land taxes
this year only produce £650,000. . . . Why then all this anger
about these taxes? I will tell you. The first reason is that they are
taxes that will grow. They only start at £650,000—and a good start
too; but year by year they are bound to grow. The [unearned]
increment duty will grow, the reversion duty will grow, the mineral duties will grow; the increment duty is bound to grow with
the growth of the prosperity of this country, and that is a certainty.
As you get advance in science and education, it strengthens and
develops the intelligence of the people and directs it; as you get advance in international ideas about peace, so that the wealth which

is produced by the industry and the people is allowed to accumulate and the harvest is not trampled down by the ravages of war, the prosperity of Britain is assured and growth of the prosperity is assured. As it grows the value of land taxes will grow, and not merely are the riches in this country growing, but there are more rich people year by year. Wealth is getting better distributed, and when a man acquires wealth he wants not merely better housing accommodation, but more elbow room, more land for recreation purposes, as well as for adornment. And it is not merely the wealthier sections of the community, the working classes are demanding better homes too. They are not satisfied with the dull, grey street of the past. They don't claim palaces, but they are tired of walbottles. They are not satisfied with promises merely that the housing problem will be settled for them on the other side of the valley, because they have observed that some of the people who insist most on that are also people who choose the best sites on this side of the valley. They are asking for more air, more light, more room, more verdure, more sunshine, to recruit energies exhausted in toil; and they will get it.

I believe this Budget will help them to get it. As these new fruitful ideas develop, more land will be required, and the more land you require, the more taxes will come from the Budget, and therefore these are taxes that will grow. That is one reason why they object to them. And that is not the chief objection. The chief objection of great landlords to this Budget lies in the fact that it has great valuation proposals. Why do they object to valuation? Because it goes to the very root of all things in the land question. There has never been a public undertaking in this country—municipal, State, or industrial—there has never been a commercial enterprise but the landlord has generally secured anything from four to 40 times as much for the value of the land as its agricultural price. When I was at the Board of Trade I saw a good deal of it.

I recollect a number of cases that were brought before me of complaints from the trading community as to the oppressive character of the railway rates from every part of the country. From every kind of business and undertaking there was complaint that the heavy character of the railway rates was interfering with the success and prosperity of that particular business. I had to go into it. I went into it very carefully in hundreds of these cases, and I found in the end that it was not the railway companies that were to blame; they had had to pay for every yard they had used, and often 50 times its real value.

Now what happens in the case of a railway company? You may get a railway passing through a perfectly barren stretch of country, passing on its way between one great hive of industry and another, the land worthless, just a few shepherds' huts here and there, and an occasional stray mountain sheep. I don't suppose the land would be worth more than sixpence or a shilling an acre, but the railway company comes along and says:—"We want to drive a railway through this wilderness." What happens? The moment they ask for that land its value goes up enormously. Every trick and chicanery of the law—and there are many of them, as my brothers in law to the right can testify—is exhausted to prove that this worthless land has enormous hidden value. . . .

There is not a railway train—goods, baggage, or passenger—in which you have not got at least one truck carrying interest on the excessive prices paid to the landlords. All this is a heavy burden upon industry at the present moment in this country. You see where valuation comes in. It is not merely that municipalities if they want land for any public purpose—a school in which to train children, waterworks, gas, electricity, anything—have to pay for it four times as much as its agricultural value to these great landlords. Start analysing the rates of any great city, and you will be surprised how much is attributable directly to the excessive prices paid by municipalities for land for purposes which are essential to the very life of the city, to the very life of a civilized community.

Then what have we in trade, in business, in commerce, in industry? If you want to found a new business or to extend an old one the charges for land are extravagant, especially if you want to extend, because you are there then. A trader in a particular locality, who for years of care and industry and a good deal of anxiety and worry has been building up a business gradually, cannot carry his trade away as if it were a coster's barrow and plant it in the next street. He has to get his extension where he is, and then comes the landlord, who has done nothing, and demands the highest price he can possibly extort. I can give you many cases of the kind; I have my bag full of them, sent to me from all parts of the country, with full particulars.

You see the value of State valuation. The State valuation for the first time places a perfectly impartial valuation upon all of the land of the kingdom. It separates the value of the land intrinsically and the value which is attributable to expenditure by its owner. It thus for the first time forces the landlords to look at the value of land, not merely from the point of view of a receiver, but of a payer. There is nothing like compelling a man to look at both sides of a question. Now that is really why they object to valuation. Whenever a great industry in the future requires land it can always quote the State valuation in answer to any extortionate and extravagant demands put forward on behalf of the landlords, and therefore they object to it very strongly.

[Lloyd George launches into a blistering attack upon Welsh landlords who do nothing but who exploit management and men with exorbitant ground rents and royalty rates.]

Landlords have no nationality; their characteristics are cosmopolitan. The case was given me the other day from Yorkshire, of all places in the world, and as it illustrates practically every tax which I propose in my Budget, if you can stand it I will tell you this story. I have it on the authority of the managing director of the concern. It is the story of a district in Yorkshire which four or five years ago was purely agricultural, receiving half its rates as agricultural land from your taxes and mine; there was not a village within four miles of it, not an industry, not a factory, not a coalmine. Some very enterprising mining investors came along and said: We think there's coal here. They went to the landlord and said: Will you allow us to dig for coal here? And he replied: For a consideration of course. He said: I will only charge a sixpence a ton on all the coal that comes up. They asked: What about the surface? Ah, certainly, he replied; I will sell you any surface land you want for a consideration. Well, what do you want, they asked; you are receiving now 15s. 6d. an acre, what will you want from us? Well, he replied, £4 an acre. Then they said to him: We must bring workmen here, and there are no cottages. We shall have to build them, and we propose building a model village. These mining investors have, in fact, built one of the most beautiful model villages in the kingdom. They said:—Will you allow us to build a few cottages? Certainly, he replied; I shall want a small return— £8 or £10 an acre. Quite moderate. I am not holding this landlord up to pillory him. He is really a most moderate landlord. The land was at 15s. 6d., and he charges £10. Well, that is only 18 times the value of the land. I can give you cases where landlords have charged 30, 40, even 100 times the value of the land. This man has been most moderate—only 18 times its value. Then he said:—

There is the fishpond rather near your model village. I do not think it will be worth much afterwards, whatever its worth is now; so I think you had better take it. The mining speculator replied:—All right; it will be rather good sport to fish either for trout or tadpoles. The landlord said:—I am getting £1 for it now; I will let you have it for 18 guineas a year, cheap.

Now they started; they spent half a million, without knowing what would happen. It was a real speculation, a real risk. They took it, spent half a million, discovered the coal, and the landowner is getting royalties now at the rate of nearly £20,000 per annum. He is getting, in addition to the £4 per annum for every acre of land on the surface used by the colliery, £6 to £10 per annum for all the cottages there; he charges £4 per annum for tipping rubbish, and £10 per annum for workmen's cottages. He is making a very good thing out of it. They have been prospering and getting more and more coal in a very short time, and they will be paying £40,000 per annum for this land for the royalties alone. They wrote to him and said:—We want more ground to build cottages on. He said:—Certainly, for £150 per acre, the land now for agricultural purposes being worth about £20 per acre, and the landlord getting half his rates paid out of the general taxation of the country in respect to the fact that it is agricultural land. Well, now, what happens? He said to them:—I will let you have this land at £150 per acre, but he said—and I am sure this will commend itself to every temperance man in this house—"No publichouse to be erected." Well, gentlemen, that is all right. Oh, I beg your pardon, here is another sentence:—"Without the consent of the landlord." If consent is given, an extra premium is required. I like a man who puts a high value on his principles. Here at any rate is a man who won't part with them without an extra premium. Well, they said to him:—Supposing the enterprise fails, supposing we cannot get coal or suppose we do not get a sufficient quantity to pay well? He said—landlords are always accommodating in these cases—I charge you a dead rent; he said, very fair, pay a dead rent for a dead failure.

So it is a growing matter, a matter of graduation, they believe in graduated receipts. I am trying to inculcate the principles of graduated payments to them; and in a few years the dead rent will be £7,900 a year. The more the mineowners sink in the mine the greater the loss, and the greater the loss of the mineowner the greater the payment to the landlord.

Where does my Budget come in? It comes in rather late. I admit it ought to have come in in one of the earlier chapters; still, it comes in soon enough to give the story a happy ending. When the £40,000 royalty comes 5 per cent. for the first time will come to the State. The land outside the land which is nominally agricultural land, but which is really now valuable building land, will pay a halfpenny in the pound. When it is sold we shall get 20 per cent. on the increase, and when the landlord passes away to another sphere we shall then get the dead rent. More than that, we have made another little provision. We have considered his case thoroughly. When these cottages fall in, and his heir comes and walks in for the whole of this beautiful model village, the State will then under this Budget say, Very well, if you really must take all that property, I think we had better get a toll of 10 per cent. from it; at any rate, we shall be able to do something for the people who live in these cottages. We have got a little provision. He has only leased one seam of coal. They have discovered, I think, four seams; some day the other three seams will probably be leased and then the 5 per cent. only applies to existing collieries, but we have got a special provision for future collieries. We shall then ask from him not 5 per cent. of the royalty, but 20 per cent. Where is the injustice there? . . . I have been listening to criticism for five months, and they could not point out a single injustice; they simply scolded at large. Let me call attention to one provision in this lease, because it really casts a strange, almost a weird, light upon the landlords' ideal of rural life in this country. There is a clause in the lease of the model village that no persons shall reside in any of these cottages if they have ever been convicted of an offence against the game laws. No person shall lodge there if he has been convicted of a game offence, no person shall reside there if the landlord or his agent has any objection to him. And this is a free country! Here is a poor miner who is guilty of what? Of doing something which the landlord spends his life in doing, and which I have done myself many a time without a licence only in Wales. What happens? Not merely is he to be fined, but he is to be deprived, as far as this gentleman is concerned, of the opportunity for all time of earning a decent living for himself and his family. All I can say is that a provision of the sort in any lease is an outrage.

Well now we are going to send the Bill up, all the taxes or none. What will the Lords do? I tell you frankly it is a matter which concerns them far more than it concerns us. The more irresponsible and feather-headed amongst them want to throw it out. But what will the rest do? It will depend on the weather. There are some who are not fair-weather sailors, and they will go on. But poor Lord Lansdowne! with his creaky old ship and his mutinous crew. There he is, he has got to sail through the narrows, with one eye on the weather glass and the other on the forecastle. But it does not depend on him. It will depend, in the first place, probably, on the reports from the country. The most important gentleman in the business is not Lord Lansdowne, with all his adroit management of the House of Lords, not even Mr. Balfour with his invaluable services to his party. The real sailing master is Sir Arthur Acland-Hood, the Chief Whip of the Tory party; and the Ancient Mariner is engaged at the present moment in trying to decide whether it is safe to shoot the albatross. He will probably not discover it until too late. But still this is the great constitutional party, and if there is one thing more than another better established about the British Constitution it is this, that the Commons, and the Commons alone, have the complete control of supply and ways and means. And what our fathers established through centuries of struggles and of strife, even of bloodshed, we are not going to be traitors to.

Who talks about altering and meddling with the Constitution? The Constitutional party—the great Constitutional party. As long as the Constitution gave rank and possession and power it was not to be interfered with. As long as it secured even their sports from intrusion, and made interference with them a crime; as long as the Constitution forced royalties and ground-rents and fees, premiums and fines, the black retinue of exaction; as long as it showered writs, and summonses, and injunctions, and distresses, and warrants to enforce them, then the Constitution was inviolate, it was sacred, it was something that was put in the same category as religion, that no man ought to touch, and something that the chivalry of the nation ought to range in defence of. But the moment the Constitution looks round, the moment the Constitution begins to discover that there are millions of people outside the park gates who need attention, then the Constitution is to be torn to pieces. Let them realize what they are doing. They are forcing revolution.

But the Lords may decree a revolution which the people will direct. If they begin, issues will be raised that they little dream of, questions will be asked which are now whispered in humble voices, and answers will be demanded then with authority. The question will be asked, "Should 500 men, ordinary men, chosen accidentally from among the unemployed, override the judgment—the deliberate judgment—of millions of people who are engaged in the industry which makes the wealth of the country?"

That is one question. Another will be, Who ordained that a few should have the land of Britain as a perquisite, who made 10,000 people owners of the soil and the rest of us trespassers in the land of our birth; who is it—who is responsible for the scheme of things whereby one man is engaged through life in grinding labour, to win a bare and precarious subsistence for himself, and when at the end of his days he claims at the hands of the community he served a poor pension of 8d. a day he can only get it through a revolution, and another man who does not toil receives every hour of the day, every hour of the night, whilst he slumbers, more than his poor neighbour receives in a whole year of toil? Where did the table of the law come from? Whose finger inscribed it? These are the questions that will be asked. The answers are charged with peril for the order of things the Peers represent, but they are fraught with rare and refreshing fruit for the parched lips of the multitude who have been treading the dusty road along which the people have marched through the dark ages, which are now emerging into the light.

General Bibliography

THIS is a highly selective list of general works. Some guide to more specialized titles can be found with each document. The student of this period is well served by journals, some historical and others interdisciplinary. *Victorian Studies* maintains a uniformly high standard of articles and reviews; it also provides an annual bibliography of works published during the year. *The Journal of British Studies, The English Historical Review, The Journal of Modern History, History, The Historical Journal, Past and Present,* and even the more popularized *History Today* may be read with profit, often with pleasure. Journals like *The Economic History Review, The Review of Politics,* and *Parliamentary Affairs,* to mention but three, often have articles touching this field. And this but begins a list.

A. BRIGGS, *The Age of Improvement* (London, 1959).

C. C. BRINTON, *English Political Thought in the Nineteenth Century* (2nd ed., New York, 1949).

A. L. BURT, *Evolution of the British Empire and Commonwealth* (Boston, 1956).

C. E. CARRINGTON, *The British Overseas* (Cambridge, 1950).

O. CHADWICK, *The Victorian Church* (London, 1966).

J. D. CHAMBERS, *The Workshop of the World* (London, 1961).

S. G. CHECKLAND, *The Rise of Industrial Society in England* (London, 1964).

J. H. CLAPHAM, *An Economic History of Modern Britain* (3 vols., Cambridge, 1927–1939).

G. D. H. COLE, *A Short History of the British Working-Class Movement* (rev. ed., London, 1948).

——— and R. POSTGATE, *The Common People* (rev. ed., London, 1946).

W. H. B. COURT, *A Concise Economic History of Britain from 1760* (Cambridge, 1954).

P. DEANE and W. A. COLE, *British Economic Growth* (Cambridge, 1962).

R. C. K. ENSOR, *England, 1870–1914* (Oxford, 1936).

E. HALÉVY, *A History of the English People in the Nineteenth Century* (6 vols., reprinted New York, 1949–1952).

E. HOBSBAWM, *Industry and Empire* (London, 1968).

W. E. HOUGHTON, *The Victorian Frame of Mind* (New Haven, 1957).

D. L. KIER, *Constitutional History of Modern Britain* (rev. ed., London, 1953).

G. KITSON CLARK, *The Making of Victorian England* (London, 1962).

D. LANDES, "Technological Change and Development in Western Europe," *The Cambridge Economic History of Europe*, Vol. VI, Part 1 (Cambridge, 1965), to be republished separately as *The Unbound Prometheus* (Cambridge, 1969).

S. MACCOBY, *English Radicalism* (4 vols., London, 1935–55).

R. B. McDOWELL, *British Conservatism* (London, 1959).

J. A. R. MARRIOTT, *England since Waterloo* (London, 1913).

R. W. SETON-WATSON, *Britain in Europe* (Cambridge, 1937).

K. B. SMELLIE, *A Hundred Years of English Government* (2nd ed., London, 1950).

D. C. SOMERVELL, *English Thought in the Nineteenth Century* (London, 1929).

D. SOUTHGATE, *The Passing of the Whigs* (London, 1962).

F. M. L. THOMPSON, *English Landed Society in the Nineteenth Century* (London, 1963).

D. THOMSON, *England in the Nineteenth Century* (Harmondsworth, 1951).

G. M. TREVELYAN, *British History in the Nineteenth Century and After* (2nd ed., London, 1937).

R. K. WEBB, *Modern England* (New York, 1968).

R. WILLIAMS, *Culture and Society* (London, 1959).

A. WOOD, *Nineteenth-Century Britain* (London, 1960).

E. L. WOODWARD, *The Age of Reform* (2nd ed., Oxford, 1962).

G. M. YOUNG (ed.), *Early Victorian England* (2 vols., London, 1934).

———, *Victorian England, Portrait of an Age* (London, 1936).

——— and W. D. HANDCOCK, *English Historical Documents*, Vol. XII, Part 1, *1833–1874* (London, 1956).

Date	Governments	Domestic Events	Some Cultural Highlights	Imperial & Foreign Affairs
1815	Liverpool (June 12–Apr. 27)	Vansittart's Corn Law Economic Distress	W. Scott, *Waverly Novels* (1814–19) J. Austen, *Emma*	Congress of Vienna
1816		Abolition of Income Tax Spa Fields Riot	Leigh Hunt, *Story of Rimini* S. T. Coleridge, *Statesman's Manual* P. B. Shelley, *Alastor*	
1817		Coercion Acts	J. Mill, *History of British India* M. Edgeworth, *Ormond* S. T. Coleridge, *Biographia Literaria*	
1818			Lord Byron, *Beppo* J. Austen, *Northanger Abbey* W. Cobbett, *Grammar of the English Language* T. L. Peacock, *Nightmare Abbey* J. Keats, *Endymion* M. W. Shelley, *Frankenstein*	Congress of Aix-la-Chapelle
1819		Owen's Cotton Mills Act Peterloo Massacre Six Acts	W. Scott, *Ivanhoe* G. Crabbe, *Tales of the Hall* P. B. Shelley, *The Cenci*	
1820	GEORGE IV	Cato Street Conspiracy Queen's Case	T. Southey, *Life of Wesley* P. B. Shelley, *Prometheus Unbound*	Congress of Troppau

Date	Governments	Domestic Events	Some Cultural Highlights	Imperial & Foreign Affairs
1821		Currency Deflation	W. Cobbett, *Rural Rides* (−30) J. Keats, *Poems* T. L. Peacock, *The Four Ages of Poetry*	Congress of Laibach
1822	Suicide of Castlereagh Liberalization of Liverpool government (Canning, Peel, Huskisson)		J. Mill, *Elements of Political Economy* P. B. Shelley, *Adonais*	Congress of Verona
1823		Relative Prosperity Criminal Code Reforms "Freer-trade" budgets	T. De Quincey, *Confessions of an Opium Eater* W. Cobbett, *Cottage Economy* L. Hunt, *Liberal* (−23)	
			Westminster Review C. Lamb, *Essays of Elia* (−33) Lord Byron, *Don Juan* W. Scott, *Quentin Durward* W. Hazlitt, *My First Acquaintance with Poets*	
1824		Repeal of Combination Acts	W. S. Landor, *Imaginary Conversations* (−29)	Recognition of Independence of Latin American states
1825			W. Hazlitt, *The Spirit of the Age* T. Hodgskin, *Labor Defended against the Claims of Capital*	
1826				Intervention in Poru-

b

		sion	
	Aug. 27)		
1828	Goderich (Aug. 27—Jan. 28) Wellington (Jan. 28—Nov. 30)	Sliding-scale Corn Law Repeal of Test and Corporation Acts for Protestant Dissenters	
1829		Catholic Emancipation	J. Mill, *Phenomena of the Human Mind* W. Cobbett, *Advice to Young Men*
1830	WILLIAM IV (b. 1765) Grey (Nov. 30— July 34)	Manchester & Liverpool Railway	Revolutions of 1830
			A. Tennyson, *Poems, Chiefly Lyrical* S. T. Coleridge, *On the Constitution in Church and State* C. Lyell, *Principles of Geology*
1831		Cholera epidemic Recession, then depression Reform Bills Irish Tithe War	Faraday's electro-magnetic experiments T. L. Peacock, *Crotchet Castle* W. Godwin, *Thoughts on Man* T. Carlyle, *Sartor Resartus*
1832		First Reform Act	R. Surtees, *Jorrocks' Jaunts and Jollities* (—34) H. Martineau, *Illustrations of Political Economy* A. Austin, *Province of Jurisprudence*
1833		Bank Charter Act Abolition of Slavery	J. Keble, *On National Apostacy*

c

Date	Governments	Domestic Events	Some Cultural Highlights	Imperial & Foreign Affairs
			A. Tennyson, *Poems*	
1834	Melbourne I (July–Nov. 34) Peel I (Nov. 34—Apr. 35)	Irish Church Temporalities Bill Althorp's Factory Act Poor Law Amendment Act Grand National Consolidated Trades Union Tolpuddle Martyrs	E. Bulwer Lytton, *Last Days of Pompeii* T. De Quincey, *Autobiographical Sketches* (—40) T. Southey, *The Doctor* (—37)	Liberal Quadruple Alliance
1835	Melbourne II (Apr. 35—May 39)	Tamworth Manifesto Municipal Corporations Act	J. Clare, *The Rural Muse*	
1836		Legalization of civil marriage Depression London Workingmen's Association	C. Dickens, *Sketches by Boz* W. Pugin, *Contrasts* G. W. Porter, *Progress of the Nation* R. Owen, *Book of the New Moral World* (—49)	
1837	VICTORIA (b. 1819)		T. Carlyle, *French Revolution* C. Dickens, *Oliver Twist*	Canadian Rebellion
1838		Irish Poor Law Conversion of Irish Tithes London & Birmingham R.R.	C. Dickens, *Nicholas Nickleby* M. Tupper, *Proverbial Philosophy*	

d

				Beagle
	(May 39–Aug. 41)	First Factory Inspectors' Reports Formation of Anti-Corn Law League Newport Rising		
1840	Marriage with ALBERT	Penny Post	C. Dickens, *Old Curiosity Shop*	Annexation of New Zealand
1841	Peel II (Sept. 41–June 46)	Economic Depression	*Punch* J. H. Newman, *Tract XC* T. Carlyle, *Heroes and Hero Worship*	
1842		Shaftesbury's Colliery Act Second Chartist Convention Reimposition of Income Tax	T. B. Macaulay, *Lays of Ancient Rome* E. Chadwick, *Sanitary Condition of the Laboring Population* F. Newman, *Phases of Faith* A. Tennyson, *Collected Poems*	Treaty of Nanking
1843		Rebecca Riots	T. Carlyle, *Past and Present* C. Dickens, *Martin Chuzzlewit* T. Hood, *Song of the Shirt* J. Ruskin, *Modern Painters* (–60)	
1844		Bank Charter Act Graham's Factory Act Rochdale Pioneers	T. Chambers, *Vestiges of the Natural History of Creation* B. Disraeli, *Coningsby* A. Stanley, *Life of Dr. Arnold*	
1845		Maynooth Grant Irish Famine	Newman to Rome B. Disraeli, *Sybil*	

e

Date	Governments	Domestic Events	Some Cultural Highlights	Imperial & Foreign Affairs
1846	Russell I (July 46– Feb. 52)	Repeal of the Corn Laws	G. Grote, *History of Greece* (–56) E. Lear, *Book of Nonsense* G. Eliot translation of Strauss, *Leben Jesu*	Spanish Marriages Dispute
1847		Fielden's Ten Hours Act Young Ireland	E. Brontë, *Wuthering Heights* C. Brontë, *Jane Eyre* W. M. Thackeray, *Vanity Fair* E. B. Browning, *Sonnets from the Portuguese*	
1848		Public Health Act	T. B. Macaulay, *History of England* (–55) Pre-Raphelite Brotherhood J. S. Mill, *Political Economy* C. Kingsley, *Yeast* Mrs. Gaskell, *Mary Barton* C. Dickens, *Dombey and Son*	Revolutions of 1848
1849		Repeal of Navigation Acts	J. Doyle, *Manners and Customs* T. De Quincey, *The English Mail Coach* C. Dickens, *David Copperfield* J. Ruskin, *Seven Lamps of Architecture*	Annexation of Punjab
1850		Amalgamated Society of Engineers Irish Tenant Rights League	A. Tennyson, *In Memoriam* T. Carlyle, *Latter-Day Pamphlets* A. H. Clough, *Dipsychus* W. Collins, *Woman in White* W. M. Thackeray, *Pendennis* C. Kingsley, *Alton Locke*	Don Pacifico

f

	ston	Tax		Napoleon

Year	Government	Events	Literature	International
		Ecclesiastic Titles Bill Great Exhibition Rapid growth in savings and productivity	J. Ruskin, *Stones of Venice* (–53) G. Borrow, *Lavengro*	
1852	Derby-Disraeli (Feb.–Dec. 52) Aberdeen (Dec. 52–Jan. 55)	Common Law Procedure Act Era of High Farming	C. Dickens, *Bleak House* M. Arnold, *Empedocles on Etna* J. H. Newman, *Idea of a University* W. M. Thackeray, *Henry Esmond*	
1853			M. Arnold, *Scholar Gypsy*	
1854			C. Dickens, *Hard Times* W. M. Thackeray, *The Newcomes*	Crimean War
1855	Palmerston I (Feb. 55–Feb. 58)	Limited Liability Act	C. Kingsley, *Westward Ho!* A. Tennyson, *Maud* F. D. Maurice, *Learning and Working* Mrs. Gaskell, *North and South* R. Browning, *Men and Women* A. Baine, *Senses and the Intellect*	
1856			C. Reade, *It's Never Too Late to Mend* J. A. Froude, *History*	Peace of Paris
1857		Divorce Act Bank Crisis	W. Buckle, *History of Civilization*	Sepoy Rebellion

g

Date	Governments	Domestic Events	Some Cultural Highlights	Imperial & Foreign Affairs
1858	Derby-Disraeli II (Feb. 58–June 59)	Jewish Emancipation Abolition of Property Qualifications for MPs S. S. *Great Eastern*	A. Trollope, *Barchester Towers* T. Hughes, *Tom Brown's School Days* C. Dickens, *Little Dorrit* G. Eliot, *Scenes of Clerical Life* G. Borrow, *Romany Rye* Darwin and Wallace on Natural Selection	India Act Orsini Plot Formation of Sein Fein
1859	Palmerston II (June 59–Nov. 65)		C. Darwin, *Origin of Species* G. Eliot, *Adam Bede* S. Smiles, *Self-Help* G. Meredith, *Ordeal of Richard Feverel* J. S. Mill, *On Liberty* W. Fitzgerald, *Rubaiyat of Omar Khayyâm* A. Tennyson, *Idylls of the King* (–72)	
1860			J. Ruskin, *Unto This Last* C. Dickens, *Great Expectations* *Essays and Reviews* G. Eliot, *Mill on the Floss*	

h

	sion on Education Uneven prosperity	*bold Management* A. Trollope, *Framley Parsonage* C. Reade, *Cloister and the Hearth* G. Eliot, *Silas Marner*	
1862	Lancashire Cotton Famine (—64)	H. Spencer, *First Principles* H. Maine, *Ancient Law* G. Meredith, *Modern Love* Colenso case	
1863	Clarendon Commission on Public Schools	J. Austin, *Jurisprudence* T. H. Huxley, *Man's Place in Nature* J. S. Mill, *Utilitarianism* C. Kingsley, *Water Babies* G. Eliot, *Romola*	
1864		J. H. Newman, *Apologia pro vita sua* A. Trollope, *Small House at Allington* R. Browning, *Dramatis Personae*	
1865	death of Palmerston Russell II (Nov. 65—June 66)	M. Arnold, *Essays in Criticism* L. Carroll, *Alice in Wonderland* W. E. H. Lecky, *Rise and Spirit of Rationalism* A. C. Swinburne, *Atalanta in Calydon* J. Ruskin, *Sesame and Lilies*	Jamaican Rebellion

i

Date	Governments	Domestic Events	Some Cultural Highlights	Imperial & Foreign Affairs
			Fortnightly Review	
			Pall Mall Gazette	
1866	Derby–Disraeli III (July 66–Feb. 68)	Liberal Reform Bill Hyde Park Riots Collapse of Overend & Gurney	G. Eliot, *Felix Holt* C. Kingsley, *Hereward the Wake* *Contemporary Review*	
1867		Second Reform Act Factory and Workshops Act	W. Bagehot, *English Constitution* A. Trollope, *Last Chronicle of Barset* J. A. Froude, *Short Studies on Great Subjects* (–83)	British North America Act
1868	Disraeli I (Feb.–Dec. 68) Gladstone I (Dec. 68–Feb. 74)	Trades Union Congress	R. Browning, *Ring and the Book* W. Collins, *The Moonstone* C. Dilke, *Greater Britain*	
1869		Disestablishment of the Irish Church	M. Arnold, *Culture and Anarchy* W. E. H. Lecky, *History of European Morals* J. S. Mill, *On the Subjection of Women*	
1870		Irish Land Act Forster's Education Act Civil Service Reform	J. H. Newman, *Grammar of Assent* T. H. Huxley, *Lay Sermons* H. Spencer, *Principles of Psychology* (–72) B. Disraeli, *Lothair*	Franco-Prussian War
1871		Local Government Board Act	C. Darwin, *Descent of Man* L. Carroll, *Through the Look-*	

Year		Political / Social	Literature	Foreign / Imperial
1872		Army Regulations Act Irish Nationalist Party Ballot Act	(—84) G. Eliot, *Middlemarch* (—72) S. Butler, *Erewhon* W. Bagehot, *Physics and Politics* W. Reade, *Martyrdom of Man* J. H. Newman, *Discussions and Arguments* *Popular Science Monthly*	Settlement of the *Alabama* claims
1873		Judicature Act "Great Depression" (—96)	J. S. Mill, *Autobiography* M. Arnold, *Literature and Dogma*	
1874	Disraeli II (Feb. 74—Apr. 80)		W. Stubbs, *Constitutional History* T. Hardy, *Far from the Madding Crowd* J. F. Stephen, *Liberty, Equality, Fraternity* E. A. Freeman, *Comparative Politics*	Ashanti War
1875		Public Health Act Artisans' Dwellings Act Conspiracy and Protection of Property Act	A. Trollope, *Way We Live Now* H. Maine, *Early History of Institutions* J. A. Symonds, *Renaissance in Italy* (—86)	Purchase of Suez shares
1876		Plimsoll's Merchant Shipping Act	G. Eliot, *Daniel Deronda* L. Stephen, *English Thought in the 18th Century* L. Carroll, *Hunting of the Snark*	Royal Titles Act

k

Date	Governments	Domestic Events	Some Cultural Highlights	Imperial & Foreign Affairs
1877			G. Meredith, *Beauchamp's Career* F. H. Bradley, *Ethical Studies*	Annexation of Transvaal
1878		Consolidated Factory Act	H. Spencer, *Principles of Sociology* (–96) W. H. Mallock, *New Republic* G. Meredith, *Idea of Comedy* *Nineteenth Century*	Congress of Berlin Afghan War
1879		Midlothian Campaign Agricultural Collapse	T. Hardy, *Return of the Native* J. Morley, *Diderot* W. H. Mallock, *New Paul and Virginia* W. E. H. Lecky, *History of England in the 18th Century* (–90)	Zulu War
1880	Gladstone II (Apr. 80—June 85)	Bradlaugh Case First Employer's Liability Act Modest industrial recovery	R. L. Stevenson, *Travels with a Donkey* G. Meredith, *Egoist* A. J. Balfour, *Philosophic Doubt*	Transvaal Revolt
1881	death of Beaconsfield (Disraeli)	Second Irish Land Act Kilmainham Pact	A. Tennyson, *Ballads* *Autobiography of Mark Rutherford* O. Wilde, *Poems* D. G. Rossetti, *Ballads and*	

Year	Political	Events	Literature / Culture	Foreign
1882		Phoenix Park Murders	E. B. Tylor, *Anthropology*	Occupation of Egypt
			Tit-Bits	
			J. A. Froude, *Carlyle* (–84)	
			W. Morris, *Hopes and Fears for Art*	
			R. L. Stevenson, *Treasure Island*	
			Gilbert & Sullivan, *Iolanthe*	
			Dictionary of National Biography (–91)	
1883		Corrupt Practices Act	A. Trollope, *Autobiography*	
		Depression again	J. R. Seeley, *Expansion of England*	
		Fabian Society organized	G. Meredith, *Joy of Earth*	
			F. H. Bradley, *Principles of Logic*	
1884		Third Reform Act	A. Toynbee, *Industrial Revolution*	
			Thorold Rogers, *Six Centuries of Work and Wages*	
			H. Spencer, *Man versus the State*	
			Oxford English Dictionary (–28)	
1885	Salisbury I (June 85 – Jan. 86)	Redistribution Act	W. Pater, *Marius the Epicurean*	
		Ashbourne Irish Land Purchase Act	T. H. Green, *Works* (–88)	
			G. Meredith, *Diana of the Crossways*	
			H. Maine, *Popular Government*	
			H. Rider Haggard, *King Solomon's Mines*	

m

Date	Governments	Domestic Events	Some Cultural Highlights	Imperial & Foreign Affairs
1886	Gladstone III (Feb.–July 86) Salisbury II (July 86–Aug. 92)	First Home Rule Bill Slow economic recovery	Gilbert & Sullivan, Mikado J. A. Froude, Oceana R. L. Stevenson, Dr Jekyll and Mr Hyde First translated edition of F. Engels, Condition of the Working Class in England in 1844 T. Hardy, Mayor of Casterbridge R. Kipling, Departmental Ditties	
1887	Jubilee of 1887	Crimes Bill Coal Mines Act Trafalgar Square Riots	S. and B. Webb, Facts for Socialists A. Conan Doyle, Study in Scarlet W. Pater, Imaginary Portraits M. Rutherford, Revolution in Tanner's Lane	Mediterranean Agreements
1888		County Councils Act Miner's Federation Match Girls' Strike	W. Morris, Signs of Change J. Bryce, American Commonwealth E. Bellamy, Looking Backward R. Kipling, Plain Tales from the Hills Mrs. Humphrey Ward, Robert Elsemere Answers Fabian Essays	
1889		London Dock Strike Technical Instruction Act Naval Defense Act	C. Booth, Life and Labor in London (–97) A. Conan Doyle, Sign of the	

n

		R. L. Stevenson, *Master of Ballantrae* A. C. Swinburne, *Poems and Ballads*, III L. Carroll, *Sylvie and Bruno* (–93)	Heligoland Treaty
1890	Fall of Parnell Failure of Baring's bank	W. Booth, *In Darkest England and the Way Out* A. Frazer, *Golden Bough* W. James, *Principles of Psychology*	
1891		G. Gissing, *New Grub Street* D. G. Ritchie, *Principles of State Interference* H. Spencer, *Principles of Ethics* (–93) A. Marshall, *Principles of Economics* O. Wilde, *Portrait of Dorian Grey* H. Sidgwick, *Elements of Politics* W. Morris, *News from Nowhere* T. Hardy, *Tess of the d'Urbervilles* A. Conan Doyle, *Sherlock Holmes* *Clarion*	
1892	Gladstone IV (Aug. 92 —March 94)	Second Home Rule Bill Gradual movement toward business	Lord Curzon, *Persia* R. Kipling, *Barrack-Room Ballads* G. DuMaurier, *Peter Ibbetson*

Date	Governments	Domestic Events	Some Cultural Highlights	Imperial & Foreign Affairs
1893		combinations and federations	A. Pinero, *Second Mrs. Tanqueray*	Armenian Massacres
		Formation of Independent Labor Party	L. Stephen, *Agnostic's Apology*	
			W. Pater, *Plato and Platonism*	
			F. Thompson, *Poems*	
			F. H. Bradley, *Appearance and Reality*	
			T. H. Huxley, *Evolution and Ethics*	
1894	Rosebery (Mar. 94— June 95)	Harcourt's Death Duties	B. Kidd, *Social Evolution*	
		Parish Councils Act	S. & B. Webb, *History of Trade Unionism*	
			F. Harrison, *Meaning of History*	
			R. Blatchford, *Merrie England*	
			G. Moore, *Esther Waters*	
			Yellow Book	
1895	Salisbury III (June 95—July 02)	Factory and Workshop Act	W. Pater, *Miscellaneous Studies*	Venezuela Dispute
			R. Kipling, *Second Jungle Book*	More Armenian massacres
			W. B. Yeats, *Poems*	Jameson Raid
			H. G. Wells, *Time Machine*	
			F. Pollock & F. W. Maitland, *History of English Law*	
1896		Slow business recovery	W. E. H. Lecky, *Democracy and Liberty*	Kaiser-Kruger Telegram
			A. E. Housman, *Shropshire Lad*	

Year	Monarch	Political	Literature / Arts	International Events
			Democracy	
1898			Havelock Ellis, *Studies in the Psychology of Sex* (—28)	Fashoda Crisis
			J. Conrad, *Nigger of the Narcissus*	
			O. Wilde, *Ballad of Reading Gaol*	
			H. G. Wells, *War of the Worlds*	
			T. Hardy, *Wessex Poems*	
			G. B. Shaw, *Plays Pleasant and Unpleasant*	
			A. Lang, *Making of Religion*	
1899			R. Kipling, *Stalky & Co.*	Boer War
			W. B. Yeats, *Wind Among the Reeds*	Hague Conference
			F. Harrison, *Tennyson, Ruskin, Mill*	
			F. W. Maitland, *Domesday Book and Beyond*	
1900		Labor Representation Committee (—02)	L. Stephen, *English Utilitarians*	Boxer Rebellion
			B. Russell, *Philosophy of Leibnitz*	
			G. B. Shaw, *Three Plays for Puritans*	
			J. Conrad, *Lord Jim*	
			G. E. B. Saintsbury, *History of Criticism* (—04)	
1901	EDWARD VII (b. 1841)	Taff Vale Case (—02)	R. Kipling, *Kim*	
			T. Hardy, *Poems of the Past and Present*	
			S. Butler, *Erewhon Revisited*	

Date	Governments	Domestic Events	Some Cultural Highlights	Imperial & Foreign Affairs
1902	Balfour (July 02–Dec. 05)	Education Act	B. Seebohm Rowntree, *Poverty* J. A. Hobson, *Imperialism* R. Kipling, *Just So Stories* J. Bryce, *Studies in History and Jurisprudence* W. James, *Varieties of Religious Experience* Times Literary Supplement	Treaty of Vereeniging Anglo-Japanese Alliance
1903		Tariff Reform League Irish Land Act	S. Butler, *Way of All Flesh* G. B. Shaw, *Man and Superman* J. Morley, *Life of Gladstone* G. E. Moore, *Principia Ethica* B. Russell, *Principles of Mathematics* Daily Mirror	
1904			T. Hardy, *The Dynasts* (–08) L. T. Hobhouse, *Democracy and Reaction* J. Conrad, *Nostromo* W. H. Hudson, *Green Mansions*	Russo-Japanese War Committee of Imperial Defence Entente Cordiale
1905	Campbell-Bannerman (Dec. 05–Apr. 08)	Unemployed Workmen Act	H. G. Wells, *A Modern Utopia* A. V. Dicey, *Law and Public Opinion in England* E. Wallace, *Four Just Men* Baroness Orczy, *Scarlet*	Moroccan Crisis

		Workingmen's Compensation Act	*erty* H. H. Joachim, *Nature of Truth* J. M. E. McTaggart, *Some Dogmas of Religion* R. S. S. Baden Powell, *Scouting for Boys* R. Kipling, *Puck of Pook's Hill*	
1907		Qualification of Women Act *Dreadnought* completed	E. Gosse, *Father and Son* Lord Acton, *Historical Essays and Studies* J. M. Synge, *Playboy of the Western World*	Second Hague Conference Anglo-Russian Entente Colonial Conference
1908	Asquith (Apr. 08—May 16)	Haldane's Army Reforms Old Age Pensions Act	A. Bennett, *Old Wives' Tale* G. Wallas, *Human Nature in Politics* E. M. Forster, *Room with a View* K. Grahame, *Wind in the Willows* W. McDougall, *Introduction to Social Psychology*	*Daily Telegraph* Affair London Naval Conference
1909		Osborne Judgment Trade Boards Act Poor Law Commission Report People's Budget	Lord Acton, *History of Freedom* J. A. Hobson, *Industrial System* C. F. G. Masterson, *Condition of England* H. G. Wells, *Ann Veronica* H. G. Wells, *Tono Bungay*	Blériot flies the Channel India Councils Act
1910	GEORGE V (b. 1865)		A. Bennett, *Clayhanger* N. Angell, *Great Illusion*	Union of South Africa

Date	Governments	Domestic Events	Some Cultural Highlights	Imperial & Foreign Affairs
1911		Parliament Act Payment of Members National Insurance Act Shop Hours Act Official Secrets Act "Syndicalist" Strikes Militant Suffragettes	H. G. Wells, *History of Mr Polly* E. M. Forster, *Howards End*	Second Morocco Crisis
1912		Minimum Wage Law Irish Home Rule Bills (–14) Welsh Disestablishment (–14)	F. W. Maitland, *Collected Papers* H. G. Wells, *New Machiavelli* A. Bennett, *Hilda Lessways* M. Beerbohm, *Zuleika Dobson* H. Belloc, *Servile State* J. Galsworthy, *The Pigeon*	First Balkan War
1913		"Cat and Mouse" Act Labor's Triple Alliance Ulster Volunteers	St. John Ervine, *John Ferguson* H. G. Wells, *Passionate Friends* J. Conrad, *Chance*	Second Balkan War
1914		Mutiny on the Curragh	B. Russell, *Our Knowledge of the External World* H. Brailsford, *War of Steel and Gold* F. H. Bradley, *Essays on Truth and Reality* G. Wallas, *The Great Society*	World War I

Index

Aberdeen, Lord, 196–197
Acland-Hood, Sir Arthur, 374
Act of Settlement and Removal, 95
Adderley, Sir Charles, 228
Adelaide, Queen, 117
Afghanistan, 168
Africa, 249 (*See also* South Africa)
Agitators, 84
Agriculture, 3, 78, 136, 139–140, 232, 290; German, 338–339 (*See also* Farmers; Tenants)
Albert, Prince, 78, 115, 172, 175, 193–194, 340; correspondence of, 197–198
Alison, Sir Archibald, 148
Amalgamated Society of Railway Servants, 293
American Civil War, 168, 171, 205, 230, 278
American revolution, 41
Anglican church (*see* Church of England)
Anglican clergymen, ordination of, 172
Anglo-Saxon superiority, 104
Annan, Noel, 170
Anti-Corn Law League, 76, 120, 137, 141, 236
Applegarth, Robert, 171, 309, 364
Ardwick Bridge conspiracy, 19
Aristocracy, 6, 8–9, 14, 47, 52, 60, 77–79, 140, 142, 148–149, 151, 170, 213, 236, 290, 295, 324; territorial, 140–141 (*see also* Peers)
Arnold, Thomas, 75
Artizans and Labourers' Dwellings Improvement Acts, 335
Askwith, Sir George, 9
Aspinall, A., 14n., 32
Asquith, Herbert H., 9, 295, 298
Atheism, 232
Australia, 104
Austria, 16, 39, 181–182, 188–191
Austro-Prussian War, 169

Bagehot, Walter, 142; on Peel, 144–167

Balfour, Arthur, 8, 347, 374; speech of, on Boer War, 352–363
Ballot Act of 1872, 198
Bank Charter Act, 2
Banking, 16
Banks, Mr., 28
Bantus, the, 351
Bedchamber crisis, 78, 114–119
Belfast, 57
Belgium, 181–183
Bentham, Jeremy, 12
Benthamite utilitarians, 17, 79, 82, 94
Bergami, 35
Bermondsey, 330
Bernstein, Eduard, 293
Besant, Annie, 309
Biggar, Joseph Gillis, 280
Bill of Rights, 44
Birmingham, 60, 290, 297, 324
Bismarck, Otto von, 169, 214, 294, 336
Bland, Hubert, 309
Blanketeers, protest march of, 19
Blatchford, Robert, 309
Bleak House, Dickens, 244, 251
Boer War, 7–9, 294, 341, 347, 350–363
Borough system, 50, 65–68
Bowring, Sir John, 168
"Boycotting," 284
Bradford, 96, 347
Bradlaugh, Charles, 232, 322
Bramwell, Lord, 316n.
Brandreth, Jeremiah, 19–21; defense of, 20; opening statement in, 21–24; sentence pronounced on, 24–25; trial of, 20
Bright, John, 175, 209, 232–233, 297; estimate of, 237–243; letter to workingmen of Rochdale, 233–236
Britain, in 1815, 11; and Europe, 16, 19, 38–41, 288, 338; in the middle of the 19th century, 168; as a world power, 169, 175–193
British army, 295, 360

British Constitution, 12, 47, 73, 75, 86, 212, 215–217, 221–222, 232, 374
British fleet, 168; navy, 295
British West Indies, 87–88
Broad Church movement, 75
Broadhurst, Henry, 346
Brook, Mr., 30
Brougham, Henry, Baron, 34, 35
Brownlow, Lord, 58
Bubble Act of 1720, 4
Buckingham, Lord, 30
Budget, the, 364, 366, 373
Buller, Charles, 80, 103
Buller, James, 56
Bureaucracy, 8, 78–79, 325
Burke, Edmund, 1, 144
Burma, 168
Burns, John, 309, 314
Byron, George Gordon, Lord, 153; quoted, 152

Cabinet, the, 116, 118, 119n., 197
Campbell-Bannerman, Sir Henry, 9, 295, 298
Canada, 80, 103–113, 351
Canning, George, 16, 37, 55, 64, 165, 168, 350
Cape Colony, 104, 350–351, 358
Capital, 139; and labor, 125–126
Capitalism and capitalists, 8, 126, 133
Carlisle, Lord, 30
Carlos, Don, 186
Carlyle, Thomas, quoted, 144, 242
Carnarvon, Lord, 60
Caroline, Queen, 13, 30–36
Carrington, Lord, 30
Castlereagh, Lord, 37, 48
Catholic Association, 42, 45
Catholic emancipation, 16–17, 42, 48, 142, 277
Catholics, Irish, 283 (See also Roman Catholics)
Cato Street conspiracy, 26, 30
Ceylon, 350
Chadwick, Edwin, 94, 324
Chamberlain, Joseph, 7–9, 290–291, 297–298, 310, 324, 336, 346, 350, 357; speech of, at Hull, 298–308
Champion, H. H., 309
Chancery Court, 243; Dickens on, 245–251
"Character of Sir Robert Peel, The," Bagehot, 144–167
Charity, 7, 315
Chartism and Chartists, 1, 5, 76, 80, 84, 96, 119–136, 237–238, 346
Chartist Petition, report on, 135–136
Chatham, Lord, 67

China, 294
Cholera, 332–333
Christian Socialists, 75
Christianity, 52, 203, 239, 314, 351
Church, 18, 41, 47; and State, 52, 222–223, 225, 239
Church disestablishment, 7–8, 251
Church of England, 41, 44–45, 75, 173, 224, 251, 314, 322
Churchill, Lord Randolph, 7, 291, 346
Churchill, Winston, 8–9, 368; quoted, 228
Civil service, 170, 172, 251, 260; permanent, organization of, 261–277
Civil Service, Board of Examiners, 269, 271–273, 276; commissioners, 261; examinations, 261, 268–274, 276
Clarke, William, 309
Class cooperation, 82–84
Class war, 232, 288, 293
Classes, 6, 76, 226, 290, 292, 295 (See also Middle classes; Working class)
Clinton, 57
Clubs, 77
Cobbett, William, 12, 47, 242, 346
Cobden, Richard, 6, 137, 175, 241–242; quoted, 164
Cold Bath Fields manifesto, 84–87
Coleridge, Sir John, 244; speech of, on judicial reform, 251–260
Coleridge, Samuel, quoted, 164
Collective bargaining, 9
Collectivism, 5, 8, 292–295, 297–309, 325
Colonial Office, 79–80, 88
Colonies, 104–113
Combination Acts, repeal of, 82
Commerce, 15 (See also Industry)
Common Law Courts, 253, 256–258
Commons, House of, 15, 18, 32–34, 36, 53–54, 77–78, 149, 159, 163, 167, 195–196, 221–222, 225, 241–242, 251, 259, 323, 348–350, 353, 356, 358, 366–374; and Irish National party, 278; Sir John Russell's speech before, 61–74
Competition, 240, 316–317, 320
Confederate States of America, 169
Congress of Verona, 37
Conservatives, 7–9, 11–12, 76–77, 137, 142–143, 148, 150–151, 157, 163, 171–172, 193–194, 203, 214–232, 238, 241–243, 289, 292, 297–298, 309, 311, 336, 364
Conservatism, 17; Disraelian, 1, 172, 214–232

Consols, 321*n*.
Constitution (*See* British Constitution)
Constitutional party, 374
Conversation, art of, 146
Conyngham, Lady, 31, 54
Conyngham, Lord, 55
Co-Operative Movement, 170–171, 314
Corn Importation Bill, 138–142
Corn laws, 15, 131, 137, 239; of 1815, 11; repeal of, 2, 5, 78, 80, 126–127, 137, 143, 193, 232, 236
Corrupt Practices Act of 1883, 199
Corruption, in Parliament, 198–199
Costs of distribution, 6
County Constables Act of 1839, 324
County Councils Act of 1888, 325
Courts, 243, 253–259
Coventry, 131
Crimean War, 168, 172, 175, 196, 230, 232, 260, 350
Cross, John, 21
Cross, Richard, 214
Crown, the, 14 (*See also* Monarchy)
Culture, 3
Cumberland, Duke of, 54
Currency Bill of 1844, 166

Death Duties Budget, 291
Debtors' prison, 244
Democratic Federation, 292, 309
Democracy, 7–9, 17, 78, 123–124, 143, 171, 233, 251, 290–291, 310–311, 325, 346; Gladstone and, 202–212; social, 233, 297, 314, 320
Denmark, 169
Derby, Lord, 88–89, 160, 194, 196, 213
Derbyshire, 19
Devonshire, Duke of, 30
Dickens, Charles, on Chancery Court, 245–251
Dietrichstein, Count, 188
Dilke, Sir Charles, 7, 298, 350
Disenfranchisement, 206–208
Disraeli, Benjamin, 9, 77, 137, 143, 146, 167, 172–173, 194, 202, 212–213, 240, 346; speeches of, on Corn Importation Bill, 138–142; at Manchester Free Trade Hall, 214–232
Disraeli's Act, of 1867, 198; of 1871, 293
Dissenters, 41, 43, 75
Divorce, 5, 30–36
Domestic policy, 16, 37
Dundas, Lord, 28

Durham, Lord, 80, 103–104
Durham Report, the, 104–113, 351
Dutch, the, in South Africa, 351, 358

Eastgate, George, 323
Economic structure, 3
Economic unrest, 19–20
Economy, the, 288–289; Germany's threat to, 336–340
Education, 76, 170, 291, 302–303, 364; popular, 1, 6, 30; religious, 224
Education Act, 224; first, 251
Edward VII, 1, 340, 348–349
Edward VIII, 347–348
Egypt, 294
Eldon, Lord, 41–42, 48, 54, 257, 277; speech of, on Roman Catholic Relief Bill, 42–46
Elections, mid-Victorian, 198–202
Elliott, Ebenezer, quoted, 241
Employers, absentee, 135
Employment, 6
Equity, law and, 252, 254–255
Equity Courts, 254–255
Estate taxes, 291
Ethiopia, 294
Europe, 350; Britain and, 16, 19, 38–41, 168–169, 181–183, 231, 234; revisionist movement in, 293 (*See also* names of countries, as France)
Exmouth, Lord, 33
Exports, 337–338
Extraordinary Black Book, The, 47–53

Fabian Essays, 292, 309
Fabian Society, 292–293, 308
Fabians, 8, 293, 308–323, 347
Factory Acts, 237; of 1819, 12; of 1833, 1, 5, 16
Factory workers, 80
Family, the, 3–5
Family boroughs, 14
Farmers, 3, 139–140, 226–227, 306, 362 (*See also* Agriculture)
Feminism, 288, 364 (*See also* Suffragettes)
Fenians, 278
Ferdinand, King, 37, 295, 341
Fielden, John, 96
Fire, 331, 335
First International, 171, 309
Fitzwilliam, Earl, 26, 29
Fletcher, Colonel, of Bolton, 19
Fletcher, J., 131
Foord, A. S., 14*n*., 32

Foreign affairs, 230–231; liberalism in, 16

Foreign Office, 172, 193–194, 261, 270–271

Foreign policy, 16, 37, 175–193, 196–197, 294, 336

Fox, 144

France, 16, 37–40, 175, 182–184, 186–187, 190, 293–294, 336 (*See also* entries under French)

Franchise Law, 206–207

Franco-Prussian War, 169

Free trade, 16, 237–239, 242, 335–336; in land, 306

French, the, 168–169, 294

French-Canadian nationalism, 103–104, 111–113

French Revolution, 12, 29, 37, 41, 47

Frost, John, 121

Garibaldi, Giuseppe, 168

Gatton, 64–65

George, Henry, 312–313, 347

George III, 1, 14, 31, 54

George IV, 13, 31–33, 36, 54–55, 114

Germany, 9, 182, 288, 293–294; Britain's fear of, 336; manufacturing strength of, 337–340; power of, 336, 364; unification of, 168–169, 336

Gibbs, Sir Vicary, 53

Giffen, Sir Robert, 305

Gilbert, W. S., 244; quoted, 245

Gladstone, William Ewart, 6–7, 143, 172–173, 175, 214, 225, 238, 243, 251, 261, 290, 297, 346–347; and democracy, 202–212; and Irish nationalism, 278–279, 281, 286, 298; letter of, to Lord Granville, 279–281

Gladstone government, second, failure of, 290

Glasgow, 207

Gold, 294, 351

Gorst, John, 214

Government, local, 301–302, 315; revolution in, 324–335; representative, 219

Graham, Sir James, 181

Granville, Lord, Gladstone's letter to, 279–281

Granville Papers, 279

Great Depression (1873–96), 7, 289, 297

Greece, 16, 37, 175, 179–180

Greenwich, 33

Grenville, Lord, 27–28, 30

Grenville, Thomas, 26; letters of, 27–30

Greville, Charles Cavendish Fulke, 32, 54, 115

Grey, Lord, 5, 17, 29, 76, 117, 119*n.*, 221

Grosvenor, Lord, 28

Hall, Sir Benjamin, 325, 327; quoted, 332–333

Hamilton, Lady Ann, 33

Hand-loom weavers, 120–121; of Coventry, 131–135

Hanover, 54

Harcourt, Sir William, 291, 347–348

Hardie, James Keir, 293, 309, 346–347; quoted, 347–350

Harney, George, 121

Harrowby, Lady, 36

Hartington, Marquis of, 279

Hastings, Lord, 58

Hobhouse, Lord, 312, 315

Hodgskin, Thomas, 85

Holland (*see* Netherlands)

Holland, Lord, 32

Holmes, Richard, quoted, 131–132

Holyoake, George Jacob, 232–233; on John Bright, 237–243

Home Office, the, 197, 214

Hong Kong, 168

Hours of labor, 2, 5, 81, 120, 131, 234

Household Franchise Bill, 208–212

Howe, Lord, 117

Howell, T. B., 21

Hownam, Lieutenant, 35

Hughes, Thomas, 75, 346

Huish, Robert, 32*n.*

Humanitarianism, 87–94

Hungary, 190

Hunt, Henry, 26

Husskisson, William, 15–16, 37

Hyndman, Henry M., 292, 309

Illiteracy, 47

Imperialism, 7–8, 278, 291, 295, 298, 309, 350–351

Imports, German, 336–340

Income, per capita, 6

Independent Labor Party (I.L.P.), 293, 347

India, 175, 214, 351; mutiny in, 168, 351

Individualism, British, 169

Industrial revolution, 41, 337

Industrialists, 3, 6, 95–96, 120, 149–151, 320 (*See also* Manufacturers)

Industry, 366; family or partnership, 3–4; service, 5

Information, 47–53; power of, 47

Institutions, rationalization of, 243–260

Investment, 6

Ireland, 69–70, 142, 173, 351, 355–356; and agrarian reform, 278, 281–287; established church in, 43, 251; famine in, 137, 143, 278; home rule for, 7, 9, 16, 104, 233, 279–281, 288, 290–291, 298, 353, 364

Irish, the, 42, 79, 114

Irish Americans, 279

Irish Land Act, 203

Irish Land League, 278, 284–285

Irish nationalism, 277–287

Irish Nationalist party, 278, 284

Irish Republican Brotherhood, 278

Italy, 188–189, 294; unification of, 168–169, 336

Jacobinism, 6, 19, 47, 82, 120, 232

Jameson's Raid, 351, 361

Jaurès, Jean, 293

Jews, 213, 241

Jingoism, 203, 294, 347, 350–363

Jowett, Benjamin, 261

Judges, 243–244, 253, 256–259

Judicial system, 243–260; reform of, 251–260

Jury trials, 125

Justices of the peace, 324

Kemp, B., 14n.

Kennington Common rally, 121

Kent, 50

"Khaki Election," 8

Knapland, P., 80n.

Kruger, Paul, 351, 356

Labor, 7, 171, 295, 320–322; capital and, 125–126; hours of, 2, 5, 81, 120, 131, 234; and management, 289, 293; organized, 346

Labor conciliation, 295

Labor movement, 290

Labor party, 292–293, 298

Labor politicians, 82

Labor relations, 293

Labor Representation Committee (L.R.C.), 8, 293–294

Laborers (see Workingmen)

Ladies of the Bedchamber, 116–119

Laissez faire, 5, 8, 166

Lambert, Royston, 325

Lancashire, 120, 139, 149, 164, 226, 228, 231; South, 96, 120

Land, 125, 141–142, 315–316, 375; in Ireland, 277–278

Land Act of 1881, 285–286

Land reform, 298, 305–308

Landlords, 137, 307, 312, 315, 318; absentee, 278; Irish, 285–287; Welsh, 371–372

Lansdowne, Marquis of, 198, 374

Latin America, 16, 37

Law, the, 244–245; and equity, 252, 254–255

Law, Andrew Bonar, 288

Lecky, William Edward Hartpole, 31

Leeds, 64, 120

Lehzen, Baroness, 117

Leopold, King, 193

Lewis, George Cornewall, 260

Liberal Unionists, 7, 290, 336, 364

Liberalism, 16, 193, 346; Gladstonian, 1, 7, 172, 202–212; limitations of, 233–243; new, 363–375; religious, 15; Victorian, 232

Liberals, 7–9, 76, 143, 172–173, 175, 194, 212, 220–221, 233, 240–241, 279, 290–292, 294, 297–299, 301, 309, 336, 364

Lieven, Madame de, 36

Lincolnshire, 139

Liquor licensing, 364

Liverpool, Lord, 14, 19, 142, 149

Lloyd George, David, 8, 78, 298, 364–365; speech of, at Newcastle-on-Tyne, 365–375

Local Government Acts, of 1858, 324–325; of 1888, 291, 311

Local Government Board, 321

Local option, 324

Lombardy, 188–189

London, 14, 19, 34–35, 37, 121, 311–312, 321n.; local government in, 324–335

London County Council, 325

London Metropolitan Board of Works, 325; report of, 325–335

London Workingmen's Association, address to the public by, 122–127

Lonsdale, Lord, 35

Lords, House of, 32, 36, 54, 78, 148–149, 218–223, 225, 251–253, 256–260, 290, 293, 364; abolition of, 310; and Pacifico affair, 176–193; reform of, 295

Lorymer, James Henry Baden, 87

Louis Napoleon, 121, 168, 238

Lovett, William, 119, 121

Lowe, Robert, 297

Luddism and Luddists, 12, 19, 22

Ludlam, Issac, 20

Macaulay, Thomas Babington, 351; quoted, 158

Mackintosh, Sir James, quoted, 165

Mallon, Dolly, 413
Management, 319; labor and, 289, 293
Manchester, 26–28, 60, 64, 71, 120–121, 139, 213, 324
Manchester School, 6, 141, 203, 297, 316, 350
Mann, Tom, 309
Manufacturers, protection of, 139–142, 316 (*See also* Industrialists)
Manufactures, English, 337–338; German, 337–340
Maria, Donna, 183–184
Marshall, Alfred, quoted, 289
Marx, Karl, 171, 292, 309
Marxism, 292
Masses, the, 6, 294, 314; emergence of, 346–350
Mechanics institutes, 6
Medical Act of 1858, 169
Melbourne, Lord, 5, 77–78, 80; Victoria and, 114–119
Metropolis Management Act of 1855, 327, 331–334
Metternich, Count, 188, 214
Miall, Edward, 225
Middle classes, 3, 5–6, 12, 76, 80, 120, 136, 150, 169–171, 175, 290, 293; radicalism of, 83–84
Midlands, the, 19, 120
Miguel, Don, 183
Mill, John Stuart, 169, 297
Milner, Alfred, 351
Miners, 346–347, 349, 371–373
Minto, Earl of, 188–189
Moira, Lord, 116
Monarchy, 217–218, 223; decline of, 30–36, 114 (*See also* Crown)
Montrose, Duke of, 55
Morley, John, 322
Morpeth, Lord, 30
Morris, William, 292, 309
Mount Charles, 56–57
Muckraking, 48
Municipal Corporations Act of 1835, 1, 79, 114, 324
Municipalities, 315–320

Namier, L. B., 14*n.*, 32
Napier, General, 121
Naples, 188
Nassau Senior, 94
National conventions, 85; circular on, 85–87
National Insurance Act of 1911, 9
National Union of Conservative Associations, 352

Nationalism, 16, 37, 238, 294; French-Canadian, 103–104, 111–113; Irish, 277–287
Negroes, 41; West Indian, 89–94
Netherlands, the, 39, 181–182
"New Unionism," 346
New Zealand, 104, 351
Newcastle-on-Tyne, 364
Newmarket, 35
Newspapers, 120; tax stamps on, 47–48, 52
Nineteenth-century world, 2–9
Nonconformists, 223–224
Norfolk, 139
North, the, 19, 80, 120
Northcote, Sir Stafford, 260–261, 277; on civil service, 261–277
Nottingham, 20, 136

O'Connell, Daniel, 42, 88, 257–258, 277
O'Connor, Feargus, 120, 136, 346
Old-Age Pension Law of 1909, 364
"Old Bailey," 243
Old Sarum, 59, 64, 71
Olivier, Sydney, 309
Opium wars, 168, 175, 350
Orange Free State, 356–360
Owen, Robert, 12, 240, 290, 314*n.*
Owenites, 85
Oxford movement, 75–76

Pacifico, David, 175, 179, 350
Pacifism, 232, 242
Palmerston, Lord, 171–172, 196–198; and Don Pacifico, 175–193, 350; Victoria and, 193–194
Pamphleteering, 47–50
Panic of 1825, 16
Pares, R., 14*n.*
Parliament, 11, 14–15, 28, 30–31, 76, 79, 170, 172; annual meetings of, 130; election to, 62–74, 77–78, 82, 119, 311; and First Reform Bill, 60–61; and Irish home rule, 278–281; and Pacifico affair, 175–193; workingmen in, 293–294, 346–347 (*See also* Commons; Lords)
Parliament Act of 1911, 9
Parliamentary Candidates Society, 82–84
Parliamentary reform, 87–88, 196–198, 203, 208, 301
Parnell, Charles Stewart, 278–279; speech of, in answer to Address from the Throne, 281–287
Paternalism, 12
Patronage, 260

Paupers in workhouses, classification of, 97; discipline and diet of, 97–101; punishment of, 101–103

Pedro, Don, 183

Peel, Sir Robert, 2, 5, 14, 37, 42, 54, 66, 76, 78, 114–115, 118–119, 137, 194; background of, 142, 149–150, 152, 161; Bagehot's estimate of, 144–167; death of, 175; and legislation, 166–167; oratory of, 160–161; quoted, 155

Peel, Sir Robert, the first, 142, 149–150, 161

Peelites, 171, 194

Peers, 78, 295, 364, 375 (See also Aristocracy)

Pensions, 275

Pentrich rising of 1817, 1, 13, 19–25

Penzance, Lord, 257

People, the, 49–53 (See also Masses)

People's Charter, 80, 119, 122, 124, 127; national petition for, 127–131

Perceval, Spencer, 147–148, 157

Peterloo massacre of 1819, 13, 26–27, 30

Picketing, 293

Pitt, William, 2, 15, 52

Pitt System, 52

Place, Francis, 82–83, 119; quoted, 83–84

Plug riot of 1842, 137

Plymouth, 34

Pole, Sir C., 57

Police, 14, 142; reform of 1829, 15

Political knowledge, 47–53

Political machines, 82

Political philosophy, 47

Political Register, The, 47

Politicians, 146

Politics, 289–290; domestic, 2, 75, 290; European, 294; local, 324; mass, 233; religion and, 232; Victorian, 172–173, 193, 213

Ponsonby, Frederick, 33

Poor Law Amendment Act of 1834, 79, 94–103, 120, 324

Poor Law Commission, 79

Poor Law Commissioners, 95–96; report of, 95–103

Poor Laws, 27

Poor relief, 95–96

Population growth, 3

Portland, Duke of, 35–36

Portsmouth, 34

Portugal, 16, 37–41, 179, 183–185

Poverty, 310 (See also Paupers; entries under Poor)

Press, the (see Newspapers)

Primrose League, 7

Privilege, assaults on, 77, 136–142, 172; elimination of, 233, 251

Production, elements of, 6

Professions, the, 169–170

Property, 366–371; private, 319–321

Prosperity, 81

Protectionism, 9, 139–142, 316

Protestants, 12, 43–46; Irish, 278, 283

Prussia, 16, 39, 181–182

Public opinion, 144, 147

Public schools, 261

Public service, 274, 276

Punch, 199

Quadrupal Treaty, 184

Quakers, 232, 242–243

Queen v. O'Connell, 257–258

Queen's Case, the, 13, 26, 30–36

Radical Platform, The, 298

Radicalism, 12, 26, 47, 82–83, 298, 311, 346; Manchester School (see Manchester School); mid-Victorian, 172, 203

Radicals, 6–7, 13, 17, 26, 30, 47, 59–60, 76–77, 79, 96, 104, 114, 116, 168, 191, 194, 232, 240–241, 260, 297, 312; agrarian, 85; middle-class, 83–84

Raffles, Sir Stamford, 350

Railroads, 3–4, 6, 370

Reactionaries, 41

Reform, 51, 172, 203, 295; chancery and judicial, 245–260; land, 298, 305–308; municipal, 7, 315–320; Parliamentary (see Parliamentary reform); police, 15; progress of, 53; radical, 11; social, 290, 364; and social stress, 75–167; university, 260–261

Reform Acts, of 1832, 1, 14–15, 17, 54, 58–74, 78–79, 114, 128, 136, 142–143, 164–166, 175, 206, 210–212, 221–222; of 1867, 7, 172, 206, 211, 221–222; of 1884, 7, 291; Gladstone's speech on, 204–212

Reform League, 232

Religion, 64; and Irish nationalism, 277; politics and, 232; and slavery, 89–90 (See also Christianity; Church; Jews; Protestants; Roman Catholics)

Rents, 278, 284–285, 290, 306–307, 311–313, 318, 371–372

Revisionist movement, 293, 310

Revolution, 16, 19–20; industrial, 41, 337; in Italy, 188–189; social, 1, 13, 297
Revolutionaries, 84–85, 297
Rhodes, Cecil, quoted, 350–351
Ricardo, David, 136–137
Richards, Lord Chief Baron, 20, 261
Roberts, Lord, 341
Rochdale, 170, 232; Bright's letter to workingmen of, 233–236
Roebuck, John Arthur, 191, 260
Roman Catholic Relief Bill, speech on, 42–46
Roman Catholics, 12, 41–43, 45–46, 277, 355
Roseberry, Lord, 347
Rotten boroughs, 14, 22
Rotundanists, 84
Royal Family, the, 217, 347–349
Ruskin, John, 292, 347
Russell, Lord John, 42, 59–60, 161, 194, 198, 204, 211; speech of, on First Reform Bill, 61–74; Victoria's correspondence with, 194–196
Russia, 16, 39, 168–169, 181–182, 190–191, 196, 294, 336

St. John-Stevas, Norman, 143
Salisbury, Lord, 291, 294
Sanderson, Colonel, 348
Sanitation, 228–229, 330
Sardinia, King of, 189
Savings, 6
Scandal, 31–32, 78, 114–119
Schleswig-Holstein, 169
Scotland, 68–70, 211; church of, 44
Scott, John (see Eldon, Lord)
Scott, Sir Walter, quoted, 146
Selborne, Lord Chancellor, 251
Sepoy rebellion, 351
Service industries, 5
Sewerage, 328–335
Shaftesbury, Earl of, 329; quoted, 329–330
Shaw, Bernard, 308–309; essay on socialism, quoted, 310–323
Sidmouth, Lord, 19, 23, 29, 37, 157
Sidney, Sir Philip, 84
Singapore, 350
Sinn Fein, 278
Six Acts, the, 26
Slavery, abolition of, 1, 5, 15, 87–94
Slaves, emancipation of, 87; speech on, 89–94
Slums, 80, 349
Small Holdings Act of 1891, 291
Smith, Sydney, quoted, 148

Social Democrats, 311, 322–323
Social divisions, pre-Victorian, 13 (See also Classes)
Social organization, 3
Social problems, 13
Social revolution, 1, 13, 297
Social security, 120
Social stress, 136–142; reform and, 75–167
Social unrest, 19–20
Social welfare, 7–8, 298
Socialism, 12, 237, 289, 292, 297, 308–323; modified, 203; revolutionary, 309; unconscious conversion to, 323
Socialist Democratic Federation (S.D.F.), 292, 309, 347
Socialist League, 292, 309
Socialists, 392; Fabian, 8, 293, 308–323, 347; revisionary, 310
Society, structure of, 324; urban, 325; village, 3
South Africa, 351–363
South Irish Volunteers, 288
Spa Fields riots, 19
Spain, 16, 37–41, 184–187
Speenhamland plan, 95
Spenceans, 85
Spencer, Herbert, 169
Staffordshire, 67
Stanley, Edward, 88; speech of, on emancipation of slaves, 88–89
State, the, 18, 47, 52, 311, 322; Church and, 222–223, 225, 239
Statesmen, constitutional, 144, 147, 151, 153, 158, 167; typical Victorian, 198
Statesmanship, 346
Stephen, Sir James, 79, 88
Stockmar, Baron, 193
Stokes, E., 80n.
Strikes, 9, 120, 288–289, 364
Suez Canal, 173
Suffrage, 232, 239–240, 324; and middle classes, 198–202; universal manhood, 119–120, 122–127, 129, 131–132, 238, 310; womanhood, 238, 288
Suffragettes, 9, 295, 364–365 (See also Feminism)
Supreme Court of Judicature Act of 1873, 243
Surrey, Lord, 30
Sussex, Duke of, 58
Swift, Jonathan, quoted, 145
Switzerland, 187–188
Syndicalism, 364

Taff Vale case, 293–294
Tamworth Manifesto, 76, 143
Tariff protection, 9
Tariffs, reciprocal, 15, 336
Tavistock, Lord, 118
Tax stamps, 47–48, 52, 120
Taxes, 86, 128, 137, 303–305, 307, 312–313, 366, 371; estate, 291; income, 312, 315–318, 320; inheritance, 292
Taylor, A. J. P., 169
Taylor, Watson, 57
Technology, 120, 289, 350
Ten-hour day, 120
Ten Hours Act, 2, 5, 81, 137
Tenants, 315; Irish, 285–287, 306; Welsh, 373
Test and Corporation Acts, 11–12; repeal of, 12, 15, 59, 75
Thames, the, 328–331, 334
Tillet, Ben, 309
Tories, 7, 9, 12, 54, 59, 84, 88, 137, 142–143, 148, 194, 213, 232, 237–242, 290–291, 297, 364, 367, 374; reforms of, 14–15, 37–41, 77
Tory Carlton Club, 77
Trade Disputes Act of 1906, 294, 364
Trade unions, 14, 79, 82, 120, 171, 289–290, 293–295
Trades Union Congress, 294
Transportation, mass, 3, 6 (See also Railroads)
Transvaal, the, 294, 351, 353–356, 358–361
Trevelyan, Sir Charles, 260–261, 277; on civil service, 261–277
Trevelyan, G. M., 1
Turkey, 190–191
Turner, William, 20
Twiss, Harold, 41, 42n.
Tyranny, 145

Uitlanders, the, 294, 351, 354–356, 358, 360
Ulster, 278, 280, 288, 291, 295
Ultra-Tories, 42
Unemployment, 289
Unemployment insurance, 120
Unions (see Trade unions)
United States, 218–219, 336; Civil War in, 168, 171, 205, 230, 278; and Ireland, 278–279; relations with, 230–231
University reform, 260–261
Utilitarianism, 94–103

Vansittart, Nicholas, 11
Victoria, Queen, 1, 13–14, 31–32, 78, 172–173, 175, 348; correspondence of, 194–196, 198, 341–346; death of, 295; Golden Jubilee of, 340–346; marriage of, 193; and Melbourne, 114–119; Parnell's answer to speech by, 281–287; power and influence of, 193–198
Victorianism and the Victorians, 1–2, 6, 143, 168–173, 340–341; and chancery and judicial reform, 245–260; and civil service, 260–277; conservatism and, 212–232; and elections, 198–202; and Irish nationalism, 277–287; liberalism and, 202–212, 232; and world power, 175–198
Villages, 3
Villiers, George, 115

Wage boards, 9
Wages, 95, 234, 236, 289; minimum, 317
Wales, 70, 74, 121, 293, 347, 349, 371–373
Wallas, Graham, 309
Walpole, Spencer Horatio, 195–196
Walter, John, 119
Wealth, division of, 132; redistribution of, 292; sources of, 125
Webb, Beatrice, 7
Webb, Sidney, 309; interview with, 323
Welfare state, 295
Wellesley, Arthur, 87, 162
Wellington, Duke of, 17, 36–37, 42, 54–56, 58, 60, 78, 137, 142, 148, 162–163, 221, 239, 257
Wetherall, Sir C., 48
Whig-Liberal Reform Club, 77
Whig-Liberals, 171
Whigs, 13, 17, 54, 59–60, 80, 114, 116–117, 147, 157, 175, 193–194, 290; reforms of, 1, 5, 77, 84, 95
Wilberforce, William, 15
William and Anne, reign of, 39–40
William IV, 13, 17, 78, 86, 114; eccentricity of, 54–58
Williams, Edwin Ernest, 336; on German industry, 337–340
Wilson, George, 137
Wilson, Sir Henry, 288
Women, 5 (See also Feminism; Suffragettes)
Wood, Alderman, 33
Worcester, Marquis of, 34
Workhouse Rules, 96–103

Workhouses, 244

Working class, 13, 75–76, 80, 83, 226–228, 297; housing of, 329–330

Working-class party, 309 (*See also* Labor party)

Workingman's Compensation Act of 1897, 291

Workingmen, 75–76, 80, 120–121, 131–135, 171, 288, 290, 292, 301–308, 346–347; and the franchise, 206–207, 239, 241–242, 293, 346–347, 364; in Parliament, 293–294, 346–347 (*See also* Farmers; Hand-loom workers)

Workingmen's compensation, 298, 364

World War I, 9, 288–289

Würtemburg, King of, 58

Wynnstay, Mr., 30

York, 28, 49; Duke and Duchess of, 347–348

Yorkshire, 96, 120, 226, 371

Yorkshire requisition, 28–30

Young, G. M., 6, 143

"Young Ireland" movement, 278

Zetland, Marquis of, 355

Zulu War, 351